Franchise Bible

Franchise Bible

How to Buy a Franchise
or Franchise Your Own Business

Fifth Edition

Erwin J. Keup

Entrepreneur.
Press

Editorial Director: Jere Calmes
Cover Design: Beth Hanson-Winter
Editing and Composition: CWL Publishing Enterprises, Inc., Madison, WI, www.cwlpub.com

This publication is designed to provide accurate and authoritative information in regard to the subject matter covered. It is sold with the understanding that the publisher is not engaged in rendering legal, accounting, or other professional service. If legal advice or other expert assistance is required, the services of a competent professional, personal franchise attorney should be sought.
—From a Declaration of Principles jointly adopted by a Committee of the American Bar Association and a Committee of Publishers

ISBN 1-932156-62-3

Library of Congress-Cataloging-in-Publication Data
Keup, Erwin J.
    Fanchise bible: how to busy a franchise or franchise your own business / by Erwin J. Keup - 5th ed.
        p.   cm.
    Includes index.
    ISBN 1-932156-62-3
    1. Franchises (retail trade)—United States—Forms. 2. Franchises (Retail trade)—Law and legislation—United States. I. Title

HF5429.235.U5K478 2003
658.8'708—dc22

                                                                    2003055837

Printed in Canada

09 08 07 06 05 04   10 9 8 7 6 5 4 3

This book is dedicated to my eight wonderful children, whom I consider gifts from God and the inspiration for my life's endeavors. As a client once said to me, "If you are not ambitious by nature, you must be ambitious by reason of your large family."

Contents

Checklists and Worksheets in this Book

Foreword

I first met Erv Keup when I was doing what you're probably doing now—standing in the business section of your local bookstore wondering which franchise you should buy or whether you should franchise your business.

When I perused *Franchise Bible* for the first time and realized exactly how complex was this new venture I was considering, I flipped to the back of the book to consider the credentials of the man who wrote it. I discovered that he and I lived a few hundred miles away from each other, so I pulled out my cell phone, played Russian roulette with Directory Assistance, and eventually got Erv himself on the phone. This was my method, as it was long ago in school, to ingratiate myself with the teacher so I wouldn't have to study the text.

Erv's tough-love instruction with me, however, began with that very first call—"Chris, read the book ... turn to so-and-so page ... see what I've done in the appendix. It's all there." Slowly, I learned Erv was right. I read every word he had written, filled the margins of his book with ideas as they came to me, and highlighted—as one might with the Bible itself—those salient points requiring more thoughtful consideration.

Working through this book as I prepared my family business to franchise, I learned that the genius of Erv Keup is his belief that the key to a successful franchise system is found not in the franchisor (a lot of great companies never scale) or in the franchise (don't expect someone else to do your work for you), but in the relationship that is created between the two of them at the first submission of the Uniform Franchise Offering Circular—which, at best, will faithfully represent the long-term, mutually beneficial business interests of both parties.

Unlike any other legal documents that I had been used to working with earlier in my career, the Offering Circular and the accompanying contract that binds the franchisor and the franchisee to the terms of the Offering Circular are generally not negotiable. I say "generally" because, though both are updated as the business evolves, they are not negotiated individually, franchise by franchise, as the uninitiated might assume. This means that the prospective franchisor must put the work in up front to understand his or her business from the outside, in order to anticipate the needs and requirements of the future franchisee, and the prospective franchisee must know the myriad different options a franchisor had while formulating the Offering Circular that could eventually govern the most minute of a franchisee's business actions for decades to come. No wonder this industry was in need of a Bible—and, thank God, Erv wrote it!

Franchise Bible allows all of us, franchisor and franchisee alike, whether we are new to the business or have been around as long as Erv, to discover the tenets of perhaps the most exciting business opportunity in America and around the world. My final advice to you is Erv's initial advice to me: "READ THE BOOK—*it's all there.*"

And if you haven't made it to the checkout line yet, just go ahead and give me a call and I'll conference Erv in.

—Christopher P. Bruno
President
Lite For Life Franchise Corporation, Inc.

What's New in This Edition? A Note from the Author

The fifth edition of *Franchise Bible* has been dramatically revised to reflect the changes since the new Uniform Franchise Offering Circular (UFOC) adopted by the Federal Trade Commission (FTC) went into effect January 1, 1995, and how the UFOC could look when and if the FTC ever makes effective its proposed revisions to the FTC rule as announced on October 15, 1999 in its "Notice of Proposed Rulemaking" for the purpose of seeking public comment.

This proposed rule disclosure has requirements that are founded on the UFOC Guidelines developed by the North American Securities Administrators Association (NASAA) in 1999. The Guidelines existing at the time of this publication have been clarified and substantively changed in a few places by the proposed rule in an attempt to reorganize and streamline the rule. (For instance, the proposed rule, if ever adopted, would change the title from "UFOC Guidelines" to "Disclosure Requirements and Prohibitions Concerning Franchising," thereby eliminating business opportunity offerings for the purpose of establishing a separate trade regulation for such ventures.) At publication, a call to Steven Toporoff, Federal Rule Coordinator, revealed that the FTC still was in the process of evaluating additional changes and indicating there will be further changes, with a staff report due possibly in the fall of 2003, with future changes to the proposed rule still very likely.

Therefore, the reader should contact the Federal Trade Commission, Division of Marketing Practices, Bureau of Consumer Protection, 600 Pennsylvania Avenue, NW, Washington, D.C. 20580, at (202) 326-2222, to inquire about the current status of the proposed rule and request a copy, if available in final form.

> The new franchisors of the 2000s are and will continue to be well-read entrepreneurs in successful home improvement product and installation sales as well as diet weight loss and other health-oriented center service businesses.

In the 1970s and 1980s, franchising was predominately seen in the areas of restaurants, retail stores in non-food products, and hotels and motels. The recessionary period in the late 1980s and early 1990s, however, caused franchisors and franchisees alike to turn to businesses involving the maintenance, reconstruction, restoration, preservation, and servicing of major consumer products—big-ticket items like automobiles, homes, furnishings, and major appliances. In addition, the 1990s saw a marked rise in the number of relatively low-cost franchises catering to the educational, business, and social needs of Americans—franchises that require a higher degree of expertise in the franchisee.

My personal experiences with registering franchisors over the past few years, which witnessed the drastic rise and fall of the stock market, have confirmed in my mind that the new franchisors of the 2000s are and will continue to be well-read entrepreneurs in successful home improvement product and installation sales as well as diet weight loss and other health-oriented center service businesses who have not only survived this volatile period but who are making a profit and wish to expand their businesses through available franchise methods. They will be choosing franchisees that have the potential management skills and motivation necessary to successfully carry out their expansion process. Nationwide layoffs of middle- and upper-management personnel will supply a more highly educated, more experienced pool of potential franchisees.

The 1990s saw a revolt by some franchisees of major franchisors concerning what they feel are "unfair and unconscionable" terms in their franchise agreements, many of which were signed in the 1980s. This has culminated not only in franchisees forming their own associations, but also in the International Franchise Association (IFA), formerly an association primarily of franchisors, now counting over 25,000 franchisees as new members. Iowa was the first state to enact legislation protecting franchisees, which became effective on July 1, 1992.

Sample Service-Oriented and Product-Oriented Uniform Franchise Offering Circulars

On April 25, 1993, the North American Securities Administrators Association (NASAA) adopted extensive revisions to the Uniform Franchise Offering Circular (UFOC) Guidelines. These revisions became binding upon franchisors on January 1, 1995, having been adopted by each of the 15 registration states and approved by the Federal Trade Commission. (See Appendix E for a listing of the 15 registration states.)

The sample offering circulars in Appendices A-1 (product-oriented franchise) and A-2 (service-oriented franchise) will give you a clearer picture of how these UFOC rules currently affect you at the time of this publication, whether you are interested in a product-oriented or service-oriented business. In addition, the present UFOC guidelines as adopted by the State of California are reproduced in Appendix F. These guidelines include specific instructions on how to prepare a UFOC and samples and illustrations for each of the items of the UFOC.

The product-oriented businesses, such as the one illustrated in Appendix A-1 (refacing of counter tops with a reconstituted granite product known as Rocksolid Granit™), are definitely in vogue today, primarily because of the "home-buying frenzy" and "fixing up craze" in this millennium. The service-oriented businesses, such as the one illustrated in Appendix A-2 (a health-oriented weight loss business featuring professional individual counseling and stressing diabetic prevention diets for all walks of life), also are in much demand now.

In the field of franchising, both parties, the franchisor and the franchisee, have one major thing in common—the franchise agreement, which is, in essence, their mutual "Bill of Rights." Whether you are a potential franchisee, independent-business buyer, franchisor, or business seller, I encourage you to read this book in its entirety. What you will learn will only help you succeed in your franchising endeavor.

—Erwin J. Keup

> In the field of franchising, both parties, the franchisor and the franchisee, have one major thing in common—the franchise agreement, which is, in essence, their mutual "Bill of Rights."

About the Author

rwin J. Keup is a practicing attorney with offices in Costa Mesa, California. For the past 45 years, Mr. Keup has specialized in franchise law, franchise consulting, and general corporate and business law, including trademarks and service marks. He has provided legal and business counseling in a variety of fields.

Mr. Keup graduated from Marquette University in 1953 with a B.S. degree in business administration and from Marquette Law School in 1958 with a J.D. degree. He also served as a member of the *Marquette Law Review* while in law school. Before establishing his private law practice in Newport Beach, California in 1975, Mr. Keup held corporate law department positions with Miller Brewing Company in Milwaukee, Wisconsin, and Glidden Paint Company in Cleveland, Ohio. He subsequently served as vice president and general counsel of Snelling and Snelling, Inc., the world's largest personnel agency franchisor.

Mr. Keup currently is a member of the American and California Bar Associations. He is admitted to the Supreme Courts of Ohio and California and a former member of the Wisconsin Bar Association. Mr. Keup is also a member of the American Bar Association's Forum on Franchising and a former member of the California Bar Association's Franchise Legislation Committee. Mr. Keup is an arbitrator/mediator with the American Arbitration Association, FAM (Franchise Arbitration and Mediation, Inc.), and British Columbia International Commercial Arbitration Centre, specializing in franchisor/franchisee disputes. He has conducted seminars on franchising and has taught the business and legal aspects of franchising at private business schools. Mr. Keup also is the author of the *Mail Order Legal Guide*, as well as numerous business articles on franchising. He is married and the father of eight children.

Acknowledgments

This work is the result of over 45 years of practicing law, much of it in the franchise- and distributorship-agreement fields, as well as dealing with the many business aspects of franchising, including serving as an executive and general counsel to a major franchisor.

I would like to thank the designer, editors, and compositors of *Entrepreneur Press*, particularly Jere Calmes, Editorial Director, for their fine work on this fifth edition of *Franchise Bible*.

My sincere gratitude also goes to my franchise clients, many of whom have become close friends, for allowing me to share in their vast business experience. I am also indebted to my clients and good friends from Sydney, Australia, Bob Smith and Colin Mackenzie, founders of Rocksolid Granit (USA), Inc, not only for allowing the reproduction of a sample version of their Granite Transformations® offering circular (Appendix A-1, for illustration purposes only, to demonstrate what a home improvement type franchise of the 2000s looks like), but also for allowing me to incorporate some of my ideas into the Granite Transformations® system.

I also am indebted to my clients and new friends, Chris Bruno, Maureen and Howard Sullivan, and Kathleen Bruno of San Mateo, California, and founders of Lite For Life franchising Corporation, Inc. for allowing me to use a sample version of their "Lite To Life" offering circular (Appendix A-2, for illustration purposes only, to demonstrate their health-enhancing service that provides personal consultation in weight loss and diabetic control at a time when such services are in great demand and will remain so for many years to come).

Introduction

hether you are interested in franchising your business or buying a franchise operation, *Franchise Bible* will be a valuable resource for you in your research and investigation of franchising.

To begin, franchising, in business language, is a method of marketing through which successful business owners (potential franchisors) expand the retail distribution of their goods or services by contracting with independent, third parties. These third parties (potential franchisees) agree to operate the retail sales or service outlets featuring the franchisor's original trademarked goods or services and implementing marketing methods at their capital costs. In exchange for this opportunity to share in the net proceeds from the sale of trademarked goods or services, the franchisees pay an initial fee and ongoing royalties to the franchisor. Franchising is not a method of generating income solely through the sale of franchises. The franchise itself is not what made a franchisor wealthy; it was the particular product or service. Any potential franchisor or franchisee should bear this fact in mind.

> The franchise itself is not what made a franchisor wealthy; it was the particular product or service. Any potential franchisor or franchisee should bear this fact in mind.

There are two main parts to the text of *Franchise Bible*. Part I is concerned with individuals who are interested in going into business by buying a franchise or existing small business. Part II of the text addresses business owners who have started a business, made it successful, and now wish to expand by franchising the business. Whether you are a successful business owner desiring to expand your market through franchising or an individual desiring to go into business for yourself, read both parts of this book thoroughly.

> Whether you are a successful business owner desiring to expand your market through franchising or an individual desiring to go into business for yourself, read both parts of this book thoroughly.

Hopefully, by reading this book, the business owner intending to franchise his or her business will gain some insight into what a franchisee looks for when evaluating a franchise agreement and initial offering circular. Likewise, the person seeking to buy a franchise can find valuable information in this book regarding the desired methods of operation a good franchisor should utilize. If a prospective franchisee has some idea of what constitutes a well-run franchise system, he or she can make an informed choice. By the same token, many successful franchisors started out as franchisees, developing franchises and subsequently selling them, using their knowledge in franchising new business entities in a role-reversal situation.

To help you in your quest for more information on franchising in general, *Franchise Bible* features several sample franchise documents and additional franchising resources. Part III contains eight appendices, each with its own unique content. Be sure to review these appendices while reading Parts I and II.

The prospect of owning a franchise or franchising your business is very exciting and challenging. Let *Franchise Bible* take some of the worry out by informing you more about the laws, documents, and responsibilities of being a franchisor or franchisee.

Many successful franchisors started out as franchisees, developing franchises and subsequently selling them, using their knowledge in franchising new business entities in a role-reversal situation.

Part I

Buying a Franchise or Small Business

Chapter 1
Buying a Franchise

re you currently working for someone but longing to be your own boss by owning your own business? Are you retired and looking for a way to get back into a new line of work? Are you a recent college graduate wanting to get into your own business? Whatever your situation, if you are looking for new business ownership opportunities, then the first part of *Franchise Bible*—Chapters 1-4—is definitely for you. This section of the book is specifically intended for the person who wants to buy either a franchise or an existing business that is not a franchise. It is not intended to help you start a business from scratch.

When looking for new business opportunities, buying a franchise or existing business may be the way for you to go. But how do you select your own business? As a new business purchaser, you must first select a particular field of business you like and then decide whether or not that endeavor is suitable to your past experience and talents. Once you have done so, you can pursue a more established course of action.

When starting a business, you have three options. First, you can start your business from scratch, using your own name, knowledge, and background. Second, you can buy an existing business, to own the business outright and operate it without any controls from a third party. Third, you can purchase a form of license to sell a product or service utilizing the name, good will, marketing techniques, and operating procedures from a franchisor.

This initial chapter is mostly concerned with purchasing a franchise, while Chapter 2 discusses the details regarding an offering circular and franchise agreement. If you are also interested in learning about purchasing an existing business that is not a franchise, Chapter 3 discusses some of the activity involved there. Chapter 4 deals with purchasing a franchise from a local franchisee and helping you evaluate potential franchisors and sellers.

> This section of the book is specifically intended for the person who wants to buy either a franchise or an existing business that is not a franchise.

> When starting a business, you have three options. First, you can start your business from scratch .... Second, you can buy an existing business .... Third, you can purchase a form of license to sell a product or service.

Once you have given adequate consideration to the advantages and disadvantages of buying outright or franchising and have carefully weighed your conclusions along these lines with your conclusions about other forms of business, you can then decide how best to invest your savings and fulfill your dream of being your own boss. According to statistics provided by the U.S. Department of Commerce, the chances of success in a franchise operation are generally recognized as much greater than those of operating a business from scratch or even purchasing an existing business. You must also realize, however, that the autonomy in operating a franchise is not necessarily less than in operating a business you start from scratch or a business you purchase.

> Any prospective business owner should remember that the risk of failure exists in purchasing any business, be it a franchise or a local business venture.

In addition, any prospective business owner should remember that the risk of failure exists in purchasing any business, be it a franchise or a local business venture. One important item to keep in mind in any business purchase is the ground rules set forth in the purchase agreement. These ground rules are often a determining factor in the success or failure of any purchased entity. It is not so much that the purchase agreement must contain legal loopholes or escape clauses that allow a buyer to regain his or her compensation if the business should fail—which is often not the case when a franchise is purchased—but the terms must be workable for both parties. To be workable and successful, the terms should include that the initial and ongoing fees and obligations provide a reasonable profit to the franchisor or seller and are also affordable to the buyer.

> Franchising can be defined from two different perspectives—the business owner's perspective and the legal statutory perspective.

To begin this discussion on purchasing a franchise, you first need to understand the two definitions of franchising. Franchising can be defined from two different perspectives—the business owner's perspective and the legal statutory perspective.

Business Owner's Definition of Franchising

The business owner's definition is the most important definition to both the franchisor and franchisee, because if the franchise entity does not succeed, any legal statutory requirements are a moot point. The business owner's definition of franchising is as follows:

> *Franchising is a method of market expansion utilized by a successful business entity wanting to expand its distribution of services or products through retail entities owned by independent operators using the trademarks or service marks, marketing techniques, and controls of the expanding business entity in return for the payment of fees and royalties from the retail outlet.*

> The success or failure of one party to this unique relationship generally determines the success or failure of the other party.

Essentially, the franchisee is a substitute for the franchisor's company-owned office in the retail distribution of the franchisor's services or products. The success or failure of one party to this unique relationship generally determines the success or failure of the other party. If the franchisor and franchisee keep this business relationship definition in mind, the self-centered attitudes that appear to arise under the legal definition can be avoided.

The Legal Definition of Franchising

The legal definition of a franchise differs among the several states that have passed franchise registration statutes and the Federal Trade Commission (FTC). California was the first state to pass a franchising law, and its definition is similar to the definition of franchise used by the other states that have franchise registration statutes. The California definition, taken from California Business and Professions Code, Section 2001, defines "franchise" as follows:

> *Franchise means a contract or agreement, express or implied, whether oral or written, between two or more persons by which:*
>
> ■ *A franchisee is granted the right to engage in the business of offering, selling, or distributing goods or services under a marketing plan or system prescribed in substantial part by a franchisor;*
> ■ *The operation of the franchisee's business pursuant to that plan or system as substantially associated with the franchisor's trademark, service mark, trade name, logotype, advertising, or other commercial symbol designating the franchisor or its affiliates; and*
> ■ *The franchisee is required to pay, directly or indirectly, a franchise fee.*

The cited business definition mentioned previously meets the elements of the legal definition; however, the attitudes of the franchisor and franchisee in looking upon the franchise as the "marketing arm" or the "independent company-owned office substitute" of the franchisor set the franchising concept in the proper business perspective.

Thus, a potential franchisee should not purchase a franchise from any franchisor that he or she would not consider for a top employment position and a franchisor should not sell a franchise to any person he or she would not consider a top choice for a lifetime manager of a company-owned office. By the same token, a franchisor should give you the same care and support as he or she would give to his or her top managers of the company-owned outlets.

Why Buy a Franchise?

With so many options available and all the potential pitfalls possible in buying a business or franchise, you may be wondering why you should invest your time and money in a franchise opportunity. To help you get an idea of some of the advantages you would enjoy as a franchisee, review the list below. As a franchisee, you will enjoy:

- Group advertising power;
- Owning your own business and making day-to-day decisions yourself, guided by the franchisor's experience;
- The ability to sell products and services to markets that cannot be serviced by company-owned outlets because of higher operational costs and lower motivation of employees in company-owned outlets;
- The benefit of identification of service marks, trademarks, proprietary information, patents, and designs;
- Systematic training from experts;
- A lower risk of failure and/or loss of investments than if you were to start your own business from scratch;

- Being a part of a uniform operation, which means all franchises will share the same interior and exterior physical appearance, the same product, and the same service and product quality;
- Assistance in financial and accounting matters from the franchisor, as well as ongoing support; and
- The enhancement of your management abilities and benefiting from an opportunity you could not have in most employment situations.

In addition, you may wonder how to ensure that you make the best decision possible. Investing in your own business takes guts and the willingness to make important decisions. As a result, you will need to carefully research the statistics regarding new business start-ups versus the purchase of an existing business from a non-franchisor. Once you have done this, compare these statistics with research on franchised endeavors. What you find may be useful in helping you make a sound business decision and helping you understand why franchising may be more beneficial for you. Here are some helpful facts of franchising.

> *Investing in your own business takes guts and the willingness to make important decisions.*

- The U.S. Department of Commerce, in an early edition of *Franchising in the Economy*, cited statistics showing that franchising had increased phenomenally over the years and it was a significant part of the present U.S. marketing system. Franchising offers tremendous opportunities to individuals and companies seeking wider distribution of their products and services. The U.S. Department of Commerce also pointed out that retail sales from franchise establishments accounted for over one-third of all U.S. retail sales.
- John Naisbitt, in the Naisbitt Group's *The Future of Franchising: Looking 25 Years Ahead to the Year 2010* (1989), predicted that more than one-half of all retail sales would be made through franchise sales by the year 2010.
- Government research over the years has indicated that the success rate for franchise-owned endeavors is significantly better than the rate for non-franchise-owned small businesses.

In short, the good news is that franchising is a growing part of the national economy and presents a better chance for success to the new franchisee. The bad news is that not every franchise is a surefire way to multiply your savings and provide you with an enjoyable occupation.

> *Not every franchise is a surefire way to multiply your savings and provide you with an enjoyable occupation.*

Buyer Beware

More and more buyers are seeking franchises from relatively unknown franchisors with little-known brand names and service marks. At the same time, an increasing number of people, particularly those who have not been in business before, are also interested in purchasing small businesses from independent business owners operating in a geographically limited neighborhood area. This scenario usually takes the form of older sellers who purportedly wish to dispose of their business as they reach retirement age. Since spending your savings on a business is one of the most important decisions of your life, if not the most important decision, always heed the classic advice, "Buyer beware."

In the late 1950s and 1960s, all kinds of charlatans jumped on the bandwagon and franchised nearly everything imaginable, on a global scale. A buyer didn't always know what he or she was getting into. Typical of our society, help eventually came from legislative enactments that swung the pendulum the other way, at least as far as paperwork is concerned. As a result, franchising today is a much more exacting and time-consuming process because of required procedures and restrictions. But all this activity has resulted in more protection for the franchise buyer.

> Franchising today is a much more exacting and time-consuming process because of required procedures and restrictions.

Franchising and the Law

Part of the flurry of new regulations and legislation that were implemented to help protect franchisees included an FTC rule, applicable before January 1, 1995, that required a written disclosure statement, referred to as an FTC offering circular. The FTC offering circular specified areas of information to be presented to prospective franchisees at certain points in time. This FTC rule regarding offering circulars applied to those states that had not passed franchise acts. Fifteen states passed their own franchise acts that require registration, while the FTC, which governs all the states, does not require registration.

Under the franchise laws effective January 1, 1995 and currently in effect at this publishing, the FTC and all 50 states use the same Uniform Franchise Offering Circular, although the states retain the right to impose stricter provisions if they so desire, including registration. In all instances, the federal and state statutes do not provide a means of deciding whether or not a franchise is of any value or even whether or not the information submitted by the franchisor is true or not. The statutes merely force the franchisor to make certain representations and reveal certain information that, if untrue, would subject the franchisor to civil and criminal lawsuits.

> All 50 states use the same Uniform Franchise Offering Circular, although the states retain the right to impose stricter provisions if they so desire, including registration.

The bottom line is that no legislation will ever eliminate crime and no legislation will ever eliminate the naiveté of some potential business owners who are obsessed with seeing only the good parts of a transaction and none of the bad. As a prospective franchisee, you must be aware of the con artists that are hard at work trying to present the best possible image of their particular opportunity and who call their business endeavors "partnerships" or "licenses."

This does not mean, however, that all partnerships or license agreements are franchises or fraudulent schemes. Because licensing and franchising have become almost synonymous, the con artists seem to consider arrangements called "partnerships" as convenient labels for circumventing the disclosure requirements of federal and state law. These types of partnerships usually offer the use of the same business name and style, but the seller is a partner whose interest is eventually purchased by the business-seeking entrepreneur. The major drawback to this type of arrangement is that the selling partner does not have the capital and does not wish to reveal information about himself or herself. This would not be the case if the seller were a franchisor. In addition, before the new business-seeking entrepreneur purchases the partnership, the business is usually subject to the control of the selling "partner."

In conclusion, beware of any offered entity that supposedly gives you a going business under a trade name and has you start out as a partner and end up eventually as a sole owner, along with other individuals who also purchased a partnership interest in other areas and became owners, using the same name as yours.

Are You Franchise Material?

> Work as if you were to live forever and pray as if you were to die tonight.
> —Russian Proverb

Now that you have a better understanding of franchising and some of its history and background, you need to consider if you are cut out to be a franchise owner and operator. To do this, you need to take a hard look at yourself and evaluate how you would handle the responsibilities and operations of a franchise. Obviously, you want to do this before you make what could be the biggest investment of your life.

Most people have the notion that in franchising a lot of money can be made with a minimum of effort. This is a serious misconception. The franchisee who works the hardest profits the most from a franchise business. Initially at least, you must be able to make sacrifices. You must lay a strong foundation even for the most successful franchise operation. Be prepared to put in long hours of hard work and, above all, to be disappointed by your employees to a certain extent. The extent of this disappointment is directly related to how good you are at selecting and supervising people. The next consideration is how well you are organized. Last, but not least, an important factor is the state of your health.

One thing is certain: if the franchisor is merely interested in your money and does not evaluate you under certain standard criteria geared to determine your potential to succeed, there is something wrong with the franchisor. However, before you even see a franchisor, evaluate yourself.

Ask yourself such questions as:

- Will your franchise be taking a considerable amount of your time away from your family? If so, how do you feel about that?
- Is your family enthused about the franchise? Will you enjoy working with them if they will be employees?
- Do you enjoy working with others?
- Do you have the background or character traits necessary to succeed in owning a business?
- Do you have the necessary capital resources? Can you make the financial sacrifices?
- Are you emotionally prepared for working long, hard hours?

Don't be afraid to ask friends and acquaintances for their opinions on your abilities along these lines. Don't rely on just one opinion; get at least several. To help determine how fit you are for buying and running a franchise operation or small business, use the Checklist for Evaluating Your Suitability as a Franchisee or Small Business Buyer, which is located at the end of this chapter.

Conclusion

Once you have determined that you want to buy a franchise and you are prepared for the franchising challenge, you need to become more familiar with the franchise transaction and protect yourself by investigating each opportunity very carefully and thoroughly. Chapter 2 is designed to help you in this endeavor by describing what is involved in an offering circular and a franchise agreement.

Checklist for Evaluating Your Suitability as a Franchisee or Small Business Buyer

Carefully consider these questions before buying your own franchise or small business.

Financial

Yes No

❑ ❑ Have you and your spouse and knowledgeable family members discussed the idea of going into business for yourselves?

❑ ❑ Are you in complete agreement?

❑ ❑ Do you have the financial resources required to buy a franchise or small business? If not, where are you going to get the capital?

❑ ❑ Are you and your spouse ready to make the necessary sacrifices in the way of money and time in order to operate a franchise or small business?

❑ ❑ Will the possible loss of company benefits, including retirement plans, be outweighed by the potential monetary and self-pride rewards that would come from owning your own business?

❑ ❑ Have you made a thorough written balance sheet of your assets and liabilities, as well as liquid cash resources?

❑ ❑ Will your savings provide you with a cushion for at least one year after you have paid for the franchise or small business, allowing a one-year period of time to break even?

❑ ❑ Do you have additional sources of financing, including friends or relatives who might be able to loan you money in the event that your initial financing proves inadequate?

❑ ❑ Do you realize that most new businesses, including franchises, generally do not break even for at least one year after opening?

❑ ❑ Will one of you remain employed at your current occupation while the franchise or small business is in its initial, pre-profit stage?

Personal

Yes No

❑ ❑ Are you and your spouse physically able to handle the emotional and physical strain involved in operating a franchise or small business, caused by long hours and tedious administrative chores?

Yes No

❑ ❑ Will your family members, particularly small children, suffer from your absence for several years while you build up your business?

❑ ❑ Are you prepared to give up some independence of action in exchange for the advantages the franchise offers you?

❑ ❑ Have you really examined the type of franchise or business you desire and truthfully concluded that you would enjoy running it for several years or until retirement?

❑ ❑ Have you and your spouse had recent physicals?

❑ ❑ Is the present state of your health and that of your spouse good?

❑ ❑ Do you and your spouse enjoy working with others?

❑ ❑ Do you have the ability and experience to work smoothly and profitably with your franchisor, your employees, and your customers?

❑ ❑ Have you asked your friends and relatives for their candid opinions as to your emotional, mental, and physical suitability to running your own business?

❑ ❑ Do you have a capable, willing heir to take over the business if you become disabled?

❑ ❑ If the franchise or new business is not near your present home, do you realize that it would not be beneficial to sell your home and buy one closer until the new venture is successful?

Business

Yes No

❑ ❑ Do you and your spouse have past experience in business that will qualify you for the particular type of franchise or business you desire?

❑ ❑ Is it possible for either you or your spouse to become employed in the type of business you seek to buy before any purchase?

❑ ❑ Have you conducted independent research on the industry you are contemplating entering?

❑ ❑ If you have made your choice of franchises, have you researched the background and experience of your prospective franchisor?

❑ ❑ Have you determined whether the product or service you propose to sell has a market in your prospective territory at the prices you will have to charge?

❑ ❑ What will the market for your product or service be like five years from now?

❑ ❑ What competition exists in your prospective territory already?

❑ ❑ From franchise businesses?

❑ ❑ From non-franchise businesses?

Other Considerations

Yes No

❏ ❏ Do you know an experienced, business-oriented franchise attorney who can evaluate the franchise contract you are considering?

❏ ❏ Do you know an experienced, business-minded accountant?

❏ ❏ Have you prepared a business plan for the franchise or business of your choice?

Chapter 2
Learning About Franchise Documents

hen you become interested enough in a franchise opportunity to start gathering information and beginning discussions with a prospective franchisor, you will need to be more familiar with two important documents—the offering circular and the franchise agreement or contract. By learning more about both of these documents and the details they require, you will be better prepared to investigate potential franchise opportunities. This chapter discusses both of these documents in detail and offers tips and strategies on what is involved with each.

The Uniform Franchise Offering Circular

As mentioned in Chapter 1, the Federal Trade Commission (FTC) implemented a rule that required franchisors to present would-be franchisees with a disclosure statement, also known as an offering circular, which contains certain information regarding a franchise.

This rule was substantially modified effective January 1, 1995, so that franchisors in all 50 states are required to provide prospective franchisees with a revised Uniform Franchise Offering Circular (UFOC). For a sample of what a UFOC looks like, refer to the sample in Appendices A-1 and A-2 and to the UFOC guidelines reproduced in Appendix F.

Specifically, the franchisor under the 1995 rules must provide you with a Uniform Franchise Offering Circular at the earliest of three times:

- At the first face-to-face personal meeting between you and the franchisor or at the time for making disclosures regarding the terms and conditions of the sale of the franchise;
- 10 business days before you make any payment to the franchisor; or

- 10 days before you sign any contract committing you to buy the franchise or any other agreement imposing a binding legal obligation on you.

(The proposed rule mentioned earlier would change the time required by the FTC Rule from *10 business* days to *14 calendar* days before a prospective franchisee may sign any binding agreement or pay any consideration for the franchise.)

In addition, the FTC requires all franchisors to furnish you with completed copies of the documents to be executed *at least five days before you sign on the dotted line*. (The proposed rule would change the time required by the FTC Rule from five *business* days to five *calendar* days. Also, the proposed rule allows for electronic delivery of the UFOC. The FTC is also working out electronic signatures.)

Examine the Uniform Franchise Offering Circular very carefully, even if you have gleaned information on your own regarding a particular franchisor and his or her franchise offering.

Before examining an offering circular more carefully, if possible, try to personally do a field investigation of all the franchises offered in the field of your choice, and compare franchisors doing business in the same area. To do a field investigation, check with current franchisees.

> If possible, try to personally do a field investigation of all the franchises offered in the field of your choice, and compare franchisors doing business in the same area.

- Ask about their experiences with their franchisor and whether the franchisor has carried out the representations made in the circular and the franchise agreement.
- Find out whether or not the franchisor keeps his or her promises.
- Try to discern the attitude of the current franchisees regarding the major people in the franchisor's hierarchy of personnel.
- Find out whether the franchisees feel that their franchise opening costs were more than what the franchisor estimated they would be.
- Determine if the franchisor provided the franchisees with adequate training or left them on their own.

Remember: competitors of a franchisor will generally be more than happy to give you all the "dirt" about that franchisor. The same is true of current franchisees. If they have a gripe against their franchisor, they will be the first to tell you in no uncertain terms. To help you gather the information you need when talking to franchisees, use the Checklist for Interviewing Existing Franchisees at the end of this chapter.

Once you have completed your field investigation, you will be better informed when examining the offering circular or prospectus. The procedures discussed in the following paragraphs will help you better examine the document. Remember: if you don't get an offering circular from a franchisor, there is something wrong; for example, your franchisor may have violated an act enforceable by the FTC or a state agency or both.

> Remember: if you don't get an offering circular from a franchisor, there is something wrong.

The Offering Circular's Cover Page

The Uniform Franchise Offering Circular has a cover page that briefly identifies the business that is being franchised and the amounts of the initial franchise fees.

On January 1, 1995, all 15 registration states and the remaining states governed by the FTC began using the same Uniform Franchise Offering Circular, including a uniform cover page. However, individual state registration regulators may require that the franchisor reveal, in capital letters, additional information regarding risk factors on the cover page. Check with your state regulators to see if your state has any additional requirements.

The cover of the Uniform Franchise Offering Circular must specify any risk factors in bold print. These risk factors must include, if applicable:

- A warning that the franchise agreement permits the franchisor to arbitrate or sue only in a particular state and whether arbitration or litigation in a state other than the franchisee's home state may force the franchisee to accept a less favorable settlement for disputes;
- The fact that arbitration out of state may cost more;
- Whether the franchise agreement designates the law of a particular state other than the franchisee's home state to govern the agreement; and
- That the out-of-state law might not provide the same protection and benefits as the franchisee's local law and that the franchisee should compare these laws.

An offering circular cover page may also include the warning that there may be other risks concerning the franchise. However, if the risks are known, they should be specified on the cover page in bold print.

(Under the proposed rule, the FTC would abandon its separate FTC cover page and use a revised form of the old UFOC cover page. The title would be changed from "Offering Circular" to "Disclosure Document" and add language that would define the differences in a disclosure document and a franchise agreement. In fact, the proposed rule would require the franchisor to reveal risk factors on the cover only if required by state law. Other new cover requirements include listing e-mail addresses, Web sites [including the FTC's], and electronic delivery notices, if they apply, and eliminating the phrases "information ... required by the FTC" and the phrase "to protect you.")

The Uniform Franchise Offering Circular as adopted by the FTC is also used in those states that do not have franchise registration laws. Some of these states with no franchise registration laws have what are called "business opportunity laws," which also might apply to franchise offerings. Franchise laws cover those business agreements that meet the following three conditions:

> *The Uniform Franchise Offering Circular as adopted by the FTC is also used in those states that do not have franchise registration laws.*

- The buyer pays money for the business;
- The buyer uses the trademark of the franchisor so the business appears to be a part of an organization; and
- The buyer is subject to marketing directives or controls or both, set forth by the seller/franchisor.

Business opportunity laws cover those businesses that are similar in some aspects to those covered by franchise laws, with the key exception being that business opportunities do not use a trademark as part of the deal between the buyer and the seller. To cover both types of businesses, some states have both franchise laws and business opportunity laws; you need to find out if your state is one of them.

You should have an experienced franchise attorney make sure that you and your franchisor comply with the franchise or business opportunity laws. Because of the complexity, don't attempt to go it alone. For specific information on state franchise and business opportunity laws, turn to Appendix E, State Franchise Information Guidelines.

The second page of the Uniform Franchise Offering Circular is a table of contents in a standard form. The table of contents normally covers a page and a half and contains 23 paragraph headings, as well as a section setting forth the exhibits. The exhibits include the franchise agreement, any other agreements signed by the franchisee, the franchisor's financials, and in many cases a directory of state administrators and agencies. (See the table of contents in the sample offering circular in Appendix A-1.)

One of the most innovative requirements under the UFOC Guidelines is that the actual disclosure portion of the UFOC be in "plain English." For example, the regulations require that the franchisor refer to itself by its corporate name or as "we" and to the franchisee as "you."

If an offering circular is not delivered on time or if it contains a false, incomplete, inaccurate, or misleading statement, it may be in violation of federal or state law and you should report this violation to the Federal Trade Commission in Washington, D.C. If your state has a registration law, you should contact the state authority that regulates franchising in your state. You can also report state registration violations to the FTC.

> If an offering circular is not delivered on time or if it contains a false, incomplete, inaccurate, or misleading statement, it may be in violation of federal or state law and you should report this violation to the Federal Trade Commission.

Additionally, you will be advised that franchise registration in a state that has a franchise registration agency does not mean that the state recommends it or has verified the information in the offering circular. You will also be advised that if you learn that anything in the offering circular is untrue, you should contact the FTC or your state authority, if any. The cover sheet should also indicate the effective date of the offering circular.

Item 1. The Franchisor, Its Predecessors and Affiliates

An offering circular will give you the franchisor's background and that of its predecessors and affiliates. A predecessor is defined as "a person from whom the franchisor acquired directly or indirectly the major portion of its assets." (The proposed rule adds to the definition "from whom the franchisor obtained a license to use the trademark or trade secret in the franchise operation.") An affiliate is defined as "a person controlled by, controlling, or under common control with the franchisor."

Examine the section on the franchisor and its predecessors and affiliates closely. Read about the background of the business and the business experiences of its principal officers. If possible, run a credit check on the company and its previous officers. In addition, any information you can obtain regarding the record of the previous businesses—including other franchise businesses—with which the principals were associated is of paramount importance. This information can also help you make some type of forecast about the possibility of your own success. To ensure that you obtain all the background information you need, use as a starting point the Checklist of Information to Secure from a Franchisor, at the end of this chapter.

Item 2. Business Experience

This section of a circular will give you some personal information on the officers and directors of the franchise company for the past five years. (The proposed rule generally mirrors the present rule, but extends the disclosure of business experience to any "director, trustee, general partner, officer, and subfranchisor of any parent who will have management responsibility relating to the offered franchises.") "Officer" is defined as "any individual with significant management responsibility for marketing and/or servicing of franchises, such as the chief executive and chief operating officers and the financial, franchise marketing, training and service officers." It also includes *de facto* officers who perform such duties but whose title does not reflect the nature of the job. If you can check out their backgrounds, both their business experience and the views of their former acquaintances or competitors, you will improve your chances of succeeding with your new endeavor. In addition, you should make every attempt to get to know these people as much as you can. Ask to see the head person before you put your money down. Remember: this person will be a vital part of your story of success, since his or her endeavors will directly affect you.

Check out any affiliates listed in the second section of the circular to make sure that all vital items or services are not supplied by relatives or friends of the franchisor. If some services are supplied by family and friends, this may drastically change the profitability of your franchise because of inflated, noncompetitive prices.

Item 3. Litigation

Pay particular attention to this section of the circular. Stay away from any prospective franchisor who is under some current effective injunction or restrictive order, particularly one that could result in a drastic change in the franchise operation, including possible cessation of the franchise. In addition, determine whether or not the franchisor or any of the franchisor's key employees has been convicted of crimes or has a record of unfavorable determinations handed down by courts or government agencies. (The proposed rule adds disclosure of litigation involving a parent and revealing any pending litigation initiated by the franchisor against franchisees on involving franchise relationship issues. The franchisor must disclose the dismissal of a material action in connection with a settlement.)

> Stay away from any prospective franchisor who is under some current effective injunction or restrictive order.

If the offering circular or prospectus mentions any such investigations, convictions, or proceedings, view these as warning signs and rethink whether or not you want to purchase the franchise. If you still wish to purchase it, at least check out the proceedings as documented in the courts or government agencies and determine what has taken place in regard to this litigation.

Always remember that the franchisor's side is only one side of the story. Beware if this section reveals any lawsuits against the franchisor by former or existing franchisees. If so, call or write the court clerks where the cases are being litigated to find out the names of the attorneys representing the plaintiffs; then contact the attorneys and their clients.

If the litigation is local, secure the information by visiting the courthouse and talking with the attorney of record. Contact the plaintiffs and ask them why they are dissatisfied with the franchisor and why they are suing or have sued.

Item 4. Bankruptcy

This section must disclose any bankruptcy in the last 10 years that involved "the franchisor, its affiliate, its predecessor, officers, or general partner." Carefully check over the section of the offering circular that refers to prior bankruptcies. It is not uncommon to find that franchise founders have started franchises in different business areas and failed in each of them. Each endeavor may be subject to a bankruptcy, but the founder may walk away with a million dollars that is not subject to the proceedings involving his or her corporate entity.

Many great people have incurred numerous failures in their lives before reaching a pinnacle of success. Abraham Lincoln is just one of many such examples. However, as a rule, people who have failed in the past will fail in the future.

Item 5. Initial Franchise Fee

Generally, you will be required to pay a certain amount of money down in order to purchase the franchise. This is commonly referred to as "the initial franchise fee" or "front money." In addition, you may be required to pay other types of money up front for certain services. This section of the offering circular should contain valuable information on the range of minimum to maximum fees that the franchisor charges up front. The basis for these ranges is stated under this section of the circular.

Examine the basis for initial franchise fees very carefully. Use the information to project how much money you will have to spend. It is very important that you determine from this section of the circular precisely what you will receive in the way of services, inventory, and other benefits in return for your front money.

Once again, you should contact the franchisor's most valued personnel and bombard them with questions regarding the benefits you will receive for this front money. If there are current franchisees, contact as many of them as you can to find out if they were satisfied with the benefits they received upon paying this front money.

A franchisor should realistically consider what it would cost to open the franchise and the wealth of the typical type of franchisee who will purchase this franchise. Franchisors need to consider these factors rather than what other franchisors in the same industry charge. If the franchisor breaks even on the sale of each franchise, he or she can still succeed with reasonable royalties and profits from goods and services sold to the "captive franchisee."

Inexperienced franchisors can create franchises that are destined to fail or that will be unmarketable because they choose high figures out of the sky. Before you purchase the franchise, ask the franchisor how the initial franchise fee is determined. If the franchisor can justify the initial franchise fee charges as necessary for the franchisor to break even and these charges are reasonable, then you can be more secure that the franchisor knows how to make a successful franchise offering. A high initial franchise fee does not necessarily mean the franchise is a better investment or even a good one.

Take the franchise expansion story of Book Rack Franchising Corporation of Fort Lauderdale, Florida, which was founded by Virginia Darnell in 1963. According to *The Franchise Redbook* by Roger C. Rule, Book Rack had 283 outlets throughout the United States that sell used and new paperback books. The initial franchise fee was only $6,000 with a straight $75-per-month royalty fee. This is quite reasonable. The moral of the story is not to judge a franchise by its initial fees!

> Remember: as a rule, people who have failed in the past will fail in the future.

> Examine the basis for initial franchise fees very carefully. Use the information to project how much money you will have to spend.

> A high initial franchise fee does not necessarily mean the franchise is a better investment or even a good one.

In your research, expect to find a wide range of initial fees and royalty payments; however, there should be a uniformity of initial franchise fees within a particular industry. Be sure you are able to determine this average fee for your industry.

Item 6. Other Fees

This section of the circular will advise you in tabular form of any other fees that you will have to pay in addition to your front money, including ongoing royalties, service fees, training fees, renewal fees, advertising fees, and other similar, one-time or ongoing charges that are payable to the franchisor or its affiliates. Check to see if the franchisor will refund these fees if you decide to back out after signing the franchise agreement. Again, it is vital that you determine these amounts and project how they will affect your operations. A good accountant is a very valuable asset when purchasing a franchise.

Also remember that if you are required to pay a royalty on gross sales, this percentage will be substantially greater in terms of the impact on your net revenues. For example, 10% of gross sales could represent a cash payment of 50% or more of your net profit after expenses, depending on your overhead expense.

> Remember that if you are required to pay a royalty on gross sales, this percentage will be substantially greater in terms of the impact on your net revenues.

Item 7. Initial Investment

This section of the circular (which the proposed rule would title "Estimated Initial Investment") presents, in tabular form, the franchisor's monetary estimate of what it will cost you to begin operations, including the initial franchise fee, equipment, inventory, rent, working capital, and other miscellaneous costs. (Under the proposed rule, all Item 7 expenses must include both pre-opening expenses and those incurred during the initial phase, extending at least three months following the opening until the franchisee can break even.) The franchisor must adjust this estimate for each particular state where the offering circular is directed. The information outlined in this section is extremely useful when trying to estimate how much of your money will go into the initial phase of the business, and how fast.

Again, if at all possible, contact current franchisees and see if these cost projections appear fairly accurate according to their experiences with the franchisor. If there are no current franchisees available, review these listed costs with local contractors and vendors. Also remember that if these figures are materially misrepresented, it may be a violation of the law that you may wish to report at a future date.

This also would be an appropriate time for you to determine whether or not you can start your own business financially. Check out the bottom line—that is, will you have enough cash to support yourself and still meet your business obligations during the launching stages of the franchise, which could span a year or more?

> If at all possible, contact current franchisees and see if cost projections appear fairly accurate according to their experiences with the franchisor.

Item 8. Restrictions on Sources of Products and Services

If the circular states that franchisees must purchase or lease from designated sources, let this be a warning sign for you to investigate the franchise further. If you are tied into purchasing a particular product or leasing your business premises from the franchisor or his or her affiliates, you may be incurring expensive costs as a result of such tie-ins. Find out if these leases or purchase contracts are competitive with unaffiliated entrepreneurs, both in costs and in benefits received. (The proposed rule requires "specifics" in explaining the legal obligations and restrictions imposed on the purchaser of a franchise.) A franchisor could set fees low enough to be very attractive, then require franchisees to contract for goods and services only with the franchisor. The costs could make the franchise a very expensive venture. Therefore, if at all possible, check with current franchisees to see how they feel about any purchase restrictions and whether or not they are receiving their money's worth. Franchisors who spend an extensive amount of time selling or leasing products, equipment, and buildings will generally spread themselves so thin that the chance of the franchise succeeding is slim. In most cases, it is a full-time operation for a franchisor to license, train, promote, and operate a franchise business, without being involved in allied businesses selling equipment, inventory, and facilities to the franchisees.

However, if franchisors can lower their royalty fee by getting a portion of the profit they need from selling ingredients or services to their franchisees at a reasonable cost, then both parties benefit. You are apt to be happier paying for tangible products you use in the business than for intangible values, such as a royalty payment.

> If the circular states that franchisees must purchase or lease from designated sources, let this be a warning sign for you to investigate the franchise further.

Item 9. Franchisee's Obligations

This section of the offering circular includes a table listing your obligations as a franchisee, with references to the sections of your franchise agreement that contain the obligations. The purpose of the table in the UFOC is to list your principal obligations under the franchise agreement and other agreements. The table should help you find more detailed information about your obligations in these agreements and in other items of the offering circular.

Read over the provisions of the agreements referred to in this section very carefully, since they constitute your contractual obligations of the franchise agreement that, if you breach, will probably be grounds for terminating you. Make sure that you are capable of complying with the obligations listed here.

If the franchisor has current franchisees, contact them and get their opinions about the obligations listed in this section. Ask them if they have encountered any difficulties complying with the obligations.

Also, be sure to study the quality of the franchisor's product or service and compare it with competitors' products and services. If you find that the franchisor's product or service suffers in comparison, forget about purchasing the franchise.

Item 10. Financing

With variable interest rates, it may be necessary for you to secure financing through the franchisor or else face the prospect of being unable to purchase the franchise. If it is a requirement to finance through the franchisor, a trip to local lending institutions is in order to determine whether or not you will be securing a loan on comparable conditions. Show a copy of the financial arrangements portion of the circular to your local banker and ask for the banker's opinion of such terms and conditions. Again, a credit check on the franchisor would be ideal. If possible, contact current franchisees to see what you can find out from them about their experiences with financing from the franchisor. Common sense is a requirement for all potential franchisees when investing hard-earned money in a franchise.

> If it is a requirement to finance through the franchisor, a trip to local lending institutions is in order to determine whether or not you will be securing a loan on comparable conditions.

Item 11. Franchisor's Obligations

(The proposed rule would change the title to "Franchisor's Assistance, Advertising, Computer Systems, and Training.")

You are not only initially paying for the right to use a trademark or service mark; you are probably also paying both a cash advance and a percentage of your future profits for other benefits to be provided to you by the franchisor. Determine whether or not you are getting your money's worth. When reviewing this part of the circular, ask yourself:

- Does the franchisor state that he or she will furnish a standard plan of specifications vital to the operation of the business or could you come up with specifications of your own if you started your own business?
- Does the franchisor provide you with starting inventory and training? If he or she provides training, how, when, and where does the training occur?
- Is a training manual provided? How detailed is the manual?
- What ongoing support does the franchisor provide to you once the franchise is operating?

Make a list of the support items you believe the franchisor needs to provide for you to succeed in the business being sold by the franchisor. The would-be franchisor should reverse this thinking and list the items of support that are necessary in order to ensure you have every possibility of succeeding. Once the list is completed, it should be included as obligations in the franchise agreement. Determine from research in the business reference sections of the public library just what training and experience you would need in order to successfully pursue this concern on your own. Answer the following questions:

- Does the franchisor offer these types of services?
- Does the franchisor offer them on a continuing basis?
- Is the franchisor obligated to offer these benefits in the offering circular and the franchise agreement?
- Does the franchisor merely offer them, even though he or she is not obligated to do so? (Remember: obligations can be enforced in court, while nonobligatory statements cannot.)
- Do the services offered fulfill the franchisee's needs?

Once again, contacting current franchisees or potential franchisees of a competitor/franchisor can give you a good idea of what to look for in the way of training and advice from a franchisor. Always remember: every franchisee went through the same things as you are going through. A telephone call to a franchisee of the franchise operation you are interested in, or to a competitor's franchisee, might give you an opportunity to meet the owner and discuss matters. Perhaps an offer of lunch would help ensure his or her cooperation.

Item 12. Territory

Exclusive areas are extremely important to the franchisee, so you need to carefully review this section of the circular. "Exclusive area" generally means that you will not have any competition in a specified area, at least as far as location of another franchise is concerned. However, the matter of exclusive areas can cause problems for the franchisor. For instance, it could be a possible antitrust violation for the franchisor to restrict any other franchisee from selling in a specified area from outside that area, as well as a costly litigation nightmare if such a provision had to be enforced by the franchisor.

In addition, the franchise system itself is concerned, because it realizes each franchisee must pursue his or her business efforts to the maximum. Therefore, if one franchisee fails to develop his or her area, it behooves the system to place another franchisee in competition in that area; this ensures that the particular franchise potential is fully achieved.

Most franchisors fear that a franchisee will not develop his or her territory, which is one reason why many franchisors will not grant exclusive areas, prohibiting putting other franchisees in that area. As an alternative to this, some franchise agreements provide that the initial franchisee must meet current minimums or lose the franchise or share the territory with another franchisee. Make sure that territories have specific formulas for determining the size of the territory, in order to have an adequate customer base to provide a reasonable profit to a franchisee in each territory. Be sure to research the impact on your sales with such a condition.

It is very unlikely that a franchisor will deliberately try to destroy an area by selling two franchises in a territory that would provide a suitable profit for only one. In many cases, you will find that you do not have an exclusive area. If not, find out whether or not the franchisor will offer you a right of first refusal so you can purchase any additional franchises that may be offered in the future adjacent to your specified territory or location. This way, you can expand in a given area without fear that someone else is operating in your area, reaping a part of your profits. One benefit for you, as a prospective franchisee, is a condition set forth by the franchisor that he or she will not open a company-owned office or another franchise in your territory under the same, similar, or different trademark. Some franchisors, however, may retain the right to sell a franchised trademark product or similar product in your territory through supermarkets or other retail outlets. This might hurt your sales.

You should give careful consideration to termination or loss-of-area-exclusivity clauses imposed by the franchisor for failing to meet a minimum sales volume. Your franchise could be withdrawn if you do not meet these minimum sales volume quotas. If the franchise you are considering imposes such minimum restrictions, you should examine them carefully to see if they are realistic. If possible, consult with current franchisees to see what their experience has been at meeting such minimums. In addition, if your state has a franchise investment act that requires the filing of offering circulars as a public record, contact the state and review the early filings to determine who the initial franchisees were. Perhaps one of these initial franchisees is no longer in business.

If you can locate a former franchisee of the particular franchise operation you are interested in, you might be able to secure a substantial amount of information from an excellent source. Listen to this person's impressions of the franchisor. If there are many

> "Exclusive area" generally means that you will not have any competition in a specified area, at least as far as location of another franchise is concerned.

> Make sure that territories have specific formulas for determining the size of the territory.

> Some franchisors may retain the right to sell a franchised trademark product or similar product in your territory through supermarkets or other retail outlets. This might hurt your sales.

former franchisees, consider this a red flag as to the merits of purchasing a franchise from this particular franchisor. This section of the circular can help you tell whether or not the franchisor favors company-owned offices rather than franchised offices. In many cases, the franchisor-owned offices may be a result of the reclamation of franchises that failed. A high record of failure by previous franchisees is another red flag in your search.

Item 13. Trademarks

One of the prime benefits you are paying for when you purchase a franchise is a well-known trade name, trademark, service mark, service name, or logotype. (The proposed rule requires the UFOC to state the franchisee's rights if the franchisee is required to modify or discontinue use of a mark under any circumstances.)

> One of the prime benefits you are paying for when you purchase a franchise is a well-known trade name, trademark, service mark, service name, or logotype.

Preferably, you wish to be a licensee of a trademark or service mark that is registered in the Principal Register of the U.S. Patent Office. A registered trademark or service mark of this nature gives the franchisor certain legal presumptions as to ownership and the right to use these marks throughout the United States, which can be very valuable to your franchise. Check with the U.S. Patent and Trademark Office in Washington, D.C. and find out if a certificate of registration has actually been granted to the franchisor. A trademark registered in the Supplemental Register does not have these presumptive legal rights. A statement to this effect must be in Item 13 of the Uniform Franchise Offering Circular.

Another consideration is the length of time that the franchisor has held such certificate of registration. An indication that the mark has been applied for but is still pending does not mean that the franchisor has or will attain the registered right to a particular name. Furthermore, the initials "TM" after the trademarks merely indicate that the franchisor uses a particular name as a trademark, not that he or she has a U.S. registration certificate. The key to utilizing a trademark or service mark is to federally register it so you can use the trademark or service mark and advertise it with the symbol ® indicating it is a U.S. registered mark. Registration of a trademark is only one element to consider. Here are some other questions to address:

- Are the trademarks and trade names well known in the market area in which you intend to operate?
- Are they well known throughout the United States?
- Is the trademark or service mark so identified with the franchisor that it will attract customers to the franchise operations?
- Do you have full use of every trademark or service mark registered to the franchisor?

Consideration should also be given to whether or not the franchisor is obligated to protect the trademark and pursue those who violate it. It behooves not only the franchisor but his or her entire franchise system to extensively police the use of the trademark or service mark and immediately stop infringers through litigation, no matter how expensive the litigation may be.

Item 14. Patents, Copyrights, and Proprietary Information

The section on patents and copyrights is important to you only if patents are material to the franchise. If so, obtain copies of the patents from the U.S. Patent Office and have your patent attorney review them for depth of coverage and length of time remaining on the patent. Examine if there are any possible limitations of the right of the franchisor to use the patent or any dissolution of the patent through licenses to others, particularly potential competitors. Carefully examine any claims of proprietary right and confidential information designated by the franchisor.

(The proposed rule requires affirmative action by the franchisor when notified of an infringement, and the franchisee's rights if the franchisee is required to modify or discontinue use of matters covered by patent or copyright must be disclosed in requirement and rights terms under the franchise agreement.)

Item 15. Obligation to Participate in the Actual Operation of the Franchise Business

This section discloses whether the franchisee must personally participate in the operation of the franchise. If there is no such requirement, this section must state whether the franchisor recommends such participation, whether the manager must complete the franchisor's training program and/or own an equity interest in the franchisee entity, and any limitations that the franchise must place on its manager.

In the opinion of many franchise professionals, the successful franchisee is the one who manages his or her own business or at least spends considerable time supervising the management of the business. The smart franchisor, in many cases, will insist that the franchisee be active in the operation of the business or at least retain qualified managers who will be active. In general, the franchisor must approve these managers. Franchisees should be obligated to train managers, preferably at their own expense. But usually, franchisors will obligate themselves to train a manager at the franchisee's expense. Be sure you can determine the frequency of the training sessions.

> In the opinion of many franchise professionals, the successful franchisee is the one who manages his or her own business or at least spends considerable time supervising the management of the business.

(The proposed rule would reduce disclosure of any limitations on whom a franchisee could hire as an on-premises supervisor and whether that person has to successfully complete the franchisor's training program in instances involving a franchisee who is an individual. In addition, the franchisor would have to disclose only agreements binding on the franchise owners that contain obligations to personally participate in the direct operation of the business.)

Item 16. Restrictions on What the Franchisee May Sell

If you wish to conduct a more extensive business while operating the franchise, this section of the offering circular will be important for you to review. It is also important if you are limited to selling services or products that alone would not give you the required return on your capital. Again, ask either current franchisees of the franchisor or current franchisees of a competitor/franchisor about their experiences.

There have been instances when franchisees were limited to one service only. In one case, for example, a franchisee who was limited to offering only a tune-up service for automobiles believed that it would be more profitable if allied services, such as oil changes, were also permitted. The question to ask yourself is whether or not such restrictions on your product sales will permit you to make a reasonable profit.

Item 17. Renewal, Termination, Transfer, and Dispute Resolution

This particular section of the circular, which is in tabular form, is of major importance to your future success, since it dictates the length of time for which you will receive a return on your investment. For many, the best franchises are those that will exist in the name of the franchisees and their heirs or their purchasers for as long as the franchisees, their heirs, successors, or purchasers perform the contracted duties as specified in the agreement. In other words, the ideal franchise agreement allows the franchisee and anyone who purchases the franchise to automatically renew the franchise agreement as long as the agreement has not been breached. A franchise agreement requiring you to spend 10 years of your time, money, and effort only to lose the franchise at the end of 10 years is not a good one.

Watch out for clauses that require you to make substantial repairs and decorations as a contingency to a renewal. Such clauses should be reasonable and have some formula so expenses do not all have to be incurred in one year. The clauses should set some type of standard so any changes in decor and refurbishing are related to staying competitive within the industry.

> Watch out for clauses that require you to make substantial repairs and decorations as a contingency to a renewal.

An ideal franchise is one you can pass on to your heirs or sell to others subject to the approval of the franchisor and possibly at a reasonable transfer fee. If a franchisor does not allow such transfers or renewals and you still wish to purchase the franchise, consider what provisions, if any, you can make for the franchisor to purchase the franchise back and the amount of consideration for such a deal.

If your state has franchise laws regulating franchise renewals and terminations, consult your attorney to see if the circular's renewal and termination clauses comply with them. See Appendix E for more on state franchise laws.

A good franchise package should definitely allow you to change legal forms of business organization—for example, from a sole proprietorship to a partnership or from a sole proprietorship or partnership to a corporation—at no extra fee or a minimum fee. Scrutinize very carefully the reasons a franchisor gives for causes of termination when examining this portion of the offering circular or prospectus.

This section also reveals whether or not the franchise business can be offered for sale. If the franchisor has the right of first refusal, that right should not be at the franchisor's discretion when the business is being sold to a blood relative. The more rights you receive regarding the continuation of the franchise, as well as its transfer and sale, the better the franchise package you are getting, from both practical and legal standpoints.

If the franchise agreement limits your choice of forum to arbitration rather than a court of law or your choice of the law to be applied is an out-of-state jurisdiction, consult an attorney regarding the effect of this on your rights. The cover page of the circular should also alert you to these restrictions as possible risks.

Item 18. Public Figures

This section requires the franchisor to disclose whether it uses a famous person to endorse the franchise. If so, it must disclose the compensation paid or promised to the person, the person's involvement in management or control of the franchisor, and the amount of the person's investment in the franchisor. If the franchisor is paying a public figure to endorse the franchise, find out whether or not you can use the person in personal appearances or in advertising without prior written approval of the franchisor, how frequently you could do so, and the cost of such use, if any.

Item 19. Earnings Claims

In most cases, the franchisor will not provide actual, average, projected, or forecasted financial sales profits or earnings because of federal and state laws requiring written substantiation of such projections. In addition, there are so many variables involved that it is very difficult to forecast projected earnings in a particular area, especially with a franchise operation that is relatively new. However, if the franchisor does provide such information, you should show it to your accountant for evaluation. This information should also be evaluated against any information that may be supplied by competitive franchisors.

Once again, contacting current franchisees of the franchisor could well provide you with considerable information as to the veracity of these projections. Even a franchisee of a competitor could give you some insight into the reliability of such projections. If it is not possible for you to contact a franchisee of either the franchisor or a competitor, a suitable alternative would be to contact someone who is not a franchisee but operates a similar business in the same geographical area. This applies to your efforts to ferret out any of the information described above. There is nothing like relying on experience when deciding whether or not to buy a business.

(The proposed rule would change the title of this section of the offering circular to "Financial Performance Representations" and allow statements about actual or potential financial performance if there is a reasonable basis for the information and if the information is included in the UFOC.)

> In most cases, the franchisor will not provide actual, average, projected, or forecasted financial sales profits or earnings because of federal and state laws requiring written substantiation of such projections.

Item 20. List of Outlets

This section of the circular provides you with the names, telephone numbers, and locations of existing franchisees. In addition to accessing this information, you can also determine whether or not a substantial number of failures have occurred within the franchised operation you are investigating. You can also project just how large the system probably will be in a few years, according to the estimates of the franchisor.

Generally, the more franchisees, the greater the franchisor's chances for success in future sales of franchises; however, don't take this at face value. Check with the franchisees themselves. It is also a general rule that the more franchisees, the more you will pay for a franchise. This is particularly true in situations where the franchisor does not have many company-owned offices. Theoretically, a higher number of franchisees indicates a more extensive distribution of the product and a better public image for the franchise.

(The proposed rule would rename this title "Outlets and Franchise Information" and require certain chart reporting changes, discussion of any confidentiality agreements ["gag clauses"], and information about certain trademark franchisee associations.)

Item 21. Financial Statements

The offering circular will contain an exhibit with audited financial statements. Take the financial statements to your accountant if you do not have the training to properly eval-

Theoretically, a higher number of franchisees indicates a more extensive distribution of the product and a better public image for the franchise.

uate them. Remember: the financial condition of the franchisor not only will affect his or her ability to run a financially successful operation in the future, but it will also determine whether or not he or she will go under, leaving you holding the bag. Most good franchisors have their own successful "pilot plant" company-owned offices, which are the basis of their franchise systems.

Most franchisors use a separate corporate entity for selling their franchises. However, if your particular franchisor doesn't, you then have an opportunity to find out whether or not these company-owned ventures actually made any income for a period of up to three years. If the franchisor can't make a go of the business, how do you expect to do so?

Financial statements are the financial track record of the franchisor. Examine, analyze, and digest this material. Feel free to ask questions of the main representatives of the franchisor concerning these financial statements. In fact, it is a good idea to take your accountant along to such meetings. Retain the services of an experienced accountant and an experienced attorney; both should be familiar with the day-to-day business operations of a franchise and specialize in franchise arrangements.

(The proposed rule would require including in the UFOC a separate, audited financial statement for a company controlling 80% or more of the franchisor.)

Item 22: Contracts

This section requires the franchisor to attach to the UFOC a copy of all form contracts the franchisees will sign, including the franchise agreement, leases, options, and purchase agreements.

Item 23: Receipt

In this final section, the franchisor is required to include as the last page of the UFOC a form for the prospective franchisee to sign to acknowledge receipt of the UFOC.

A Comparison of a Circular and Franchise Agreements

Attached to the circular, as required in Item 22, you will find a copy of the current franchise agreement or contracts and possibly other ancillary agreements issued by your franchisor. Carefully examine these agreements and compare them with the statements that are made in the circular. Make sure that the statements coincide and there is nothing missing from the agreement or contract and nothing additional that is not in the circular as previously discussed. See Appendix B-1 for a sample franchise agreement. The rest of this chapter discusses those areas of the agreement you should be aware of, in addition to those that have been discussed in this section.

The Franchise Agreement

In the trade, the franchise agreement or contract is sometimes referred to as "money in the bank" because a good agreement that protects the best interests of the franchisee and franchisor will be a major factor in ensuring future revenues from the franchise business for both parties. Every franchise agreement provides certain basic provisions and conditions. They may be numbered differently, be placed in different locations, or even have different subtitles, but they are basically the same in nature. This section discusses some additional provisions to look for in the agreement and some suggestions of how to handle them.

Generally, franchisors will not agree to negotiate any terms of their agreement, particularly those terms that are material to them. Before the passage of state franchise registration laws, this was not the case. Today, any substantial changes in the agreement require a change in the circular, so many franchisors may be reluctant to make material changes, particularly if they must first obtain approval from a state franchise regulator. However, there is no harm in asking.

The rules differ from state to state. For instance:

> Generally, franchisors will not agree to negotiate any terms of their agreement, particularly those terms that are material to them.

- California allows a restricted type of negotiation. The franchisor must provide a notice of negotiated sales with the California Commissioner of Corporations within 15 business days after the sale and must amend his or her registered UFOC in order to disclose the terms of the particular item negotiated before making another sale. The latter disclosure must be made if the negotiated sale occurred within 12 months of the offering being made.
- Illinois allows a one-time-only negotiation without a formal amendment.
- Indiana requires a temporary amendment for negotiating franchises only.
- North Dakota and South Dakota seem to favor negotiated franchise agreements and appear not to require an after-amendment referring to the negotiations. This should be checked out periodically with the state authorities.
- Virginia requires the franchisor to negotiate.
- Minnesota requires an amendment prior to selling the franchise.
- New York doesn't permit negotiation prior to filing.

However, these regulations and rules change as often as the weather, so a franchisor should check with the particular state authority before beginning any negotiations, each time the occasion arises.

Use of Trademarks

As previously indicated, one of the prime benefits you receive when you purchase a franchise is the use of a well-known and registered trademark or service mark. Examine the portion of the agreement that is entitled "License" or "Trademark" and make sure you are getting your money's worth. Consider the following:

- Is the trademark well known?
- Has it been in use for a substantial amount of time?
- Does the franchisor have an unrestricted right to use and license such trademark or service mark?
- Are there other trademarks, service marks, or logos you are entitled to use?
- Will the franchisor enforce the trademark registration to the exclusion of infringers?

Location of the Franchise

Another factor influencing the success of almost any business is location. Franchising is no exception. You will need to ask yourself these questions when reviewing this section of a franchise agreement:

- Do you have an exclusive right to operate a facility within a franchised area? If not, do you have the right of first refusal to open other locations within the area?
- Is the franchisor required to advise you on site selection? If not, are you qualified to select your own site?
- Will the franchisor assist you by providing information and statistics concerning a suitable location? Included at the end of this chapter is a Franchise Site Evaluation Form to assist you in selecting a site.
- How close is the nearest franchise outlet (whether owned by a franchisee or the franchisor) to the site proposed for you?
- How close are your competitors?
- If you are unable to renew your lease at its expiration, will the franchisor make every reasonable effort to relocate you in another premise in the same location?
- Who will pay for relocation, the franchisor or you?

Term of the Franchise

Regarding the term of your potential franchise, consider these questions:

- Do you have the franchise as long as you live?
- Is your franchise subject to an option to purchase by the franchisor before it expires? If it is, are you to be paid an amount equal to market value or a certain multiple of earnings or must you take a lower book value?
- If the franchise is for a stated term, do you have a right to renew? If you have a right to renew, is there a renewal fee? What is the renewal fee? Is it reasonable?

Front Money and Royalties

The answers to the following questions are very pertinent to your decision regarding whether or not to invest in the franchise offered for sale. Some of these concerns are touched upon in other sections of this book as well.

- Is there any front money (initial fee) that you must pay? If so, can you afford the front money?
- What do you receive in the way of services, inventory, and other fringes for the front money?
- When is the front money payable? Will the franchisor finance the front money? Have you calculated your debt service obligations on the total amount borrowed in your projected pro forma financial statements?
- Do you have to pay a royalty? If so, is it based on net income or gross sales? If based on gross sales, what is the effective percentage on your net income before taxes? After taxes? How often do you have to pay the royalty?
- What records of your earnings must you submit to the franchisor?
- Is the amount of the front money and the royalty consistent with the working capital that you have available?
- What type of investment would you have to provide if you started your own business in competition with the existing franchisees of the franchisor?

Leases

The portion of the franchise agreement that pertains to leases is another important area to review. Here are some sample questions you may want to ask yourself.

- Are you required to lease the location from the franchisor? If so, is the lease reasonable in its term and the monthly payment to the franchisor? Have you checked with landlords to determine if the rent is reasonable, comparable with what they would charge?
- Is this a "net lease"? That is, do you have to pay—in addition to rent—utilities, parking lot improvement costs, and wage increases based on the standard-of-living clause, and increases in property taxes? If so, have you checked out the actual or probable amount of these additional costs?
- Must you lease fixtures, signs, or equipment from the franchisor? If so, are the prices reasonable? Have you compared costs of fixtures, signs, and equipment offered by suppliers other than the franchisor?
- Are you required to buy a certain amount of inventory? Is the cost of the inventory comparable with the cost of an inventory purchased from a third party?
- Are you required to follow certain customs and standards? Are these customs and standards consistent with the good management of the business and the quality of the products?

Obligations and Duties of the Franchisor

Ask yourself the following questions regarding the franchisor's responsibilities to you:

- Will you receive adequate training from the franchisor? If so, when, where, and for how long?
- Do you have to pay for such training? Is such training offered at a convenient location not requiring extensive travel expenses?
- Are you entitled to continuous training throughout the term of your franchise?
- Will you be provided with an operations manual? (See Chapter 10.)
- Will the franchisor give you some idea of the extent of the coverage of the manual before you sign the contract?
- Will the franchisor provide you with advertising at his or her expense? If not, must you submit any advertising copy to the franchisor to approve in advance?
- Are you required to pay an additional fee for advertising? If so, is the franchisor bound to place such an advertising fee in a special account in your name and utilize it for local advertising?
- What are the franchisor's obligations to you after you are in operation? Are they worth the royalty you will be paying?

Obligations and Duties of the Franchisee

Be sure and ask about your responsibilities as a franchisee.

- Are your obligations and duties under the contract reasonable?
- Do other franchisees have the same obligations and duties?

- Are the obligations necessary to help ensure the uniformity and quality of the service or product?
- Are you required to participate in the franchisor's training?
- Are other franchisees required to participate in initial and ongoing training by the franchisor?
- Are you obligated to actively participate in the franchise? If not, are you obligated to have a manager approved by the franchisor?
- Is there any provision regarding the days that your franchise must be kept open?
- Are there provisions that help ensure that all franchised entities will be clean and kept in an attractive manner?
- Are you subjected to revisions in the contract at various times or when you transfer the contract by sale to others?
- Are you required to keep adequate records and books?
- What records must you submit to the franchisor and how often?
- What are the penalties for not submitting such records?

Transfer of Agreement and Termination

Regarding the transfer of the franchise agreement or termination of the franchise, consider the following questions:

- Can you transfer the license to your heirs or to a corporation formed by you for that purpose? If so, must you pay a fee? Is such a fee reasonable?
- If you die and you are operating as a sole proprietorship or a partnership, will your personal representative be able to carry on the business?
- Are you required to give a right of first refusal to the franchisor? If the franchisor has a right of first refusal, is the formula for payment of your interest adequate? Will it include a price for goodwill?
- If the franchisor has a right of first refusal, is the purchase price payable in a lump sum rather than spread out in installments?
- When can the franchisor terminate the franchise? Can this be done only with good cause? If so, are the causes listed in the franchise agreement reasonable?
- If the franchisor can terminate for breach of contract, has he or she specified which terms of the agreement are considered material terms, the breach of which will automatically constitute termination?
- What are your rights upon termination? What are the penalties? Can you terminate this venture without cause prior to its term without any liability? Can you compete after termination?
- Are there applicable laws regulating the termination of franchises or distributorships in your state?

Arbitration and Court Jurisdiction

Review the agreement to see if there is a provision relating to the arbitration of disputes. Generally, arbitration is much less costly and certainly quicker than court. It is also ideal if the arbitration can be held in the state where you are located. The downside to arbitration is that it normally does not allow for discovery procedure and is binding and final.

You would benefit greatly from the insertion of a paragraph stating that the laws of the state in which the franchise is operated prevail. Usually, the franchisor will attempt to have controlling law in the state where he or she is located, thus causing you a great deal of hardship and expense if legal action takes place away from your franchise area.

Attorney Fees

In addition, review the agreement to see if there is a clause providing that, in the event of litigation of a dispute under the franchise agreement, the winning party shall be entitled to an award for his or her attorney fees. This clause often encourages both parties to litigate, each feeling he or she will be victorious and reimbursed for his or her fees by the loser. However, each party is obligated to pay his or her respective attorney fees as litigation progresses. At the conclusion of the trial, the judge can award whatever he or she deems as reasonable attorney fees, no matter the amount of the actual bill, and the losing party may well be bankrupt at the time of the final award. For cost-saving tips on attorney fees, refer to Chapter 11.

> You would benefit greatly from the insertion of a paragraph stating that the laws of the state in which the franchise is operated prevail.

Helpful Publications and Tips to Prospect for a Franchise

To help you get more information on franchises in general, you may want to obtain some of the following publications:

- *Entrepreneur Magazine*—This monthly magazine has published comprehensive franchise information for more than 20 years. *Entrepreneur* publishes "The Annual 500," a ranking of the top franchises in the industry, and maintains a comprehensive Web site, with a "Franchise Zone"—www.entrepreneur.com/franchise—that lists more than 1,000 franchises and provides comprehensive information on how to buy a franchise. *Entrepreneur* publishes "Be Your Own Boss" in February (Spring), May (Summer), and September (Winter). To subscribe to this helpful magazine, contact:

  Entrepreneur Magazine
  2445 McCabe Way, Suite 400
  Irvine, CA 92614-6244
  phone: 800 274-6229
  e-mail: entmag@entrepreneur.com

- *The Franchise Handbook*—This is a handy publication that will provide useful information on available franchise opportunities. For more information on this handbook, contact:

  1020 North Broadway, Suite 111
  Milwaukee, WI 53202
  phone: 414 272-9977
  fax: 414 272-9973
  www.franchisehandbook.com

- The *Franchise Opportunities Guide* (biannual) is another source of information on available franchise opportunities. Contact:

  International Franchise Association
  1350 New York Avenue, NW, Suite 900
  Washington, DC 20005-4709
  phone: 202 628-8000
  fax: 202 628-0812
  www.franchise.org

- *Entrepreneur Magazine's Ultimate Book of Franchises* by Rieva Lesonsky and Maria Anton (Entrepreneur Media, 2004).

You will find that most franchise offerings are advertised in either the business opportunity section of *The Wall Street Journal* on Thursdays or the Sunday classified section of your local newspaper. When you answer such ads, the franchisor will probably respond by sending you a brochure and franchisee business application and net worth form. Refer to the end of Chapter 11 for a sample of this form. Once the franchisor determines that you have the financial wherewithal, the offering circular will be sent and franchise salespersons will come knocking.

Another way of discovering franchise opportunities is to attend franchise trade shows. Some of the best franchise trade shows are those sponsored by the International Franchise Association (IFA). IFA trade shows take place in major U.S. cities every year.

Conclusion

To help you investigate and research, review the Checklist of Information to Secure from a Franchisor located in the following pages.

With the help of some of the resources above and your own investigating and researching, you will have a good start on prospecting for and purchasing a franchise. To help you investigate and research, review the Checklist of Information to Secure from a Franchisor located in the following pages. If you are evaluating more than one franchise, make enough copies of this checklist so you can use a form for each franchise offering.

Checklist for Interviewing Existing Franchisees

Use this questionnaire when trying to investigate franchise opportunities by interviewing existing franchisees.

Financial

Yes No

❑ ❑ Are you satisfied with the franchisor?

❑ ❑ Is your franchise profitable?

❑ ❑ Have you made the profit you expected to make?

❑ ❑ Are your actual costs those stated in the offering circular?

❑ ❑ Is the product or service you sell of good quality?

❑ ❑ Is delivery of goods from the franchisor adequate?

❑ ❑ How long did it take you to break even?

❑ ❑ Was the training provided to you by the franchisor adequate?

❑ ❑ What is your assessment of the training provided?

❑ ❑ Is your franchisor fair and easy to work with?

❑ ❑ Does your franchisor listen to your concerns?

❑ ❑ Have you had any disputes with your franchisor? If so, please specify.

❑ ❑ If you have had disputes, were you able to settle them?

❑ ❑ How was settlement accomplished?

❑ ❑ Do you know of any trouble the franchisor has had with other franchisees? If so, what was the nature of the problem?

❑ ❑ Do you know of any trouble the franchisor has had with the government?

❑ ❑ Do you know of any trouble the franchisor has had with local authorities?

❑ ❑ Do you know of any trouble the franchisor has had with competitors?

❑ ❑ Are you satisfied with the marketing and promotional assistance the franchisor has provided?

❑ ❑ Have the operations manuals provided by the franchisor helped you?

❑ ❑ What do you think of the manuals?

❑ ❑ Are the manuals changed frequently? If so, why?

❑ ❑ Other comments you would like to make.

Checklist of Information to Secure from a Franchisor

Use this checklist when doing your own investigation and information gathering.

Yes No

❑ ❑ Is the franchisor a one-person company? or

❑ ❑ Is the franchisor a corporation with an experienced management that is well trained?

Yes No

☐ ☐ Is the franchisor offering you an exclusive territory for the length of the franchise? or

☐ ☐ Can the franchisor sell a second or third franchise in your market area?

☐ ☐ Do you have the right of first refusal to adjacent areas?

☐ ☐ Will the franchisor sublet space to you? or

☐ ☐ Will he or she assist you in finding a location for your franchise operation?

☐ ☐ Does the franchisor provide financing? If so, what are the terms?

☐ ☐ Does the franchisor require any fees—other than those described in the offering circular—from the franchisee? If so, what are they?

☐ ☐ Has the franchisor given you information regarding actual, average, or forecasted sales?

☐ ☐ Has the franchisor given you information regarding actual, average, or forecasted profits?

☐ ☐ Has the franchisor given you information regarding actual, average, or forecasted earnings?

☐ ☐ What information have you received?

☐ ☐ Will the franchisor provide you with the success rates of existing franchisees?

☐ ☐ Will the franchisor provide you with their names and locations?

☐ ☐ Are there any restrictions on what items you may sell? If so, what are they?

☐ ☐ Does your prospective franchisor allow variances in the contracts of some of his or her other franchisees? What is the nature of the variances?

☐ ☐ In the event you sell your franchise back to your franchisor under the right of first refusal, will you be compensated for the goodwill you have built into the business?

☐ ☐ Does the franchisor have any federally registered trademarks, service marks, trade names, logotypes, and/or symbols?

☐ ☐ Are you, as a franchisee, entitled to use them without reservation? or

☐ ☐ Are there restrictions, exceptions, or conditions? If so, what are they?

☐ ☐ Does the franchisor have existing patents and copyrights on equipment you will use or items you will sell?

☐ ☐ Does the franchisor have endorsement agreements with any public figures for advertising purposes? If so, what are the terms?

☐ ☐ Has the franchisor investigated you carefully enough to assure himself or herself that you can successfully operate the franchise at a profit both to him or her and to you?

❏   ❏   Has the franchisor complied with FTC and state disclosure laws?

Yes   No

❏   ❏   Does the franchisor have a reputation for honesty and fair dealing among the local firms holding his or her franchise?

Other Questions

- How many years has the firm offering you a franchise been in operation?
- Describe the franchise area offered you.
- What is the total investment the franchisor requires from the franchisee?
- How does the franchisor use the initial franchise fees?
- What is the extent of the training the franchisor will provide for you?
- What are your obligations for purchasing or leasing goods or services from the franchisor or other designated sources?
- What are your obligations in relation to purchasing or leasing goods or services in accordance with the franchisor's specifications?
- What are the terms of your agreement regarding termination, modification, and renewal conditions of the franchise agreement?
- Under what circumstances can you terminate the franchise agreement?
- If you decide to cancel the franchise agreement, what will it cost you?
- What are the background experience and achievement records of key personnel (their "track records")?
- How successful is the franchise operation? (Use Dun & Bradstreet reports or magazine articles to supplement information the franchisor gives you.)
- What is the franchisor's experience in relation to past litigation or prior bankruptcies?
- What is the quality of the financial statements the franchisor provides you?
- Exactly what can the franchisor do for you that you cannot do for yourself?

Franchise Site Evaluation Form

When trying to evaluate suitable site locations for your potential franchise, use this form as a guideline.

Name of person making report:

Address:

Phone:

Date of report:

Address of site:

Information on Site, Customers, and Street Traffic

Type of site (strip center, mall, free-standing, drive-through, or other):

Nearest intersections:

Distance of nearest intersections from site: _____, _____,

_____

Nearest stop sign and name of street: _____ ft. _____

Number of lanes on front and side streets:

_____ on _____

_____ on _____

_____ on _____

_____ on _____

Description and number of parking spaces (front, side, and back, as applicable):

_____ spaces _____

_____ spaces _____

_____ spaces _____

_____ spaces _____

Condition of adjacent streets: _____

Observations of traffic on streets at peak hours, including time of day observed:

Description of adjoining business, including type of building, and products or services offered:

	Left Building	Right Building

Frontage measurements:
Depth of site:
Total square footage:

Customer traffic count of adjacent buildings or businesses:

	Left Building	Right Building
6:00-8:00 a.m.		
8:00-10:00 a.m.		
10:00-noon		
noon-1:00 p.m.		
1:00-2:00 p.m.		
2:00-4:00 p.m.		
4:00-6:00 p.m.		
6:00-7:00 p.m.		
7:00-8:00 p.m.		
8:00-midnight		
midnight-6:00 a.m.		

Major competition within one and a half miles of site:

Name	Address	Type of Business

Observations made from surveillance of adjacent businesses and discussions with businesspeople regarding general business conditions, customer traffic, parking availability, center advertising, promotions, reasonableness of rent, possible rent increases, possible construction, and other:

Disadvantages	Advantages

Visibility of site from street:

North _____ feet   West _____ feet

South _____ feet   East _____ feet

Ingress and egress observations:

General access:

Excellent _____ Good _____ Poor _____

Purchase of Real Estate

Purchase price: $ _____

Terms of purchase:

Base Rental

Monthly: $ _____

Date and amount of increase: _____ $ _____

Percentage rental: Yes _____ No _____ If yes, describe:

Common area costs: Yes _____ No _____ If yes, brief description:

Description of utility costs that must be paid and estimated amounts:

Description of other costs:

Term of Lease

Renewal term and increased rental or other increased costs associated therewith:

Lease can be canceled _____ years _____ months from date of possession or on:

_____, 20 ___.

Price Comparisons with Competitors within One Mile

Prime competitor:

Secondary competitors:

List each of your major products or services and insert competitors' price:

_____ $_____

_____ $_____

_____ $_____

_____ $_____

_____ $_____

_____ $_____

Population—Demographics (Minimum Two-Mile Radius)

Population: _____ Year: _____ + ___ Increase in last 12 months: _____ %

Per-capita income: $ _____ Median family income: $ _____

Type of housing:

Average home, condo, or apartment value: $_____

General comments:

Zoning and Restrictions

Present zoning class:

Permissible uses:

Required setbacks:

Front: _____ Rear: _____

Right side: _____ Left side: _____

Number and size of parking places:

Front: _____ Back: _____

Left side: _____ Right side: _____

Fire zone: _____

Nearest fire hydrant: _____

Address and distance of closest fire station: _____ feet or miles

Sign Restrictions

Freestanding: _____

Exterior: _____

Interior: _____

Utility and Regulatory Agency Information

	Company Name	**Phone Number**
Electric		
Natural gas		
Water		
Telephone		
Health department		
Zoning		
Other		

Problems discovered when contacting utilities:

Nearest Industrial Developments

Name and Address	**Type of Business**	**Estimated # of Employees**	**Distance**

Possible Area Business Draws

List all convention facilities, colleges, high schools, grade schools, parks, or churches in the area.

Shopping Areas

Location	**Size**	**Distance from Site**	**Comparable Rents**

Exhibits

1. Strip map showing site in relation to competitors within a one-mile radius.
2. Videotape of location from all directions.
3. Demographic profiles from one- and two-mile radius.
4. Traffic count sheet.

5. Plot plan of site.
6. Other business and development information from brokers, landlords, and others.
7. Names and addresses of real estate brokers used.

Your Evaluation of Suitability of Site

Chapter 3
Buying a Local Business

If you are considering purchasing a local business rather than a franchise, you will find the factors you need to consider are similar to those for purchasing a franchise; however, you will also find some dissimilarities. For instance, the local business owner is not going to supply you with an offering circular or prospectus detailing his or her background and that of the business you are buying. Consequently, you will have to secure this information yourself. To do this, you can have a qualified attorney prepare an agreement that would, in essence, make the seller warrant and represent certain necessary facets of the business which, if untrue, would allow you to bring an action for fraud or rescission or both. Thus, many of the provisions discussed in Chapter 2 can be incorporated into these warranties and representations.

This chapter focuses on some of the factors you need to consider when purchasing a local business. Review each discussion carefully to get a better idea of what types of actions and responsibilities you will have as a prospective business purchaser.

> If you are considering purchasing a local business rather than a franchise, you will find the factors you need to consider are similar to those for purchasing a franchise; however, you will also find some dissimilarities.

Purchase Agreements

Many people are under the impression that escrow instructions are the only contracts they need when purchasing a business. This is not true. The escrow agreement is merely an instructional type of agreement wherein both parties advise the escrow agent of what he or she must do to complete the closing, such as which payments are in order and which documents must be received and exchanged. This is not a true sales agreement.

A true sales agreement should require the seller to put in writing and warrant every essential part of the business that will make it a success or failure. This includes warranting that the financials are true and correct, that there are no hidden income tax claims or litigation, that the business has made a certain amount of money and will continue to make a certain amount of money (if that information can be obtained from the seller), and that there are no pending lawsuits. There will be many other details you will want to

> A true sales agreement should require the seller to put in writing and warrant every essential part of the business that will make it a success or failure.

know about as well, but unless you put them in writing and have them warranted by the seller, they will get lost in the shuffle.

Exhibits of purchase agreements should include:

- Financial statements;
- The type of note that you will sign;
- A list of creditors and accounts receivable;
- A list of claims and pending litigation; and
- A complete list of the outstanding contracts, inventory, fixtures, and equipment you are purchasing, together with their value and the basis of evaluation. (Valuable contracts should be examined to determine if you can assume them.)

The passage of the Clinton Deficit Reduction Act has created certain opposing tax advantages between the seller and the buyer of a business on how the purchase price of a business is allocated to various assets being acquired. This tax legislation, which was passed in August 1993, simplified the allocation process by creating a broad new category of amortizable assets, called Section 197 Intangibles. Consequently, intangible assets purchased after August 1993 may now be amortized over a 15-year period by the purchaser. Intangibles include covenants not to compete, know-how, customer lists, goodwill, and going concern value. For the first time ever, a buyer can amortize goodwill and going concern value as Section 197 Intangibles over a 15-year period. See your accountant before signing a purchase agreement that attempts to allocate the purchase price.

> See your accountant before signing a purchase agreement that attempts to allocate the purchase price.

Review Financial Statements

The name of the game in any business is the bottom line—profit. The seller should provide you with updated financial statements and warrant and represent that they are true, accurate, and the basis for your purchase. Don't be afraid to run a credit check on your seller or ask his or her creditors and competitors what they know.

Audited financial statements, including a balance sheet and a profit and loss statement, are extremely desirable. Unaudited statements prepared by a CPA or an accountant are less desirable and unaudited statements prepared by the seller are much less desirable. In many cases, the seller will contend that an audit would be too expensive. If this is the case, you may want to offer sharing the audit's expense.

> An experienced CPA familiar with business acquisitions should examine not only the current financial statements of the seller, but any projections or forecasts he or she has made.

You should have all statements reviewed by a qualified, experienced, business accountant. I cannot emphasize too forcefully that an experienced CPA familiar with business acquisitions should examine not only the current financial statements of the seller, but any projections or forecasts he or she has made. It would be a good idea to attempt to get the seller to set forth in writing his or her sales and earnings projections.

If the financials are not audited, the purchase agreement should contain a clause in which the seller warrants that such financials are true and correct. Any such warranty should indicate that it will survive the closing of the purchase and sale. Having this warranty could certainly save you from disaster and prevent you from buying "a pig in a poke." Sometimes, the best investment is the investment that is not made.

Beware the seller who refuses to give you a financial statement, audited or not.

Bulk Sales Laws

When a business sells all or substantially all of its assets or enters into a major transaction that is not part of its ordinary business activities, the bulk sales law applies. While many states have repealed this law, some states still have a bulk sales law, so you need to find out if yours is one of them.

The bulk sales law is of particular importance to you, because if you purchase a business, this law requires you to perform certain duties to ensure that the rights of the seller's creditors are protected.

To comply with this law, both you and the seller have certain responsibilities. The recommended approach is to consult your attorney and escrow agent, if one is involved. In fact, retaining an attorney to research bulk sales law requirements, as well as to help write a purchase agreement, is imperative to protecting yourself from potential pitfalls and liabilities. Preferably, try to find an attorney who specializes in business law.

> If you purchase a business, the bulk sales law requires you to perform certain duties to ensure that the rights of the seller's creditors are protected.

The Purchase Price

Always remember: the purchase of a business is like an investment in any other type of endeavor—you are seeking a fair and reasonable return on your investment. With interest rates fluctuating, investments in relatively safe endeavors many times can return an annual rate of 5%. In other words, in a safe investment, within 20 years, you can obtain a return equal to your original investment. The same is true when you are buying a business. If possible, find out how the seller arrived at the sales price and compare it with the sales price of comparable businesses.

Currently in California, business brokers recommend a sales price equal to one year's gross sales, plus the value of the assets on the books. Have your accountant carefully check over the financial statements, including the all-important cash-flow analysis, and have him or her estimate when you should be able to secure back your investment. The better the investment, the faster you will recover your initial investment.

> Always remember: the purchase of a business is like an investment in any other type of endeavor—you are seeking a fair and reasonable return on your investment.

You must ask yourself whether you can afford the down payment and, in many cases, the installment payments that you will be required to make in future years. Will your payments make it difficult to support your family? Will your new business provide enough money to make the current payments and at the same time support your family? A cash-flow analysis will at least give you some idea about the prospects you face along these lines. Check your seller's cash-flow analysis and his or her financial statements and determine how much he or she had left over after expenses. In all probability, you will find that the seller did not have the expenses you have since he or she did not have to pay someone else for the business.

Look not only at the costs of operating the business but also at the contracts that accompany such costs. For example, you should carefully examine the lease to see if it has escalation costs that are not payable now, but will be in the future. In addition, you should make sure that you will have the premises for a sufficient number of years to recoup your investment.

Location of the Business

Seriously consider the location of the business you are thinking of buying. Here are some of the questions you may want to raise:

- Will this location be available for a substantial number of years?
- Is there any possibility of a major competitor coming to the immediate area? If so, what effect would this have on the business that is for sale?
- Can the business be relocated without loss of profit? Is the present lease assignable?

You can answer the last question by making a personal visit to the landlord with the understanding that you wish to have the same terms and conditions as those of the seller. Most leases provide that an assignment cannot be made without the consent of the landlord. In many cases, the landlord is given the right to raise the rent if there is a sale.

Not only is it important to examine the lease's contents, assignability, and duration, but it is also imperative to check with the landlord to determine whether or not he or she will abide by such assignment and its existing terms and conditions. See the section in Chapter 2 entitled "Leases." This section raises additional questions that should be asked by franchise or independent-business buyers.

Market Analysis

As with all businesses, the life or death of a local business depends on its market. Major companies that are generally successful in opening a new location normally conduct a market feasibility study beforehand. There is no reason why you should not make your own market feasibility study.

> Major companies that are generally successful in opening a new location normally conduct a market feasibility study beforehand.

There is a wealth of information available from the U.S. Department of Commerce regarding the buying patterns of Americans in relation to particular businesses, including service- and product-oriented businesses. A trip to your local library can provide you with appropriate statistical information. Business publications such as *The Wall Street Journal* will give you an idea of the quickly changing attitudes of the American consumer public.

You can also acquire information about the customers of a particular business, either by phone or by requesting that the seller make questionnaires available to his or her customers for 30 to 60 days before you purchase the business. You could establish a contingency that the closing be delayed for a certain period of time until you can conduct your own survey.

If the seller will not go for this, your best bet is to tell him or her that you would like a trial period with the business, during which you will contact customers to obtain their viewpoints on the establishment and why they patronize it. If you are buying a small business, you should have permission to contact its customers. To prevent any type of panic, you can do this without indicating that you would be the new owner. With the help of the seller, you can introduce yourself as someone merely seeking to find out for the owner how the business can be improved.

If you are buying a business whose particular trade name is the key to the purchase, make sure your purchase agreement contains a provision stating that:

- You can use the name; and
- The seller represents and warrants, subject to a fraud action, that such name is his or hers and is not subject to litigation by any third party claiming to have rights to the name.

Competition

You should check the market area thoroughly for current and potential competitors. Most real estate agents will advise you of buildings that might be available to competitors in your line of business. Personally canvass the area for existing or potential competing businesses that may lessen your future profits.

In addition, ask the seller if he or she will include in writing a covenant not to compete that ensures he or she will not compete with you in a specific geographical area and for a period of time that is reasonable and enforceable under your state laws. Here again, an experienced attorney is a necessity.

> Most real estate agents will advise you of buildings that might be available to competitors in your line of business.

Checking the Seller's Background

It is a good idea for every potential purchaser to study the local county court records to determine whether or not any litigation has been brought against the seller.

You can do this by going to the local courthouse and providing clerks with the last names of the sellers and/or the name under which the business entity has operated. Once any case numbers are secured, you should review the file to determine what the litigation involved. Follow-up conversations with the plaintiffs and their attorneys are also in order. You should then confront the seller to get his or her side of the story regarding these litigated matters. If real property is part of the deal, a title policy should be secured as part of the transaction so you know you are getting clear title to the property.

In all cases where inventory, fixtures, and other items are passing hands, check with the office of the secretary of state or an applicable state or county agency to determine whether or not a Form UCC-1 has been filed. A Form UCC-1 is a Uniform Commercial Code, which is a financing statement that is signed by a debtor indicating that a creditor has a lien on certain enumerated items.

The secretary of state or an applicable state or county agency can also provide a Form UCC-3; for a small fee, the secretary of state will forward copies to you of any financing statements indicating liens that are on file in the name of the particular seller or business entity.

If the seller has not revealed any existing liens, you should confront him or her with these forms, since liens are a cloud on your title to such items. There are some private agencies that, for an additional fee, will check the secretary of state's files or other appropriate state or county files for you in considerably less time than if you submitted a Form UCC-3 to the secretary of state.

When checking the background of a seller, you may wish to use the checklist at the end of this chapter. This checklist will help you obtain some of the information discussed in this chapter.

Conclusion

To help ensure a good purchase of a local business, there are several tips you can follow.

- Determine what the seller is providing you for your money. Does this include a starting inventory, training, promotional advice, customer lists, and other such vital information necessary to your continued success?
- Check with competitors and, particularly, with suppliers, to see if the seller has priced up the inventory to you. A high price to which you add your normal markup could price you right out of the retail market. The suppliers can attest to the price that was paid for the inventory and what inventory prices will be in the future.
- Try to persuade the seller to allow you to watch him or her operate the business for a suitable period of time. You might be taking one giant step toward ensuring a good purchase.
- Encourage the seller to advise you fully as to whether or not his or her own personality has made the difference between success and failure. If it does, make sure you have a similar personality. A successful restaurant that attracts a multitude of people because of the outgoing personality of the owner might become a dismal failure for the purchaser who is much more introverted.
- Truly shop for your local business. Investigate several businesses and compare their profit and loss statements. Talk to other small business owners who are in the same line, even if they are not direct competitors, and consider what they have to say. This may cost you a lot of lunches or dinners, but it could prove very beneficial.
- Determine whether or not the business will make a profit under your ownership. To help do this, prepare a business plan. Such a plan will also be useful to your bank or investor if you are seeking funding. It also acts as a written confirmation of your long-term business goals.

> Determine whether or not the business will make a profit under your ownership. To help do this, prepare a business plan.

There are more than 900 small business development center offices providing free and/or low-cost counseling on starting, running, and operating a business, including information on business plans, finance, and marketing for those wishing to start a business. The SBDC Web site is www.sba.gov/sbdc.

With this brief overview of what factors to consider when buying a local business, you will be better prepared to work with your attorney and accountant when investigating, evaluating, and negotiating the purchase of a small business.

Checklist of Information to Secure from the Seller of an Existing Business

- ❏ Obtain information on the background of the business and its owner.
- ❏ Obtain the seller's financials for the past three years.
- ❏ Obtain copies of all leases on location and equipment.
- ❏ Obtain an accurate list of all equipment, fixtures, inventory, and supplies.
- ❏ Determine the condition of equipment, fixtures, inventory, and supplies—particularly heating and air conditioning.
- ❏ Obtain copies of all maintenance agreements on equipment.
- ❏ Ask about potential or actual liability claims against the current business.
- ❏ Find out if a bulk sale law is applicable.
- ❏ Run a credit check on the seller.
- ❏ Question current and past employees on their views of the business.
- ❏ Check the seller's cash-flow analysis charts.
- ❏ Determine whether the seller's present prices for his or her products or services are competitive.
- ❏ Check with suppliers to verify actual prices of inventory and stock items.
- ❏ Prepare pro forma sales projections in the form of profit and loss statements for the next two years.
- ❏ Make sure the business's past success was not due to the personality of the seller.
- ❏ Secure a valid not-to-compete covenant from the seller.
- ❏ Do a market study of the area or hire a qualified person to do this for you.
- ❏ Find out if any competitors, particularly high discounters, are looking for locations in your area. Make it a practice to contact local real estate and commercial brokers in your area as the source for this important information.
- ❏ Talk to the seller's customers and find out why they patronize the business and their thoughts on improving the business.
- ❏ Check with owners of similar businesses for their opinions on the merits of making money in their line.
- ❏ Check with your bank on the availability of funds to you and the cost.
- ❏ Find out if the seller's present lease is assignable on the same rental terms.
- ❏ Check county records for lawsuits and claims against the seller.
- ❏ Check with the local county or state agency where liens are filed—usually in the secretary of state's office—and determine whether any liens have been filed against the seller and the seller's premises.
- ❏ Find out why the seller is selling his or her business.

Chapter 4
Buying a Local Franchise Operation

 aving read the previous chapters, you have a better understanding about purchasing a franchise from a franchisor or purchasing a business that is not a franchise from a local business owner. This chapter examines the scenario of purchasing an existing franchise business from a local franchisee.

The big difference between purchasing a franchise from a franchisor and purchasing a franchise from an existing franchisee is that, if it is truly a sale by a franchisee, the franchisee is not bound by restrictions on revealing actual or projected revenue figures. By the same token, the franchisee/seller is also not bound by any disclosure laws, such as the one issued by the Federal Trade Commission. Therefore, you should extensively review the previous chapters of this book regarding both purchasing a franchise and purchasing a business from a local business owner and consult the checklists at the end of Chapters 1-3 for additional information on what you need to know and research when purchasing a franchise or an existing business.

In essence, ensure that you secure a written purchase agreement in which the franchisee selling produces accurate, truthful financial statements and warrants their veracity. Because the business is also a franchise, familiarize yourself with the terms and conditions of the franchise agreement and with the information in the circular concerning the franchisor.

> Ensure that you secure a written purchase agreement in which the franchisee selling produces accurate, truthful financial statements and warrants their veracity.

Reviewing the Disclosure Document

As stated above, in the sale of a franchise that is strictly between the franchisee and the prospective buyer and does not involve the franchisor, the franchisee/seller is not required to provide you with the franchisor's disclosure document. However, since most franchise agreements provide that a franchisee can transfer his or her franchise only with the franchisor's consent and upon the execution of a then-current franchise agreement by the purchaser, it is extremely wise for the franchisor to provide you with a disclosure document that contains the updated franchise agreement. Therefore, thoroughly examine the disclosure document, as indicated in Chapter 2. In addition, follow all of the suggestions made in Chapter 3 pertaining to the purchase of a non-franchise business. Additionally, find out whether you must pay for training sessions required by the franchisor or if your training can be obtained from the selling franchisee at no cost to you. This is extremely important to know.

You must realize that your relationship with the selling franchisee is only temporary and short term and that assuming his or her franchise agreement or executing a new franchise agreement means a long-term relationship with the franchisor. Therefore, before you sign any documents or part with any money, familiarize yourself with the franchisor and contact other franchisees to determine answers to the many questions you will have. In addition, find out why the franchisee is selling. In many instances, a franchisee places the business on the market because he or she is unable to make it profitable. This is why it is so important that you dig out all information available on the franchise you seek to buy, including the financials, the franchisee's reasons for selling the franchise, and the seller's relationship with and opinion of the franchisor.

> Before you sign any documents or part with any money, familiarize yourself with the franchisor and contact other franchisees to determine answers to the many questions you will have.

Because the franchisee/seller could jeopardize any sale by being too frank about the shortcomings of the franchisor, information from the franchisee/seller is often slanted to avoid any criticism of the franchisor. Other franchisees of the same franchisor will not have this reservation when you approach them regarding the franchisor's performance with the franchisees.

Selling Price of an Existing Franchise

Since this purchase is of an ongoing business as well as a franchise, the transaction is going to be much more costly than buying a new franchise and starting it from scratch. There doesn't seem to be any set formula for determining a fair price for an existing franchise.

Years ago, before inflation, a business would generally sell for three to five times its annual earnings, with all parties assuming that the investment could be recouped in three to five years. In more modern times, businesses generally are sold at one year's net earnings, plus the value of the equipment, fixtures, and inventory on the books. In reality, most businesses sell for a price the seller is willing to accept and the buyer is willing to pay. Anybody buying a business, however, should first consult an accountant or real estate agent familiar with the purchase and sale values of the business in question.

> If the franchise you are thinking about buying is successful, be sure to find out why it has succeeded.

You may want to make arrangements to observe or work in the particular business for several weeks before making any written contractual commitment. However, if there are other prospective purchasers interested in the business, it is unlikely that the franchisee selling the business will entertain such an arrangement.

If the franchise you are thinking about buying is successful, be sure to find out why it has succeeded. If it is a service-oriented business and the sales or technical ability of the franchisee/seller is the primary reason for the business's success, make sure you have some of the same qualities.

The success of the business may stem from competent employees. Therefore, although a franchisee/seller cannot "sell" his or her employees, the purchase agreement could be drafted with a warranty and representation by the seller that he or she will do everything within his or her power to convince the employees to stay on with you. In addition, a restriction that the seller will not compete with you should also be incorporated into a written buy and sell agreement.

In purchasing any existing business, you should make sure there is a long-term assumable lease and the landlord will consent to the transfer. More businesses have been sunk when the purchaser took over a business only to find a few months later that the rent had been doubled or that the lease would shortly expire without any possibility of renewal.

Helpful Tips

Here are some tips for anyone interested in buying an existing franchise or business.

- Current federal and state franchise laws offer you what you need the most— information about the seller's franchisor. If you are interested in buying a franchise, utilize this source of information.
- If you are interested in buying a local non-franchise business, read over the material in Chapters 1 and 2 to get an idea of the type of information required of franchisors and ask for the same type of information from the owner.
- The less information you get from the seller, the greater the risk you may be buying a "lemon."
- Remember to personally investigate the deal. Common sense is the key here. Why take a bigger risk than necessary? Check, check, and double check.
- Anybody purchasing a business should seek out competent legal counsel versed in the practical business aspects of buying and selling a business.
- Use the checklists at the end of Chapters 1-3 to evaluate every franchise or business you are seriously considering buying.
- Research and review all state and federal franchise laws and any state business opportunity laws. (See Appendix E.)

Conclusion

The following chapters that constitute Part II, although written for someone who owns a business and is considering franchising it, can also be viewed from the standpoint of purchasing a franchise. These chapters examine the factors that contribute to a good franchise business from a franchisor's viewpoint. The prospective franchisor will soon find that whatever makes the franchisee successful makes the franchisor successful as well.

If you are considering buying a franchise, compare the terms of your potential franchise purchase with the information in Part II to determine whether your potential franchisor has done his or her homework. In addition, remember that today's purchaser of an ongoing business may be tomorrow's franchisor.

Part II

Franchising Your Business

Chapter 5

Franchising Basics

s a new franchisor, you need to realize that franchising is a method of marketing and therefore entails a business operation in and of itself. Before beginning the franchise process, you will need to know how to:

- Structure a workable franchise agreement with franchisees;
- Choose and train your franchisees; and
- Market not only the product or service the franchisee will sell, but the franchise concept itself to prospective franchisees.

Too often, many new, potential franchisors seek out an attorney—who perhaps has worked on only one or two franchise deals at the most—to draw up a franchise agreement. In most cases, these new franchisors are very successful in running their own businesses, but they don't know the first thing about franchising. For example, many first-time franchisors don't know some of the franchising basics, such as:

- What a franchisee is or what to expect from one,
- How to provide ongoing support to a franchisee,
- How much money is needed to capitalize the franchise venture, or
- How much to charge as an initial franchise fee and as an ongoing royalty.

Part II of this book—Chapters 5-11—provides you with this type of information so you can set up a franchising operation with some prior knowledge of the most common business mistakes inexperienced franchisors make in franchising. As a result, you will hopefully avoid making the same mistakes and improve your chances for success. Before deciding if your business can be franchised, you may want to review some of the advantages and disadvantages of doing so.

Advantages of Franchising

When discussing the advantages of franchising for the franchisor, it is inevitable to discuss the advantages available to the franchisee as well. This is because many advantages for one are also considered advantages for the other. So, even though the following list specifies the advantage to the franchisor or the franchisee, most of them are generally held to be advantages for both:

- There is a strong possibility for rapid maximum expansion with minimum capital expenditures.
- Direct managing responsibilities become the franchisee's obligation and allow the franchisor more freedom to do other things.
- The franchisee generally has pride of ownership and self-motivation because of his or her capital investment and stake in future profits. (This self-motivation generally results in the franchisee's lowering his or her costs, resulting in higher profit margins for the franchisee and greater consumer markets for the franchisor than normally attainable by company employees.)
- A franchisee will generally have a minimum amount of line-management employees and a greater amount of staff advisory employees.
- National and local advertising fund dollars are available for franchisees in far greater amounts than could be generated by the franchisor or franchisee alone.
- There is increased buying power, resulting in a lower possible purchase price to the franchisee than for a company-owned entity.
- Research and development facilities are available to the franchisor through reports from franchisees.
- The franchisor can have a steady cash flow from royalties.
- The franchisor enjoys greater control over franchisees through wise and fair contract provisions.
- Some limits of liability extend to the final consumer. (Franchisees generally are not held to be agents of the franchisor in the event of injuries due to negligence of the franchisee, as opposed to sure liability to the company for injuries suffered in a branch store.)

Other advantages a franchisor may enjoy can be directly attributed to the advantages that a franchisee will enjoy. In short, if the franchisee is happy, the franchisor will be happy. For more on franchisee advantages, refer to Chapter 1.

Disadvantages of Franchising

Of course, as is the case with most things in life, there is usually a downside to every decision you make or every venture you pursue. And when it comes to franchising, you need to be aware of some of the disadvantages. This section of the chapter details some of the downsides of franchising so you are better informed and more prepared in making your franchising decision.

Decreased Net Receipts

Net receipts from franchisees could be less than net receipts from successful, company-owned operations. In reality, only a few new franchises break even immediately. Most franchises take six months to a year to break even. This is also true of most new company-owned retail outlets. Although the company-owned office retains 100% of its net profits, it has obligated itself to an initial capital indebtedness that it would not have if the office were a franchise.

> Only a few new franchises break even immediately. Most franchises take six months to a year to break even.

If you are relatively sure that company-owned retail outlets can produce an immediate profit and you have the capital and labor to staff them, you will certainly make much more money with company-owned outlets than if you franchised an equal number of franchises that made the same amount of profit. Your main problem will be to raise the necessary start-up capital and secure and retain qualified, hard-working managers and employees while hoping that sales will immediately exceed the substantial start-up costs for company-owned outlets. Capital and qualified employees are very hard to get—and the latter are even more difficult to retain.

Independence of Franchisees

As a franchisor, you will be dealing with independent operators rather than with company employees. The key is to treat all franchisees fairly. Franchisees should be subject to only enough control to ensure that your franchised service or product will be marketed to the consumer with the same quality that made you a success.

For example, if the franchisees feel they are overpaying for services they receive from you or that the services are not what were represented to them, they will become disgruntled and eventually may group together, withholding payment of their franchise fees. Most franchisees who withhold payment of fees and sue are those who feel that the franchisor has breached their contracts. And usually, these franchisees have experienced a personality conflict with someone in the franchisor's operation.

Be extremely careful in selecting a franchisee or allowing a franchisee to transfer his or her franchise to someone else. Furthermore, continue to look upon each of your franchisees as an economical substitute for a company manager insofar as assisting and supporting that franchisee.

> Many franchisors seem to have the attitude that they now are in the business of making money by selling franchises instead of selling their services or products.

Many franchisors seem to have the attitude that they now are in the business of making money by selling franchises instead of selling their services or products. Their attention is more attuned to advertising and marketing the franchises rather than marketing the product or service to the consumer.

The primary goal of any franchisor is to sell his or her services or wares. The use of franchisees is a method of attaining this goal.

Difference in Required Business Skills

The business skills you will need for operating a franchisor system are entirely different from those you needed in running your original retail business. Most of the franchisors who fail in the franchising business are those who did not know what they were doing when they first started their franchisor corporation. They were experts at operating an initial retail business and tried to franchise because of their extensive trial-and-error experience in such a business; however, they did not know how to be franchisors.

> The business skills you will need for operating a franchisor system are entirely different from those you needed in running your original retail business.

Overspending

Franchisors tend to spend too much money on show. There seems to be a tremendous temptation for franchisors to immediately "put on the dog." High-rise office buildings, overstaffing, company cars, expensive hotels, elaborate trade show booths, and costly classified advertising are some of the first mistakes many new franchisors make. Franchisors have a tendency to undercapitalize by not budgeting themselves.

No matter what your capital is, be it $20,000, $100,000, or $1,000,000, wisely budget the cost of your office, the marketing of your franchises, the training of your franchisees, and the maintenance and support of your franchise outlets.

Costs Can Be High

In the United States, franchisors are required to have written offering circulars containing copies of all proposed contracts for signing up franchisees. (See Chapter 2 for more on offering circulars.) To prepare a circular, you will need to retain the services of an attorney and an accountant. As pointed out in Chapter 11, the costs of preparing a circular and audited financial statements sometimes are not in direct proportion with the value given.

> In the United States, franchisors are required to have written offering circulars containing copies of all proposed contracts for signing up franchisees.

Try to get the most for your dollar, but be careful in selecting the attorney and the accountant. Rely heavily upon the references of a particular attorney's or accountant's past clients. Under no circumstances should the costs of setting up the franchise be greater than the costs you would incur if you were to set up company-owned offices with qualified management personnel. When trying to control service costs of attorneys and accountants, complete the questionnaires in both Appendix C and Appendix D. You should complete these questionnaires before your first meeting with an attorney.

In addition to legal and professional fees, the cost of franchising in multiple states is high because of the individual legal costs for disclosure filings in the 15 states that have franchise registration laws that stipulate your legal requirements as a franchisor. In 17 other states, your requirements are governed by business opportunity statutes. (See Appendix E, State Franchise Information Guidelines, for more on these state statutes.) In the remaining 18 states and Washington, D.C., you will need to comply with the Federal Trade Commission's rules on disclosures.

Unfortunately, the registration states differ and one registration state will not allow an offering circular approved by another state without changes. The same is true in those states having business opportunity laws that require filing. Even the FTC rules require the circulars to differentiate regarding the individual non-compete, renewal, and termination laws of each of the FTC states, although they are generally incorporated in one disclosure form.

This cost disadvantage can be minimized if you have a business plan of slow growth that concentrates on one or two states for the first few years and gradually expands to bordering states. By doing this, you will incur attorney fees and filing costs over a period of time rather than all at once. Thoroughly evaluate the particular advantages and disadvantages of franchising as compared with alternatives for expansion before making the franchise decision. Refer to Chapter 6 for more on alternative expansion methods.

Can Your Business Be Franchised?

If you have a successful business that is susceptible to a regional or national system of marketing and you do not wish to share control or risk the personality conflicts that come with bringing in investors who would become your equals in making business decisions, then franchising may be your best course of action. To help you determine if your business could be franchised, review some of the qualifiers and considerations described below.

Are You Franchisor Material?

Before you evaluate your business as a potential franchise, be sure to evaluate yourself as a potential franchisor. Often, a person who might successfully operate a business that is susceptible to franchising may not be cut out to be a franchisor. Consider your qualities and remember that franchising is more than the business of selling services and/or products to a consumer. In addition, as a franchisor, you will be an educator, trainer, psychologist, minister, and perpetual hand-holder to your franchisees. You will also be their Uncle Sam, extracting an initial fee to put them in a higher income tax bracket and then continually taxing them through the form of a royalty throughout their careers.

> Before you evaluate your business as a potential franchise, be sure to evaluate yourself as a potential franchisor.

You will need to be aware of the franchisee-franchisor relationship and always remember to allow your individual franchisees to become their own persons in having their own businesses and always treat them as independent business owners. It is important you carefully set forth the guidelines of this independent contractor relationship clearly in the initial contract, the offering circular, and all further communications to franchisees.

Is There a Market for Your Particular Product or Service?

Do not consider franchising your business unless you have a known, local market for your product or service. Marketability is determined by need, and need is determined by competition.

> Do not consider franchising your business unless you have a known, local market for your product or service.

For example, if you are running a hamburger stand, your chances of finding a market for your franchise and a market for your franchisees are relatively small in today's business community. However, if you have a unique way of running a hamburger stand, it is entirely possible to franchise it. Take the Wendy's operation, for example, which has gained steam by introducing the system of in-line preparation of hamburgers as the consumer watches and waits for his or her order. This is in contrast with the traditional method of preparing hamburgers out of view and then setting them on a warming tray until someone places an order. Wendy's gives consumers the impression that it is making the hamburger to order right before their eyes.

Demand is the crucial force here. It is just as important as uniqueness. Your unique product or service must be desired not only by the people who wish to buy franchises from you, but also by the people who will buy from the franchisees.

What Market Research Must You Do?

If your product or service is relatively new and not extensively offered by anyone else but has proven extremely salable, your first task is to determine those sections of the country that would most likely buy your products or services, based on needs similar to those of your present customers. For example, a new type of thermal underwear would not go over well with residents of California's Palm Springs area; however, a successful gas-saving device might take hold anywhere in the world.

If your product or service is not relatively new, you can retain market research firms to prepare extensive reports concerning the types of consumers in various regions and their needs and buying power. This could be rather expensive, so an alternative is to do your own research by visiting the reference department of your local library. Study the Yellow Pages of phone books of the various cities in which you would like to offer your product or service to determine if any competition exists in those areas.

You will also want to interview existing franchisors and franchisees for their insights on franchising. People enjoy telling others of their business accomplishments, so this should be a particularly enjoyable aspect of researching the franchising potential of your business.

Government agencies are also very helpful in providing demographic information and market research data. In particular, the U.S. Department of Commerce and the U.S. Department of Labor have conducted extensive studies on the regional consumer habits of Americans. You can use this information in your research.

It is always necessary to do an initial study of the existing demand for the products or services you are thinking of offering through a franchise system. A more extensive study can be conducted by potential franchisees. If you feel an initial market is out there, utilize potential franchisees by encouraging them to make their own market study as a prerequisite to receiving a license from you.

Do You Have a Registrable Trademark?

If you have a product or service that is unique or in demand, you must capture this uniqueness through the use of a trademark (if it is a product) or service mark (if it is a service). The idea is to get the American public to associate your product with a particular trademark.

For many years, purchasers of a certain type of transparent tape would not go into the local stationery store and ask for transparent tape but would instead automatically ask for the trademarked "Scotch" tape. In looking around, you will see that all of the big companies utilize this concept. The producers of cola drinks do not want you to ask for just "a cola," thereby allowing the local dispenser of the product to make the choice for you. The Coca-Cola Company wants you to ask for a Coke and the Pepsi-Cola Company wants you to ask for a Pepsi.

As a result, you will want to apply for a registered trademark or service mark on your product or service as soon as possible. You will most certainly want to do this before the first franchise agreement is negotiated and consummated. Keep in mind that the trademark or service mark must be used in intrastate and interstate commerce before the owner can apply to the U.S. Patent and Trademark Office in Washington, D.C. to register it.

Before spending any money to advertise or promote a trademark or service mark, determine that no other entity has already secured the registered rights of that particular trademark or service mark. You can do so for less than $400 by contacting one of many trademark search firms. Be aware that some search firms will provide their services only to attorneys. Since your application for federal trademark or service mark registration will be reviewed and determined by a government attorney, you should retain a trademark attorney.

If you do not wish to utilize such a search, you can file an application to the U.S. Patent and Trademark Office for a trademark. Examiners will review your application and advise you as to whether or not there is an existing trademark that might be confused with yours. Then, after determining that you have a unique product or one that is in demand, your next step is to register your service mark or trademark with the U.S. Patent Office. This can be done by a trademark attorney, who will normally charge between $750 and $1,000.

The filing fee for such an application is currently $335. For more information on trademark registration, obtain the free booklet, *Basic Facts About Trademarks* by writing:

U.S. Patent and Trademark Office
2900 Crystal Drive
Arlington, VA 22202-3513
phone: 202 512-1800
fax: 202 512-2250
www.uspto.gov

If the examiner determines that your trademark will not cause confusion with the trademarked goods of others, your application will be published in the *Federal Register*, allowing third parties to object if they disagree with the examiner. If there are no objections, you will receive a certificate of trademark registration approximately three or more months after your application has been published in the *Federal Register*. Your registered trademark will be in effect for 10 years before it needs to be renewed.

Once you have received your certificate of trademark registration, you should let the world know you have it. Remember that once you have obtained a certificate of registration, you are eligible to seek enforcement of your trademark or service mark against infringers through litigation in federal district courts. In addition, you may register your trademark with state agencies, although this is not necessary if you have a federal registration. Registration laws vary from state to state, but in most states, a nominal fee (some less than $20, but some $200 and higher) can secure registration of your trademark for a period of years, in many cases, for up to 10 years.

> Once you have obtained a certificate of registration, you are eligible to seek enforcement of your trademark or service mark against infringers through litigation in federal district courts.

The Final Decision to Franchise

Before you make your final decision to franchise, you need to know the following:

- You have what it takes to be a franchisor.
- Your product is unique and in demand, and your business is profitable and promising to prospective franchisees.
- You have a market for your product or service.

■ Your service or product is associated with a registrable trademark.

In addition, you have probably already decided you do not wish to share your control with any investors in the form of partners or shareholders and you have investigated other business expansion alternatives. (See Chapter 6.) You should also have a strong idea of what to look for in your future franchisees. (See Chapter 7.)

Before you launch your plan to expand by franchising, prepare a thorough business plan so you can realistically look at the financial outlay each new outlet will require to get up and running; then compare that with the revenue you can expect to receive from fees, royalties, and sales of ingredients and services. Some of the costs specific to franchising that you will want to include in your business plan are overhead costs of your franchise operation, such as salaries and benefits for yourself and employees in your head office and trainers and sales staff, as well as normal office expenses like rent, office equipment, car allowances, and travel. Plan in the cost of finding franchisees. This could include buying ads, traveling to franchise shows, preparing brochures and videos, and entertaining. In addition, add a healthy allowance for start-up and ongoing legal, accounting, and advertising fees.

> Be overly conservative as you project the timing and amount of income you expect to receive from your franchise outlets.

Be overly conservative as you project the timing and amount of income you expect to receive from your franchise outlets. You will have determined the mixture of franchise fees, royalties, and product sales that will bring you income from your franchisees. Pad your expectations of how soon these revenues will flow back to you, instead of basing your predictions solely on how your business worked in the past.

Another important factor you should have investigated before making your franchise decision is the advantages and disadvantages of each legal form of business organization—sole proprietorship, partnership, or corporation. If you form either a sole proprietorship or a partnership, your operation will be subject to unlimited liability: if the business fails and its debts exceed its assets, the sole proprietor or the partners can be held individually liable for unpaid debts. Because of this liability issue, most franchisors choose a corporate entity, in order to limit their liabilities to the assets of the corporation. To find out more on legal forms of business organization, especially incorporating, consult an attorney and a certified public accountant.

Conclusion

Franchising has grown in leaps and bounds in recent years, and so have the related state and federal regulations. Before making the final decision to franchise in your state, check the state and local regulations with which you will have to comply. Refer to Chapter 8 and Appendix E for more on state and federal franchise laws.

Chapter 6
Franchising and Alternative Methods of Expansion

During the last 10 years in the United States, well-organized company programs that are short of adequate expansion capital have turned into efficient, highly profitable networks of franchised outlets. The desired end result of this popular marketing system called franchising is a highly motivated, cost-cutting, quality-conscious retailer who provides a product or service to the customer in a manner far more efficient and profitable than the often poorly managed, high-cost, poor-service marketing system known as the "company store."

Franchising, simply put, is a means of expanding a business operation by licensing a third party to engage in a franchise system under a required marketing plan or system using a common trademark, service mark, or trade name, for a fee. Franchising is available to businesses distributing both products and services and to those distributing services only. Today, the latter is by far the most popular category.

This chapter is written for the potential franchisor who has built a profitable business that craves expansion before it becomes stagnant or dies when an aggressive competitor captures the available expansion markets by franchising first. It is also aimed at the potential franchisor who wishes to set up the best operating franchise system at the lowest possible cost. This chapter is set up to help you explore your best expansion options, be it franchising or its alternatives, such as the "as is" alternative, the company-owned outlet alternative, and the agreements of association alternative. As mentioned in the previous chapter, it is valuable to explore all your expansion options before making your final franchise decision. Take the time to review these alternatives and see if any seem applicable to you.

> Franchising is a means of expanding a business operation by licensing a third party to engage in a franchise system under a required marketing plan or system using a common trademark, service mark, or trade name, for a fee.

61

The "As Is" Alternative

The primary alternative to franchising is to let your business continue "as is," without franchising or expanding. This option, however, raises the possibility that your business will be eliminated by the competition and you will never reach your full potential. Profits are limited to the amount of gross revenues that can be generated from one location. In many cases, unless a business expands, it dies. In addition, if you choose to continue your company "as is," your advertising budget remains minimal compared with that of a franchisor, whose local, regional, or national advertising fund is fed by a multiple number of franchise entities.

Above all, you must remain on the firing line. In other words, you are still the day-to-day manager and your life is spent hiring, firing, purchasing, and selling on the lower level. As a franchisor, you would direct a sizable operation with franchisees performing these duties. Franchising can give a business owner the opportunity to realize his or her full executive ability.

Selling products or services through the Internet is an alternative to many businesses, particularly those selling products, instead of expanding by franchising. Of course, the owner bears all the expenses involved in selling direct and receives no franchise fees or royalties, but avoids the possibility of difficult relationships with franchisees.

> The primary alternative to franchising is to let your business continue "as is," without franchising or expanding.

The Company-Owned Outlet Alternative

The second alternative—formerly considered the only method of expanding a marketing system before the advent of franchising—is opening company-owned outlets. This normally requires a considerable capital investment and handling the difficult problem of securing capable, willing, and hard-working managers.

In addition to the amount of capital necessary to expand your own business through company-owned offices, the amount of time spent in such company expansion is likewise very demanding. Site location, general administration, lease negotiation, and interviewing and hiring managers and employees all require considerable time and money that are not anywhere near the amount required for expansion through franchising.

When opening a company-held retail distribution outlet, you spend money for a considerable time while receiving little, if any, profit in return. In franchising, by comparison, you immediately receive a franchise fee at the outset and then possible royalties if the franchise can generate sufficient sales during the first six months to a year. It is true that you must train the franchisees, but you would also have to train managers and employees of company-owned outlets. It seems that franchising has an advantage, since as the franchisor you do not have to pay the franchisees or their employees any wages or salary while they are being trained.

> The second alternative—formerly considered the only method of expanding a marketing system before the advent of franchising—is opening company-owned outlets.

The Agreements of Association Alternative

A third and perhaps less common alternative to franchising is association through dealerships, licenses, incentive programs, partnerships, and joint ventures. Most dealerships, partnerships, joint ventures, and licenses come about through negotiations between two parties having some adverse interest, resulting in a compromise agreement. In most such cases, to satisfy the whims of both parties, control will be split, even though it should be centered in the hands of one. Often, when one party is supplying only the money, that party will insist upon some control over major decisions, even though he or she may be totally unqualified in management abilities. In many cases, when the money provider exercises that control, it results in a decision based on money rather than on what is the most beneficial to the enterprise in the long run. This type of agreement is in contrast to the development of a franchising agreement, in which the franchisor unilaterally prepares his or her contractual arrangements from an objective standpoint, without being pressed into compromises.

Associating with others is even more difficult, since only very loose agreements, exerting practically no marketing control, can be worked out without violating franchise laws. In most such relationships, the entities in a joint venture or a partnership have equal control, which, in many cases, may cause either a stalemate or compromised business decisions. A good business decision is never one that is the result of a compromise between two or more people. With a compromise, the best you will have is a partially correct arrangement that could easily result in the loss of a lot of money and loss of market share.

If an entrepreneur expanding through any joint venture or association intends to exert any type of control or even suggests certain marketing methods while receiving compensation for the right of the venture to use his or her particular trademark or service mark, he or she could easily be in danger of civil and criminal penalties for violating various state and federal franchise laws. These laws generally set forth the elements of a franchise as the existence of an agreement wherein one party licenses the other to use a trademark or service mark, exerts some type of control over the person using the trademark or service mark (usually in a form of suggested or required marketing methods), and then receives compensation for such rights.

In essence, many state regulators hold that if it looks like a franchise, it is a franchise. Thus, if you license another to use your trademark or service mark and set him or her up in a business that operates like your other licensees, you are most likely franchising your business. This is especially true if you receive any form of consideration for these rights or require compliance with your marketing plan. In some states, just the suggestion of such marketing procedures is sufficient for government agencies to find a franchise law violation.

A partnership is a limited alternative to franchising, at best. If one partnership composed of one set of partners is the owner of all the retail stores, restaurants, or outlets operating under the partnership trademarks, the state registration authorities and FTC probably will not consider it a franchise. However, if an entrepreneur enters into general partnership agreements with different partners for each additional outlet utilizing the entrepreneur's trademark at each outlet, the arrangements between the entrepreneurial partner and the operating partners are, in essence, a franchise.

If you think about this, you will find that the partner for each store generally will put some money into the partnership, pay the entrepreneurial partner an initial and ongoing

A third alternative to franchising is association through dealerships, licenses, incentive programs, partnerships, and joint ventures.

If you license another to use your trademark or service mark and set him or her up in a business that operates like your other licensees, you are most likely franchising your business.

A partnership is a limited alternative to franchising, at best.

fee, salary, or draw for his or her expertise or supervision or both, and operate the outlet under the trademark of the entrepreneur. The same danger of violating franchise laws exists if the entrepreneur sets up different corporate entities and exercises shareholder control of the separate corporations, each operating outlets with different minority shareholders but the same trademark.

The key to a potential violation of the franchise laws is the trademark license agreement that must exist between the corporation holding the trademark registration and the sister corporations. These license agreements might constitute a franchise in the eyes of some state franchise legislation agencies. Such an arrangement should have prior clearances from the appropriate state and federal franchise authorities.

Before using any type of general partnership or majority-controlled, affiliated corporation or sister corporation, consult a competent franchise attorney.

> If expanding through company-owned offices or an association, an entrepreneur also must evaluate the efficiency of his or her own personnel, since he or she most probably will be transferring this personnel to the expansion location.

Anyone wishing to expand through company-owned offices, an association, or franchising must look first to available capital and then prepare a business plan that delineates the amount of capital needed to attain the desired level of expansion and the availability of efficient and loyal management personnel.

If expanding through company-owned offices or an association, an entrepreneur also must evaluate the efficiency of his or her own personnel, since he or she most probably will be transferring this personnel to the expansion location. If available capital is limited and/or management personnel for company-owned offices or an association with third parties is insufficient, the entrepreneur should then consider the advantages and disadvantages of franchising as compared with the alternatives just discussed.

Conclusion

Hopefully, this brief discussion of several alternatives to franchising has helped you get a better idea of how you will want to expand your business. Once you have made your final franchise decision, it will be time to begin searching for well-qualified franchisees.

Chapter 7 discusses some of the issues you will need to explore when recruiting prospective franchisees.

Chapter 7
Building a Strong Franchising Foundation

As a would-be franchisor, you must realize that your current management and operating and marketing techniques probably are insufficient in many ways for a successful franchise operation. For instance, a good computer sales employee is not necessarily a good computer franchise salesperson. A good field manager is not necessarily a good franchise manager, particularly when it comes to supervising multiple, independently operating franchisees. Company managers who have trained company employees informally, one on one, might not be qualified to adequately train a group of potential franchisees who have a significant amount of their savings at stake.

In addition, present advertising media suitable for selling a product or service at the retail level is not necessarily suitable for attracting qualified people with adequate capital interested in purchasing franchises. In short, your previous experience and knowledge of your business may not necessarily be the same experience and knowledge required to successfully operate a franchise business.

> Your previous experience and knowledge of your business may not necessarily be the same experience and knowledge required to successfully operate a franchise business.

To be successful, a potential franchisor must have built his or her own business, no matter what size, on a sound foundation of well-trained personnel, good marketing techniques, and an adequate working capital structure. These foundation blocks are the same for a successful franchise operation as well, but as a franchisor you will need to view them from a different perspective and utilize different skills.

Well-Trained Personnel

Your success really lies in your ability to recognize the business insight necessary to operate a smooth-running, successful franchise. To help you do this, carefully review your

65

current management, marketing, training, advertising, and sales personnel to determine whether or not you should provide franchise management training, engage specialized consultation for present personnel, and/or hire new personnel. The capabilities of current personnel—such as in the case of the very small entity, consisting of the founder and his or her spouse—should be carefully reviewed and, where they are found lacking in franchise experience, they should be properly trained in franchise operating and marketing techniques.

Staffing a well-run franchise operation with knowledgeable, competent personnel can be achieved at a reasonable expense in one of four ways:

- Educating current personnel;
- Hiring experienced franchise personnel;
- Subcontracting for franchise functions; and
- Retaining an all-purpose franchise consultant.

Educating Current Personnel

> If current personnel are not only capable of performing franchising duties, but also available for such duties without overextending themselves, franchise-oriented business seminars and literature should be sought out as educational tools.

First, if current personnel are not only capable of performing franchising duties, but also available for such duties without overextending themselves, franchise-oriented business seminars and literature should be sought out as educational tools. Many such courses are offered by specific professional business symposiums or community colleges and take one or two days. Courses and seminars are usually individual efforts presented by specialists with hands-on experience in their particular franchise fields and should not be confused with the all-purpose franchise consultants discussed later in this section.

Check the business opportunities section of your local Sunday newspaper regularly for listings of upcoming business events and seminars. These listings often contain goldmines of information for new franchisors and their inexperienced staff. The International Franchise Association (IFA) in Washington, D.C. can also provide you with a wealth of information regarding franchising:

International Franchise Association
1350 New York Avenue, NW Suite 900
Washington, DC 20005-4709
phone: 202 628-8000
fax: 202 628-0812
Web: www.franchise.org
e-mail: ifa@franchise.org

Hiring Experienced Franchise Personnel

> The second method of ensuring adequate personnel familiar with current franchising methods is to hire experienced personnel who have worked for other franchisors.

The second method of ensuring adequate personnel familiar with current franchising methods is to hire experienced personnel who have worked for other franchisors. You should review thoroughly not only each applicant's franchise expertise, but also his or her character and knowledge of strict franchising laws. Pay particular attention to any substantial experience gained by an applicant before 1971. This is when the first franchise act was passed in California. This might indicate that the applicant's basic knowledge of franchising was formulated on methods now prohibited by franchise laws—methods such as providing actual or projected revenue and sales figures to potential franchisees and/or negotiating material terms of a franchise agreement without applicable government approval. Thus, ensure that employee applicants are familiar with current franchise marketing techniques, particularly the numerous legal restrictions franchises face.

Hiring additional experienced franchise personnel is costly and it may be affordable, or even necessary, only for the larger franchisor. In many cases, the smaller franchisor will handle all the administrative, management, and marketing functions of his or her new franchise operation, at least initially. Therefore, if your franchise will be small or medium-sized, you may prefer educating current personnel about franchising rather than hiring high-priced new personnel with franchise experience.

Subcontracting for Franchise Functions

The third and highly recommended way of educating yourself and your staff on the business aspects of franchising is to subcontract the job to individual franchise specialists in the fields of law, training, advertising, public relations, and marketing. These consultants will evaluate your needs and, instead of providing a complete package, will give you only what you actually need.

The one outside professional always required is an experienced franchise attorney with vast experience not only in franchise law but in the everyday business aspects of franchising. Talk to the attorney's past franchise clients about the his or her legal expertise and hands-on knowledge of franchising. Refer to Chapter 9 for tips on how to choose a franchise attorney.

When selecting an advertising agency, make sure it is one that specializes in franchising as well as general business. The same holds true with financing and marketing specialists. Carefully check each specialist's references.

> The third and highly recommended way of educating yourself and your staff on the business aspects of franchising is to subcontract the job to individual franchise specialists in the fields of law, training, advertising, public relations, and marketing.

Retaining an All-Purpose Franchise Consultant

The fourth method of obtaining franchise business guidance is to retain an "all-purpose" franchise-consultant entity—that is, an entity claiming to provide the franchisor with the entire "franchise package," from legal work to marketing and advertising, all under one roof.

Most such "package" and multi-purpose consultants do not actually sell franchises but offer to train the franchisor's sales force. A multi-purpose consultant is one who offers so-called "complete services" to would-be franchisors, including preparing the franchise circulars and other legal documents at costs ranging from $37,500 up to $150,000 or more for the complete package in phases. Such consultants require their clients to retain their own counsel to review the legal documents and secure any required state registration of them, at additional cost to the clients, since a corporation consultant who would do so without the proper legal qualifications would be practicing law illegally.

In addition, the all-purpose consultant provides operations manuals, video training films, and feasibility market and business plan studies that normally can be provided by local specialists in each field at much lower costs, often with a better final product. Never retain any consultant without thoroughly investigating his or her background and contacting his or her references and clients.

Individual franchise consultants who provide various specific functions—such as training, marketing, advertising, sales, business planning, or financing—are generally far more likely to be not only better organized and informed, but less costly and much faster than an all-purpose, high-priced consultant. If you go the way of a consulting firm, compare the costs of all-purpose consultants with those of individual specialists in the legal and marketing franchise field. By farming out jobs to specialists, such as Kushell Associates, who concentrate in individual areas, you might discover you can receive faster and better franchise work at a much lower price. Again, the best way to evaluate a consultant or marketing specialist is to thoroughly investigate the person's references, particularly clients who have hired the consultant for assistance in franchising a similar business. It is vital to know about the results, as explained by clients, and the worth of those results compared with the price.

Never retain a consultant just because the consultant was once a franchise executive. First, find out if he or she was a good executive, why he or she left the franchise, and whether or not he or she is a good consultant. There are many former franchise executives who are out of work because of their lack of expertise. Evaluate the consultant's versatility.

In a new and diversified industry, such as computer software and hardware franchising, the experience required might not be compatible with the background of a consultant who had a lifelong career in the restaurant business, for example. A penny-wise but profit-motivated franchisor can retain various specialists as needed for specific functions and end up with less expensive, more suitable, and more extensive franchising services. An experienced, franchise-oriented consultant specializing in advertising will work perfectly with any experienced, franchise-oriented business planning or training consultant or employee. Both should be able to work effectively with an experienced, marketing-oriented attorney, since they will all be somewhat of like minds.

Marketing Techniques

Once you have been licensed to sell franchises as required by registration states or have obtained from your attorney a suitable offering circular and disclosure for other states, you must initiate advertising, sales, marketing, and public relations programs geared for launching your franchise operations. Selling your product or service to the final user or consumer of that product or service is drastically different from selling a person on becoming a franchisee.

A small mom-and-pop franchise could easily be sold by a one-person franchisor operation where the franchisor has a pool of good, qualified potential franchisees. An example of this would be the franchising of skilled trade services under a common trademark. The market consists of independent operators or skilled tradespeople working for

> The all-purpose consultant provides operations manuals, video training films, and feasibility market and business plan studies that normally can be provided by local specialists in each field at much lower costs, often with a better final product.

> Individual franchise consultants who provide various specific functions are generally far more likely to be not only better organized and informed, but less costly and much faster than an all-purpose, high-priced consultant.

> Once you have been licensed to sell franchises ..., you must initiate advertising, sales, marketing, and public relations programs geared for launching your franchise operations.

companies engaged in that trade. For such a franchisor, marketing, advertising, and public relations can consist of working through trade papers or trade association meetings.

Even current employees of the franchisor can be a good source of franchisees in a certain situation, depending on the financial status of the employees and the cost of the franchise. A small franchisor capable of using current efficient staff could commence franchising at an initial outlay of amounts as low as $20,000. This amount encompasses:

- The costs of suitable brochures;
- An experienced, business-minded franchise attorney; and
- The use of the franchisor's existing facilities.

The cost of the existing facilities would be incurred as part of the franchisor's prevailing or existing business being franchised, making the business a "pilot plant" and training facility. However, never capitalize at this low amount unless you have carefully worked out a realistic estimation of your projected income and costs during the initial years of your franchise company.

> Even current employees of the franchisor can be a good source of franchisees in a certain situation, depending on the financial status of the employees and the cost of the franchise.

The Ideal Franchisee

It is a growing trend among some franchisors not to sell a franchise to anyone who has not worked for the franchisor for at least one year. This is a company rule of one of today's leading franchisors, Domino's Pizza. However, if you are not in a position to offer franchises only to persons who have worked for you for at least one year, you must incur the cost of identifying potentially good franchisees and establishing communications with them. In other words, you will need to formulate a profile of the type of franchisee who would have the best chance of succeeding in selling your product or service. The best franchisee is one who:

> You will need to formulate a profile of the type of franchisee who would have the best chance of succeeding in selling your product or service.

- Is a hard worker,
- Follows instructions,
- Will enjoy working in that particular type of business,
- Has a background suitable to it,
- Has adequate financial resources,
- Has a family that supports the new venture, and
- Is able to follow orders.

Generally, franchisees who continually wish to change systems or have suggestions for change based purely on theory do not make the best franchisees. The ideal franchisee should have advisory input abilities but not the stubbornness to insist upon changing the franchise system, at least until you have an opportunity to test-market the franchisee's theories or can show, based on your experience, that such theories do not work.

In any potential franchisee, look for the same qualities that made you successful in operating your retail business. There are business consultants who research and identify the profile of ideal franchisees for various industries and companies. It might be a good idea to retain such a consultant if his or her clients have provided good references. In many ways, good common sense and an objective view of what is necessary, as determined by your past experience or your operational personnel, might be the ticket to determining the best profile for the ideal franchisee.

Selecting an Advertising Agency

In situations where it is not a simple matter to attract franchisees and knowledge of the market for such franchisees is limited, an experienced, franchise-oriented advertising agency should be retained and a market survey initiated. The more difficult it is to attract the first franchisee, the more expensive advertising will be. The more extensive the franchising program is in the number of franchisees sought and the tightness of the timetable of expansion, the greater the necessity for a good, experienced, franchise-oriented advertising agency.

> Marketing products and services to the retail consumer is not the same as marketing a business to potential franchisees.

The cost of such an agency's services normally runs about $4,000 to $6,000 or more in fees on a monthly basis, according to the number of hours of work. Each franchisor is judged individually according to marketing needs and the fee is set accordingly.

Remember to select an agency or hire an employee with franchise business experience. Marketing products and services to the retail consumer is not the same as marketing a business to potential franchisees.

Most smaller franchisors initially will market their franchises on their own. They usually do this by advertising in the classified section of the Thursday edition of *The Wall Street Journal* or the Sunday edition of local metropolitan newspapers. Franchise trade shows, particularly those sponsored by the International Franchise Association, are another good way to recruit franchisees.

Working Capital Considerations

The costs involved in franchising will vary according to geographic areas, expansion time, and availability of potential franchisees, as well as the complexity of the product or service being sold.

> A small, one-person operation that has a profitable product or service with controlled lower costs and an ever-increasing market can franchise just as well as a larger competitor.

A small, one-person operation that has a profitable product or service with controlled lower costs and an ever-increasing market can franchise just as well as a larger competitor, provided the small business offers consistent services or products or both to its franchisees in a manner that will motivate the franchisees to remain in the franchise family. This usually means that the franchisor either performs a service or provides a product to the franchisee that the franchisee cannot obtain elsewhere or offers the product or service to the franchisee at a price lower than any price the franchisee could secure elsewhere or at a quality unavailable anywhere else.

This is necessary at least until the franchisor's trademark attains the recognition that will automatically generate continuing business for the franchisee or until the common franchisee advertising fund grows big enough to enhance the franchisee's business through customer recognition.

As a would-be franchisor, you must have a "glue" or "hold" on the franchisee that will be strong enough to keep the franchisee interested in remaining a licensed franchisee. In addition to providing the franchisee with products at lower prices and of the best available quality, as described above, such additional holds include supporting the franchisee's success. To demonstrate such ongoing support, you can provide continued training sessions, co-op advertising, billing and accounting services, discounted inventory prices from third-party suppliers, and exclusive product distribution.

The amount of working capital you need to start a franchise operation will vary depending on your size, rate of expansion, complexity of training, necessity of site selection and architectural planning, extent of marketing, attractiveness of the franchise, the capital investment required from franchisees, and other factors.

Carefully planned, slow expansion by a franchisor with a small, but efficient franchise-oriented staff or consultants and a product or service attractive to potential franchisees can be capitalized for as low as $20,000 to $50,000 by utilizing the existing franchise-trained staff.

Do not franchise your business without first developing a well-thought-out business plan. In this plan, you should set forth realistic marketing goals along with expansion plans, advertising programs, capital outlay, and projected costs for a five-year period. Don't rely on initial franchise fees and royalties to support you in the first few years of your business.

Realistic financial forecasts and iron-clad budgets, including necessary ongoing support systems for the franchisees, should be the keys to any franchise endeavor.

> As a would-be franchisor, you must have a "glue" or "hold" on the franchisee that will be strong enough to keep the franchisee interested in remaining a licensed franchisee.

> Do not franchise your business without first developing a well-thought-out business plan.

Conclusion

To build a strong foundation for your franchise operation, ensure that you:

- Obtain well-qualified and well-trained personnel to run and operate the business efficiently, as needed;
- Recognize the strategies for marketing your franchise opportunity to potential franchisees; and
- Determine the income and cash outlays of your first initial years as a franchisor, so you understand the numbers behind the venture.

If you use these resources and information in your franchising investigations and preparations, your franchise opportunity will have a much better chance for success.

Chapter 8
Franchise Laws—A Trap for the New Franchisor

s discussed earlier, in Chapter 6, many successful business owners decide to expand their businesses through distributorships, licensees, or joint venture/partnership arrangements to distribute and sell their products or services and, as a result, save themselves a considerable amount of capital investment in building or leasing company-owned and -backed outlets. The third parties—whether they are called distributors, licensees, partners, or joint venturers—all have one thing in common: they may constitute arrangements that are in violation of federal and state franchise laws.

These industrious and sincere business owners, in their desire to adopt a successful marketing system and expand their businesses, may very well be entering into a nightmare of litigation and government agency investigations resulting in considerable civil damages and government penalties. In most cases, the business owner is unaware of the impending danger and perhaps has even consulted an attorney not experienced in or aware of the ramifications of federal and state franchise and business opportunity laws.

It is entirely possible that an entrepreneur may purchase or an uninformed business owner may market a company that is actually engaged in franchising without being registered under applicable state law or without following the appropriate directives set forth in federal law.

A typical example of this is the business owner who has developed a new or improved product or service and has experienced a certain degree of success in marketing it. He or she must now decide whether or not to raise and risk additional capital to provide more marketing outlets for the expanding line of products or services, which would include hiring people to conduct his or her business in these new locations. All of this takes a considerable amount of time and money. In most cases, either the money is

> The third parties ... all have one thing in common: they may constitute arrangements that are in violation of federal and state franchise laws.

unavailable or the interest rates are prohibitive and it is almost impossible to find additional competent employees who will feel motivated to market the product or service properly. The business owner then decides that he or she will teach others to market the product or service and charge them for his or her expertise. The recipients of this training will, of course, want the right to use the name of the business owner, which, in almost all instances, is an integral part of the sales success of the product or service. The business owner, by the same token, will want to exert some type of control or limitations on the use of his or her name by third parties, so that it can be used only under certain controlled circumstances, avoiding any chance of bringing the name into disrepute.

If any of these restrictions are violated, the business owner will want to call off the deal and revoke the right to use the trademark. In addition, in order for the fledgling business to succeed financially, it will be necessary for the business owner to teach the third-party licensee, distributor, or joint venturer methods of marketing the product or service that will bring a degree of success to the third party's operation. This marketing plan or scheme will be such as to correspond to the methods used by the business owner in gaining his or her initial success.

The end result desired by both the third party and the business owner is to maintain an operation engaged in marketing a product or a service that will look to the public as if it is one big organization with a single identity and universal continuity of service. The business owner, of course, is going to want some type of remuneration for training the third party and allowing him or her to become part of what looks like a "big happy family." The consideration is usually in the form of an initial fee to cover the training and, in many cases, a percentage of future gross profits. In some cases it may be the outright sale of a facility and the right to use the name for a one lump sum payment. Such an arrangement is clearly a franchise under federal and state franchise law.

> The end result ... is to maintain an operation engaged in marketing a product or a service that will look to the public as if it is one big organization with a single identity and universal continuity of service.

The legal reality of the situation—that this is a franchise—is even less apparent to the business owner who is selling a third party a product rather than a service, such as an image-engraving system or coin-stamping equipment.

Federal Law

The federal government entered into regulating franchises on October 21, 1979, when the Federal Trade Commission (FTC) published its interpretive guides to the agency's trade regulation rule entitled "Disclosure Requirements and Prohibitions Concerning Franchising and Business Opportunity Ventures." In essence, the rules are an attempt to remedy the problems of nondisclosure and misrepresentation that arise when people purchase franchises without first obtaining reliable information about them. The rules thus require franchisors and franchise brokers to furnish prospective franchisees with information about the franchisor, the franchisor's business, and the terms of the franchise agreement in one single document—the basic disclosure document or offering circular.

> The rules are an attempt to remedy the problems of nondisclosure and misrepresentation that arise when people purchase franchises without first obtaining reliable information about them.

Additional information must be furnished if any claims are made about actual or potential earnings. This is referred to as the *earnings claim document*. The franchisor must also give the franchisee a copy of the proposed franchise agreement. The disclosures must include important facts in terms of the franchisor-franchisee relationship.

The FTC does not require registration, but does require that you provide the potential franchisee with certain written disclosures at your first face-to-face meeting with him or her, at least 10 days before taking any consideration for the franchise and five days before executing any franchise agreement.

The FTC rule requires that the franchisor update the disclosure documents at least quarterly when there is a material change in the franchisor's or subfranchisor's business during the quarter. Additionally, the FTC rule requires that disclosure documents be completely rewritten and updated once a year within 90 days of the fiscal year-end for distribution to prospective franchisees.

Due to the multifaceted complexity of creating a disclosure document that meets all levels of legal requirements, it is not safe to attempt to complete this yourself. By following the sample franchise documents in the appendices, you can start to build the framework for your franchise documents that can be reviewed and completed by professionals. By doing this preliminary work, you most likely will reduce your attorney fees.

Prior to January 1, 1995, federal law preempted certain state laws where the provisions of both overlapped. To prevent the duplication of disclosure requirements with state statutes, the FTC rules permitted use of a disclosure format known as the Uniform Franchise Offering Circular (UFOC) to comply with state registration laws on disclosure requirements. Under the new law, effective January 1, 1995, the same UFOC format is required by the FTC and state authorities. The revised and updated UFOC guidelines are reproduced in Appendix F of this book.

On October 22, 1999, the FTC formally requested public comment on proposed revisions to the existing franchise disclosure rule. It is doubtful that these proposed changes—involving exclusion of applicability of the FTC rules to business opportunities, time changes for making disclosures, clarification of application to foreign sales, certain additional changes regarding franchisor-initiated lawsuits, etc., electronic media disclosures, and expanding the rule's exemptions of sophisticated investors—will become official for several years (64 *Federal Register* 57293-57350). Your franchise attorney should keep you abreast of any formal changes.

A violation of the rules set forth by the FTC for failure to provide the required circular or for misrepresentation will constitute an unfair or deceptive act or practice within the meaning of Section 5 of the Federal Trade Commission Act. It subjects the violator to civil penalty actions brought by the FTC of up to $10,000 in fines per violation per day. The courts have held that the FTC rule does not create a private right of action in wronged franchisees. However, franchisees have successfully sought enforcement through "Little FTC Acts," which are state unfair practice acts.

Under federal law, as the franchisor, you must provide prospective franchisees with a circular that conforms to the law, but you do not have to send a copy to the FTC or register the circular with the FTC. In states requiring registration, such as California, you must complete an application for registration that contains, among other things, information regarding the background of the salespersons authorized to sell the franchise.

> The FTC does not require registration, but does require that you provide the potential franchisee with certain written disclosures.

> Under federal law, as the franchisor, you must provide prospective franchisees with a circular that conforms to the law, but you do not have to send a copy to the FTC or register the circular with the FTC.

State registration fees vary from $50 to $750. See Appendix E for more specifics on filing fees of franchise registration states.

State Law

Fifteen states have also passed franchise registration or notice of filing acts. If you want to sell franchises, these acts require that you file and gain approval of an application that contains information about who you are, submit a copy of your proposed contract, and prepare a proposed circular that is to be given to the franchisee at least 10 days before he or she purchases the franchise and pays any money for it.

As mentioned above, the offering circular required by the applicable state governments is referred to as a Uniform Franchise Offering Circular and requires the franchisor to state the following:

- Background information regarding the franchisor, predecessors, and affiliates;
- The identity and business experience of key personnel;
- Pending franchisor litigation;
- Prior franchisor bankruptcies;
- Details of franchise fees and other fees;
- An outline of the franchisee's initial investment;
- Restrictions on sources of products and services;
- Territory;
- Trademarks;
- Patents, copyrights, and proprietary information;
- Obligations of the franchisee to participate in the actual operation of the franchised business;
- Restrictions on what the franchisee may sell;
- Renewal, termination, transfer, and dispute resolutions;
- Arrangements with public figures;
- Earnings claims;
- Identification of franchisees of the franchisor; and
- Financial statements of the franchisor.

In addition, a copy of the franchise agreement and an explanation of its more pertinent provisions are also required. Many of these topics are discussed in greater detail in Chapter 2.

You can also refer to Appendices B-1 and B-2, which are sample franchise agreements corresponding to the UFOCs in Appendices A-1 and A-2, respectively.

In most cases, if you are in a registration state, you will submit your application with the franchise agreement and circular to a state official, who will then determine whether or not it has any filing deficiencies from a state standpoint and will advise you accordingly.

In essence, these state statutes, like the federal statutes, require a complete disclosure of certain enumerated items. The states do not determine whether or not the statements in the offering circular are true or false, but, in the event that a stated item is not true, the state gives the franchisee an additional legal right for damages.

In some cases, a violation may result in administrative or criminal sanctions or both, in addition to the civil remedies afforded to the franchisee. States having franchise investment laws have statutes that can be used in seeking damages through the courts or arbitration for both loss of profit and return of monies spent in the event that a franchisor violates these laws. This is in addition to remedies for fraud that are available to any victimized business owner.

In addition, the states with franchise registration laws and the FTC under its rule on franchising have given government authorities certain powers to seek criminal remedies against franchisors violating the franchise acts and, in some instances, the power to order the franchisor to pay back franchise fees received in violation of the acts.

> The states with franchise registration laws and the FTC under its rule on franchising have given government authorities certain powers to seek criminal remedies against franchisors violating the franchise acts.

If you insist upon doing your own disclosure documents—which franchise experts do not recommend—you should familiarize yourself with the laws of the state in which you intend to franchise. At the very least, contact the various state agencies to see whether or not you are required to comply with their laws if you are selling to a franchisee residing in that state or if you want to operate franchises in that state.

In all states with franchise registration laws, if the prospective franchisee is a resident of the state and the franchise is to be operated in that state, the franchise laws of that state will apply. Also remember that you can make no claims regarding existing franchisees' earnings or potential earnings unless you provide an earnings claim document. Those states with franchise registration laws also require an approved earnings claim document of a similar sort.

Conclusion

Before selling your business in any way that will involve third parties—such as distributors, licensees, or partners—be sure to review federal and state franchise laws so you are informed on their requirements. In particular, you are going to want to make sure your legal counsel is aware of these franchise requirements. It is amazing how many business attorneys are unaware of such requirements and legislation.

> Before selling your business in any way that will involve third parties ..., review federal and state franchise laws .... In particular, ... make sure your legal counsel is aware of these franchise requirements.

Ask your attorney if he or she is experienced with FTC Rule 436, as well as the acts in your state regulating franchise investment, business opportunities, and seller-assisted marketing plans—in short, franchises and other business ventures that are short of being franchises but are close enough to require a specific type of disclosure form. If your counsel is unfamiliar with these rules and regulations, seek counsel specializing in this area. Even if counsel is familiar with these laws, request the names of previous clients that he or she has helped franchise and call them for their opinion of his or her knowledge and ability.

For further information on state franchise laws and resources, refer to Appendix E, State Franchise Information Guidelines.

Chapter 9
Choosing a Franchise Attorney

T hroughout this book, you are advised to consult a competent attorney, who preferably specializes in franchise law, to assist you in the franchising arena— be it as a potential franchisor or as a prospective franchisee. Their assistance can range from putting together the required offering circular to researching federal and state franchise laws.

Because franchise attorneys have gone through the franchise process before, they can be of particular help to new franchisors who are not familiar with the training, marketing, administrative, and sales functions that are unique to a franchising operation.

Another important area where franchise attorneys can be of assistance is in the marketing of your potential franchise. For many potential franchisees, the offering circular is the first point-of-sale piece they see. Your offering circular introduces you, presents your background and those of your predecessors, and outlines all the services, products, and obligations. Having an experienced, business-oriented attorney help you prepare your circular effectively and accurately could prove very valuable, both in terms of marketing and in terms of complying with federal and state franchise laws.

Select an Experienced, Business-Oriented Attorney

An offering circular must have provisions that are practical, time-proven, business-oriented, workable, and, above all, fair. Because most executives of a prospective franchisor entity, whether large or small, have no prior experience in operating a franchised business and not much if any know-how in selling franchises, training franchisees, or opening and servicing franchises, they are of little help to the franchise attorney from a business standpoint. Therefore, the situation arises in which the attorney is required to know

> An offering circular must have provisions that are practical, time-proven, business-oriented, workable, and, above all, fair.

Find out whether your franchise attorney is more than a legal technician whose only function is to file a legally acceptable document suitable only to get you a permit from the state authority to sell franchises.

much more about franchising than his or her client does. This is in addition to knowing the legal requirements. Therefore, find out whether your franchise attorney is more than a legal technician whose only function is to file a legally acceptable document suitable only to get you a permit from the state authority to sell franchises.

When you and your experienced, market-oriented attorney begin work on the offering circular and franchise agreement, other business issues will have been decided, including the franchise fee to be charged, the type of training to be given the franchisees, the continuing royalty and service fees to be charged, and the duties and obligations of both the franchisor and the franchisee. All such business policies must be established on time-proven, practical terms that will work.

If you fail to properly prepare yourself for operating a franchise system, including selecting either a business-minded, franchise-oriented attorney or an experienced, business-oriented franchise consultant, you may be launching your new franchise the same way as you started the business you intend to franchise, with absolutely no practical knowledge of how to operate it.

Chances are the attorney you have used in the past will be in the same boat when it comes to franchising the business. You both may have started out as novices in the business start-up world, but through trial and error and working together, you have gained business know-how and developed proven procedures for business success. Now that you have reached the point of expanding your business through franchising, that attorney may not be the one you want to rely on for determining such franchise factors as suitable franchise fees and royalties, setting up and operating a franchise, and the franchise agreement. Trial-and-error methods of operating a franchise company do not succeed, because such companies are operating with other people's money and lives and on a limited time basis.

If you have knowledge and experience in opening a franchise or you have guidance from a consultant or a new employee who has actual experience in running a successful franchise company, you or your employee or consultant can tell the attorney what procedural rules are necessary for a workable franchise agreement.

Legal Fees—What to Expect

Attorney fees vary according to each attorney's overhead expenses and desire for profit. An experienced attorney who runs a cost-efficient operation can easily make a fair return on a $20,000 to $30,000 legal fee (depending on the business and knowledge of the franchisor) for preparing and filing a marketable, workable, and well-coordinated offering circular registration in the initial state of registration.

Attorneys should be able to complete their work within 30 to 40 days, barring any unforeseen circumstances. Legal fees for each additional state (since the circular will have to be amended in certain states) will vary anywhere from $250 to $2,500, depending on the state. Filing fees range from $50 to $750. You should obtain from the attorney a complete fee quotation for the initial state and for additional states, along with his or her scheduled date of completion. Completion of the franchisor-background questionnaires in Appendix C and Appendix D may help you save legal fees and expedite the timetable for completing the offering circular and franchise agreement. Refer to Chapter 11 for other tips on how to save on attorney fees.

Aside from legal costs, remember the cost of a certified audit, which is an initial necessity in certain states and an ultimate necessity in others. Generally, a good franchise attorney will have a client start a corporation for the purpose of franchising; the audited financials of the new corporation will be nominal—from $950 to $1,950, depending again upon the accountant and his or her cost-effectiveness.

> Aside from legal costs, remember the cost of a certified audit, which is an initial necessity in certain states and an ultimate necessity in others.

Conclusion

As with any professional consultant, you cannot necessarily judge a good franchise attorney by his or her legal fees, but you can, however, judge franchise attorneys by what their franchise clients say about them, not only in terms of complying with certain statutory laws but also in terms of familiarity with the time-proven and correct methods of operating a franchise in a particular industry. Insist upon references from the attorney and call each reference. Ask each client's opinion of the attorney's legal abilities and his or her ability to draft an offering circular and franchise agreement that are fair, marketable, and marketing-oriented—all of which are necessary elements of a successful franchise operation.

Chapter 10
Making Your Franchise Operation Work

To make your franchise operation work more smoothly and succeed, you will want to ensure you do a couple of important activities. These activities include:

- Helping your franchisees find a suitable location for the franchise so it has a better chance of success;
- Preparing an operations manual to provide the franchisee with guidelines and instructions on how to operate the franchise on a day-to-day basis;
- Selecting a franchise office that is practical and economical; and
- Reviewing franchise agreement clauses regarding transfer, renewal, and termination of the franchise, to keep your franchise's reputation positive despite a potential franchisee's dissatisfaction and desire to leave your organization.

All of these activities are discussed in this chapter in hopes you, as the potential franchisor, will have much of this information and knowledge before dealing with potential franchisees, thus creating a better franchisee-franchisor relationship and, most likely, a more successful franchise operation.

Assisting Franchisees in Selecting a Site

If your franchise involves a restaurant or other business in which location is a key factor in franchise sales, you will want to have someone assist your franchisees in selecting sites. Most franchisors require their franchisees to conduct preliminary research on potential sites. In most cases, real estate brokers or shopping-center managers can provide the demographics and other commercial information pertaining to each potential site.

The primary reason for making your franchisees responsible for site selection is not only to make the franchisee thoroughly familiar with the pros and cons of each potential site location, but also to help alleviate any liability you may face if you are the sole selector of the site and the franchisee subsequently fails. Many franchisees who fail will blame the choice of site location as the primary reason for their failure, even though the failure may be entirely the franchisee's own fault. Therefore, most franchisors require the franchisees to make their own site selection, with the franchisor acting as the final approving authority.

To ensure that the franchisee has picked an appropriate site, however, you should have a qualified broker or other expert evaluate the suitability of the chosen site. This person should be qualified in real estate matters and have some experience in franchising and in the particular business being franchised. In some cases, a new franchisor may act as the site selection appraiser assisting the franchisee; however, most franchisors retain real estate consultants rather than hire full-time personnel, at least in the initial stages. These agents normally are compensated by brokers' fees from the landlord. Again, carefully check out references and accomplishments of the brokers or individuals you hire to help your prospective franchisee find a franchise location. For help in rating potential sites, use the Franchise Site Evaluation Form at the end of Chapter 2.

> Many franchisees who fail will blame the choice of site location as the primary reason for their failure, even though the failure may be entirely the franchisee's own fault.

Site Selection Costs

If you are knowledgeable regarding the elements necessary for a good site for your business and conduct the site selection yourself, costs will be minimal. If contacts are made with local real estate brokers who are familiar with your franchisees' needs and territories, costs will also be minimal. Hiring a professional, full-time site selector could be expensive, depending upon your location. In most cases, an employee hired as a site selector will hold other positions in a franchise company, including marketing or training responsibilities. Again, try to keep your costs at a minimum without sacrificing the effectiveness of your organization.

> If you are knowledgeable regarding the elements necessary for a good site for your business and conduct the site selection yourself, costs will be minimal.

Preparing the Operations Manual

As part of the operational function in a well-developed franchise system, you should prepare and provide an effective operations manual that documents the functions of the franchise business in a written, chronological, step-by-step format, so that the franchisee can easily follow them after completing the initial franchise training program.

You can have an all-purpose consultant prepare your operations manual or, if you are an experienced business owner, you can do it yourself by following the Operations Manual Outline in this book and merely listing, in chronological order—perhaps by talking into a tape recorder—the steps that complete the operations of your business. This account of basic business practices details the specific elements that made your business unique and successful. If you feel awkward in doing this, you can have someone else record and subsequently type up what you have said regarding the basic functions of the business. The operations manual is generally the framework that you will use for your training sessions. Thus, the substance of the training sessions will be based on whatever is in the operations manual.

> You can have an all-purpose consultant prepare your operations manual or ... do it yourself by following the Operations Manual Outline in this book.

If you feel you do not have the necessary dictation and writing skills to create a training manual and if you do not have a family member or employee who can do so, hire a qualified person to write one. Even individuals who specialize in writing manuals can be hired for fees ranging anywhere from $2,000 to $5,000. If any confidential information is to be contained in the manual, take steps to get a confidentiality nondisclosure agreement from the person retained to write and/or type the manual and consider obtaining copyrights for the manual.

Contents of an Operations Manual

> Each franchisor's operations manual is unique, because in a given industry, each successful franchisor has a quality that distinguishes his or her business from those of his or her competitors.

Each franchisor's operations manual is unique, because in a given industry, each successful franchisor has a quality that distinguishes his or her business from those of his or her competitors. For example, a Wendy's operation featuring orders made up as they are given to the cashier differs from a McDonald's, where food is prepared in advance. Another illustration of this is Subway's method of making sandwiches at the direction of the customer, who deals with the individual preparer instead of ordering through a cashier.

Some franchisors have two operations manuals. One might deal with site selection, the initial opening of the store, bookkeeping, accounting, advertising, and grand-opening procedures. The second manual may address the duties of individual employees and, in the case of a restaurant, preparation of the food. A second manual could also cover such everyday duties as opening and closing procedures, accepting checks, making daily reports, hiring employees, preparing time sheets, receiving and transferring goods, preparing supply lists, and maintaining inventory procedures, security measures, and banking procedures.

Selecting Your Office

> Your success or failure can be determined in many instances by how well you plan your initial operation.

In many cases, one of the first things new franchisors do is commit themselves and their new franchise to a costly new office showplace. This can be fatal. You must do the same thing for yourself as you do for the franchisee: establish a highly capable, efficient organization at the lowest cost possible. You should have a pilot plant of the operation you are intending to franchise. Often, you can initially work from this location by using a back room and a new telephone number. If this workplace is not feasible because it does not present an attractive appearance, then you can rent, preferably month to month, a location and office furniture in an attractive, but economical building.

In many situations, executive suites that will provide services such as photocopying, faxing, telephone answering, and reception services can be rented by the month at an economical cost. It is suggested that this avenue be taken, at least initially, until the franchise business has taken hold.

Budget, budget, budget! Your success or failure can be determined in many instances by how well you plan your initial operation. Thus, plan your franchise operation in the same careful way as you have planned your business and the future business operations of your franchisees.

Reviewing Transfer, Renewal, and Termination Clauses

You must select each of your franchisees carefully. Never sell a franchise to anyone you do not consider completely qualified for the job. The franchisee is also a manager of your business extension, so you should never choose as a franchisee someone you would not hire as a manager. A good selection of franchisees will diminish the chance of franchise failure, especially early transfers and terminations. Treat the franchisee like a member of your team and regard the franchising system as an extension of your marketing arm. It is your services or products that are being sold under your service mark or trademark. You would not hesitate to assist one of your company managers when in trouble or even to remove him or her if it were in the best interest of the company-owned office.

If you look upon the franchisee as a replacement for your company-owned office, your attitude will be positive when concentrating on assisting him or her. Your franchise agreement should allow for transfers, with your consent, which you should not withhold unreasonably. Examples of transfer and termination provisions are contained in the sample franchise agreements in Appendices B-1 and B-2.

If a franchisee is dissatisfied, the best procedure is to allow him or her to transfer or for you to buy out the franchisee. Lawsuits are costly and time-consuming and you must report them in the offering circular. Therefore, a lawsuit could be detrimental to the future sale of franchises, since potential franchisees will be made aware of the dissatisfied franchisees who are suing or have been terminated and probably will receive negative information about you from them.

> If a franchisee is dissatisfied, the best procedure is to allow him or her to transfer or for you to buy out the franchisee.

Franchise agreements are generally drafted by an attorney with provisions that are applicable in the state where the franchisor and the attorney are located. In many cases, the termination and transfer provisions may be contrary to the laws of other states where the same franchise agreement is being utilized. The cost of tailoring each clause to abide by changing laws in each state is almost prohibitive. In addition, new state laws become effective from time to time after the initial franchise agreement has been drafted. Therefore, before any transfer is made, your attorney should check over the particular state law pertaining to transfers or terminations—even if there is a clause in your agreement stating that the laws of the state of the franchisor apply.

State Renewal and Termination Laws

Laws regarding the termination and transfer of franchisees are commonly referred to as "franchise relationship laws." Some of these termination and transfer laws are contained in state franchise investment or disclosure acts. Others are contained in a deceptive franchise act, pyramid scheme act, or retail franchising act and, in Wisconsin, the fair dealership law. For a complete list of such laws, see Appendix E, State Franchise Information Guidelines.

> Laws regarding the termination and transfer of franchisees are commonly referred to as "franchise relationship laws."

In the absence of a state statute to the contrary, a fixed-term franchise that does not provide for general renewal will expire upon its expiration date. However, some of the state statutes require good cause for termination. The good-cause requirements in some of these franchise laws may mandate renewal of a fixed-term agreement, even one that clearly states that no renewal is allowed, thereby resulting in the perpetual renewal of the agreement unless the franchisor can prove that the franchisee did something that constituted good cause for termination of the agreement. At the time of this writing, Arkansas, Connecticut, Delaware, the District of Columbia, Hawaii, Indiana, Iowa, Nebraska, New Jersey, Virginia, and Wisconsin require good cause for the franchisor not to renew the franchise agreement.

California permits nonrenewal upon receipt of 180 days' notice for several specified reasons, including failure by the franchisee to agree to the standard terms of the renewal franchise. Some other states that affect the right to renewal are Arkansas, Connecticut, Indiana, Mississippi, Missouri, Nebraska, New Jersey, Minnesota, Illinois, Michigan, Washington, and Wisconsin. Mississippi and Missouri currently have notice requirements regarding nonrenewal of a franchise agreement. Virginia has passed an act that makes it unlawful for a franchisor to cancel a franchise without reasonable cause or to use undue influence to induce a franchisee to surrender any right given to him or her by any provision contained in the franchise agreement.

These laws change from time to time and, therefore, any franchisor who does not intend to renew or has a franchisee who is transferring his or her franchise should consult experienced legal counsel before issuing any communication to the franchisee.

Excessive Transfer Fees

> It is recommended that transfer and renewal fees be geared more to compensate the franchisor for expenses rather than to make a huge profit.

Franchise attorneys have a tendency to draft provisions that require substantial transfer fees for the franchisee. Some of these high-figured transfer fee provisions have been attacked as unconscionable in court lawsuits. In fact, the states of Iowa and Washington prohibit a transfer fee in excess of an amount necessary to compensate the franchisor for expenses incurred as a result of the transfer. Therefore, it is recommended that transfer and renewal fees be geared more to compensate the franchisor for expenses rather than to make a huge profit. After all, a good franchisee should bring good royalties to the franchisor.

Conclusion

If you take the time to research and compile much of the information pertaining to this chapter's activities before organizing your franchise operation and recruiting potential franchisees, you will be much better off than many other prospective franchisors who haven't done their homework.

> The more knowledge you have on franchising ... the more secure and confident you will appear to potential franchisees.

The more knowledge you have on franchising—such as good site location data and resources for your particular business or writing a thorough manual on how to operate your type of franchise operation—the more secure and confident you will appear to potential franchisees. In other words, you will make a better impression on the prospects you talk to when getting your franchise operation going.

In addition to creating a more confident appearance, your research will also make you more aware of the costly mistakes frequently made by new franchisors, such as spending money too extravagantly on new franchise headquarters or making fees too high so they backfire on you. You will be a much wiser franchisor by doing research and investigation on your own and in conjunction with potential franchisees or franchise attorneys.

Operations Manual Outline

I. Introduction

A. Welcoming Letter from Chief Operations Officer

B. Introduction to Manual

C. Biographical Information on Franchisor's Key Personnel

II. Pre-Opening Requirements

A. Preparation of Chronological Chart by Franchisee, with Franchisor's Assistance, Setting Dates and Time Periods for:
   1. Selection of the site by franchisee
   2. Approval of the site by franchisor
   3. Approval of the lease by franchisor
   4. Execution of a lease
   5. Commencement of construction within required number of days after execution of the lease
   6. Finalization of construction

B. Preparation of Pro Forma Financial Statements by Franchisee and His/Her Financial Advisors and Accountants

C. Checklist of All Necessary Permits and Registration Forms

D. Review of Franchisor's Specifications Regarding Construction and Decor

E. List of Equipment, Inventory, and Fixtures

F. Procurement of Necessary Documents, Items, and Services
   1. Suppliers
   2. Telephone systems
   3. Security systems
   4. Cleaning agencies
   5. Trash removal agency
   6. Pest control service
   7. Map services
   8. Fire extinguishers
   9. Background music installation
   10. Bank services
   11. Appropriate licenses
   12. Sales tax permit
   13. Minimum wage and equal opportunity literature
   14. Cleaning supplies
   15. Hand tools
   16. Office forms

III. Pre-Opening and Post-Opening Training Procedures

   A. General Daily-Business Operational Policies

   B. Product or Service to Be Sold
      1. Development of menu
      2. Specifications
      3. Purchase lists

   C. Preparation of Personnel to Sell Product or Service

   D. Decor and Dress Code of Restaurant Personnel

   E. Customer Service Procedure Deliveries

   F. Delivery Requirements and Techniques

   G. Preparation of Sales and Financial Reports
      1. Daily business forms
      2. Inventory strategy
      3. Preparation of daily, weekly, and monthly financial statements

   H. Security Procedures

   I. Cash Register Operation

   J. Store Policy on Tipping

   K. In-Store Promotion, Advertising, and Mandatory Direct Mailings

   L. Periodic Amendments to Operation Procedures

IV. Bookkeeping and Accounting Methods

V. Grand Opening Procedures

VI. Daily Operational Function

VII. Troubleshooting

VIII. Conclusion

Chapter 11
Final Thoughts on Franchising

In this final chapter, you will find several helpful tips and information on franchising your business. Areas include subfranchising, saving on attorney fees, determining capital requirements, and avoiding litigation. By this point, you hopefully have gained enough information to understand your responsibilities as a franchisor and perhaps have even begun some of your research and investigation. Take the time here to learn ways to cover all your bases and save money at the same time.

Subfranchising or Area Franchising

Subfranchising, sometimes referred to as area franchising, is a procedure by which a franchisor tries to clone himself or herself. In other words, for a substantial fee, a franchisor sells to a third party, usually a group of investors, the right to use the franchisor's trademarks, trade secrets, and training, administrative, and marketing procedures in designated regions of the United States and the world. Thus, the purchaser of a region will act in the place of the franchisor in that particular region. Usually, the consideration of subfranchising does not come up until a franchisor has successfully franchised in a particular area.

Before embarking upon this approach, however, thoroughly consider the positive and negative aspects of such an arrangement.

A pioneer of subfranchising has been the Century 21 system. The cloned subfranchisees did not have to provide a great deal of training to their new franchisees, since they were brokers who knew how to sell real estate. For the most part, they simply changed their coats when they joined the nationwide Century 21 system.

Unlike franchisees, subfranchisees are usually a group of wealthy individuals who are looking for a return on their investment. It is extremely difficult to get one or more

> Subfranchising, sometimes referred to as area franchising, is a procedure by which a franchisor tries to clone himself or herself.

> It is extremely difficult to get one or more investors of a subfranchise to carry on the everyday activities required for a successful subfranchise company.

investors of a subfranchise to carry on the everyday activities required for a successful subfranchise company. Therefore, this avenue should be reviewed very carefully before any decision is reached. Selling a subfranchise territory is also expensive. The market for subfranchisors is limited to a person or persons with a considerable amount of money—anywhere from a quarter of a million dollars to several million dollars.

Generally, this type of individual is looking for an investment and does not want to be taught the exhaustive, highly difficult job of marketing franchises and following through by providing supportive services to the franchisees. It is much easier to find qualified franchisees than it is to find qualified subfranchisees with huge capital resources. In addition, subfranchisors tend to make changes in the franchise system and often feel they are as competent as the original franchisor or more so, since they usually become more active than the franchisor in the actual operation of the franchise.

In addition, in order to sell subfranchises, a franchisor must prepare an offering circular and a subfranchise contract detailing the terms and conditions of the arrangement between the franchisor and the subfranchisee, including the splitting of royalties and initial franchise fees, the delegation of someone as a trainer, and more.

Once the subfranchisee has purchased a subfranchise that qualifies in the FTC states, he or she must in turn register his or her own circular before selling franchises in registration states. In nonregistration states, the subfranchisee must still provide prospective franchisees with an offering circular containing pertinent disclosure. If you are considering subfranchising as an option, take great care in selecting each subfranchisee and think through all the pros and cons.

Saving on Attorney Fees

As mentioned in Chapter 9, many new franchisors have little personal knowledge of how to run a franchise company; therefore, they have definite ideas of what they want to charge as franchise fees, royalties, and advertising fees. They generally base their ideas on what they would like or what others have been doing—that is, seeking franchisees more as a method of making a lot of money rather than as a way to extend their marketing arm by adding franchised retail outlets.

> To help you in your first meeting with your franchise attorney, you will want to complete the two background questionnaires in Appendices C and D.

It is the job of an experienced, knowledgeable franchise attorney to interview his or her franchisor clients and determine certain biographical information as well as their business desires, particularly those pertaining to royalties and franchise fees, and to reconcile the information so he or she can give a more objective, realistic view of what each new franchisor should do. To help you in your first meeting with your franchise attorney, you will want to complete the two background questionnaires in Appendices C and D. Both of these questionnaires make you think about what you want contained in the offering circular and the specific terms you want in the franchise agreement. By completing these questionnaires before your first visit to a franchise attorney, you may be able to convince him or her to lower the bill because of the time you have saved in securing such information.

In addition, if you can supply your attorney at this first meeting with further written documentation of the estimated costs of opening and operating one of your franchises, the number of such franchises that will be sold within the ensuing year, and a complete breakdown of what the franchisee will be required to spend in order to open one of your franchise outlets—including franchise fees, rent, fixtures, equipment, payroll, utilities, insurance, and working capital—you will hasten the preparation of your circular and thus possibly reduce your legal expenses.

Determining Your Capitalization Requirements

One of the first items you, as a potential franchisor, must determine is the amount of money necessary to capitalize your franchise operation. In a registration state, the minimum amount of capital that a franchisor should have is a sufficient amount of liquid cash (current assets) so that he or she can open the number of franchises he or she projects opening in the forthcoming year. However, your capitalization amount should be equal to the amount you have projected to carry you to your break-even point—where income will begin to equal payables. In addition, the higher your capitalization, the easier it will be for you to sell franchises, since your audited financials are part of your offering circular.

> One of the first items you, as a potential franchisor, must determine is the amount of money necessary to capitalize your franchise operation.

Impounds

If you are in a registration state and the attorney for the state examining your application for franchising determines you do not have sufficient capitalization to open the franchises you plan to open, the applicable state agency will generally grant you a permit to sell franchises. To do this, however, you must open an impound account in a bank chartered in that particular state for the direct deposit of all franchise fees. In essence, an impound is a trust account: the franchisor is required to have the franchisee write a check to the designated depository bank, to be held in trust until the franchisee provides a written declaration to the registration state that his or her franchise is open and that the franchisor has performed all of his or her opening obligations under the franchise agreement.

Once this declaration is received, it is filed with the appropriate state registration agency; if the agency approves the declaration, it will prepare an order allowing the franchisor to remove the franchisee's funds from the bank. The franchisor then submits this order to the bank and the bank pays that particular franchise fee to the franchisor.

Unfortunately, there are not too many banks familiar with these trust account procedures and most such escrow accounts are extremely expensive—$1,000 to $2,000 in some cities for each franchisee escrow account. In some instances, your franchise attorney may be able to convince the state authority that you will provide in your franchise agreement that you will not require payment of the initial franchise fee until the franchisee has opened his or her store and advised you that he or she agrees you have fulfilled all your opening obligations under the franchise agreement. Many registration states will allow this type of provision in lieu of impounds.

Franchise Taxes

As a franchisor, you will definitely need to retain the services of a competent accountant who is versed in franchise taxation. Presently, franchise income has generally been held

Since you will need annual audited statements, your CPA will advise you of the current tax regulations on these tax matters.

not to be passive income if the franchisor has ongoing responsibilities. In addition, the Internal Revenue Service places certain restrictions on when the franchisor can report income as earned. Generally, the franchisor can report the franchise fee as earned only during the time the franchise is operating. Since you will need annual audited statements, your CPA will advise you of the current tax regulations on these tax matters.

Besides the federal tax regulations on franchise income, many states have franchise tax regulations. To get more information on your tax obligations and reporting requirements, see an experienced accountant or certified public accountant. You don't want any nasty surprises that could cost you money. Be as informed as possible on franchise income taxation.

Franchisee Associations and Advertising Councils

Most registration states have laws that prohibit a franchisor from interfering with the right of franchisees to have their own associations.

Most registration states have laws that prohibit a franchisor from interfering with the right of franchisees to have their own associations. Franchisees can have an association, but it is in your best interests as a franchisor to form that association and you should be involved in its operations. Generally, a franchisee association will not be formed until seven to 10 franchisees are operating in a given area.

A franchisee association should be an advisory body only, since you, as the franchisor, should still determine the specific procedures to be followed by the franchise system. Many successful franchisors, including McDonald's, have improved their systems by implementing suggestions from franchisees and making changes within the entire system after they have been proven successful at one or two test-franchise operations.

Like franchisee associations, franchisee advertising councils can be effective too. Each franchisee usually has his or her own idea of what the ideal advertising media should be—and most of the ideas are cost-prohibitive. For instance, almost all franchisees want local, regional, and national television exposure, which is much too costly in most cases and clearly in excess of the advertising fund fees collected from franchisees. It would be better to poll the franchisees from time to time in order to get an idea of which local advertising media they have found effective in their operations.

Do not indiscriminately pass out your disclosure document or offering circular, because this document can be ... 80 to 100 pages long and is costly to reproduce.

A good franchise agreement should compel the franchisee to provide written reports of all types, particularly covering sales data. This information could then be compiled into meaningful results for each franchisee in the system. This is one of the major benefits of the franchise system—the experiences of each franchisee, rather than his or her theories, can be compiled, analyzed, and passed on for the benefit of the entire system.

Cost-Saving Tips for the Offering Circular

Do not indiscriminately pass out your disclosure document or offering circular, because this document can be anywhere from 80 to 100 pages long and is costly to reproduce. In addition, circulars shouldn't be easily disassembled, but you should not heavily staple or bind these documents in any way, shape, or form. This is because you will be revising your disclosures quite often, particularly if you have registered in more than one state. You can save yourself the cost of completely replacing your current supply of official circulars by substituting a revised page for the old page. A three-ring, loose-leaf binder might be a good alternative.

All franchise registration laws and the FTC rule require that the disclosure be modified at least once a year or at any time a material modification is made or both. Audited financials, for all practical purposes, must be updated yearly, so you will be amending and filing them annually in the registration states. To save on significant copying costs, screen your potential franchisees by using a customized Franchisee Business Application and Net Worth Form, such as the sample form set forth at the end of this chapter, before sending out any offering circular.

> All franchise registration laws and the FTC rule require that the disclosure be modified at least once a year or at any time a material modification is made.

Steps to Take Before Sending the Circular

Following a prospective franchisee's initial inquiry, you should send him or her an informational brochure. Brochures can cost anywhere from a few dollars to thousands of dollars to prepare. Depending on your personal taste and budget, it may be preferable to use a simple letter-form brochure stating many of the items that are in the disclosure—but painting a nice picture of the attributes of the particular franchise system.

In California and a few other states where registration is necessary, the brochure, like any advertisement, must be submitted to the appropriate registration authority for prior approval. An ad is generally required to be submitted in duplicate anywhere from three to seven days before publication, with a duty upon the agency to disapprove it within such time or the ad is deemed approved.

> A sample of a Franchisee Business Application and Net Worth Form is located at the end of this chapter.

In addition to sending a brochure, you should make an attempt to find out if the franchisee is financially qualified to buy a franchise. Therefore, the first document forwarded to the franchisee should be a franchise application seeking background information and the net worth of the franchisee. A sample of a Franchisee Business Application and Net Worth Form is located at the end of this chapter. This type of application seeks net worth financials of the prospective franchisee and should be tailored to your needs and reviewed by your legal counsel.

Acknowledgment Receipt

After a prospective franchisee has completed the background application and net worth financial form, use the document to assess his or her suitability to your franchise by checking out every disclosure that you can. If you determine a franchisee to have the necessary qualifications, the next step is to forward your disclosure document (UFOC) to the prospective franchisee or meet with him or her and present the circular at the first face-to-face meeting, as required by the franchise laws. The prospect acknowledges receiving the disclosure by signing a document called an acknowledgment receipt and returning it to you, as the franchisor. At the end of Appendix A-1 and A-2 are examples of acknowledgment receipts.

> The prospect acknowledges receiving the disclosure by signing a document called an acknowledgment receipt and returning it to you, as the franchisor.

Always prepare two acknowledgment receipt forms, one copy for the prospective franchisee to keep and the other for him or her to sign and return to you. If the franchisee signs one and returns it to you but doesn't retain a copy for his or her own records, he or she may at some time in the future, particularly if the situation involves legal proceedings, contend that he or she didn't receive the disclosure at least 10 business days before execution of the agreement or payment of any deposit or franchise fee. This initial accusation might be avoided if you provide the franchisee with a copy of his or her acknowledgment receipt at the time it is executed.

Restrictions on Offer of Circular

In the 15 registration states, you are precluded from offering to sell a franchise to a prospective franchisee and discussing any of the substantive disclosure terms until the franchisee has received the disclosure document; however, the FTC rule does allow some discussion by telephone before the franchisee actually receives the document. Keep in mind the FTC rule is quite nebulous as to the permitted extent and nature of this discussion. It is a much better practice to provide the potential franchisee with the required offering circular before any discussion about it.

> If the franchise is to be operated in another state, you will be required to register in the other state before offering your franchise.

If the franchisee is out of state and the franchise is to be operated in your registration state, the offering circular to be sent to the prospective franchisee would be your in-state offering circular. However, if the franchise is to be operated in another state, you will be required to register in the other state before offering your franchise.

Deposit and Lease Agreements

After the prospect has reviewed the disclosure and indicated a desire to purchase the franchise, you may have him or her execute a deposit agreement and make a partial franchise fee payment, called a deposit, while he or she evaluates possible franchise locations. Many franchisors prefer to have the franchisee sign the franchise agreement and immediately pay the entire franchise fee. The use of the deposit agreement, when a franchisee does not yet have a location and may be a little reticent, is one way to get your foot in the door. This is a marketing theory based on the premise that once a person pays something down, he or she is more likely to pay the balance and not back out of the deal. A copy of the deposit agreement must be part of the circular.

You should be knowledgeable in lease negotiations or at least able to assist the franchisee in lease negotiations, making sure to inform him or her that final approval of the lease is at your discretion.

The landlord should give the franchisee certain information, such as definite construction completion and opening dates. Many franchisees have leased locations with leases that allowed the landlord to complete construction, for periods up to 18 months or even two years, before the franchisee was allowed to cancel the lease.

The franchisee tenant should have an escape clause so he or she can cancel the lease if the particular building or structure is not completed within the time frame set by the franchisee. Depending on whether there is a seller's or buyer's market, it may be difficult to get a choice location under these conditions. One last warning: never allow the franchisee and his or her spouse to quit their jobs or sell their house and move until it is absolutely certain that their particular franchise will be opened shortly.

Some franchisors require that franchisees have their landlords execute a lease assignment agreement allowing the franchisor to take over the franchisee's location in the event the franchise agreement is terminated.

Avoiding Litigation and Arbitration

Avoid litigation if at all possible. Not only is litigation expensive—although less so if an arbitration provision is included—but the facts of the litigation or arbitration must be reported in the franchise offering circular. This includes furnishing the name, address, and phone number of each litigating franchisee. It also makes the marketing of future franchises much more difficult, since prospective franchisees can contact the listed litigating franchisees and, in all probability, will receive negative information about the franchise operation.

> One last warning: never allow the franchisee and his or her spouse to quit their jobs or sell their house and move until it is absolutely certain that their particular franchise will be opened shortly.

Breach of Contract

Some registration states provide that if a franchisor fails to properly register an offering circular, the franchisee can automatically file an action for rescission and get his or her money back. However, many other states merely make this a possible criminal violation while upholding the validity of the franchise agreement. The general rules of agreement regarding substantial breach would then apply—that is, a franchisee would have the burden to prove to a judge, jury, or arbitrator that the franchisor made a specific written commitment and failed to follow through on that commitment. If this were proved, it would constitute a substantial breach of the franchise agreement. There is a fine line between a "substantial" breach and an "insubstantial" breach, wherein a verdict for rescission would not be granted, but rather a judgment for whatever money damages the franchisee may have proven. In addition, most franchisors, in their franchise agreements, present a minimum amount of written obligations that apply after the franchisee has opened his or her operation.

> Some registration states provide that if a franchisor fails to properly register an offering circular, the franchisee can automatically file an action for rescission and get his or her money back.

If you are proven to have committed a fraud—making fraudulent promises that were not true that induced the franchisee to enter into the franchise agreement—he or she may seek to rescind the agreement based on what is called "common-law fraud." It is not the purpose of this book to be a franchise legal manual; therefore, you must take every precaution to make sure your employees, particularly your franchise salespeople, make no representations that are not set forth in the written circular. In addition, actively abide by all after-opening obligations to the franchisee, as provided in the franchise agreement.

Pros and Cons of Arbitration

The positive aspect of arbitration is that you can generally select an arbitrator who has a firm knowledge of franchising from the standpoints of both franchisor and franchisee, as opposed to a judge or jury who know little, if anything, about franchising. The ideal arbitrator is one who has a legal and a franchising background, because arbitrators who are businesspeople tend to give both parties some type of award. Therefore, neither party wins. As a straight legal rule in the judicial system, if a contract is breached or a franchisee has been defrauded, only one party should win and the other party should get nothing. In a major arbitration, three arbitrators may be selected, so as to eliminate the chance of selecting a totally outrageous sole arbitrator who will render a bad decision.

The negative side of arbitration is that it is final and binding and, in most cases, the decision cannot be appealed. However, most court appeals are won by the party that won at the lower level. In addition, court appeals are extremely expensive and time-consuming.

Franchise Fees and Royalties

Many franchisors fail because they expect to immediately profit by charging high initial franchise fees, high royalty fees, and high advertising fees. However, if you look at what is happening in the American market, you will find that discounters who charge lower fees and bank on volume to make profits have overtaken the retail market. Most franchisees cannot handle high initial franchise fees and even higher royalty fees based on their gross sales. So, keep your expenses at a minimum while maintaining a high level of services to the franchisee. The franchisee is the marketing arm of the franchisor; if the franchisor can set up a franchisee by breaking even, he or she has already accomplished a great feat.

> The franchisee is the marketing arm of the franchisor; if the franchisor can set up a franchisee by breaking even, he or she has already accomplished a great feat.

Many franchisors who set their fees higher are unable to sell many franchises—and the franchises they sell have such high fees that they soon go out of business. In some states where franchisees have brought lawsuits against franchisors with excessive fees and royalties, the courts have sided with the franchisees! So having 1,000 franchisees paying $50 a month is much more profitable than having 10 franchisees paying $1,000 a month.

Always make detailed projections regarding how much profit you can make with a minimum amount of franchise fees and royalties, taking into consideration the profit you will make from the sale of your products and services to your franchisees. It will be time well spent.

Making the Decision

Now that you are more familiar with franchising in general, you are better prepared to make your final decision. Here are a couple of franchising factors to consider. Be sure of the following:

- The advantages of franchising outweigh the disadvantages.
- Your business has a market and a registrable trademark.
- Your current personnel or outside consulting personnel familiar with franchising are well qualified and available.
- You have no problem with selecting sites or preparing the manual.
- You have the working capital necessary to start the franchising process.
- You have sufficient capital to market your franchise.
- You have prepared a realistic business plan and budget for your franchise entity.
- You have an attorney who is not only experienced in franchise law but also familiar with the business aspects of franchising and the necessary relationship with the franchisee.

If these statements apply to you, you are ready to move ahead to a new way of conducting business and an exciting way of life.

Franchisee Business Application and Net Worth Form

This information is confidential. We will not contact your present employer without your consent.

Name of Franchise and Franchisor: _____

Name of Applicant Franchisee: _____

Personal Information on Potential Franchisee

Single ❑ Separated ❑ Married ❑ Divorced ❑

Number of minor children: _____ Ages of children: _____

Other dependents: _____

Own/buying home ❑ Rent ❑ Live with parents ❑ Live with spouse ❑ Live with relatives ❑

Home Payments $ _____ per month

Rental payments $ _____ per month

If buying, monthly payments $ _____ Paid to: _____

Applicant

Name: _____

Home telephone: _____

Business telephone: _____

Home address: _____

City/state/ZIP: _____

Social Security number: _____

Birth date (day/month/year): _____

Physical Information

Height: _____ Weight: _____

Physical limitations or health concerns: _____

_____

Educational Record

High school: _____

Last grade completed: 8 9 10 11 12 _____

College/university: _____

Major: _____

Degree received: _____ Year: _____

Employment Record

Current employer: _____

Address: _____

City/state/ZIP: _____

Position: _____

Present salary: _____

Started (year): _____ to _____

Description of work: _____

_____

Previous employer: _____

Address: _____

City/state/ZIP: _____

Position: _____

Salary: _____

Started (year): _____ to _____

Description of work: _____

_____

Employment Record of Applicant's Spouse

Current employer: _____

Address: _____

City/state/ZIP: _____

Position: _____

Present salary: _____

Started (year): _____ to _____

Description of work: _____

_____

Previous employer: _____

Address: _____

City/state/ZIP: _____

Position: _____

Salary: _____

Started (year): _____ to _____

Description of work: _____

Previous Business Owned

Have you ever owned your own franchise or other type of business? If so, give the following details:

Business 1 name: _____How long owned? _____

Address: _____

How many employees? _____

Type of business: _____

Describe how the business changed over the time you owned it. _____

_____

Business 2 name: _____ How long owned? _____

Address: _____

How many employees? _____

Type of business: _____

Describe how the business changed over the time you owned it. _____

_____

Financial Information (Note: Additional financial information may be required.)
Net Worth Summary

	Current Assets		**Current Liabilities**
Cash in checking account		Notes payable	
Cash in savings account		Amount owed on real estate	
Total		Total	

	Fixed Assets		**Long-Term Liabilities**
Real estate, home			
Other real estate		Describe	
Listed stocks and bonds			
Automobile(s)			
Your own business			
Money due you			

	Fixed Assets		Long-Term Liabilities
Insurance (cash value)			
Other assets (describe)			
Total		Total	
Total Assets		**Total Liabilities**	
Net Worth (assets less liabilities)			

How much capital can you allocate from the above sources to buy this franchise?

$ _____

What is the cash down payment you can make for a franchise? $ _____

If the required amount is not available, how would the investment be obtained?

_____

If you own your home, do you plan to sell it? Yes ❑   No ❑ Equity $ _____

Do you plan to convert any of the above assets into cash? Yes ❑   No ❑

Do you plan to have a partner? Yes ❑   No ❑

If so, will the partner be active? Yes ❑   No ❑

Do you plan to have investors? Yes ❑   No ❑   If so, to what extent?

Thoroughly explain your answers and any other strategies you have for obtaining the required funds. Use a separate sheet if necessary.

What is the minimum income you need to maintain your family during the first year of business? $ _____

From what sources will it come? _____

References

Business References

Name	Address	Years Known
_____	_____	_____
_____	_____	_____
_____	_____	_____
_____	_____	_____
_____	_____	_____

Character References (other than employers or relatives)

Name	Address	Years Known
_____	_____	_____
_____	_____	_____
_____	_____	_____
_____	_____	_____
_____	_____	_____

Former Addresses for the Past Five Years

1. _____

2. _____

3. _____

4. _____

5. _____

Business Goals

In order of priority, list which specific types of business you prefer to become involved with.

1. _____

2. _____

3. _____

4. _____

Are you willing to relocate? Yes ❑   No ❑   If so, state locations in order of priority.

1. _____

2. _____

3. _____

4. _____

When do you want to start your franchise operation? _____

How did you become interested in this particular franchise? _____

_____

What are your realistic personal and professional goals ...

Three years from now? _____

_____

Five years from now?_____

_____

10 years from now? _____

_____

State your reasons for believing you will be able to successfully operate one of our franchises. _____

_____

_____

_____

_____

Do there appear to be any disadvantages to owning one of our franchises? If so, please state your concerns. _____

_____

_____

_____

_____

I certify that the enclosed information as given is complete and correct. _____

_____

_____

_____

_____

_____   _____
Applicant's Signature   Date

It is understood that the purpose of this questionnaire is to gather general information and is in no way binding upon either the company or the applicant. It is, however, understood that the applicant supplies the information contained herein to the best of his or her knowledge and ability and that the company relies on this fact in assessing the desirability and qualifications of the applicant.

Part III

Appendices

Appendices A-1 and A-2
Uniform Franchise Offering Circular

These Appendices contain samples of offering disclosures that conform to guidelines of the Uniform Franchise Offering Circular (UFOC), effective January 1, 1995. These samples illustrate how the cover page and table of contents should appear and how the many tables outlining fees, investment costs, and obligations might appear in a UFOC. They also illustrate the differences between a *product* franchise (A-1) and a *service* franchise (A-2).

Appendix F contains the present UFOC Guidelines, which will give you further information about how to prepare or interpret a Uniform Franchise Offering Circular. Since these UFOC guidelines were last promulgated in 1995, the examples use pre-1995 dates.

Most people, whether seeking to become franchisors or franchisees, initially have no idea what an offering circular looks like until they contact an attorney. Examine the sample circulars, whether you are a potential franchisor or a prospective franchisee, and compare them with the information in Chapters 2 and 8.

Pay particular attention to Item 11 of the circulars, entitled "Franchisor's Obligations." As a franchisee, you will receive important benefits from a good franchise agreement that you could not receive if you started the particular business on your own. For the franchisor, these obligations "glue" the franchisee to the franchise. For example, if the franchisee can purchase inventory at the lowest competitive price from the franchisor, this glues the franchisee to the franchisor for the term of the franchise agreement. The franchisee cannot purchase the inventory at that low price without the franchisor. Other benefits attractive to a franchisee, which serve as glue to the franchisor, may include the exclusive use of a patented process or product, low-cost health plans, secret recipes, or access to national purchasing accounts.

Look for the "glue" when you review the following sample offering circulars. Using the information you learned from this book, decide for yourself whether the UFOC you are signing is a good offering circular.

Granite Transformations® is a trademark of Rocksolid Granit (USA) Inc. Further reproduction or use of this registered trademark without the permission of Rocksolid Granit (USA) Inc. is prohibited.

The following Offering Circular is included for illustration purposes only with the consent of Rocksolid Granit (USA) Inc.

GRANITE TRANSFORMATIONS®

Franchise Offering Circular
Rocksolid Granit (USA) Inc.
A Delaware Corporation.
11098 Inland Avenue, Mira Loma, California 91752
(909) 685-5300

The franchisee will operate an independently owned professional business providing the marketing, sales and installation of various approved products as ROCKSOLID GRANIT™, a reconstituted Granite slab, applied to new and existing surfaces including countertops, kitchens, bathrooms, fireplaces, etc. to housing units. The amount of the initial franchise fee is based on an equation equal to $2,500 per each 10,000 occupied housing units and therefore can vary from $25,000 to $75,000. At our sole discretion, where a territory of less than 100,000 housing units warrants a franchise, the initial franchise fee will be based on an equation equal to $2,500 per each 10,000 occupied housing units in such small territory. The estimated initial investment required ranges from $74,500 to $251,000. (See Item 7 for more details.)

Risk Factors

THE FRANCHISE AGREEMENT REQUIRES THAT ALL DISAGREEMENTS BE SETTLED BY ARBITRATION IN MARYLAND WITH MARYLAND LAW APPLYING SO YOU DO NOT HAVE THE RISK IN HAVING AN OUT-OF-STATE LAW APPLYING THAT MAY DIFFER FROM YOUR LOCAL LAW.

THERE MAY BE OTHER RISKS CONCERNING THIS FRANCHISE.

INFORMATION ABOUT COMPARISON OF FRANCHISORS IS AVAILABLE. CALL THE STATE ADMINISTRATORS LISTED IN EXHIBIT D OR YOUR PUBLIC LIBRARY FOR SOURCES OF INFORMATION. REGISTRATION OF THIS FRANCHISE WITH THE STATE DOES NOT MEAN THAT THE STATE RECOMMENDS IT OR HAS VERIFIED THE INFORMATION IN THIS OFFERING CIRCULAR. IF YOU LEARN THAT ANYTHING IN THIS OFFERING CIRCULAR IS UNTRUE, CONTACT THE FEDERAL TRADE COMMISSION AND/OR STATE AUTHORITY.

EFFECTIVE DATE: (5/22/03)(6/22/03)

Uniform Franchise Offering Circular

Table of Contents

* **Note:** In your actual document, page numbers must be filled in, but they have been omitted in this publiication to avoid confusion with the book's page numbers.

ITEM 1. THE FRANCHISOR, ITS PREDECESSORS AND AFFILIATES

To simplify the language in this offering circular, "we" or "us" or "ROCKSOLID GRANIT™" or "Rocksolid Granit (USA) Inc." means Rocksolid Granit (USA) Inc., the Franchisor. "You" means the person who buys the franchise and includes owners/partners, etc., in cases when the franchise is a business entity. Rocksolid Granit (USA) Inc. is a Delaware Corporation that was incorporated on March 15, 2001 and was licensed to do business in California on June 4, 2001 and does business as the Franchisor of a franchise network system known as GRANITE TRANSFORMATIONS®.

Our principal business address is 11098 Inland Avenue, Mira Loma, California 91752. Our agent for service of process is Maryland Securities Commissioner, 200 St. Paul Place, Baltimore, Maryland 21202-2020.

We have offered and sold franchises of the type to be operated by you in other states prior to the effective date of this Offering Circular. We currently operate a business of the type being franchised at this time, having done so since June, 2001. We use this location as our franchise training location. Our affiliate company, Granite Transformations Pty. Ltd. (an Australian company located at 5/224 Headland Road, Dee Why, New South Wales 2099, Australia), has been conducting a similar type of business since April, 1996, when it was known as Rock Solid Products Pty. Ltd. It re-invented itself as Granite Transformation Pty. Ltd in late 1997 at the same location and concentrated sales on a unique technique of applying a reconstituted Granite slab as an overlay over existing household surfaces such as countertops, bathrooms, fireplaces and floors providing a quick, cost effective way of revamping an old kitchen countertop or bathroom vanity. Granite Transformations Pty. Ltd. has been franchising in Australia since 1997 with 28 Granite Transformations® franchises in Australia that provide kitchen/bathroom refacing. Our other affiliate company, Trend Group SPA, an Italian company located at Viale dell'Industria, 42, 36100, Vicenza, Italy, has been processing ROCKSOLID GRANIT™ Granite slabs and sells product to us for resale to you. The principals of Trend Group SPA have over 40 years experience in supplying product to the building industry. Trend Group SPA is the co-owner of Rocksolid Granit (USA) Inc., along with Tessina Holdings Pty. Ltd., an Australian company located at 5/224 Headland Road, Dee Why, New South Wales 2099, Australia. We have no other business activity. Neither we nor our predecessor and affiliate have offered or sold franchises in any other line of business.

Our franchisees are independent operators of a professional business which markets, sells, and installs our ROCKSOLID GRANIT™ reconstituted slabs primarily to new and existing surfaces, including vanities, countertops in bathrooms, kitchens, and fireplaces to occupied housing units located within their designated territories. You will receive a comprehensive training program with our unique system and procedures enabling you to market reconstituted Granite slabs to new and existing surfaces. We have a true commitment to customer service. We fully utilize the supervisory services of our founders in our training and ongoing operations. Our franchisees are distinguished by the service mark GRANITE TRANSFORMATIONS®.

We have no predecessor. Our system was developed by the founders of Rocksolid Granit (USA) Inc. to create a high-quality, duplicable system in order to offer franchise opportunities to other potential business owners who desire to provide existing kitchens and bathroom countertop refacing services.

A state contractor's license will apply in many states, such as California, but should be satisfied if held by an employee of yours or by a licensed independent contractor performing the installations on your behalf. You should contact your applicable Illinois state licensing authority and confirm that no licenses are required before purchasing the franchise.

Your market consists of all housing units (single-family homes that are or have been occupied) according to the 2000 U.S.A. Census (as currently updated by our demographic services) located in your designated territory. To the best of our knowledge, our procedures, installation methods, and concept are new and unique to the U.S.A. market. We believe that there is no real competition for our resurfacing products and techniques when applied to existing surfaces including countertops, kitchens, bathrooms, and fireplaces in the U.S.A. Your competitors primarily will be in the new countertop installation industry, particularly local sellers and installers of natural Granite, solid surfaces, and similar surfaces including laminates for entirely new kitchens, countertops, bathrooms, and fireplaces. Head-to-head competition with this type of competition that supplies new kitchens and bathrooms should be the exception rather than the rule, since your focus will be on refacing an existing kitchen or bathroom countertop with a fast, high-quality reface at a very competitive price of a new kitchen or bathroom countertop. You can purchase additional franchises under the then prevailing franchise agreement terms provided you are in good standing and we feel you have demonstrated that you can successfully operate more than one franchise.

ITEM 2. CORPORATE OFFICERS, BUSINESS EXPERIENCE

CHIEF OPERATING OFFICER AND SECRETARY: MARK J. JOHNSON

Mark J. Johnson has been our General Manager since September 3, 2001 and Chief Operating Officer and corporate Secretary since October 23 2001. Prior to September 3, 2001, he was co-owner of a retail specialty shop called "The Ruffled Tulip" located and operated in Tustin, California. He held the position of Director of Operations, General Manager-Training Store and Store Opening Coordinator for Great Earth Companies, Inc. operating out of Rancho Cucamonga, California from June 1996 to November, 2000.

PRESIDENT AND DIRECTOR: ROBERT BRUCE ARUNDEL SMITH

Robert Bruce Arundel Smith is our President and Director. He has held these positions since our inception on March 15, 2001. He has held (and currently is holding) the position of Director, Granite Transformations Pty. Ltd., our Australian affiliate, since September 26, 1997. From June 24, 1996, until September 26, 1997, he held the position of Director of Rocksolid Products Pty. Ltd, the forerunner of Granite Transformations Pty. Ltd. He is also a director and 50% shareholder of Tessina Holdings Pty Ltd. He brings over 25 years of business experience to our franchise company.

TREASURER AND DIRECTOR: COLIN DOUGLAS MACKENZIE

Colin Douglas Mackenzie is one of our directors and treasurer. He has held this position since our inception on March 15, 2001. He has held (and currently is holding) the position of Director, Granite Transformations Pty. Ltd., our Australian affiliate) since September, 1997. From June 24, 1996, until September, 1997, he held the position of Director of Rocksolid Products Pty. Ltd., the forerunner of Granite Transformations Pty. Ltd. He is also a director and 50% shareholder of Tessina Holdings Pty

Ltd. He brings over 20 years of experience in business to our franchise company.

DIRECTOR: GIUSEPPE BISAZZA

Giuseppe Bisazza is one of our directors. He has held this position since our inception on March 15, 2001. He currently holds the position of Managing Director of Trend Group SPA, address: Viale dell'industria, 42, Vicenza, Italy. He has held this position since January 21, 2000 to the present. He held the position of Managing Director of Gruppo Bisazza, Viale Milano, 56, Montecchio Maggiore, Vicenza, Italy from January 1, 1996 until January 18, 2000. He brings over 40 years of experience in business to our franchise company.

SENIOR VICE PRESIDENT AND DIRECTOR: ANDREA DI GIUSEPPE

Andrea Di Giuseppe is one of our directors and is senior vice president. He has held this position since our inception on March 15, 2001. He currently holds the position of Director, Trend Group SPA, Viale dell'industria, 42, Vicenza, Italy. He has held this position since February 1, 2000. He held the position of Director of Repla SRL, Calusco d'Adda, Bergamo, Italy from February 1, 1997 to January 12, 2000. Previously he was a Director of Todini Italceramiche SPA, Via A. Crivellucci 31, Roma, Italy from January 1, 1996 to January 31, 1997. He brings over 12 years of experience in this business to our franchise company.

DIRECTOR: GIORGIO PAVANETTO

Giorgio Pavanetto is one of our directors. He has held this position since our inception on March 15, 2001. He currently holds the position of General Manager of Trend Hong Kong Ltd., Room 801-3, Asian Orient Tower, 33 Lockhart Road, Wanchai, Hong Kong. He has held this position since June 1, 2000. Previously he was employed as General Manager of Bisazza Hong Kong Ltd. Room 701, Beverly House, 93-102 Lockhart Road, Wanchai, Hong Kong from 16 February 1998 until 31 May 2000. Previously to that he was employed as General Manager of Breton Machinery H.K. Ltd, 17th Floor, Wall Park Commercial Building, 10?12 Chatham Court T.S.T. Kowloon, Hong Kong from 1 July 1989 to 15 February 1998. He brings over 12 years experience to our franchise company.

ITEM 3. LITIGATION

No litigation is required to be disclosed in this offering circular.

ITEM 4. BANKRUPTCY

Neither the Franchisor or any predecessor, officer or general partner of the Franchisor during the preceding 10 (ten) year period is currently or has been the subject of any bankruptcy proceeding, either under U.S. Bankruptcy Code or under the laws of foreign nations relating to Bankruptcy proceedings, or was the principal officer of any company or general partner in any partnership that is currently or was the subject of any Bankruptcy proceeding, either under U.S. Bankruptcy Code or under the laws of foreign nations relating to Bankruptcy proceeding, during or within one year after this person held such a position.

ITEM 5. INITIAL FRANCHISE FEE

The amount of your initial franchise fee is nonrefundable and payable in a lump sum that is based on an equation equal to $2,500 per each 10,000 housing units in your designated territory, with a minimum of 100,000 in a designated territory and, therefore, your initial franchise fee will be between $25,000 (100,000 housing units) to $75,000 (300,000 housing units), depending on the number of housing units in the territory of your choice. At our sole discretion, where a territory of less than 100,000 housing units warrants a franchise according to our discretion, we will charge an initial franchise fee equal to $2,500 per each 10,000 housing units with a 20,000 housing unit minimum in such small territories. Your initial franchise fee is payable in a lump sum and is non-refundable.

ITEM 6. OTHER FEES

Name of Fee	Amount	Due Date	Remarks
Service Fee (no minimum payment)	2% of gross sales (1) per month	By the 10th calendar day after the end of the previous month	Payable to us
Local Advertising	3% of monthly, gross sales.	Per month	Payable to local media
Cooperative Advertising: we may decide to form a cooperative advertising program if future circumstances so dictate. The fees you contribute can only be increased by the controlling vote of the majority vote of the franchisee members with no voting on such matters by franchisor-owned outlets.	Not to exceed 2% of monthly gross sales without consent of majority of cooperative members)	Due and payable the last calendar day of each month	Payable to us in trust for deposit in our Cooperative Trust Account (or the cooperative's trust account) to be used for new campaigns or modifications to existing campaigns, production of art work, any national campaigns, i.e., national magazines, syndicated radio or television programs, including personnel, etc.
Transfer Fees (*)	$1,500	Upon any assignment, sale or transfer of the franchise except to a spouse or child	The transfer fee may increase to reflect increases in the local applicable Consumer Price Index
Renewal (*)	$1,000	Upon renewal	You must be in good standing

Name of Fee	Amount	Due Date	Remarks
Audit Fee (*)	Cost of audit plus legal interest rate from date of any underpayment	Upon Billing	Payable only if under-statement of at least 2% due. Late payments bear legal rate of interest
Additional Training (*)	$125 per person per day subject to increases in the Consumer Price Index pertaining to our headquarters location.	Prior to or after initial training	The costs of your travel, lodging and meals are your responsibility

* All monies are payable directly to us and are non-refundable.

(1)The term "gross sales" is defined to include all sums or things of value received by you in and from your business from all sales of services, goods, and products whether for cash, check, credit, barter or otherwise without reserve or deduction for inability or failure to collect same including, without limitation, such sales and services where the orders thereof originated at or accepted by you at one location or site but delivered or performed at any other location or site. Gross sales do not include refunds to customers or the amount of any sales taxes or any similar taxes collected from customers to be paid to any federal, state, or local taxing authority. All such items, including non-collectible accounts, which are claimed as deductions to gross sales must be supported by proper documentation.

ITEM 7. INITIAL INVESTMENT

Investments	Amount Low-High	Method of Payment	When Due	To Whom Payment Is Made
Initial Franchise Fee	$5,000 to $75,000	In full	Upon signing franchise agreement	Us
Travel and living expenses while training	$1,000 to $5,000	As incurred	Prior and during training	Airlines, hotels, restaurants etc.
Initial Opening Advertising	$5,000 to $10,000	Lump sum	30 days before opening	Advertising supplier
Vehicle (1) (a) Personal car or light truck for sales and general traveling if do not presently own.	$0 To $25,000 ($0 to $300 per month, approxi-mately) lease to interest payment	Lump sum or installments as negotiated plus interest.	Upon purchased or as negotiated	Vehicle Seller, Finance Company, Leasing Agency;
(b) Working truck and forklift (1)	$0 (If you retain a subcontractor's crew and its vehicle, since cost included in cus-tomers' billing.) $6,000 to $15,000 refurbished or new 4-ton forklift ($0 to $600 per month if leased).	Lump sum or installments as negotiated plus interest.	Upon purchased or as negotiated	Vehicle Seller, Finance Company, Leasing Agency, applicable Subcontractor

Investments	Amount Low-High	Method of Payment	When Due	To Whom Payment Is Made
Real Estate Rental: business office/ showroom/factory Monthly rental approx. 2,000 sq. ft. to 4,000 sq. ft.(2)	$1,000 to $4,000 per month rent Plus first and last month deposit of $2,000 to $8,000	Per Month Lump sum	Monthly Before opening	Landlord Landlord
Leasehold Improvements, i.e., showrooms, building	$2,500 to $10,000	Lump sum	Upon completion	Amount only if fabricated
Business Licenses/ Permits	$0 to $1,000	In full	Before opening	Government agencies (may be more than one city at time of contracting)
Equipment, Furniture, and Fixtures (desks, chairs, small copier and fax machine, etc.)	$2,000 to $10,000	Lump sum or as negotiated	Before opening	Designated supplier
Complete Signage (Interior and Exterior)	$2,000 to $5,000	As required by vendor	As required by vendor	Vendor
Tools	$1,000 to $4,000	Lump sum or as negotiated	Before opening	Designated supplier
Initial Granit Inventory and Supplies including stationery, letterhead, contract documents and diagram papers, job site signage, Granite slabs etc. Minimum Granite inventory maintenance require-ments is ___ sq. ft.	$10,000 to $25,000	As negotiated	Before opening	Us or designated supplier
Contractor's License Fee	$0 to $6,000	Lump sum	Before opening	Government agency
Public Liability Insurance and Worker's Compensation; Liability; Fire Extended Coverage, Errors and Omissions Insurance	$1,000 to $3,000	Monthly	Upon opening	Insurance agent

Investments	Amount Low-High	Method of Payment	When Due	To Whom Payment Is Made
Miscellaneous Costs (organizational expenses, etc.)	$2,000 to $5,000	As needed	Upon opening	Various suppliers
Working Capital (3) (additional funds for expenses, including gas, payroll, petty cash, construction manager's salary, and car allowance; fuel expenses; additional tools; pagers, utilities; truck lease or payment; telephone, equipment mainte-nance; rent for first 3 months, advertising for months 2 and 3; recruiting for first 3 months and miscellaneous costs for first 3 months, in addition to above expenses, paid prior to opening)	$20,000 to $40,000	As required	As required	Suppliers, etc.
Estimated Total Initial Investment and Initial Advertising Requirements	**$74,500 to $251,000**			

No allowance has been made for inflation, debt service, or interest payment on borrowed money, but you should consider this, particularly if part or all of your startup costs are to be financed.

(1) You can lease or finance your car or light truck for sales and general travel if you presently do not have a suitable car/light truck at $300 to $600 per month and you can lease or finance a working truck generally selling new from $20,000 to $30,000 with 10% payment approximately $500 with payments over 36 to 60 months, thus incurring a substantial saving in initial cash outlay. However, you can pass the cost of the truck and the labor to the customer if you retain the services of a subcontractor and his tools and crew, since the cost of using same is included in the particular customer's estimate and contract sheet. If you do not retain a subcontractor's crew and its vehicle, the estimated cost of 15% to 25% is added to the customer's estimate and passed on.

(2) You can secure acceptable office/showroom spaces for between $0.30 and $1.00 per sq. ft. per month in most areas. You should confirm this in your local area.

(3) Working capital does not include any draw or compensation for the franchise owner or employee wages or payroll except for the field operations manager's salary. We have not calculated labor into the above costs as it forms a cost of sale as part of your gross profit on any job. No revenue = no labor.

ITEM 8. RESTRICTIONS ON SOURCES OF PRODUCTS AND SERVICES

You are required to purchase a minimum of 1,243 square feet (30 sheets) of ROCKSOLID GRANIT™ and specified adhesive each month from us or an approved supplier designated by us in writing at a later date. We presently are the exclusive supplier of ROCKSOLID GRANIT™ with a dimension of over 1 meter (39.37 inches) x 1 meter (39.37 inches). We are the only approved supplier of Rocksolid Glue and Festool Installation Tools and other persons affiliated with us are currently the approved suppliers of other items. If you desire to purchase any equipment and materials (other than ROCKSOLID GRANIT™, Rocksolid Glue, and Festool Installation Tools) from someone other than our designated supplier, you must submit a complete description of the history and credit rating of the supplier and the items desired to be purchased. You also must supply us with specifications and tests which will prove to our sole satisfaction that the equipment and materials are of equal or superior quality to those which we or our designated supplier may offer for sale to you at what we feel are competitive prices and the supplier's ability to stand behind the supplier's product warranty, which warranty must meet or surpass those of our then current designated supplier. We will approve or disapprove a prospective supplier according to our complete and final discretion within 10 business days of receipt of your request to purchase from alternate suppliers. We will provide written standards and specifications including but not limited to sales methods, reporting and documentation, installation methods, etc. We may modify our specifications if changes occur in the industry based on our research and we will make this known to you in writing as the changes occur.

We will provide you with a written list of approved suppliers in advance of your purchases. Your required purchases of computer hardware and software include a computer system capable of handling and loaded with Word, QuickBooks, Excel, and an Internet package.

Our total revenue from all sources ending in fiscal year end of December 31, 2002 was $2,476,279. Accordingly, the revenues from all required purchase and leases of products and services sold to our franchisees by us was $1,147,882 for the same period or 46.35% of our total revenues.

We will negotiate purchase arrangements with potential suppliers including price at our discretion for your benefit. We do not provide our franchisees with material benefits such as the right to purchase additional franchises or to renew based on your use of our designated supplier. Our criteria for supplier approval are available to you upon request. There are designated suppliers that may make rebate payments to us because of transactions that you may make with such suppliers. All such rebates will be retained by us and used for our general operating expenses. Festool Installation Tools has a rebate program with Rocksolid Granit (USA) Inc. and pays us a rebate of 20% on all purchases from them. We offer a franchisee a 10% discount on all Festool tools purchased and the other 10% is used for our training center for installation classes. There are presently no other approved suppliers that make rebates to us.

We estimate that you will purchase or lease from us approximately 50% of all of the goods and services, which you will need in the establishment and operation of your franchise business.

You may only offer services and sell products designated by us in writing in order to be consistent with our theme and offer these services and products as we deem necessary in writing. We will loan you a confidential Operations Manual that will contain specifications and parameters developed by us and that you must strictly follow. The goods and services which you supply must be used for the installation of our ROCKSOLID GRANIT™ slabs to new and existing surfaces including countertops, bathrooms, kitchens, fireplaces, etc. Granite Transformations system is unique in the trade and an intrinsic part of our system that offers a new, innovative, uniform, quality product throughout the world and is not to be confused with any other product on the market nor should these products be substituted for ours under our marks.

If we decide to install a system of a centralized telephone service, you must use our approved telephone number in all promotions identifying your business so that we can provide a uniform system of distributing the calls to your area along with whatever assistance we can be in facilitating your servicing these calls.

We reserve the right to designate or consent to the content, themes, materials, and placement of all advertising programs by you. You must submit all advertising to us for our approval at least seven (7) business days before publication (subject to deadlines) unless specifically waived in writing by us as to each particular ad or advertising campaign. You are to complete our required order forms in amounts not less than 414 square feet per order unless otherwise agreed in writing with us. There are no purchasing or distribution cooperatives.

Obligation	Section in Agreement	Item in Offering Circular
A. Site Selection and Acquisition	Articles 2 and 8	Items 7, 11, and 12
B. Pre-Opening Purchases and Leases	Articles 6 and 7	Items 7, 8, and 10
C. Site Development and Other Pre-Opening Requirements	Articles 2 and 8	Items 7, 8, and 11
D. Initial and Ongoing Training	Articles 4, 5, and 8	Items 6 and 11
E. Opening	Articles 2, 5, 7, and 9	Items 5, 7, 8, 9, and 11
F. Fee	Article 6	Items 5, 6, and 7
G. Compliance with Standards	Articles 3, 4, 5, 6, 7, and 9	Items 8, 4 and 15, 16 and 17
H. Trademarks and Proprietary Information	Articles 1, 2, 3, 4, 12, and 13	Items 8, 13, and 14
I. Restrictions on Products/Services Offered	Articles 7 and 9	Items 8 and 16
J. Warranty and Customer Service	Articles 6 and 7	None
K. Territorial Development and Sales	None	None
L. Ongoing Product/Service Purchases	Articles 6, 7, and 9	None
M. Maintenance, Appearance, and Remodeling Requirements	None	Items 7 and 8
N. Insurance	Article 6	Items 6, 7, and 8
O. Advertising	Articles 6, 7, and 8	Items 6, 7, and 1
P. Indemnification	Article 15	None

Obligation	Section in Agreement	Item in Offering Circular
Q. Owner's Participation, Management, Staffing	Article 7	Item 15
R. Records/Reports	Articles 6 and 7	Item 6
S. Inspections/Audits	Article 6	Item 6
T. Transfer	Articles 6 and 11	Items 6 and 17
U. Renewal	Articles 6 and 11	Items 6 and 17
V. Post-Termination Obligations	Article 11	Item 17
W. Non-Competition Covenants	Articles 7, 11, and 12	Item 17
X. Dispute Resolution	Article 23	Item 17
Y. Other (Describe)	None	None

ITEM 9. FRANCHISEE'S OBLIGATIONS

This table lists your principal obligations under the franchise and other agreements. It will help you find more detailed information about your obligations in these agreements and in other items of this offering circular.

ITEM 10. FINANCING

We do not offer direct or indirect financing or guarantee your note, lease, or obligation.

ITEM 11. FRANCHISOR'S OBLIGATIONS

Except as disclosed below, we need not provide any other guidance to you. Before you open your business, we will:

(1) Assist you in obtaining the necessary information and advise you on the best approach in the selecting of your base site within the territory and assist you with your showroom office layout plan. (We will pre-approve your operational site with emphasis on the facility. This approval will not be unreasonably withheld by us.) Each territory purchased is outlined on a map attached to the Franchise Agreement. If we cannot agree on a site for you within sixty (60) days of receipt of your down payment, our agreement will be terminated. Factors which we consider in approving an area for your site include a neighborhood conducive to a proper show room fit, and adequate parking and showroom space in this area. We will approve or disapprove an area in which you propose to open your site within 10 days of receiving written notice thereof from you. **(Franchise Agreement, Paragraph 8.1)**

(2) Loan you one set of the Confidential Operations Manual covering the operational procedures. **(Franchise Agreement, Paragraph 8.2)**

(3) Provide you with a detailed list of all necessary equipment, supplies, and inventory and a list of approved suppliers. (Franchise Agreement, Paragraph 8.4)

(4) We will train you and/or your sales and installation personnel for 3 to 5 days a week up to 13 days exclusive of Saturdays and Sundays (8 hours per day) to be scheduled by us as we deem necessary as follows. **(Franchise Agreement, Paragraph 5.3 and 8.3)**

Subject	Day and Time Begun	Instructional Material	Hours in Class and on-the-Site Training	Instructor
Sales Advertising and Promotions. This section includes the selling process, measuring, scheduling appointments, and developing leads through ads and promotions	Days 1-3 9 AM	Sales Success Manual Sales Kit	Classroom and in-House Sales Presentations Minimum 8 hours	Broderick
Operations. This section includes scheduling jobs, paperwork, follow-up mailings, verifying payments, and ordering products	Day 4 8 AM	Operations Manual Operations Training Manual Installation Manual	Classroom and Shop Minimum 8 hours	Mindreau and/or Mackenzie
Finance. A complete discussion and introduction of balance sheets, P&L, and appropriate support material	Day 5 8:30 AM	Excel and Quickbooks Laptop (Optional)	8 class hours	Roberts
Home Shows and/or Sales Calls	Days 6 and 7 10 AM	Home Show or Field Manual	8 hours	Sales Staff
Installation Training Everything related to installation including templating, cutting, fabrication, and installation, also tools and shop	Days 8-12 7 AM	Installer Manual Evaluation Manual Certifications	Shop and Field 8 hours minimum	C. Johnson and Saad
Final Exam	Day 13	Final Test and Certification	Office 4 to 8 hours	M. Johnson

Our instructors have up to seven years' experience and up to five years of experience in marketing, sales methods, and installation of ROCKSOLID GRANIT™ reconstituted Granite slabs. The training is at our headquarters over the three-week period.

DURING THE OPERATION OF THE FRANCHISED BUSINESS, WE WILL PROVIDE:

(1) Three to five days of continued training regarding hands-on sales methods and construction methods and efficiencies, etc. at your location and local work sites all to be conducted by us in the first five days from the opening of your business, with our trainers' travel, subsistence, and lodging at our expense for this period. Any training requested by you exceeding the initial five days of training shall be at your expense for our instructors' travel, subsistence, lodging, and reasonable per diem charges. **(Franchise Agreement, Paragraphs 5.5 and 8.6)**

(2) A continuing advisory service and available service and product informational updates regarding the industry. **(Franchise Agreement, Paragraph 8.7)**

(3) A system of distributing telephone calls/leads to the nearest Granite Transformations Franchisee. **(Franchise Agreement, Paragraphs 7.5 and 8.8)**

(4) Existing and available advertising brochures and point of sale material supplied to you at cost price plus a small shipping and handling fee. **(Franchise Agreement, Paragraph 8.9)**

(5) Operating and service consulting and support via phone and e-mail for your business and provide relevant data and information to ensure that you have the benefits of the exploitation and use of the system and its products. **(Franchise Agreement, Paragraph 8.8)**

(6) Suggested uniform, proprietary computer software system of record-keeping techniques to manage your customer base and customer contracts and software updates and software maintenance. **(Franchise Agreement, Paragraph 8.10)**

(7) Later training classes, both mandatory and non-mandatory, offered from time to time at your costs of travel, lodging, and subsistence unless any such mandatory training classes exceed one (1) per calendar year, wherein we shall then reimburse you for the airfare of the required attendee. **(Franchise Agreement, Paragraph 8.11)**

(8) We, at our discretion, will provide you with newsletters regarding current industry trends and marketing updates as well as business recognition. (**Franchise Agreement, Paragraph 8.12**)

We must approve all of your advertising and promotional materials in advance. **(Franchise Agreement, Paragraph 8.9)**

You must buy the hardware and software identified as follows, by brand, type, and principal functions: a quality desktop computer and accounting software package, i.e., Quickbooks and Excel. The software is proprietary property of a third party. The third party having proprietary interest in the software is Intuit and Microsoft. **(Franchise Agreement, Paragraph 8.10)**

We may, at our discretion, require the use of new, updated software. There are no current annual costs of any optional or required maintenance support contracts with the seller or manufacturer of the hardware required by us.

Franchisees typically open their business within 90 days after signing the Franchise Agreement and paying the fees.

You may be required to make contributions to a cooperated advertising fund set up by us. In the future you must join any future national or local advertising cooperative when we direct you at our sole discretion. You are obligated to contribute to any such cooperative fund. We are not obligated to contribute to the fund but may do so at our complete discretion. The managers of the cooperative are selected by us. We or our designee may manage the cooperative fund. The 2% that you contribute can only be increased by a majority vote of the franchisee members and is payable to us or a cooperative account to be used on corporate branding and national marketing. We have the power to terminate the cooperative. You may use your own advertising material if approved by us in writing. There is no advertising council nor are there any provisions being made for the establishment of an advertising council. The source of our advertising is an in-house advertising department. We will have independent access to leads and sales information without limitation through any computer networking. Fees relating to advertising are raised through your monthly contributions and an annual accounting of adverting expenditures will be given upon your written request. The media in which the advertising may be disseminated include print, radio, internet, and television, which will be local, regional, and national in scope through local or national advertising agencies. We do not require an electronic cash register but require computer system hardware capable of running Excel, QuickBooks, and Word and sending and receiving e-mail.

There is no hardware or software component to us or an affiliate or to a third party so none are identified herein. The following is a description of each software program and how it will be used in your business and the types of business information that will be collected and generated. Any such information we may have access to without limitation. QuickBooks is used to provide financials, including monthly profit-and-loss statements and balance sheets. Excel is used to support the financial program. We also suggest Microsoft Word to receive written forms and reports via the e-mail.

The following are the factors that we consider in approving operational site selections and time limit for approval, which include visibility, centrally located, a mandatory showroom space, back work area, landlord and city approval of fabrication functions, parking, and safety features. Pictures, maps, and details of location must be submitted for approval. The time limit for selecting a location site is 60 days from the signing of the franchise agreement. If we felt that the potential franchisee had made a good-faith effort to find a suitable location but failed to do so, we reserve the right to terminate the franchise agreement and retain a portion of the initial franchise fee equal to our costs, including any training, which costs will in no event be less than $10,000.

The table of contents of our Confidential Operations Manual, including the number of pages devoted to each subject matter, will be provided to you prior to your signing your franchise agreement, and its format will be substantially the same as follows, with the applicable number of pages included:

Confidential Operations Manual

Chapter Title	Number of Chapters Dedicated to Each Chapter
Chapter 1. Introduction	6
Chapter 2. Location and Layout of Premises	6
Chapter 3. Sales and Marketing—Retail	27
Chapter 4. Sales and Marketing—Wholesale	5
Chapter 5. Operating Management	12
Chapter 6. Installation	10
Chapter 7. Administration	10
Appendix. Folder 2	48

ITEM 12. TERRITORY

Your exclusive retail domestic territory is determined primarily by a population of at least a minimum of 100,000 housing units (single-family homes that are or have been occupied) and a maximum of 300,000 housing units (as defined in the 2000 U.S. Census as a house, an apartment, a mobile home or trailer, a group of rooms, or a single room that is occupied as a separate living quarters, or, if vacant, has been occupied as a separate living quarters) located only in your exclusive retail domestic territory. The amount of the initial franchise fee is based on a formula equal to $2,500 per each 10,000 housing units. At our sole discretion, where a territory of less than 100,000 housing units warrants a franchise, the initial franchise fee will be based on a formula equal to $2,500 per each 10,000 housing units in such smaller territory. Your territory is exclusive in that we will not operate company-owned stores, nor will we designate or allow a franchise-owned site offering the same service to be physically opened or operated from an approved site location within your territory nor will we service or grant other franchisees the right to service occupied or vacant domestic housing units located in your territory. However, your retail domestic territory is non-exclusive in that we or any other franchisee may solicit and service units such as commercial housing buildings, hotels, motels, new housing developments, commercial buildings including offices, etc. within your territory. These are the restrictions on us from soliciting or accepting orders inside your defined territory. By the same token you may solicit or service any such units or other buildings as mentioned in the previous sentence in other territories. We will pre-approve your operational site based on the facility. Such approval will not be unreasonably withheld by us. Each territory purchased is outlined on a map attached to the Franchise Agreement. If we cannot agree on a site for you within sixty (60) days of receipt of your down payment, our agreement will be terminated. There are no minimum sales quotas, market penetration, or other contingencies that would alter your territory. You maintain the rights to your territory even if the population increases. There are no provisions in the franchise agreement allowing the alteration of your territory without your written approval. Your franchise fee is not refunded in the situation where we can not agree on a site. There are no circumstances that permit us to modify your territorial rights. There are no options, rights of first refusal, or similar rights for you to acquire additional franchises within your territory or contiguous territories. Your territorial exclusivity is not dependant upon achievement of certain sales volume, market penetration, or any other contingency and there are no circumstances where your territory may be altered while your franchise agreement is in effect. Neither we nor any affiliate will establish other franchises or company-owned outlets or other channels of distribution selling or leasing products or services under the same/or different trademarks.

The typical length of time between your signing, initial payment, and your opening is three months.

ITEM 13. TRADEMARKS

We grant you the exclusive right to open and operate your business under the principal service mark GRANITE TRANSFORMATIONS®. On June 18, 2001 applications for the service mark GRANITE TRANSFORMATIONS® were filed by us with the Commissioner of Patents and Trademarks on the Principal Register in the U.S. Trademark Office in Class 37 for installation services, namely the installation of reconstituted slabs; and Class 41, the education and training services, namely teaching and training others how to install reconstituted Granite slabs. On October 29, 2002, we were issued Registration No. 2,644,309 for the service mark "GRANITE TRANSFORMATIONS®" in Class 41. On February 3, 2003, we were issued Registration No. 2,652,638 for the service mark "GRANITE TRANSFORMATIONS®" in Class 37.

In addition, applications for the service mark "Rocksolid Granit" were filed on May 14, 2001 with the Commissioner of Patents and Trademarks on the Principal Register in the U.S. Trademark Office in Class 19 for reconstituted slabs and titles; Class 37 for installation services, namely the installation of reconstituted slabs and titles; and Class 41 for education and training services, namely teaching and training others how to install reconstituted Granite slabs and titles by us which are on hold pending approval or disapproval of applications filed by an affiliate. By "trademarks," we mean trade names, trademarks, service marks, and logos used to identify your installation service.

You must follow our rules when you use these marks. You cannot use a name or mark as part of a corporate name or with modifying words, designs, or symbols except for those which we license to you. You may use our service marks in your d.b.a. but only with our written permission. You may not use our pending or registered name in connection with the sale of an unauthorized product or service or in a manner not authorized in writing by us.

There are no agreements that limit our right to use or license the use of our trademarks. You must make your own independent investigation of the demographics of your proposed area before making a final determination. In the event of a challenge to your use of our trademark, we will take the action we think appropriate. We, alone, have the sole right to control any legal action or proceeding including settlement involving service maker infringement or unfair competition against you or others. We will prosecute or defend an action at our sole discretion.

You must notify us immediately upon learning about any infringement or challenge so we can take whatever action we deem is necessary. We may take over the defense of a claim at any time and settle it, as we think fit.

You must modify or discontinue the use of a trademark if we modify or discontinue it. If this happens, we will reimburse you for your tangible costs of compliance for the cost of changing your stationary, ads, or signs. You must not directly or indirectly contest our right to our trademarks, trade secrets, or business techniques that are part of our business. We do not know of any infringing uses or litigation that could significantly affect the ownership or use of our principal trademark.

There are currently no material determinations of the Patent and Trademark Office, Trademark Trial and Appeal Board, the Trademark Administrator of this State of any court; pending infringement, opposition, or cancellation; and pending material litigation involving the principal trademarks. We do not know of any infringing use or litigation that could significantly affect the ownership or use of a principal trademark.

ITEM 14. PATENTS, COPYRIGHTS, AND PROPRIETARY INFORMATION

No patents or copyrights are material to the Circular. We reserve the right to copyright our proprietary confidential information manuals in the future.

ITEM 15. OBLIGATION TO PARTICIPATE IN THE OPERATION OF THE FRANCHISE BUSINESS

You must devote your best efforts and full dedicated time to the management of the franchised business in your office and in the field conducting both sales calls and at the job site visits unless a designated job site manager is employed to handle job site supervision. Corporate or partnership franchisees must designate an individual upon whom we may rely for the personal and direct management of the franchised business at the job site. Such individual does not have to have an equity interest in the franchised business if you are a business entity but must successfully complete our training. You shall conduct your business in an efficient and businesslike manner and at all times maintain the highest commercial and ethical standard and a high level of quality and service, thereby enhancing the reputation of the system and its name. You are encouraged to have your employees execute confidential, personal guarantees and/or non-competing agreements with you at your expense, if valid under your state law, but we have not placed these obligations on you, your owners, or your spouses in your Franchise Agreement.

ITEM 16. RESTRICTIONS ON WHAT THE FRANCHISEE MAY SELL

You may sell or offer for sale to the public only goods and services of the kind and quality which comply with the reasonable standards designated in the Operations Manual or directives in writing provided by us from time to time, including affiliated services. All products and services used or offered must be from our approved vendor or us. We have the unlimited right to change the types of authorized goods or services where we believe are in the best interests of our franchisees in order to upgrade and improve such goods or services.

ITEM 17. RENEWAL, TERMINATION, TRANSFER, AND DISPUTE RESOLUTION

This table lists important provisions of the franchise and related agreements. You should read these provisions in the agreements attached to this offering circular.

Provision(s)	Section(s) in the Franchise Agreement	Summary
A. Term of the Franchise Agreement	Article: 10.1	Term is 10 years from the date of execution of the Franchise Agreement, with the opportunity to renew for like periods of 10 years each if in good standing under the Franchise Agreement.

Provision(s)	Section(s) in the Franchise Agreement	Summary
B. Renewal or extension of the term	Article: 11.1	You can renew for unlimited additional periods of 10 years each if: (1) you are not in default or violation of the Franchise Agreement or any other agreement with us; and (2) upon execution of the then current Franchise Agreement, or if no agreement is in effect, extension of the last agreement executed by the parties within the applicable state, under the terms in effect at that time, including new royalty rates, advertising fees, etc., with the exception that the length of term or renewal terms shall not change your territory. The renewal fee to you is $1,000.00. Any required general release required as a condition of renewal, sale, and/or assignment/transfer shall not apply to any liability under the Maryland Franchise Registration and Disclosure Law.
C. Requirements for you to renew or extend	Article: 11.1	Sign a new agreement and pay the fee and not be in default.
D. Termination by you	Article: 11.2	You may terminate the franchise for good cause only if we have immediately breached the Franchise Agreement. Before you terminate the Franchise Agreement for good cause, you must serve a written notice of default upon us, specifying the grounds for default and granting us a reasonable opportunity to cure. We should have at least no less than 30 days in which to cure the default or in which to commence diligent efforts to cure the default (if the default cannot reasonably be expected to be cured within 30 days). You may also terminate on any grounds available by law.
E. Termination by us without cause	Article: 11.3	We can terminate only if you default and fail to cure.
F. Termination by us with cause	Article: 11.4	We can terminate for cause (see [G] and [H]). However, the provision allowing us to terminate the franchise may not be enforceable under federal bankruptcy law. (11 U.S.C. Section 101 et seq.)

Provision(s)	Section(s) in the Franchise Agreement	Summary
G. "Cause" defined: defaults which can be cured	Article: 11	30 days or less to cure: Attachment of involuntary lien over $1,000; adverse conduct affecting goodwill; default of Franchise Agreement; failure to make timely payments after 5 days' notice or as guarantor; conduct damaging to goodwill; transfers without our prior consent; failure to cure a default within 10 business days; failure to pay for or conduct an audit after 10 days' notice; failure to supply reports on gross sales; failure to use our techniques; failure to put in work hours managing during such days and hours as may be specified in accordance with the Franchise Agreement; failure to keep accurate business records; failure to maintain good conduct standards; failure to maintain confidential information; operating out of territory; failure to participate in a cooperative ad group and failure to pass training or open within 180 days after paying franchise fee; failure to spend required funds on your local advertising.
H. "Cause" defined: defaults which cannot be cured	Article: 11.4	Judicially declared insolvent; abandons business for 5 consecutive days; we mutually agree in writing; material misrepresentations; your failure after 10 days' notice to comply with laws; engage in same conduct after cured or not; repeated failure to comply with terms; franchised premises are seized and judgment unsatisfied for 30 days; conviction of felony or any criminal misconduct; failure to pay franchise fee within 5 days after notice; we determine your business is a danger to public health.
I. Your obligations on termination/non-renewal (also see R below)	Article: 11.5	Obligations include complete identification removal and payment.
J. Assignment of contract by us	Article: 11.12	No restriction on our right to assign.
K. Transfer by you (definition)	Article: 11.8	Includes transfer of contract and sole assets or ownership change.

Provision(s)	Section(s) in the Franchise Agreement	Summary
L. Our approval of transfer by franchisee	Article: 11.8	We have the right to approve all transfers but will not unreasonably withhold approval.
M. Conditions for our approval of transfer	Article: 11.8-11	30-day notification of intent to sell given to us, new franchisee qualifies, transfer, training and software fees paid, purchase agreement approved, training arranged, and release signed by you and current agreement signed by new franchisee.
N. Our right of first refusal to acquire your business	Article: 11.6	We can match any offer.
O. Our option to purchase your business	Article: 11.6	We have the right of first refusal except the transfers to approved qualified children and/or spouse exercisable within 30 days of receipt of your notice to us. We can purchase the franchise at any time that you attempt to cause a transfer to any other person.
P. Your death or disability	Article: 11.9	The estate must assign the franchise to an approved buyer in 3 months.
Q. Non-competition covenants, term of the franchise	Articles: 11 and 12.2	You cannot directly or indirectly operate a business similar to your franchised business.
R. Non-competition covenants after the franchise is terminated or expires	Articles: 7.13 and 12.2	No competing business for 2 years following the termination in your territory and within a 50-mile radius from your territorial boundaries.
S. Modification of the Agreement	Articles: 18.1 and .2	No modifications generally but Operation Manual subject to change.
T. Integration/merger clause	Article: 25.2	Only the terms of the Franchise Agreement are binding (subject to state law). Any other promises may not be enforceable.
U. Dispute resolution by arbitration or mediation	Article: 23.3 (1), (5)	Except for certain claims, all disputes must be arbitrated in the state of Illinois before the Franchise Arbitration and Mediation, Inc. (FAM) or the American Arbitration Association.
V. Choice of forum	Article: 19.1	Litigation must be in the State of Maryland.

Provision(s)	Section(s) in the Franchise Agreement	Summary
W. Choice of law	Articles: 19.1 and 23.3 (1), (5)	Maryland Law. All claims arising under the Maryland Franchise Registration and Disclosure Law must be brought within 3 years after the grant of the franchise and any limitation of claims provision will not act to reduce the limitation period under this Maryland law.

States having laws or laws concerning termination or non-renewal include Arkansas (Stats. 70-807), California (Bus. and Prof. Code Sections 20000-20043), Connecticut (Gen. Stat. Section 42-1130 at s2g), Delaware (Code, tit.), Hawaii (Rev. Stat. Section 482E-1), Illinois (815 ILCS 705/19 and 705/20), Indiana (Stat. Section 23-2-2.7), Iowa (Code Sections 523H.1-523.17), Michigan (Stat. Section 19.854(27)), Minnesota (Stat. Section 80C.14), Mississippi (Code Section 75-24-51), Missouri (Stat. Section 407.400), Nebraska (Rev. Stat. Section 87-401), New Jersey (Stat. Section 56:10-1), South Dakota (Codified Laws Section 375A-51), Virginia (Code 13.1-557-574-13.1-564), Washington (Code Section 19.100.180), Wisconsin (Stat. Section 135.03). These and other states may have court decisions that may supersede the franchise agreement in your relationship with the franchisor, including the areas of termination and renewal of your franchise. The laws of the applicable state where the franchisee will operate regarding termination of franchises should be checked thoroughly by franchisee's counsel.

ITEM 18. PUBLIC FIGURES

We do not use any public figure to promote our franchise at the time of this offering but may do so in the future.

ITEM 19. EARNING CLAIMS

We do not furnish or authorize our salespersons to furnish any oral or written information concerning the actual or potential sales, income, or profits of Rocksolid Granit (USA) Inc. franchised or company-owned units. Actual results vary from unit to unit and we cannot estimate the results of any particular franchise.

ITEM 20. LIST OF OUTLETS FRANCHISED

Franchised Site Center Status Summary for Last Three Calendar Years (2002/2001/2000)

State	Transfers	Canceled/ Terminated	Not Renewed	Reacquired by Franchisor	Left the System	Total Left Columns	Franchises Operating at the End of Year
Alabama	0/0/0	0/0/0	0/0/0	0/0/0	0/0/0	0/0/0	0/0/0
Alaska	0/0/0	0/0/0	0/0/0	0/0/0	0/0/0	0/0/0	0/0/0

State	Transfers	Canceled Terminated	Not Renewed	Reacquired by Franchisor	Left the System	Total Left Columns	Franchises operating at the end of year
Arizona	0/0/0	0/0/0	0/0/0	0/0/0	0/0/0	0/0/0	0/0/0
Arkansas	0/0/0	0/0/0	0/0/0	0/0/0	0/0/0	0/0/0	0/0/0
California	0/0/0	0/0/0	0/0/0	0/0/0	0/0/0	0/0/0	0/0/0
Colorado	0/0/0	0/0/0	0/0/0	0/0/0	0/0/0	0/0/0	0/0/0
Connecticut	0/0/0	0/0/0	0/0/0	0/0/0	0/0/0	0/0/0	0/0/0
Delaware	0/0/0	0/0/0	0/0/0	0/0/0	0/0/0	0/0/0	0/0/0
Dist. of Col.	0/0/0	0/0/0	0/0/0	0/0/0	0/0/0	0/0/0	0/0/0
Florida	0/0/0	0/0/0	0/0/0	0/0/0	0/0/0	0/0/0	0/0/0
Georgia	0/0/0	0/0/0	0/0/0	0/0/0	0/0/0	0/0/0	0/0/0
Hawaii	0/0/0	0/0/0	0/0/0	0/0/0	0/0/0	0/0/0	0/0/0
Idaho	0/0/0	0/0/0	0/0/0	0/0/0	0/0/0	0/0/0	0/0/0
Illinois	0/0/0	0/0/0	0/0/0	0/0/0	0/0/0	0/0/0	0/0/0
Indiana	0/0/0	0/0/0	0/0/0	0/0/0	0/0/0	0/0/0	0/0/0
Iowa	0/0/0	0/0/0	0/0/0	0/0/0	0/0/0	0/0/0	0/0/0
Kansas	0/0/0	0/0/0	0/0/0	0/0/0	0/0/0	0/0/0	0/0/0
Kentucky	0/0/0	0/0/0	0/0/0	0/0/0	0/0/0	0/0/0	0/0/0
Louisiana	0/0/0	0/0/0	0/0/0	0/0/0	0/0/0	0/0/0	0/0/0
Maine	0/0/0	0/0/0	0/0/0	0/0/0	0/0/0	0/0/0	0/0/0
Maryland	0/0/0	0/0/0	0/0/0	0/0/0	0/0/0	0/0/0	0/0/0
Massachu.	0/0/0	0/0/0	0/0/0	0/0/0	0/0/0	0/0/0	0/0/0
Michigan	0/0/0	0/0/0	0/0/0	0/0/0	0/0/0	0/0/0	0/0/0
Minnesota	0/0/0	0/0/0	0/0/0	0/0/0	0/0/0	0/0/0	0/0/0
Missouri	0/0/0	0/0/0	0/0/0	0/0/0	0/0/0	0/0/0	0/0/0
Montana	0/0/0	0/0/0	0/0/0	0/0/0	0/0/0	0/0/0	0/0/0
Nebraska	0/0/0	0/0/0	0/0/0	0/0/0	0/0/0	0/0/0	0/0/0
Nevada	0/0/0	0/0/0	0/0/0	0/0/0	0/0/0	0/0/0	0/0/0
New Hamp.	0/0/0	0/0/0	0/0/0	0/0/0	0/0/0	0/0/0	0/0/0
New Jersey	0/0/0	0/0/0	0/0/0	0/0/0	0/0/0	0/0/0	0/0/0
New Mexico	0/0/0	0/0/0	0/0/0	0/0/0	0/0/0	0/0/0	0/0/0
New York	0/0/0	0/0/0	0/0/0	0/0/0	0/0/0	0/0/0	0/0/0
North Car.	0/0/0	0/0/0	0/0/0	0/0/0	0/0/0	0/0/0	0/0/0
North Dakota	0/0/0	0/0/0	0/0/0	0/0/0	0/0/0	0/0/0	0/0/0
Ohio	0/0/0	0/0/0	0/0/0	0/0/0	0/0/0	0/0/0	0/0/0
Oklahoma	0/0/0	0/0/0	0/0/0	0/0/0	0/0/0	0/0/0	0/0/0

State	Transfers	Canceled/ Terminated	Not Renewed	Reacquired by Franchisor	Left the System	Total Left Columns	Franchises Operating at the End of Year
Oregon	0/0/0	0/0/0	0/0/0	0/0/0	0/0/0	0/0/0	0/0/0
Pennsylvania	0/0/0	0/0/0	0/0/0	0/0/0	0/0/0	0/0/0	0/0/0
Rhode Island	0/0/0	0/0/0	0/0/0	0/0/0	0/0/0	0/0/0	0/0/0
South Car.	0/0/0	0/0/0	0/0/0	0/0/0	0/0/0	0/0/0	0/0/0
South Dakota	0/0/0	0/0/0	0/0/0	0/0/0	0/0/0	0/0/0	0/0/0
Tennessee	0/0/0	0/0/0	0/0/0	0/0/0	0/0/0	0/0/0	0/0/0
Texas	0/0/0	0/0/0	0/0/0	0/0/0	0/0/0	0/0/0	0/0/0
Utah	0/0/0	0/0/0	0/0/0	0/0/0	0/0/0	0/0/0	0/0/0
Vermont	0/0/0	0/0/0	0/0/0	0/0/0	0/0/0	0/0/0	0/0/0
Virginia	0/0/0	0/0/0	0/0/0	0/0/0	0/0/0	0/0/0	0/0/0
Washington	0/0/0	0/0/0	0/0/0	0/0/0	0/0/0	0/0/0	0/0/0
West Virginia	0/0/0	0/0/0	0/0/0	0/0/0	0/0/0	0/0/0	0/0/0
Wisconsin	0/0/0	0/0/0	0/0/0	0/0/0	0/0/0	0/0/0	0/0/0
Wyoming	0/0/0	0/0/0	0/0/0	0/0/0	0/0/0	0/0/0	0/0/0
Totals	0/0/0	0/0/0	0/0/0	0/0/0	0/0/0	0/0/0	0/0/0

PLEASE REFER TO EXHIBIT C ENTITLED "FRANCHISE LIST."

The names and last known addresses and telephone number of every franchisee who has had an outlet canceled or terminated or not renewed or reacquired by the franchisor or otherwise voluntary or involuntary ceased to do business under the Franchise Agreement during the most recently completed fiscal year or has not communicated within 10 weeks of the application date with the franchisor is as follows: NONE

Status of Company Owned* Centers for the Last 3 Years (2002/2001/2000)

State	Sites Closed During the Year	Sites Opened During the Year	Total Sites Operating at Year End
California (California office opened in 2001)	0/0/0	0/1/0	1/1/0

* The date of the information disclosed above is May 22, 2003.

Projected Openings as of May 22, 2003

State	Franchise Agreements Signed but Site Center Not Opened	Projected Franchised New Site Centers in the Next Fiscal Year	Projected Company-Owned Center Openings in the Next Fiscal Year
Arizona	0	1	0
California	0	15	0
Florida	0	1	0
Illinois	0	1	0
Michigan	0	1	0
Nevada	0	1	0
New York	0	1	0
Texas	0	1	0
Totals	0	22	0

ITEM 21. FINANCIAL STATEMENTS

The following financial statements are attached to this Offering Circular: Exhibit A Audited Balance Sheet and Related Statement of Income as of December 31, 2002.

ITEM 22. CONTRACTS

Attached, as Exhibit B, is a copy of the Franchise Agreement proposed to be used in this state.

ITEM 23. RECEIPT

The last page of the Offering Circular is a Detachable Document Acknowledging Receipt of the Offering Circular by the prospective franchisee and is attached as Exhibit E.

EXHIBIT A. FINANCIAL STATEMENTS

Financial statements are purposely omitted. This circular is not an offering, but included for illustration purposes only.

EXHIBIT B. FRANCHISE AGREEMENT

Please see Appendix B-1 of this book for a full illustration of a Franchise Agreement.

EXHIBIT C. LIST OF FRANCHISEES OF THE OFFERING CIRCULAR FOR GRANITE TRANSFORMATIONS®

Franchisee's I.D. Number	Location	Owner	Address/Phone

EXHIBIT D. STATE ADMINISTRATORS AND AGENCIES

Listed here are names, addresses, and telephone numbers of state agency personnel having responsibility for franchising disclosure/registration laws and selected business opportunity laws.

California
Commissioner of Corporations
Department of Corporations
320 West 4th Street, Suite 750
Los Angeles, CA 90013-1105
213 576-7500

Connecticut
[Business Opportunity Investment Act]
Assistant Director
Securities and Business Investments Division
Connecticut Department of Banking
44 Capitol Avenue
Hartford, CT 06106
203 566-4560

Florida
[Sale of Business Opportunities Act]
Department of Agriculture and Consumer
   Services
Division of Consumer Services
Mayo Building, 2nd Floor
Tallahassee, FL 32399-0800
800 HELP-FLA
Fax: 850 410-3804

Hawaii
Department of Commerce and Consumer
   Affairs
1010 Richards Street, 2nd Floor
Honolulu, HI 96810
808 586-2722

Illinois
Office of Attorney General
500 South Second Street
Springfield, IL 62706
217 782-4465

Indiana
Franchise Section
Securities Division

Secretary of State
Room E-111
302 West Washington Street
Indianapolis, IN 46204
317 232-6681

Iowa
[Business Opportunity Promotions Law]
Supervisor of Regulated Industries
Iowa Securities Bureau
Second Floor
Lucas State Office Building
Des Moines, IA 50319
515 281-4441
Fax: 515 281-6467

Maryland
Franchise Examiner
200 St. Paul Place
Baltimore, MD 21202-2020
410 576-6360

Michigan
Franchise Administrator
Consumer Protection Division
Antitrust and Franchise Unit
Michigan Department of Attorney General
670 Law Building
Lansing, MI 48913
517 373-7117

Minnesota
Registration Unit
Minnesota Department of Commerce
85 7th Place East, Suite 500
St. Paul, MN 55101-2198
651 296-6328

Nebraska
[Seller-Assisted Marketing Plan Law]
Department of Banking and Finance Unit
1200 N Street, Suite 311

P.O. Box 95006
Lincoln, NE 68509
402 471-3445

New York
State of New York
Office of the Attorney General
23rd Floor
120 Broadway
New York, NY 10271
212 416-8236

North Dakota
Office of Securities Commissioner
Fifth Floor
600 East Boulevard
Bismarck, ND 58505
701 328-2910

Oregon
Department of Consumer and Business Services
Division of Finance and Corporate Securities
Labor and Industries Building
Salem, OR 97310
503 378-4387

Rhode Island
Securities Examiner
Division of Securities
Suite 232
233 Richmond Street
Providence, RI 02903
401 277-3048

South Dakota
Franchise Administrator
Department of Commerce and Consumer
    Regulations
Division of Securities
c/o 118 West Capitol
Pierre, SD 57501
605 773-4013

Texas
[Business Opportunity Act]
Statutory Document Section
Secretary of State
P.O. Box 12887
Austin, TX 78711
512 475-1769

Utah
[Business Opportunity Disclosure Act]
Division of Consumer Protection
Utah Department of Commerce
160 East Three Hundred South
P.O. Box 45804
Salt Lake City, UT 84145-0804
801 530-6601
Fax: 801 530-6001

Virginia
State Corporation Commission
Division of Securities and Retail Franchising
P.O. Box 1197
Richmond, VA 23218

Washington
Adminstrator
Department of Financial Institutions
Securities Division
P.O. Box 9033
Olympia, WA 98507-9033
306 902-8760

Wisconsin
Commissioner of Securities
345 W. Washington Avenue, 4th Floor
Madison, WI 53703
Mail:
P.O. 1768
Madison, WI 53701-1768
608 266-1064

EXHIBIT E. RECEIPT

Franchisee's Copy

THIS OFFERING CIRCULAR SUMMARIZES PROVISIONS OF THE FRANCHISE AGREEMENT AND OTHER INFORMATION IN PLAIN LANGUAGE. READ THIS OFFERING CIRCULAR AND ALL AGREEMENTS CAREFULLY.

IF ROCKSOLID GRANIT (USA) INC. OFFERS YOU A FRANCHISE, ROCKSOLID GRANIT (USA) INC. MUST PROVIDE THIS OFFERING CIRCULAR TO YOU BY THE EARLIEST OF:

1. THE FIRST PERSONAL MEETING TO DISCUSS OUR FRANCHISE; OR
2. TEN BUSINESS DAYS BEFORE SIGNING A BINDING AGREEMENT; OR
3. TEN BUSINESS DAYS BEFORE ANY PAYMENT TO ROCKSOLID GRANIT (USA) INC.

YOU MUST ALSO RECEIVE A FRANCHISE AGREEMENT CONTAINING ALL MATERIAL TERMS AT LEAST TEN BUSINESS DAYS BEFORE YOU SIGN ANY FRANCHISE AGREEMENT.

IF ROCKSOLID GRANIT (USA) INC. DOES NOT DELIVER THIS OFFERING CIRCULAR ON TIME OR IF IT CONTAINS A FALSE OR MISLEADING STATEMENT, OR A MATERIAL OMIS-SION, A VIOLATION OF FEDERAL AND STATE LAW MAY HAVE OCCURRED AND SHOULD BE REPORTED TO THE FEDERAL TRADE COMMISSION, WASHINGTON DC 20580.

ROCKSOLID GRANIT (USA) INC.'S AGENT FOR SERVICE OF PROCESS IS MARYLAND SECURI-TIES COMMISSIONER, 200 ST. PAUL PLACE, BALTIMORE, MARYLAND 21202-2020.

I HAVE RECEIVED A FRANCHISE OFFERING CIRCULAR DATED _____

THIS OFFERING CIRCULAR INCLUDED THE FOLLOWING EXHIBITS:

A. FINANCIAL STATEMENTS
B. FRANCHISE AGREEMENT
C. FRANCHISEE LIST
D. ADMINISTRATORS AND AGENCIES
E. RECEIPT (FRANCHISOR AND FRANCHISEE)

AND SCHEDULE TO FRANCHISE AGREEMENT WITH TERRITORY MAP

SIGNED:_____

PRINT NAME:_____ DATE: _____

Note: The same document is also prepared as the "Franchisor's Copy."

Lite For Life

Franchise Offering Circular
Lite For Life Franchising Corporation, Inc.
A California Corporation
1199 Howard Ave., Suite 102
Burlingame, California 94010
(650) 685-LIFE

You, as our Franchisee, will operate a weight loss center using a proprietary diet that has been proven effective for over 25 years. Your key services are providing your dieters with a nutritional and behavioral approach to lifetime weight management specializing in blood sugar stabilization and sugar addiction avoidance through private daily counseling and nutrition education, along with the sale of daily nutritional supplements and fresh and frozen food products to be used in conjunction with a diet designed to achieve permanent weight loss.

The initial franchise fee is $20,000. The initial franchise fee is payable upon signing the Franchise Agreement. There are no refunds.

The estimated initial investment required ranges from $58,972 to $122,700. See Item 7 for specifics.

THE FRANCHISE AGREEMENT REQUIRES THAT ALL DISAGREEMENTS BE SETTLED BY ARBITRATION ONLY IN BURLINGAME, CALIFORNIA. OUT OF STATE ARBITRATION MAY FORCE YOU TO ACCEPT A LESS FAVORABLE SETTLEMENT FOR DISPUTES. IT MAY ALSO COST YOU MORE TO ARBITRATE WITH US IN CALIFORNIA THAN IN YOUR HOME STATE.

THE FRANCHISE AGREEMENT STATES THAT CALIFORNIA LAW GOVERNS THE AGREEMENT AND THIS LAW MAY NOT PROVIDE THE SAME PROTECTION AND BENEFITS AS LOCAL LAW. YOU MAY WANT TO COMPARE THESE LAWS.

THERE MAY BE OTHER RISKS CONCERNING THIS FRANCHISE.

Information about comparison of franchisors is available. Call the state administrator listed in Exhibit D or your public library for sources of information.

Registration of this franchise with the state does not mean that the state recommends it or has verified the information in this offering circular. If you learn that anything in this offering circular is untrue, contact the Federal Trade Commission and/or state authority.

Effective Date: California: (2/9/03) (2/10/03) (2/16/03) (/2/17/03) (2/18/03) (2/24/03) (2/25/03) (2/26/03) (2/27/03) (3/21/03) (3/24/03) (3/25/03) (4/3/03) (4/14/03) (4/15/03) (4/16/03)

Table of Contents

* **Note:** In your actual document, page numbers must be filled in, but they have been omitted in this publication to avoid confusion with the book's page numbers.

ITEM 1. THE FRANCHISOR, ITS PREDECESSORS AND AFFILIATES

To simplify the language in this offering circular, "we" means the Franchisor, Lite For Life Franchising Corporation, Inc. "You" means the person who buys the franchise. Lite For Life Franchising Corporation, Inc., is a California corporation incorporated on April 7, 2003. It does franchising business using its trademark "Lite For Life." We have no predecessor or affiliate. Our principal business address is 1199 Howard Ave. Suite 102, Burlingame, California 94010.

Our agent for service of process in this state is the Commissioner of Corporations, 320 West 4th Street, Suite 750, Los Angeles, CA 90013-2344, and Christopher P. Bruno, 2107 Ensenada Way, San Mateo, CA 94403.

Our franchisees are independent operators of weight loss centers. You, as our Franchisee, will operate your weight loss center using a proprietary diet that has proven effective for over 25 years. Your key service is to provide your dieters with a nutritional and behavioral approach to lifetime weight management with specialization in blood sugar stabilization and sugar addiction avoidance through private daily counseling and nutrition education along with the sale of daily nutritional supplements and fresh and frozen food products to be used in conjunction with a recommended diet designed to achieve permanent weight loss. You will receive comprehensive training that will enable you to provide a complete permanent weight loss service to your dieters. You will sell nutritional supplements and food products in conjunction with the individual diets. The service mark "Lite For Life" and other of our trademarks, logos, designs, and systems distinguish your business.

Maureen and Howard Sullivan founded and are the sole owners of Lite For Life, Inc., a California corporation incorporated on December 20, 1991, which presently operates "Lite For Life" weight loss centers in Burlingame and Los Altos, California. In addition to these two "Lite For Life" weight loss centers, Maureen's daughter, Elizabeth Schermer, operates a "Lite For Life" weight loss center in Redmond, Washington, started on September 31, 2002, and Maureen's sister has operated a "Lite For Life" weight loss center in San Francisco, California since December 20, 1991. Both centers operate under previous oral trademark arrangements from Lite For Life, Inc. It is our intention to offer both parties a franchise agreement after we are registered to sell franchises in California.

The market for "Lite For Life" weight loss centers is quite literally growing. As continuously reported and confirmed in the national media for the past several years, obesity and its consequences, especially adult onset diabetes, have reached epidemic proportions in this country. It is now estimated that over 60% of American adults and 20% of the nation's children are overweight. The health costs associated with obesity are now believed to equal those associated with smoking. A recent landmark study reported in the *New England Journal of Medicine* linked obesity with one out of every six cancer deaths in the United States. Earlier studies have found that excess weight contributes to cancers of the breast and uterus, colon and rectum, kidney, esophagus, and gall bladder. This study also linked obesity to cancers of the cervix and ovary, multiple myeloma, non-Hodgkin's lymphoma, pancreas, liver, and, in men, the stomach and prostate. The flood of irrefutable evidence of the health risks of obesity points to the necessity of attitudes toward being overweight changing much the way attitudes toward smoking have. Lite For Life is poised to profit from this change in attitude.

The diet market is well developed, with a perennial crop of books touting new diet plans as well as numerous weight loss service businesses available to the consumer. Our system is unique in that it focuses on long-term sustainable changes through personal daily nutrition education and counseling emphasizing blood sugar stabilization through the consumption of real foods.

Your competition includes such national chains or franchises as Weight Watchers, a group support meeting-based program with some online dieting information; Jenny Craig, a lifestyle-based program focusing on a low-fat diet with weekly counseling and a mandatory purchase of prepared foods; and Diet Center, Inc., part of a health-oriented conglomerate offering a diet based on nutritional supplements and daily counseling coupled with fabricated foods such as meal replacement shakes and bars and fat-burning thermogenic pills. In addition, most local markets support independent medically supervised weight loss clinics as well as weight loss "boutiques" offering services as hypnotherapy, guided meditation, cellulite endermologie, acupuncture, and herbs.

We have not offered or sold franchises of the type to be operated by you prior to registering in California. We have no predecessor or affiliate. We have not offered or sold franchises in any other line of business and are not engaged in any other business activity. We do not operate the type of business being franchised but our founders and their families have extensive experience as described below.

ITEM 2. BUSINESS EXPERIENCE

HOWARD A. SULLIVAN: CHAIRMAN OF THE BOARD AND DIRECTOR

Howard A. Sullivan has been Chairman of the Board of Lite For Life Franchising Corporation, Inc. located in Burlingame, California since the inception of the corporate entity on April 7, 2003. He is responsible for the guiding the board in the creation of the franchise business and in its execution. Howard has held the position of Vice President of Lite For Life, Inc. since 1991 and has been involved in the weight loss business since 1986. Previously, Howard was in medical equipment sales with Foremost McKesson, Whitaker General Medical, and Will Ross, Inc. He attended Stanford University before enlisting in the Army in World War II. Assigned to the Army Air Corps of the 3rd Army under General Patton, Howard was a fighter pilot in the Mediterranean Theater, flying P-40's, 41's, and 51's and leaving the service with the rank of Captain. He was a member of the Civil Air Patrol for over 30 years.

MAUREEN A. SULLIVAN: CHIEF EXECUTIVE OFFICER AND DIRECTOR

Maureen A. Sullivan has been President and Director of Lite For Life Franchising Corporation, Inc. since the inception of the corporate entity on April 7, 2003. Maureen also is President of Lite For Life, Inc., a California corporation, and has held that position since its incorporation on December 20, 1991. She has been a weight loss professional since 1978. Maureen has a BA from Seattle University, a Master's in Education and is a Certified Nutrition Consultant.

CHRISTOPHER R. BRUNO, PRESIDENT AND DIRECTOR

Christopher P. Bruno has been President of Lite For Life Franchising Corporation, Inc. since the inception of the corporate entity on April 7, 2003. Most recently he was Vice President, Sales, at Full Degree in Palo Alto, CA. Prior to that Chris worked as sales consultant in high technology in San Francisco, CA and was a Director of Sales at Scient Corp from May of 1999 to December of 2001. For the three years prior to that Chris ran and consulted to his own company, CTI Solutions, in San

Francisco, CA. Chris opened his first weight loss center in Santa Barbara, CA in 1983. He has a BA in English from Santa Clara University.

EDWARD T. KENNEDY, VICE PRESIDENT, OPERATIONS AND FINANCE, DIRECTOR

Edward T. Kennedy has been Vice President, Operations and Finance of Lite For Life Franchising Corporation, Inc. since July 15, 2003. Previously, Ed was Vice President, Channel Sales for Navisite, Inc. from November 2001 to June 2003, where he managed Accenture and other key outsourcing relationships. From June 2001 to November 2001 Ed consulted to start-up high-technology companies. Prior to that he was Director in the Telecommunications Business Unit at Scient Corporation in San Francisco from July 1999 to June 2001. He held various sales and marketing management roles at IBM from 1995 to July 1999 and was a Senior Consultant at Price Waterhouse from 1989 to 1994, where he earned his CPA. Ed graduated from the University of Notre Dame with a BBA in accounting and a minor in psychology and from Stanford Graduate School of Business with a master's in business administration.

KATHLEEN M. BRUNO, VICE PRESIDENT, BUSINESS DEVELOPMENT, DIRECTOR

Kathleen M. Bruno has been Vice President, Business Development of Lite For Life Franchising Corporation, Inc. since the inception of the corporate entity on April 7, 2003. From June of 1999 to April of 2003, she was with Ariba, Inc., where she closed the single-largest software sale by a sales representative, and from 1994 to 1999 she worked on Wall Street for Sybase, Inc., selling to financial institutions. Kathleen previously managed her own weight loss center in Millbrae, CA. She holds a BA in Psychology from Santa Clara University and for her Master's degree in Counseling Psychology, her practicum was performed at Stanford University's Center for Disease Prevention. Kathleen was honored by Mercy Burlingame High School with The Founder's Award of "Alumna of the Year" in 2002.

LYNN M. BRUNO, SECRETARY AND TREASURER

Lynn M. Bruno has been Secretary and Treasurer of Lite For Life Franchising Corporation Inc. since the inception of the corporate entity on April 7, 2003. She has a diverse background in communications, design, and small business. She began her career as an editor and writer for *The Wall Street Journal*. She owned and operated her own design business for 10 years. From 2000 to the present she has been director of a mentoring program she founded. She has a BA in English from Santa Clara University.

ELIZABETH A. SCHERMER, DIRECTOR

Elizabeth A. Schermer has been a Director of Lite For Life Franchising Corporation, Inc. since the inception of the corporate entity on April 7, 2003. Liz owns and operates the Redmond, Washington Lite For Life, which she opened in September 2002 after parenting her two children to school age. Liz previously managed the Burlingame Lite For Life for a period of 10 years. Liz holds the all-time rebounding record for men's and women's basketball at Santa Clara University. She holds a BA in Psychology and a Master's in Counseling Psychology.

ITEM 3. LITIGATION

No litigation involving a predecessor or a person identified in Item 2 is required to be disclosed in this offering circular.

ITEM 4. BANKRUPTCY

No person previously identified in Items 1 or 2 of this offering circular has been involved as a debtor in proceedings under the U.S. Bankruptcy Code required to be disclosed in this Item.

ITEM 5. INITIAL FRANCHISE FEE

You will be required to pay $20,000. This initial franchise fee is payable upon signing the Franchise Agreement. There are no refunds.

ITEM 6. OTHER FEES

Name of Fee	Amount	Due Date	Remarks
Service Fee	5% of gross	On or before the 7th day after the close of each calendar month based on "gross sales" for the previous month	The term "gross sales" is defined to include all sums or things of value received or receivable by you in and from the business from all sales of goods, products, and services whether for cash, check, credit, or otherwise, without reserve or deduction for inability or failure to collect same including, without limitation, such sales and services where the orders thereof originated at or accepted by you at one location but delivered or performance thereof made from or at any other location. Gross sales do not include rebates, promotional sales coupons, or refunds to customers or the amount of any sales taxes or any similar taxes that you might be required to and do collect from customers to be paid to any federal, state, or local taxing authority. All such items, including non-collectible accounts which are claimed as deductions to gross sales, must be supported by proper documentation in accordance with the operating manual provided by us to you.
Local Operating Advertising and Promotional Fee	$1,000 per month (Additional $1,000 also to be spent within 60 days of opening)	Commencing from the first date that you open for business	You must prove that you have spent this amount each month.

Name of fee	Amount	Due Date	Remarks
Transfer Fee	$4,500	Upon any assignment, sale, or transfer of the franchise	Fee covers the cost of training and transfer including credit checks, legal work, etc. No charge if franchise is transferred to a corporation owned by you, to a trained and qualified family member, or another franchisee in the system.
Renewal Fee (Subject to Consumer Price Index)	$1,000	Upon renewal	Should the Consumer Price Index (CPI) that is based on the annual inflationary rates in your territory increase, your Renewal Fee may be increased as compared with the year of opening of your franchise by the same increased CPI percentage.
Additional Training Fee	Prevailing, reasonable per diem rates for training personnel at home office or requested at-site training.	Prior to the training	Annual seminars as we deem necessary with travel, lodging, and meals at your cost.
Audit Fee	Cost of audit plus interest at the maximum legal rate of interest allowed by law from	As incurred	We reserve the right to audit you at least once a year at your cost if the audit reveals a discrepancy of 2% or more. Payable only if you understate by at least 2% of what is due. Late payments bear legal rate of interest allowed by law.

Description	Amount	Method of Payment	When Due	To Whom Payment to Be Made
Non-refundable Initial Franchise Fee	$20,000	Cashier's check	On signing of Franchise Agreement.	Us
Leasehold improvements (1)	$1,700 to $20,000	Progress payments until completed	By agreement.	General contractor
Telephone, fax, computer equipment, Visa machine, additional scales	$2,350 to $7,000	Lump sum	Prior to opening.	Dealer

Description	Amount	Method of Payment	When Due	To Whom Payment to Be Made
Telephone, fax, computer equipment, Visa machine, additional scales	$2,350 to $7,000	Lump sum	Prior to opening.	Dealer
Furniture	$2,000 to $5,000	Lump sum	Prior to opening	Dealer
General liability insurance (per month)	$300 to $500	Quarterly	Prior to opening	Dealer
SSI/Medicare/Worker's Compensation Insurance	$129 to $1,000	Quarterly	Prior to opening	Government agency, insurance agent
City business license	$100 to $500	Lump sum (renewable annually)	Prior to opening	City
Initial Inventory (perishable and non-perishable) and operating supplies (office supplies, stationery, brochures) (2)	$3,500 to $5,500	Lump sum	Prior to opening	Vendor
Signage with permits (Interior and exterior strip mall)	$250 to $7,500	As required by vendor	As required by vendor	Sign vendor
Rental per month (approximately 1,200 square feet)	$1,200 to $3,500	In full	Monthly	Landlord
Security deposits (Usually first and last months' rent) including lease utilities	$3,300 to $8,000	Lump sum	As required	Landlord, utility, licensor, etc.
Utilities and equipment lease deposits	$1,000 to $2,500	Lump sum	As required	Utility, licensor, etc.

Description	Amount	Method of Payment	When Due	To Whom Payment to Be Made
Freezer and refrigerator leases; utilities, truck rental, 4 telephone lines and toll, postage, bottled water, insurance (per month)	$2,343 to $6,500	Lump sum	Monthly	Licensor, etc.
Professional fees, bookkeeping, 1 employee (monthly)	$300 to $1,800	Lump sum	Monthly	Professional and bookkeeper
Miscellaneous Pre-Opening Costs (travel and living expenses while training; permits; organizational expenses)	$1,500 to $4,000	As incurred	As incurred	Vendors, etc.
Initial grand pre-opening advertising requirement	$2,000	As incurred	Once the office is open for business	Media
Advertising (magazines, yellow pages)	$1,000 to $5,000	Lump sum	Monthly	Media
Additional funds to commence or continue operation for 3 months, i.e., working capital, etc. (2,3)	$12,500 to $17,500			

ESTIMATED TOTAL INITIAL INVESTMENT: $54,972 to $ 117,800 (4)

The sources listed above are amounts to be supplied from your own funds.

No allowance has been made for inflation, debt service, or interest payment on borrowed money, but you should consider this, particularly if part or all of your start-up costs are to be financed.

Notes

1. Please note that if you are able to wholly or partially able to finance the entire leasehold improvements and/or the initial inventory, the initial cash requirements will be reduced by the amounts financed, but the monthly interest and principal debt service must be calculated in its place according to the terms

of the lender. Additionally, on occasion, some or all of the tenant improvements may be paid by the lessor of the property. If fixtures, furniture, and/or equipment is rented or leased, the amount of the minimum and maximum initial cash requirement may be decreased depending on local terms.

2. Working capital does include wages for one (1) employee but no draw or compensation for the franchise owner.

3. This estimates your initial start-up expenses. These expenses do include payroll costs for one (1) employee. These figures are estimates and we cannot guarantee that you will not have additional expenses starting your business. Your costs will depend on factors such as how much you follow our methods and procedures; your management skill, experience, and business acumen; local economic conditions; the local market for our service; the prevailing wage rate; competition; and the sales level reached during the initial period.

4. We relied on over 25 years of experience of our Chief Executive Officer in the weight loss profession to compile these estimates. You should review these figures carefully with a business advisor before making any decision to purchase the franchise.

We do not offer direct or indirect financing to franchisees for any items.

ITEM 8. RESTRICTIONS ON SOURCES OF PRODUCTS AND SERVICES

We have not been in existence for a full fiscal year nor have we sold franchises prior to the effective date of this Disclosure, so neither we nor any affiliate has revenues from the sale or lease of any products or services and therefore we are unable to represent a percentage of our franchisees' total purchases from us as compared to our total revenues for the last fiscal year. Our fiscal year ends every March 31st. To the extent known or estimable, we estimate that your purchases and leases of all goods, services, supplies, fixtures, equipment, or inventory that you must purchase from us in relation to all of the purchases of goods and services that you will make or enter into for the establishment and operation of the franchise will be approximately 10% or less of your overall purchases in operating your franchise.

We are the designated supplier for diet supplements, paper forms, and dieting booklets at this time. Any scales in addition to the two (2) scales that are provided to you by us as part of your initial franchise fee must be purchased from a supplier approved by us and must include professional assembly and calibration. At this time, we are the only approved supplier for the nutritional supplement used in conjunction with the conditioning and reducing diets.

All Franchisees will be required to purchase or lease a commercial freezer and refrigerator with glass front doors from suppliers approved by us in writing. In the event that you believe that any such product of an equal quality can be purchased at a lower price, you must present us backup studies and data indicating the price of such items and the quality characteristics. Our sole testing procedures determine whether such items equal or exceed the quality and price reasonableness over the items purchased from us. Our review typically is completed in 60 business days.

If you desire to purchase any products, including supplements and food, services, equipment, and materials, from someone other than our designated supplier, you must submit a complete description of the history and credit rating of the supplier and the items you wish to purchase. You also must supply us with specifications and tests which will prove to our sole satisfaction that the products, equipment, and materials are of equal or superior quality to those which we or our designated supplier may offer for sale to you at what we feel are competitive prices and the supplier's ability to stand behind the supplier's product warranty, which must meet or surpass that of our then current designated supplier. We also require you to submit proof that the product meets USDA and FDA regulations pertinent to the type of product submitted, and the name, address, history, and ownership of the provider, along with your brief business analysis of the cost, retail pricing, inventory requirements, needs justification, break-even point, and marketing sales plan for the product. Suppliers of food, vitamins, and nutritional supplements also will be evaluated by compliance with appropriate USDA and FDA regulations for the type of food that you wish to provide, i.e., approved kitchen products, etc. Product ingredients will be evaluated by Maureen Sullivan, Certified Nutrition Consultant, for healthfulness and appropriateness for the particular diet. In her absence another certified nutritionist will be designated. We also evaluate for taste, product appearance and packaging, cost, and inventory requirements, as well as the manner in which the manufacturer plans to market the product to other vendors. Six (6) samples of each product should be submitted to us for testing purposes. We will approve or disapprove a prospective supplier according to our complete and final discretion within 60 business days of receipt of your request to purchase from alternate suppliers. We may charge a fee for our time to cover our costs in researching the product. If the product you submit is accepted for sale in your franchise, we will provide written standards and specifications including, but not limited to, sales methods, reporting and documentation, installation methods, etc. We may modify our specifications based on our research and industry changes and we will make this known to you in writing as the changes occur. We also may seek out and test suppliers on our own.

You might have to purchase other trademarked items to be used in the franchised business according to the specifications set forth by us in the operating manuals from time to time. We formulate and modify our specifications and standards for products and services through observations and testing that are made available to you. We see no need for a purchasing cooperative in our present line of business. We have the option to drop any supplier from our approved list. You must notify us in the event you discover that any supplier has dropped a service or product. We will provide you with a list of our approved suppliers after you have satisfactorily completed your initial training.

We do not derive income from purchases that you make from approved suppliers. We do not now receive but reserve the right to receive rebates or promotional fees in the future from approved suppliers from whom you may purchase products. These fees may be used by us to defray overhead costs and for advertising at our sole discretion. We do not derive direct income from rebates. These fees may or may not be credited to you for any fees owed to us at our sole discretion. You are not required to purchase from suppliers that give rebates or promotional fees to us. However, it may be beneficial for you and other franchisees to purchase from this type of vendor. We do not provide renewals, grant additional franchises, or bestow any other material benefits to our franchisees based on a franchisee's use of a designated or approved source of supply.

You must purchase an IBM compatible computer running a current version of Windows and possessing a CD-ROM or DVD drive, modem or DSL connection, and printer with fax capabilities. Internet Service Provider (ISP), anti-virus software, Internet browser, and e-mail provider to be approved and compatible with our existing network systems. Current versions of QuickBooksPro and Microsoft Office software and one (1) database program for tracking client information are required. You will update your software and hardware as we update ours and additional software may be required from time to time.

You may only offer such services and sell products designated by us in writing in order to be consistent with our theme. We will loan you a Confidential Business Operations Manual that will contain specifications and parameters developed by us including signage, advertising, personal appearance of personnel, location, size, and appearance of location, product display, etc., which you must strictly follow. Modifications to specifications, grants, and revocation of supplier approval will be issued by mail as required.

We reserve the right to designate or consent to the content, themes, materials, and placement of all advertising programs by you, which must be tailored to your local market and without inappropriate or misleading content. You must submit all advertising to us for our approval at least five (5) business days before publication (subject to deadlines) unless specifically waived in writing by us as to each particular ad or advertising campaign. Although there are no restrictions on the areas in which you may advertise, we recommend that you concentrate on advertising in your local area as a matter of good business practice.

The site you select must have our written approval both as to the outside and inside as well as decor and appearance as spelled out in more detail in your Business Operating Manual.

ITEM 9. FRANCHISEE'S OBLIGATIONS

This table lists your principal obligations under the franchise and other agreements. It will help you find more detailed information about your obligations in these agreements and in other items of this offering circular.

Obligation	Section in Franchise Agreement	Item in Offering Circular
a. Site selection and acquisition/lease	II (A) (5)	Items 7 and 11
b. Pre-opening purchases/lease	II (A) (1) and (3)	Items 5, 6, 7, and 8
c. Site development and other pre-opening requirements	II (A) (5)	Items 6, 7, 8, and 11
d. Initial and ongoing training	II (A) (2), (4), and (5)	Items 6, 7, and 11
e. Opening	II (A) (1), (2), and (3)	Items 5, 6, 7, 8, 9, and 11
f. Fee	III (A) and (C); IV (A), (B), and (C)	Items 5, 6, and 7
g. Compliance with standards and policies/operating manual	II (A) (1), V, VI, and VII (A), VIII, IX	Items 8, 9, 11, 14, 15, 16, and 17
h. Trademarks and proprietary information	I (A), (B), (C) and (D), VII (A)-(C)	Items 13 and 14
i. Restrictions on products/services offered	V (A) and VII (D)	Item 16

Obligation	Section in Franchise Agreement	Item in Offering Circular
j. Warranty and customer service	None	None
k. Territorial development and sales	None	None
l. Ongoing product/service purchases	V (A) and VII(D)	Items 16
m. Maintenance, appearance and remodeling requirements	V (H)	Item 9
n. Insurance	IX (A)	Item 7
o. Advertising	II B (5), (6); IV (B) (H)	Items 6, 8, and 11
p. Indemnification	VIII, IX	None
q. Owner's participation/management/staffing	VI	Item 15
r. Records/reports	V (B), (C), (D)	None
s. Inspections/audits	V (C), (J)	Item 6
t. Transfer	IV (C); X (A)-(F)	Items 6 and 17
u. Renewal	III (B) (C)	Items 6 and 17
v. Post-termination obligations	X (G)-(K); XI (A)-(D)	Item 17
w. Non-competition covenants	VII (A)-(D)	Item 17
x. Dispute resolution	XIII (A), (B), (M)	Item 17
y. Other (describe)	None	

ITEM 10. FINANCING

We do not offer direct or indirect financing or guarantee your note, lease, or obligation.

ITEM 11. FRANCHISOR'S OBLIGATIONS

Except as disclosed below, we need not provide any other assistance to you.

Before you open your business, we will provide:

1) Operating Manuals We will loan you one or more sets of the franchise operating manual that specifies the guidelines for site selection, decor, signage, fixtures, inventory, supplies, names of approved suppliers, suggested budgets, pre-opening advertising guides, operational techniques, financial and accounting information, marketing plans, and other items and procedures relevant to the operation of the franchised business. All of our manuals are considered confidential trade secrets. This manual is confidential and remains our property. We will modify and upgrade this manual as the occasion warrants but the modification will not alter your status and rights under the Franchise Agreement. (Franchise Agreement, Paragraph II. A.1)

2) Initial Franchise Training. Within 10 to 60 days of your signing the Franchise Agreement, we will provide a minimum of 25 hours of training in the management and operation of the franchised business. You must attend and successfully complete the training prior to the opening of the franchised business. The training will be conducted at our main office or at the location of our choice. The training schedule outlined below will cover all aspects of the franchise operation including but not limited to:

(1) Nutrition Fundamentals
(2) Handling inbound calls about the diet
(3) Types of Dieters
(4) Fluctuating Blood Sugar
(5) Handling Difficult Dieters
(6) Marketing
(7) Local Advertising
(8) Vendor Negotiation
(9) Community Involvement
(10) Newsletters, Specials, PR, and Buzz
(11) Inventory, vendors, and suppliers
(12) Time Management
(13) Competition

Subject	Time Begun	Learning Materials	Hours: Classroom Training	Hours: On-the-Job Training	Instructor
Weight Loss Industry	8 AM Day 1	Handouts	3	4	Staff
Fluctuating Blood Sugar	8 AM Day 2	Handouts, Books provided	5	2	Maureen
Dieting Behavior	8 AM Day 2	Manual	4	3	Maureen
Telephone Sales	8 AM Day 3	Audio	2	5	Kathleen, Staff
Diabetes, Eating Disorders, etc.	8 AM Day 4	Manual, Handouts	7	0	Staff

Subject	Time Begun	Learning Materials	Hours: Classroom Training	Hours: On-the-Job Training	Instructor
Community Involvement	8 AM Day 5	Handouts	5	2	Staff
Vendor Negotiation	8 AM Day 6	Books provided	4	0	Staff

This training is included in the franchise fee. You must pay all of your living expenses and travel, lodging, and sustenance. All training occurs at our Los Altos or Burlingame, CA and Redmond, WA centers or a designation of our choice and the initial training is mandatory. Initial training is for one owner/manager and one other employee. Any additional employees or persons to be trained will be charged a per diem training instructor's fee of $200 per instructor. This charge is subject to consumer price increases based on annual rates as determined by the applicable CPI (Consumer Price Index) for your territory covering the inflationary price increases as compared with the year of opening of the Franchise.

Additional training will be conducted as we deem necessary. (Franchise Agreement, Paragraph II.A.2)

It is at our sole discretion as to whether or not you have successfully completed the initial training program or any subsequent training program.

Subsequent training classes, both mandatory and non-mandatory, will be offered from time to time at our discretion, with you required to bear all costs of travel to and lodging and sustenance at the training sites. (Franchise Agreement, Paragraph II.A.2)

3) Initial Supplies. We will provide initial supplies of proprietary and confidential materials. (Franchise Agreement, Paragraph II.A.3.)

4) Additional Trainees. Training is for one owner/manager and one other employee. Any additional employees or persons to be trained will be charged a per diem training instructor's fee of $200 per instructor. This charge is subject to consumer price increases based on annual rates as determined by the applicable CPI (Consumer Price Index) for your territory covering the inflationary price increases as compared with the year of opening of the Franchise. (Franchise Agreement, Paragraph II.A.4)

5) Territorial and Site Assistance. We will advise you in obtaining the necessary demographics, including number of people in your territory, and assist you locating your site. (Franchise Agreement, Paragraph II.A.5)

During the operation of the franchised business, we will:
1. provide, according to the extent required by us, in our sole judgment, a continuing advisory service which shall include consultation on promotional, business, or operations problems and analysis of your services, sales, marketing, and financial data at times and places and to the extent designated by us. (Franchise Agreement, Paragraph II.B.1)
2. provide from time to time a list of updated suppliers or manufacturers of supplies and products approved, but not purchased from us. (Franchise Agreement, Paragraph II.B.2)
3. provide you with evaluations of sources of supplies and products recommended by you for

use in the franchise system. (Franchise Agreement, Paragraph II.B.3)

4. develop institutional public relations, advertising, and promotional campaign designed primarily to benefit and assist all franchisees and to promote and enhance the value of all of our franchisees where possible. (Franchise Agreement, Paragraph II.B.4)

5. supervise the advertising in accordance with our advertising standards. Any dispute regarding the direction of advertising between us and you will be resolved on the following basis: all advertising is to bring name recognition first to our national prominence and secondly to our franchisee in any individual area. (Franchise Agreement, Paragraph II.B.5 and 6)

6. provide you with a uniform system of accounting and record keeping including standardized forms. (Franchise Agreement, Paragraph II.B.7)

7. provide subsequent training classes, both mandatory and non-mandatory, offered from time to time, with you required to pay all costs of travel, lodging, and sustenance. Mandatory trainings will not be held more than twice a year. If you request special training, and we agree, a charge for the instructor(s) may be added. (Franchise Agreement, Paragraph II.B.8)

The Table of Contents of our Confidential Operation Manual as of our last fiscal year end, including the number of pages devoted to each subject, is as follows:

1.	Lite For Life History and Philosophy	10 pages
2.	The Lite For Life Weight Reduction Program	90 pages
3.	Telephone Sales	15 pages
4.	The Initial Consultation	45 pages
5.	Marketing Your Center	50 pages
6.	Eye on the Bottom Line	20 pages
7.	Center Management	60 pages
8.	Business Management	25 pages
9.	Personnel Leadership	45 pages
		360 pages

Our instructors have a minimum of 5 years' experience in this business.

Franchisees must open their business within one to three months after signing their franchise agreement or first payment. The factors that affect the selection of your site within your territory include the square footage and layout, potential for signage, ample parking, easy access, appearance of building, lease terms, improvements, etc.

It normally takes us 10 days to approve your requested territory.

Factors that may affect the time period in your opening schedule include financing availability and delays in equipment and/or inventory delivery.

There is no advertising council or a co-op advertising group at this time. If we decide to form a co-op advertising group of franchisees with our stores, we and all franchisees will contribute equally, with us as the administrator under written governing documents made available to all. Monthly accounting of the funds will be made. None of these funds will be used for the solicitation of franchisees. (Franchise Agreement, Paragraph II.B.9)

ITEM 12. TERRITORY

The size of your exclusive territory is determined primarily by a population of at least a minimum of 100,000 middle-income persons living within an acceptable radius that would allow for daily visits by the dieter, unless demographic constraints naturally limit this number. The map attached to the franchise agreement shows the agreed upon boundary outlined in red for contract purposes.

You are granted a designated territory wherein only you will have a center and where we cannot open or operate a similar operation or appoint a franchised operation to operate a location within this designated area for the purpose of servicing customers.

There is no minimum sales quota, market penetration, or contingency requirements that would alter your territory. You maintain the same rights to your area even if the population increases or decreases.

ITEM 13. TRADEMARKS

You have the right to operate your business under the principal service mark "LITE FOR LIFE" trademark that identifies your business. A "LITE FOR LIFE" service mark application for registration was filed on February 19, 2003 by Lite For Life, Inc. and was in turn the subject of an exclusive service mark license to us by them with the right to sublicense subject to reserving to the Licensor the use of the mark for their company-owned offices with the U.S. Patent and Trademark Office. By not having a Principal Register federal registration for "LITE FOR LIFE," we do not have certain presumptive legal rights at this time granted by registration for this mark only.

By "trademarks," we mean trade names, trademarks, service marks, and logos used to identify your weight loss center.

You must follow our rules when you use these marks. You cannot use a name or mark as part of a corporate name or with modifying words, designs, or symbols except for those which we license to you. You may not use our registered name in connection with the sale of an unauthorized product or service or in a manner not authorized in writing by us.

No agreements limit our right to use or license the use of our trademarks. You are restricted to use the name and service mark in your dba in such a format and with such a suffix or prefix as the law and/or we may, from time to time, designate, including such designations as "LITE FOR LIFE of _____" and to indicate the required trademark, service mark, or copyright notices in the form specified by us.

You must notify us immediately when you learn about an infringement of or challenge to your use of our trademark. We will take the action we think appropriate. While we are not required to defend you against a claim against your use of our trademark, you must notify us immediately when you learn about the infringement or challenge. However, we may take over the defense of such claim and settle it as we think fit.

You must modify or discontinue the use of a trademark if we modify or discontinue it. If this happens, we will reimburse you for your tangible costs of compliance in such matters as the reasonable cost of changing your exterior signs only. You must not directly or indirectly contest our right to our trademarks, trade secrets, or business techniques that are part of our business. We do not know of any infringing uses or litigation that could significantly affect the ownership or use of our principal trademark.

There are no currently material determinations of the Patent and Trademark Office, Trademark Trial and Appeal Board, the Trademark Administrator of this State or any court; pending infringement, opposition, or cancellation; and pending material litigation involving the principal trademarks. We do not know of any infringing use or litigation that could significantly affect the ownership or use of a principal trademark.

ITEM 14. PATENTS, COPYRIGHTS, AND PROPRIETARY INFORMATION

No patents are material to the franchise. We presently have proprietary rights in numerous items, such as advertising designs and the like, relating to the operation of our business, which are suitable for copyright protection. We reserve to ourselves or our designee any and all rights which we have in and to such items. We may, in our sole discretion, obtain copyright registrations for any unregistered items.

Although we have not filed an application for a copyright registration for the Operations Manual, we claim a copyright and the information is proprietary. Item 11 describes limitations on the use of this manual by you and your employees. You must also promptly tell us when you learn about unauthorized use of this proprietary information. We are not obligated to take any action but will respond to this information as we think appropriate.

ITEM 15. OBLIGATION TO PARTICIPATE IN THE ACTUAL OPERATION OF THE FRANCHISE BUSINESS

You, if a sole proprietor or the principal owner or owners of the Franchise (if a partnership or corporation is the franchisee), are required to personally supervise the direct operation of the franchised business for at least 40 hours per week divided equally between all locations owned. Franchisees are prohibited from the delegation of operational responsibility of the franchised business to any other person except as may otherwise be set forth in a written agreement between us and you or approved in writing by us. Only qualified, trained citizens meeting our standards of experience and background may be hired by you and you are responsible to see that your employees and independent contractors sign confidentiality agreements enforceable in your state. Preferably, the facility should be supervised by personnel that have participated in the program successfully.

The shareholders of a corporate franchisee must sign the Franchise Agreement individually assuming and agreeing to discharge all of the obligations of the "Franchisee" under the franchise agreement.

ITEM 16. RESTRICTIONS ON WHAT THE FRANCHISEE MAY SELL

You may sell or offer for sale to the public only prior approved products, including supplements and food, goods, and services of the kind and quality that comply with the reasonable standards designated in the Operating Manual or by written directives provided by us to you from time to time. You may not use our name, marks, or symbols in any business other than the franchised business. All products must be from an approved vendor.

ITEM 17. RENEWAL, TERMINATION, TRANSFER, AND DISPUTE RESOLUTION

Provision	Section in Franchise Agreement	Summary
a. Term of the franchise	III	10 years from time you commence business
b. Renewal or extension of term	III	You can renew for unlimited additional five-year periods, providing: (1) you are not in default or in violation of the Franchise Agreement or any other agreement with us, and (2) upon execution of the then current Franchise Agreement under the terms in effect at that time, including new royalty rates, advertising fees, etc., with the exception that the length of term or renewal shall not change nor your territory. We may refuse to renew the Franchise Agreement if you are in default or violation of your Franchise Agreement and/or fail to execute the then current Franchise Agreement. The renewal fee charged to you by us is estimated at $1,000 to cover our legal fees and administrative and overhead cost associated with the renewal. The renewal fees are subject to Consumer Price Index increases based on annual inflationary rates as determined by applicable CPI in your territory.
c. Requirements for you to renew or extend	III	Sign new agreement, pay fee, and good standing.
d. Termination by you	X (K) (1) and (2)	With our consent or for cause with 30 days to cure.
e. Termination by us without cause	None	
f. Termination by us with cause	X (G)	We can terminate only if you default or are in default.

Provision	Section in Franchise Agreement	Summary
g. "Cause" defined— defaults which can be cured	X	You have 30 days to cure: (a) attachments; (b) adverse business conduct; (c) defaults between us; (d) unapproved assignment; (e) failure to pay after five days' notice; (f) guarantor default; (g) failure to cure franchise agreement default within 10 days after notice; (h) failure to pay or conduct a required audit after 10 days' notice; (i) non-submission of reports; (j) failure to follow directives or attend mandatory training; (k) failure to work 400 hours per week; (i) failure to keep true and correct business records and books or to open same for inspection or provide us with tax returns; (m) failure to maintain fixtures, etc.; (n) failure to maintain confidentiality; (o) failure to operate a weight loss center outfitted to our specifications; (p) failure to purchase from approved vendors; (q) failure to participate in any approved purchasing or distribution cooperative or purchase required equipment.
h. "Cause" defined— defaults which cannot be cured	X (G)	Non-curable defaults: (a) you file any form of bankruptcy; (b) you abandon your franchise by failing to operate the business for five consecutive days or by mutual written agreement; (c) you make any material misrepresentations relating to the operation of the franchise; (d) you, for a period of 10 days after notice, fail to comply with any federal, state, or local law or regulation; (e) you, after curing any failure in accordance with the franchise agreement, engage in the same non-compliance, whether or not such non-compliance is corrected after notice; (f) you repeatedly fail to comply with one or more requirements of the franchise, whether or not corrected after notice; (g) the franchise business or business premises are seized, taken over by government, or foreclosed by a creditor; (h) you are convicted of a felony or any other criminal misconduct which is relevant to the operation of the franchise; (j) you fail to pay any franchise fees or other amounts due us or our affiliate within five days after receiving written notice that such fees are overdue; and (j) we make a reasonable determination that the continued operation causes an imminent danger to public health or safety.

Provision	Section in Franchise Agreement	Summary
i. Your obligations on termination/non-renewal	XI	You will promptly and immediately cease using our trade names, service marks, or trademarks and will cease identifying the business as a member of our system; will forthwith cease operating a franchise; will promptly remove all signs bearing our names and identification; will cause any registration of said names to be cancelled or withdrawn or, in the alternative, if requested by us, will assign such registered names to us or our nominee; will return to us or our representatives immediately upon written demand, all customer lists, records, and books of account pertaining to your business and all training films, forms, materials, and manuals belonging to us or bearing our name or service mark, with delivery being made directly to us or our authorized representatives. You will immediately cancel all telephone listing, yellow page ads, and discontinue the use of any telephone numbers used in conjunction with the franchise business. However, upon our written request, you will assign said telephone numbers to us or our designee and will use your best efforts to secure the cooperation of the telephone company in assigning such numbers to us or our designees.
j. Assignment of contract by us	XIII (K)	No restriction on our right to assign.
k. "Transfer" by you—definition	X (A to F)	Includes transfer of contract and/or assets or ownership change.
l. Our approval of transfer by franchisee	X	We have reasonable right to approve.
m. Conditions for our approval of transfer	X	New franchisee qualifies, transfer fee paid, purchase price paid by franchisee, agreement signed by new franchisee (also see r, below).
n. Our right of first refusal to acquire your business	X (A), (B), and (C)	We can match any offer for the franchisee's business.
o. Our option to purchase your business	X (A), (B), and (C)	We have the right of first refusal to your business except for transfers to approved issue and/or spouse exercisable within 30 days. We can purchase anytime you attempt to transfer.

Provision	Section in Franchise Agreement	Summary
p. Your death or disability	X (A) (1) (2)	The franchise must be assigned by the estate to approved buyer in six months.
q. Non-competition covenants during the term of the franchise	VII (A) (D)	You cannot operate similar business.
r. Non-competition covenants after franchisee is terminated	VII (B)	No competing businesses for three years following termination within 50 miles of another franchisee.
s. Modification of the agreement	XIII (D)	None.
t. Integration/merger-clause	XIII	Only the terms of the agreement are binding (subject to state law). Other promises may not be enforceable.
u. Dispute resolution by arbitration or mediation	XIII	Except for certain claims, all disputes arbitrated and mediated in Burlingame, California before AAA or FAM.
v. Choice of forum	XIII (M)	Litigation must be in California.
w. Choice of law	XIII (N)	California law applies.

States having laws or laws concerning termination or non-renewal include Arkansas (Stat. 70-807), California (Bus. & Prof. Code Sections 20000-20043), Connecticut (Gen. Stat. Section 42-113e et seq.), Delaware (Code, tit.), Hawaii (Rev. Stat. Section 482E-1), Illinois (815 IL CS 705/20), Indiana (Stat. Section 23-2-2.7), Iowa (Code Sections 523H.1 - 523.17), Michigan (Stat. Section 19.854(27)), Minnesota (Stat. Section 80C.14), Mississippi (Code Section 75-24-51), Missouri (Stat. Section 407.400), Nebraska (Rev. Stat. Section 87-401), New Jersey (Stat. Section 56:10-1), South Dakota (Codified Laws Section 37-5A-51), Virginia (Code 13.1-557-574-13.1-564), Washington (Code Section 19.100.180), Wisconsin (Stat. Section 135.03). These and other states may have court decisions which may supersede the franchise agreement in your relationship with the franchisor, including the areas of termination and renewal of your franchise. The laws of the applicable state where the franchisee will operate regarding termination of franchises should be checked thoroughly by Franchisee's counsel. If you are purchasing a franchise in California, please read Exhibit D, entitled "California Appendix."

ITEM 18. PUBLIC FIGURES

We do not use any public figure to promote our franchise.

ITEM 19. EARNINGS CLAIMS

We do not furnish or authorize our salespersons to furnish any oral or written information concerning the actual or potential sales, costs, income, or profits of any Lite For Life franchise or company-owned units. Actual results vary from unit to unit and we cannot estimate the results of any particular franchise.

ITEM 20. LIST OF OUTLETS

Franchised Center Status Summary for Last 3 Fiscal Years (2002/2001/2000)

State	Transfers	Canceled/ Terminated	Not Renewed	Reacquired by Franchisor	Left the System/ Other	Total Left Columns	Franchises Operating at Year End
Washington	0/0/0	0/0/0	0/0/0	0/0/0	0/0/0	0/0/0	0/0/0
California	0/0/0	0/0/0	0/0/0	0/0/0	0/0/0	0/0/0	0/0/0
Total	0/0/0	0/0/0	0/0/0	0/0/0	0/0/0	0/0/0	0/0/0

Note: All numbers are as of effective date of this UFOC and as of March 31. for each year thereafter."

The numbers in the "Total" column may exceed the number of franchises affected because several events may have affected the same franchise.

There have been no transfers, cancelled or terminated or not renewed or reacquired franchises by the franchisor.

Please refer to Exhibit F for the list of franchisees.

Status of Company-Owned Centers for the Last Three Fiscal Years (2002/2001/2000)

State	Centers Closed During Year	Centers Opened During Year	Total Centers Operating at Year End
Washington	0/0/0	1/0/0	1/0/0
California	0/0/0	0/0/0	3/3/3
Total	0/0/0	1/0/0	4/3/3

Note: The above new company location is owned and operated by an affiliate.

Projected Openings as of July 1, 2003

State	Franchise Agreements Signed but Center Not Opened	Projected New Franchises Next Fiscal Year	Projected Company Owned Center Openings Next Fiscal Year
Washington	0	0	0
California	0	8	0
Total	0	8	0

ITEM 21. FINANCIAL STATEMENTS

Audited financial statements in accordance with generally accepted accounting principles have been prepared for the period ending June 15, 2003 and are attached to this offering circular as Exhibit B.

ITEM 22. CONTRACTS

Attached as Exhibit A is a copy of the Franchise Agreement proposed to be used in this state.

ITEM 23. RECEIPT

Exhibit G is a detachable document prepared in duplicate acknowledging receipt of the offering circular by the prospective Franchisee. You must sign both copies. Keep one copy for your records. Please return the other copy to: Attention: President, Lite For Life Franchising Corporation, Inc., 1199 Howard Ave., Suite 102, Burlingame, California 94010.

Note: In the actual document you will find the exhibits at this part of the document.

Appendix B-1
Franchise Agreement
Rocksolid Granit (USA)

sample document of a *product*-type franchise agreement (where a unique product is sold and installed) is included in this Appendix B-1 to illustrate typical terms and restrictions contained in most product/installation-type franchise agreements.

As either a potential franchisor or a prospective franchisee, acquaint yourself with the evaluation pointers discussed in Chapter 2, Learning About Franchise Documents, and other portions of this book, and make your own evaluation of the sample franchise agreement.

As a franchisor, be aware of your franchisee's needs, because if the franchisee fails, so will you. You will want to supply all the support necessary to ensure the possibility of your franchisee's success.

Franchise Agreement
ROCKSOLID GRANIT (USA) INC.
11098 Inland Avenue
Mira Loma, California 91752
866 685-5300 or 909 685-5300
Table of Contents

***Note:** In your franchise agreement, you must provide page numbers. They have been omitted in this sample to avoid confusion with the book's page numbers.

ROCKSOLID GRANIT (USA), INC.
FRANCHISE AGREEMENT

THIS FRANCHISE AGREEMENT is entered into and effective this _____ day of _____, 200__ by and between ROCKSOLID GRANIT (USA) INC. 11098 Inland Avenue, Mira Loma, California 91752 (hereinafter called "we," "us," etc.) and _____ (hereinafter called "you").

WHEREAS, you hereby acknowledge that this Franchise Agreement was accompanied by a Uniform Franchise Offering Circular which you received at the earlier of: (1) the first personal meeting with us; (2) 10 business days prior to the signing of any franchise agreement; or (3) 10 business days before any payment by you. In addition, you acknowledge receipt of this Franchise Agreement containing all material terms at the time of the delivery of the Uniform Franchise Offering Circular. These representations are not intended to nor will they act as a release, estoppel, or waiver of any liability incurred under the Maryland Franchise Registration and Disclosure Law.

WHEREAS, you are desirous of obtaining a franchise system for the purpose of joining a network of independently owned professional businesses providing the marketing, sales and installation of various approved products such as "Rocksolid Granit®," a reconstituted slab applied to new and existing surfaces including vanities, countertops, kitchens, bathrooms, and fireplaces to occupied housing units. The Franchisees are distinguished by the service mark "GRANITE TRANSFORMA-TIONS®" and other trademarks, service marks, trade names, logo types, commercial symbols, unique forms and materials, centrally coordinated advertisements, relatively low overhead operating expenses as well as our true commitment to customer service.

NOW THEREFORE, we and you, intending to be legally bound, for and in consideration of the mutual covenants hereinafter following, do mutually covenant and agree:

ARTICLE 1. GRANT OF FRANCHISE LICENSE

1.1 License Rights. We hereby grant you the right, during the term of this agreement, to use the service mark "GRANITE TRANSFORMATIONS®" within your territory. You are licensed to operate the franchised business under such names and such other trademarks, service marks, trade names, logo types, commercial symbols, and copyrights as we may designate from time to time solely for the purpose of identifying and advertising the franchised business. You are designated as a participant in our system while operating your franchise. Such business will be conducted by you from your approved site, which may feature our trademarks, service marks, trade names, logotypes, or commercial symbols and approved material within a designated exclusive territory. You have no right to delegate, franchise, or sub-franchise the right to use the marks or to authorize independent contractors or any third party with whom you transact business to use the marks.

1.2 Office Site. We grant you the right to use and operate from a single, approved office site within your designated territory with the service mark "GRANITE TRANSFORMATIONS®" as the primary identity of your business.

1.3 Use of Marks. You will use the marks in signage, business cards, stationery, promotional materials, and advertising only in the form, manner, and extent required or permitted as set forth herein, or by the Confidential Business Operations Manual or by us. You will not use any of the marks as part of your trade or corporation name but file appropriate notices required under an applicable fictitious or assumed name law.

1.4 Trade Practices. You agree that we have the sole rights to certain trade practices pertaining to our business practices and procedures and that no goodwill associated with any of the trade practices will vest in or inure to you. It is further agreed that the items of this trade practice constitute our trade secrets, which are revealed to you in confidence, and you will not, at any time during the term of this Agreement or anytime thereafter, use or attempt to use the trade practices in connection with any other entity or business in which you have an interest, direct or indirect, nor will you disclose, duplicate, reveal, sell, or sub-license the trade practices or any part thereof or any way transfer any rights in the trade practices except as authorized by us.

1.5 Reservation of All Rights. We reserve all rights, except as precisely provided herein, including the right to offer or open additional company-owned sites and additional franchises.

ARTICLE 2. EXCLUSIVE AREA OR TERRITORY

2.1 Exclusive Territorial Aspects and Minimums. Your territory is exclusive in that we will not designate or allow a franchise-owned site offering the same service to be physically opened or operated from an approved site location within your territory nor will we service or grant other franchisees to service occupied domestic housing units located in your territory. However, your retail domestic territory is non-exclusive in that we or any other franchisee may solicit and service any units such as commercial housing buildings, hotels, motels, new housing developments, commercial buildings including offices, etc. within your territory. By the same token, you may solicit or service any such units or other buildings as mentioned in the previous sentence. We will pre-approve your operational site based on the facility. Such approval will not be unreasonably withheld by us. Each territory purchased is outlined on a map attached to the Franchise Agreement. If we cannot agree on your site for you within sixty (60) days of receipt of your down payment, our agreement will be terminated.

2.2. Franchisee's Exclusive Territory. The exclusive territory boundaries will be as follows:
Territory: _____
_____
_____

See outlined map of your territory boundaries attached as Schedule 1.

ARTICLE 3. TRADEMARKS, SERVICE MARKS, TRADE NAMES, LOGOTYPES, AND COMMERCIAL SYMBOLS

3.1 Federal Service Mark Registrations. We grant you the right to operate and use at one location and only within the boundaries of your defined territory our service mark "GRANITE TRANSFORMATIONS®" as your identifying mark as well as other service mark designs that we may develop for your business.

3.2 Restrictions on Use. You are restricted to use the name and service mark "GRANITE TRANS-FORMATIONS®" in your "d/b/a" in such a format and with such suffixes as the law and/or we may from time to time designate, including such designation as "GRANITE TRANSFORMATIONS®" of: "_____" (name of city, town, or county where you are located).

3.3 Fictitious Name Filing. You are required to file the necessary fictitious name affidavit applicable to your county or state for your approved d/b/a. However, you cannot use our trademarks or service marks in your corporate or business trade name.

3.4 Service Mark Protection. We are not required to protect you against claims of infringement or unfair competition arising out of the use of our trademarks, service marks, or logos or defend you in any legal action arising thereof. However, we will take such action that we think is appropriate under the circumstances, provided you have promptly notified us in writing of the facts of such claims or challenges and if you have used such service marks, trademarks, or logos in strict accordance with the provisions of the Franchise Agreement and all rules, regulations, directives, and procedures provided by us. However, we may take over the defense of the action at any time if we initially declined to take over the defense.

3.5 Control of Actions and Service Mark Usage. We alone have the sole right to control any legal actions or proceedings including settlements involving service mark infringement or unfair competition against you or against others using our marks without our permission. We may, at our sole discretion, prosecute or defend any infringements or unfair competition involving our marks or any other actions or proceedings which we deem necessary or desirable for the protection of our service marks, trademarks or logos and you agree not to contest our right, title, or interest in such marks and logos. If it becomes advisable at any time in our discretion to modify or discontinue the use of any such logos, names, or marks or institute the use of one or more additional or substituted names or marks, you must do so at our sole expense for reasonable and tangible costs.

ARTICLE 4. OPERATIONS MANUAL

4.1 Operations Manual. You will be lent a Confidential Operations Manual at your training which will contain specifications, instructions, and specified parameters developed by us, which are to be strictly followed.

4.2 Confidential Operations Manual Prerequisites. You acknowledge and understand that you will receive one copy of the Confidential Operations Manual ("Manual") and subsequent updates and agree to abide by all policies and rules set forth therein and to require any employees to abide by all such policies and rules. The Manual and systems remain our property and all rights therein and must be returned to us promptly upon expiration or termination of this Franchise Agreement. The Manual and systems are considered to contain proprietary information and our trade secrets.

4.3 Additions and Modifications. We may, in our reasonable business judgment, add to or otherwise modify the Manual and systems, from time to time, for all franchisees uniformly and on a nondiscriminatory basis, if possible, whenever we consider such additions or modifications desirable to improve or maintain the standards of our franchise system and to effectuate the efficient operation or to protect or maintain the goodwill associated with the marks, or to meet the demands of competition.

ARTICLE 5. TRAINING

5.1 Training. We will provide you with training in operating the franchise as set forth in the following paragraphs to enable you to independently operate your franchised business.

5.2 Training Programs. We will provide initial, mandatory, and optional training programs. We will conduct training programs at our designated training facilities in various locations and at various times to be named by us.

5.3 Initial Training. We will provide an initial training at our headquarters site for a period of three to five days a week exclusive of Saturdays and Sundays up to 14 days, eight hours per day including one hour for lunch, to be scheduled by us at our discretion. We will train you prior to the opening of your franchise as further specified in Article 8.3. The initial training will cover all aspects of the franchise operation and will include hands-on classroom training.

5.4 Failure to Complete Initial Training or Open. If you and your designated manager fail to complete the initial training program to our satisfaction or to open within 120 days of payment of the franchise fee, we may terminate this agreement. You must complete this required training at least 10 days prior to your opening date. You and your manager must attend and complete the training to our satisfaction.

5.5 On-Site Training. We will provide three to five days of continued training regarding hands-on sales and construction methods and efficiencies at your location and local work sites, all to be conducted by us at a mutually agreed time with our trainers' travel, subsistence, and lodging at our expense. Any training requested by you exceeding the initial five days of training will be at your expense for our instructors, travel, subsistence, lodging, and reasonable per diem charges. (See Article 8.6.)

5.6 Subsequent Mandatory and Optional Training Programs. We will also provide, from time to time, subsequent mandatory and optional training programs on selling techniques, services, preferred suppliers, management skills, customer service standards, and other aspects of business operations which we believe are useful to franchisees. These programs are conducted for various lengths of time and at various locations selected by us. Certain programs will be offered at no charge, while others may require a fee. (See Articles 6.8, 8.6, and 8.11.)

5.7 Additional Special Training Requested by You. Additional, optional, or special training may be requested by you. If you request additional or special training, and we agree, a charge for the special training may be required by us. (See Article 6.8 below.)

5.8 Franchisor's Initial Training Expenses. We provide and pay only for the training instructors, facilities, and training material in connection with our initial training programs at the time you purchase and open your franchise business.

5.9 Franchisee's Initial Training Expenses. You must pay all expenses incurred by you, your designated manager, and your employees in connection with all training programs including, without limitation, the cost of your travel, entertainment, room, board, and wages for the duration of all training programs.

ARTICLE 6. FRANCHISEE'S FEES AND OTHER PAYMENTS

6.1 Initial Franchise Fee. You will pay us a uniform, non-refundable initial franchise fee of $ _____ payable upon signing this Agreement. All fees and payments referenced in this agreement will be paid in US dollars.

6.2 Monthly Service Fee and Minimum Payment. In consideration of the franchise granted, you are required to pay us a continuing Monthly Service Fee of 2% of your gross monthly sales during the term of the franchise agreement. The Monthly Service Fee is nonrefundable and due and payable by the 10th calendar day after the end of the previous month based on gross sales for the previous month.

6.3 Gross Sales Defined. The term "gross sales" is defined to include all sums or things of value received by you in and from your business from all sales of services, goods, and products, whether for cash, check, credit, barter, or otherwise without reserve or deduction for inability or failure to collect same including, without limitation, such sales and services where the orders thereof originated at or accepted by you at one location or site but were delivered or performed at any other location or site. Gross sales do not include refunds to customers or the amount of any sales taxes or any similar taxes collected from customers to be paid to any federal, state, or local taxing authority. All such items, including non-collectible accounts, which are claimed as deductions to gross sales must be supported by proper documentation.

6.4 Local Advertising and Possible Cooperatives. You are also required to spend a minimum sum equal to 3% of your monthly gross sales on advertising to generate leads and enhance the reputation of your service on a local level due and payable to advertising media during each month. In the event we negotiate a contract with national accounts such as hotels, motels, government authorities, national office complexes, hardware chains, home improvement chains, or other nationwide or regional stores with facilities in your territory identifying you as an authorized installer of our reconstituted slab systems, any commission charged by same for any referral resulting in a proven installation by you will be credited against your 3% minimum monthly advertising obligation and you agree to abide by such contracts. All advertising must be approved by us. You are required to substantiate the minimum advertising required by supplying such written information as we may require on a weekly, monthly, quarterly, annual, or other basis. You may be required to make contributions to a comparative advertising fund set up by us of a minimum of 2% of your gross monthly sales which will be credited against your minimum monthly advertising obligation. In the future you must join any future national or local advertising cooperative when we direct you at our sole discretion. You are obligated to contribute to any such cooperative fund. We are not obligated to contribute to the fund but may do so at our complete discretion. The managers of the cooperative may be selected by us. We or our designee may manage the comparative fund. The 2% that you contribute can only be increased by a majority vote of the franchisee members and is payable to us or a cooperative account to be used on corporate branding and national marketing.

6.5 Transfer Fee. You will be required to pay a nonrefundable transfer fee (except where a transfer is to your spouse, your adult child [18 years or older], or your corporation or entity in which you own the majority of stock or interest) of $1,500 upon any assignment, sale, or transfer of the franchise to cover our costs of research, administration, and, where we deem necessary, the cost of training the new franchisee in our system. This transfer fee may be increased to reflect increases in your local applicable Consumer Price Index.

6.6 Renewal Fee. The term of the franchise commences from the date the Franchise Agreement is executed for a ten (10) year period. The renewal fee is $1,000 for each renewal period. You can renew for unlimited additional periods of ten (10) years each providing you are not in default or in violation of the Franchise Agreement and upon execution of our then-current Franchise Agreement (or if no agreement is in effect in the state, then the last agreement, at our sole discretion, executed by the last franchisee within the United States) under the terms in effect at that time, including new service fee rates, advertising fees, etc., with the exception that the length of a term or renewal term will not change nor will your territory change without your prior consent.

6.7 Yellow Pages Advertising by Franchisee. We may require you to advertise in the yellow pages and any such advertising by you will be first approved by us.

6.8 Special or Additional Training Program Expenses. Special or additional training programs may be implemented by us at our discretion or at your special request to help you effectively succeed in the operation of your franchised business where we deem a particular franchisee or franchisees are in need of such training. The expenses for special or additional training programs will be borne by you, including all expenses for instructors, facilities, and training manuals in addition to you or your designee's personal expenses, including travel, meals, or lodging. These expenses will not be uniform, but will vary according to your location or in relation to the training facilities and other variables. (See Article 5.7 above.)

6.9 Audit and Late Payment Fee. You agree that we have the right to verify the information contained in your reports to us by inspecting and auditing your records. If any such inspection or audit discloses a deficiency in payments exceeding 2% due to us under the Franchise Agreement, you must immediately pay the deficiency and you must also pay travel, lodging, meals, salaries, and reasonable professional service fees and other expenses of the inspecting or auditing personnel. Such payments are not refundable under any circumstances. If any such inspection or audit discloses an overpayment, we will credit the overpayment to your account. Any payment owed to us but not paid when due bears interest at a rate equal to the maximum contract rate allowed by the governing state law.

6.10 Delinquent Payments and Fees. Any payment or fee not received on time payable from you to us will bear interest at the rate equal to the maximum contract rate allowed by governing state law from the date due until the date received by us.

6.11 Insurance. At all times during the term of the Franchise Agreement, you will maintain in effect a policy or policies of insurance naming us as an additional insured on the face of each policy at your sole cost and expense, subject to change from time to time, including the following:

(A) Professional public liability policy that includes comprehensive general liability coverage in the amount of $1,000,000 per occurrence and errors and omissions coverage.

(B) Additional insurance, including fire extended coverage, worker's compensation insurance, and unemployment compensation for any employees you may choose to hire.

(C) All insurance coverage required by city, county, state, or federal agencies.

6.12 Acceptable Insurance Companies. All insurance will be with insurers acceptable to us.

Insurance amounts may be changed from time to time upon receipt of written demand from us. All policies of insurance will be renewed timely and copies of all policies and certificates, together with evidence of payment of premiums, will be delivered to us at least thirty (30) days prior to the expiration of such policies by certified mail or by hand delivery with receipt.

6.13 Customer Disputes. You will use your best efforts to resolve satisfactorily any customer disputes and refund any amounts disputed by the customer for services that the customer deems unsatisfactory. (See also Article 7.9 for further details.)

6.14 Reports, Agencies, and Organizations. You are also required to compile and report certain information to us as required by us or the Operations Manual. You also must maintain any membership and/or filing requirements with agencies and organizations necessary to enable your continued functioning as a franchisee. You must file duplicate copies of reports with us when filed with any agency or organization.

6.15 Monthly Financial Statements. You must submit to us, no later than the 10th day of each month during the term of the Franchise Agreement, a monthly gross sales and revenue statement and a detailed report evidencing the advertising that you purchased on forms prescribed by us accurately reflecting all gross sales and revenues during the preceding month and such other data and information regarding the operation of the franchised business as we may require.

6.16 Annual Financial Statements. Annually, within sixty (60) days after the close of your fiscal year, you are to submit to us, if we so request it in writing, an income and expense statement and a balance sheet as well as any other statement that we may request reflecting the operation of your business as it stands at the end of the fiscal year, setting forth in each case corresponding figures in comparative form for the preceding year and compiled by you or by your accountant. All statements must be in reasonable detail and in accordance with generally accepted accounting practices and accompanied by a declaration from you with reports of information required by us each year for completion by you.

6.17 Franchisee's Tax Returns. Annually, within 120 days after the close of your fiscal year, you are required to submit to us, if we so request it in writing, a copy of your federal and state tax returns and all amendments thereto prepared for the franchise business and a letter from you or your accountant stating as applicable whether or not (1) all payroll tax returns have been filed and payroll taxes paid to the end of the fiscal period, (2) all federal returns have been filed and taxes, and (3) all state income tax returns have been filed and any payments due have been paid.

6.18 Cost of Accounting Services. The costs of your accounting services for the above requirements are your responsibility and may vary substantially upon your size and location, but the requirements are imposed uniformly on all franchisees.

ARTICLE 7. OBLIGATIONS OF FRANCHISEE

Your obligations include:

7.1 Franchise Services. You will render the services specified in your Franchise Agreement, Operations Manual, and in writing by us. You will offer services and products to the general public, will maintain the highest professional and ethical standards, will observe any preferred suppliers program requirements, and will conduct no other business under our marks without our consent.

7.2 Full-Time Effort. You are obligated to devote your best efforts and dedicate your full time to the management of the franchised business in your office and in the field conducting both sales calls and at-the-job-site *supervision* unless a competent designated manager is employed to handle job-site supervision. Corporate or partnership franchisees must designate an individual upon whom we may rely for the personal and direct management of the franchised business.

7.3 Advertising Approvals. We reserve the right to designate or consent to the content, themes, materials, and placement of all advertising programs by you. You must submit all advertising to us for our approval at least twenty-one (21) business days (subject to deadlines) before publication unless specifically waived in writing by us as to each particular ad or advertising campaign. We may receive *and retain* rebates from national suppliers of materials purchased by our franchisees. You will not permit any advertising, including Web sites and links to and from the site, to be produced or published unless such material is furnished by or approved by us in writing. We do not currently grant you the right to use the name of a public figure or celebrity in your promotional efforts or advertising.

7.4 Employees. If you hire employees, you will use your best efforts to properly train or procure qualified and competent personnel in keeping with the standards established by us through our Operations Manual and our periodic directives, including the standards set for all services and products sold by you.

7.5 Leads. We will provide a system of distributing leads. (See also Article 8.8 for more details.)

7.6 Administrative Codes. You and your employees will adhere to any *applicable* administrative and *building* codes at all times when serving a customer.

7.7 Quality Control and Purchases of Rocksolid Granit® from Franchisor. You will operate the franchised business in accordance with our standards of quality, production, appearance, cleanliness, and service as prescribed by the Operations Manual and in writing by us. You may be required to purchase certain proprietary software and marketing materials from us. It is understood and agreed that proprietary software licenses are not transferable. You are required to purchase a minimum of 1,243 square feet (30 sheets) of Rocksolid Granit® each month *for your business needs* from us or an approved supplier subsequently designated by us in writing. We presently are the exclusive supplier of Rocksolid Granit® with a dimension of more than 1 meter (39.37 inches) x 1 meter (39.37 inches).

7.8 Customer Service Policies. You will conform to our customer service policies as set forth in the Operations Manual or as we may change as from time to time.

7.9 Customer Complaints. Any complaints from dissatisfied customers will receive prompt attention. Whenever possible, you will initiate contact within 24 hours after a complaint is received. Should you be unable to equitably resolve the complaint within seven (7) days after the complaint, you will contact us for advisory assistance in handling the complaint. (See also Article 6.13 above.)

7.10 Permits and Licenses. You will maintain all permits and licenses required for the operation of the franchised business.

7.11 Records and Reports. You will maintain all county, state, and federal records and reports and file them with the appropriate agency and provide copies of the same to us. Also, all records and reports as are required herein and by the Operations Manual must be filed expeditiously with us.

7.12 Annual Conventions. Each year an annual franchisee convention may be held to provide additional and current updates for the benefit of the franchisees and to award franchisees who have operated exceptional franchises. Franchisee attendance may be mandatory at all annual conventions.

7.13 Agreement Not to Compete. You agree that during the term of this Agreement or any extension hereof you will not compete with us. You further agree that for two (2) years after the termination hereof, you will not, without our prior written consent, either directly or indirectly as principal, agent, servant, or otherwise, carry on or engage in or have financial interest in the same or similar business in your territory as set forth in this agreement or within a 50-mile radius from your territorial boundaries. You acknowledge and agree that the damage caused to us by your violation of this Section shall constitute irreparable injury and accordingly, acknowledge and agree that we may enforce this section by applying for a temporary and/or permanent restraining order, temporary and/or permanent injunction, and any such other legal or equitable relief as may be appropriate.

7.14 Adherence to Franchisor's Policies and Procedures. It is understood and agreed that a material part of our consideration granting your license to you, without which we would not execute this Agreement, is that you agree to adhere strictly to the specifications, methods, policies, practices, and systems established by us in our matters and written directives for the management, marketing, and operation of the franchised business.

7.15 Timely Fees Payable. You are required to pay all fees herein in a timely manner.

7.16 Alternate Supplier Qualifications. In the event that you desire to purchase your required equipment and materials from someone other than us or our approved suppliers, you must submit a complete description of the history and credit rating of the supplier and satisfactory evidence that the supplier has the ability to stand by its product warranty, which must meet those of our designated suppliers, as well as a detailed description of such items, together with specifications and tests which will prove to us, at our satisfaction, that the equipment and materials are of equal or superior quality to those which we or our designated supplier may offer for sale to you at reasonable prices. We will approve or disapprove a prospective supplier according to our complete and final discretion within 10 business days of receipt of your request to purchase from alternate suppliers.

ARTICLE 8. OBLIGATIONS OF FRANCHISOR

Our obligations *prior to opening* of the franchised business are:

8.1 Territorial and Site Assistance. We will assist you in obtaining the necessary information and advise you on the best approach in the selecting of your base site within the territory and assist you with your showroom office layout plan. We will pre-approve your operational site based on the facility. Such approval will not be unreasonably withheld by us. Each territory purchased is outlined on a map attached to the Franchise Agreement. If we cannot agree on a site for you within sixty (60) days of receipt of your down payment, our agreement will be terminated. Factors which we consider in approving an area for your site include a neighborhood conducive to a proper show room fit and adequate parking and showroom space in such area. We will approve or disapprove an area in which you propose to open your site within 10 days of receiving written notice thereof from you.

8.2 Confidential Operations Manual. We will loan you one set of the confidential Operations Manual covering our operational procedures consisting of suggested, sales and marketing, operating management, installation, and administration procedures and follow-up programs.

8.3 Initial Franchisee Training. We will provide initial training at our headquarters and at local sites as we deem necessary to you and your sales personnel for three to five days a week up to 14 days (exclusive of Saturdays and Sundays), eight hours per day, including one hour for lunch, to be scheduled by us at our discretion. (See also Paragraph 5.3.)

8.4 List of Supplies and Equipment. We will provide you with a detailed list of all necessary tools, equipment, supplies and inventory and a list of approved suppliers.

The obligations performed by us during the operation of your business are in the following paragraphs.

8.5 On-Site Follow-Up Training. We will provide three to five days of continued training regarding hands-on sales methods, construction methods, and efficiencies at your location and local work sites, all to be conducted by us on mutually agreed dates with our trainers' travel, subsistence, and lodging at our expense for this period. Any training requested by you exceeding the initial five days of training shall be at your expense for our instructors' travel, subsistence, lodging, and a reasonable per diem charge. (Franchise Agreement, Paragraph 5.5)

8.6 Franchisor Consultations. We will provide, according to the extent required by us in our sole judgment, a continuing advisory service which shall include consultation on promotional, business, or operations problems, an analysis of your services, sales, marketing, and financial data at time and places and to the extent designated by us. We also will provide service and product information updates regarding our industry which we feel are necessary to the operation of your franchise, as such information becomes available to us.

8.7 Telephone Calls/Leads. We may provide a system of distributing telephone calls/leads to the nearest Granite Transformations Franchisee. We also may provide you with operating and service consulting via phone and e-mail for your business, and provide relevant data and information to ensure the benefits and the exploitation and use of the system and its products. You will sign any documentation needed by us for your applicable telephone authority to assign ownership of your business phone number or your domain name if requested by us.

8.8 Advertising Materials. We will provide you with all existing and available brochures and point-of-sale material at cost price plus a small shipping and handling fee. We must approve all of your advertising and promotional materials in advance.

8.9 Software. We will suggest a uniform, proprietary computer software system of record-keeping techniques to manage your customer base and customer contracts and software updates and maintenance. We require you to purchase a quality desktop computer and an accounting package entitled "Peachtree" prior to opening.

8.10 Subsequent Franchisor Training. We may provide subsequent training classes, both mandatory and non-mandatory, offered from time to time with you also required to pay all costs of travel, lodging, and subsistence unless any such mandatory training classes exceed one (1) per calendar year, wherein we shall then reimburse you for the airfare of the required attendee. If you request special training, and we agree, a charge for the instructor may be added. (See Article 5.6 above.)

8.11 Newsletter. We, at our discretion, will provide you with monthly or quarterly newsletters regarding current industry trends and marketing updates as well as business recognition.

ARTICLE 9. RESTRICTIONS ON GOODS AND SERVICES OFFERED BY FRANCHISEE

9.1 Restrictions. You may sell or offer for sale to the public only services and goods of the kind and quality which comply with the reasonable standards designated in the Operations Manual or directives in writing provided by us from time to time. You may not use our name, trademarks, service marks, trade names, logotypes, or commercial symbols in any business other than the franchised business. All products and services used or offered must be from us or an approved vendor. (See also Articles 1 and 7.3, 7.4, 7.7, 7.14, and 7.16 above.)

ARTICLE 10. TERM

10.1 Term. The initial term of the Franchise Agreement is ten (10) years from the date of execution of this agreement, with the opportunity to renew for similar terms of 10 years each if in good standing under your current franchise agreement and, upon your execution of the then current franchise agreement provided by us.

ARTICLE 11. RENEWAL, TERMINATION, REPURCHASE, MODIFICATION, AND ASSIGNMENT OF THE FRANCHISE AGREEMENT AND RELATED INFORMATION

11.1 Renewal. This Franchise Agreement may be renewed for unlimited additional renewal periods of time by your execution of a new Franchise Agreement at the end of each 10-year term, providing: (1) you are not in default or in violation of the Franchise Agreement or any other agreement with us; and, (2) upon execution of the then-current Franchise Agreement or, if no current agreement is in effect, then the last agreement executed by the last franchisee within the United States, under the terms in effect at that time, including new service fee rates and advertising fees, with the exception that the length of term or renewal terms shall not change nor your territory. The renewal fee charged to you by us is $1,000.00.

11.2 Termination by Franchisee. You may terminate the Franchise Agreement by obtaining our written consent, which consent we are not obligated to give. You may terminate the Franchise Agreement for good cause only if we have materially breached the Franchise Agreement, provided that, prior to your terminating the Franchise Agreement for good cause, you must serve a written notice of default upon us, specifying the grounds for default and granting us a reasonable opportunity, but in no case less than thirty (30) days, in which to cure the default or in which to commence diligent efforts to cure the default (if the default cannot reasonably be expected to be cured within thirty [30] days).

11.3 Franchisor's Termination Rights After Failure to Cure. The conditions under which we may terminate, subject to a thirty (30) day notice to cure, unless otherwise specified include:

(1) The attachment of any involuntary lien in the sum of $1,000.00 or more upon any of your business assets or property, which lien is not promptly removed.

(2) Conduct of the franchised business in such a manner so as to affect materially and adversely your goodwill or reputation or your products and services.

(3) Default by you of any provision of the Franchise Agreement or under any other agreement between you and us not subject to earlier termination as agreed by the parties.

(4) Any purported assignment, transfer, or sub-license of the franchise, or any right hereunder, without prior written consent.

(5) Failure to make timely payment to us of any and all sums payable to us pursuant to the Franchise Agreement after five (5) days' written notice of such failure to pay.

(6) Failure to make timely payment upon any obligation of you upon which we are acting as a guarantor or default upon or a breach of any provision of any promissory note or other evidence of indebtedness or any agreement relating thereto.

(7) Failure to cure a default under the Franchise Agreement, within ten (10) business days after receipt of notice thereof, which default materially impairs the goodwill associated with our trade names, trademarks, service marks, logotypes, or other commercial symbols.

(8) Failure to pay for or conduct any audit required by us or failure to secure and maintain the required insurance, including but not limited to fire, public liability, and worker's compensation insurance after ten (10) days, written notice requiring such deficiency to be cured.

(9) Failure to supply reports on gross sales, receipts, and business activities or other information required in such reports, including but not limited to advertising performed and results thereof, description, and number of leads.

(10) Failure to use the techniques, training, and methods promulgated by our manuals or attend seminar sessions required by us, which are limited to one required session per calendar year.

(11) Failure to put your best efforts and full dedicated time to the management of the franchised business in your office and in the field, conducting both sales calls and job site visits unless a designated job site manager is employed to handle job site supervision or, in your excused absence, to have the franchised business managed by a designated office manager approved and accepted by us for the office supervision, who has the proper training and aptitude in the procedures and systems as prescribed by us, or failure to designate an individual upon whom we may rely for the personal and direct management of the franchised business, if you are a corporate or partnership entity. All "job sites," i.e., "premises where your services are performed," must be under your direction or that of a designated, qualified job site manager hired by you to handle job site construction supervision.

(12) Failure to keep true and accurate business records and books in accordance with our procedures or failure to make available those items deemed necessary for inspection or provide federal and state income tax returns as requested by us or upon discovery of a deficiency in payments exceeding two percent (2%) or more in any audit of your business.

(13) Failure to maintain the standards of good conduct and appearance designated by us for the success of the franchise in order to ensure continuity of quality, appearance, and professionalism.

(14) Failure to maintain confidential any information designated as confidential by us.

(15) Having relatives, agents, representatives, or employees operating any similar business center from a permanent base location other than the location address approved herein by us.

(16) Personally operating any similar business center from a permanent base point location other than the location approved by us herein.

(17) Failure to participate in any approved cooperative advertising group or to be listed in the dominant telephone directory in your territory.

(18) Failure of you and your designated office manager to complete the initial training program to our satisfaction and/or begin operation within 120 days of payment of the franchise fee.

(19) Failure to spend the required funds on your local advertising or at least 3% of your gross receipts in your cooperative advertising or failure to cease and desist in servicing job sites in the territories of other franchisees.

(20) Failure to cease soliciting and servicing occupied housing units in another franchisee's exclusive territory after written notice.

11.4 Franchisor's Termination Rights Without Notice. If, during the period in which the franchise is in effect, there occurs any of the following events which is relevant to the franchise, immediate notice of termination without any opportunity to cure shall be deemed reasonable:

(1) You or the business to which the franchise relates is declared or judicially determined to be insolvent, or all or a substantial part of the assets thereof are assigned to or for the benefit of any creditor, or you admit your inability to pay your debts as they become due.

(2) You abandon the franchise by failing to operate the business for five (5) consecutive days, during which time you are required to operate the business under the terms of the franchise, or any shorter period after which it is not unreasonable under the facts to conclude that you do not intend to continue to operate the franchise, unless such failure is due to fire, flood, earthquake, or other similar causes beyond your control.

(3) We and you agree in writing to terminate the franchise.

(4) You make any material misrepresentations relating to the acquisition or operation of the franchise or you engage in conduct which reflects materially and unfavorable upon the operation and reputation of the franchise system.

(5) You fail, for a period of ten (10) days after notification of noncompliance, to comply with any federal, state, or local law or regulation applicable to the operation of the franchise.

(6) You, after curing any failure in accordance with Article 11.3 above, engage in the same conduct or noncompliance, whether or not such conduct or noncompliance is corrected after notice.

(7) You repeatedly fail to comply with one or more requirements of the Franchise Agreement, whether or not corrected after notice.

(8) The franchise business or business premises of the franchise are seized, taken over, or foreclosed by a governmental official in the exercise of his duties, or seized, taken over, or foreclosed by a creditor, lien holder, or lessor, provided that a final judgment against you remains unsatisfied for thirty (30) days (unless supersedes or other appeal bond has been filed); or a levy of execution has been made upon the license granted by the Franchise Agreement or upon any property used in the franchised business, and it is not discharged within five (5) days of such levy.

(9) You are convicted of a felony or any other criminal misconduct that is relevant to the operation of the franchise.

(10) You fail to pay any franchise fees or other amounts due to us or our affiliate within five (5) days after receiving written notice that such fees are overdue.

(11) We make a reasonable determination that continued operation of the franchise by you will result in an imminent danger to public health or safety.

11.5 Obligations of Franchisee After Termination. In the event of termination of the franchise agreement for any reason:

(1) You lose all rights to all fees and may no longer use our trademarks, service marks, trade name, copyrights, systems, manuals, displays, your telephone numbers, or any other property connected with the franchise.

(2) You must immediately cease use of all trade names, systems, service marks, trademarks, training manuals, and other proprietary property of ours, which must be returned to us immediately upon written notice.

(3) We have the right to enter the premises of the franchised location and to recover and remove training material and all other proprietary property of ours.

(4) Any amounts due or owing to us by you, including unpaid royalties and fees remaining on the unexpired portion of your Franchise Agreement when terminated by you without our permission, shall be paid immediately.

(5) You, in executing the Franchise Agreement, agree to assign all right, title, and interest to all of your business telephone numbers upon termination, for any reason, of your franchise and to execute any further documents or instruments or instructions necessary to further effect such transfer.

(6) You, after termination of the Franchise Agreement, will have no interest in the franchised business and all rights and privileges are terminated.

(7) All Confidential Manuals and systems must be returned to us by you within 24 hours after notice.

11.6 Franchisor's Right of First Refusal upon Sale or Termination or Breach. We have the right of first refusal exercisable within thirty (30) days after receipt of notice by us from you of the proposed sale or assignment, in which we may repurchase the franchise at any time that you attempt to transfer to any other person or entity except a qualified spouse or child. This also includes a transfer by will or intestate upon the death of a sole proprietorship, partner, or shareholder. Any attempt to transfer the assets and/or business without assigning the Franchise Agreement to the potential purchaser shall constitute a default and breach of the Franchise Agreement. The purchase price is determined by the amount of a bona fide offer from a third party in the event of a sale or transfer. Such repurchase price will recognize goodwill and other tangibles associates with the normal sale of a going business if same is included in the bona fide offer of a third party.

On any termination due to your default or breach of the Franchise Agreement or an attempted cancellation by you, we shall have the right, at our option, for thirty (30) days after such termination, to purchase your interest in all or a portion of equipment, inventory, supplies, or fixtures at a purchase price equal to the fair market value of such items. If the parties do not agree to any such purchase price within such thirty (30) day period, such prices shall be set by an independent appraiser designated by us.

11.7 Provisions of Applicable Law. The provisions herein shall be subordinated to and conformed with the provisions of any valid applicable law or regulation affording you any more favorable rights or remedies.

11.8 Franchisee Assignment. You may not sell, assign, or transfer, in whole or part, your interest in the Franchise Agreement without first obtaining our written consent, which consent will not be unreasonably withheld subject to your rights set forth herein. We will require, as a condition to any transfer, that you deliver to us the complete financial statements of the proposed transferee, and you make payment in full for all obligations outstanding or accruing to us through the date of such sale, assignment, or transfer and the new franchisee must sign a current Franchise Agreement. You must pay us transfer, training, and software fees and the transferee (new franchisee) must assume your complete obligations under the Franchise Agreement. The new franchisee's net worth must be sufficient enough, in our sole discretion, to pay all current liabilities out of current assets and to have a reserve necessary for the continued operation of the franchise.

11.9 Unauthorized Transfer of Franchise Agreement and Death and Probate of Franchisee. A transfer or attempt to transfer your interest in this Franchise Agreement, without our written consent and the payment of the transfer fee, constitutes abandonment of this Franchise Agreement by you. If you, a sole proprietor, or a partner or a shareholder of a corporation dies, your estate may sell the franchise to a transferee acceptable to us within three (3) months after the death of the original franchisee. If the franchise is stalled in probate for more than three (3) months, we have the right to place our personnel in your area and all necessary support systems required to maintain the franchise as we deem necessary on a cost plus twenty percent (20%) basis to the deceased franchisee's estate.

11.10 Resignation, Removal, Non-Performance. The resignation, removal, non-performance, death, or permanent disability of you or your designated manager is treated as a proposed assignment by you of your rights and obligations, and you or your estate must promptly request approval of a replacement franchisee or designated manager.

11.11 Current Standards on Transfer. The purchaser or assignee will be required to update the franchised business to our then-current standards and will be required to fulfill all training and testing requirements at the assignee's or purchaser's expense for travel, lodging, and meals. The new owners will be required to participate in our training program.

11.12 Assignment by Franchisor. This Franchise Agreement may be assigned in whole or in part by us without your consent or prior approval and such assignment shall not modify or diminish your obligations hereunder.

11.13 Banking. You will establish a bank account exclusive to Granite Transformations and not attached or associated with any other business or personal accounts. You will instruct your bank or trust company that we and our financial and legal advisors will at all times be entitled to information as to such accounts and to examine all bank statements and cancelled checks and other bills of exchange and supporting documents. You will sign and deliver such directions, authorizations, and other documents as we or such bank or trust company may require in order to permit access and inspection by us and our financial and legal advisors.

11.14 Credit Card Accounts. You will establish credit card accounts with VISA, MasterCard, AMEX, and Discover and any other additional financial institutions selected by us for purposes of accepting payments from customers.

ARTICLE 12. CONFLICTS OF INTEREST

12.1 Affiliations. To maintain our confidentiality of marketing and/or operational plans and programs, commission rates, and other information, you shall not during the term of this agreement: (1) be a member of or otherwise be associated with any consortium or other organization engaged, directly or indirectly, in the purchase or arranging for the purchase of a competing business for or on behalf of its members, or (2) personally, directly, or indirectly or through a family member, partner, or affiliate, maintain any ownership or leasehold interest in or business affiliation with any franchise system other than a franchise operated under a direct franchise agreement from us, without our prior written consent, which consent may be withheld at our discretion with or without cause, or (3) authorize or allow independent contractors or any third party with whom you transact business to use or have access to our confidential marketing and operational plans and programs without our prior written consent, which consent may be withheld with or without cause. However, you may be a member of or otherwise be associated with trade associations or an association among you and other franchisees and/or us.

12.2 Confidentiality. You shall keep strictly confidential our marketing and operational plans and programs, suggested pricing, commission rates, proprietary materials or information access, retrieval, storage and management systems, and other information contained in the Operations Manual or otherwise conveyed to you by us. If requested by us, you shall cause your officers, directors, and employees to execute written agreements to keep such information strictly confidential.

ARTICLE 13. COPYRIGHTS

13.1 Copyrights and Patents. We do not own any rights in or to any patents which are material to the franchise. We presently have proprietary rights in numerous items, such as your manuals, systems, advertising designs, and the like relating to the operation of our business, which are suitable for copyright protection. We reserve to our designee or ourselves any and all rights that we have in and to such items. We may obtain copyright registration on our confidential Operations Manual and any future manuals and may, at our discretion, obtain copyright registration for any now unregistered items that are a part of this agreement.

ARTICLE 14. RIGHT OF OFFSET

14.1 Right of Offset. You authorize us to retain monies by us on your behalf or due to you to off-set amounts owed to us by you.

ARTICLE 15. INDEMNIFICATION

15.1 Indemnify. You shall indemnify and save us harmless from and against all costs, damages, expenses, claims, and other losses and liabilities, in tort or contract, including reasonable legal and accounting fees incurred directly or indirectly out of or in connection with, or alleged to have been caused by, the operation of your business or arising or alleged to have arisen against you, including all costs incurred as a result of claims or suits against us arising therefrom, unless such claim is due to our negligence or willful act or that of our agents, employees, or representatives. We may take steps we deem necessary to protect ourselves from such claims or suits, and you shall reimburse us for all expenses incurred in connection therewith, including reasonable attorneys' fees, within ten (10) days from the date of an invoice from us to you for such expense.

15.2 Attorneys' Fees. If any provision of this Agreement is enforced at any time by us or if any amounts due from you to us or our affiliates are at any time collected by or through an attorney at law, you are liable to us for all costs and expenses of enforcement and collection, including court costs and reasonable attorneys' fees.

ARTICLE 16. NOTICES

16.1 Written Notices. Any notice required or permitted by this Agreement shall be deemed given if sent postage prepaid, registered, or certified mail, or overnight express service and addressed to the following address or to such other address as may be provided by either party upon written notice to the other party or published in the Operations Manual.

Franchisor: Franchisee:

Chief Operating Officer   _____

Rocksolid Granit (USA) Inc.   _____

11098 Inland Avenue   _____

Mira Loma, California 91752   _____

ARTICLE 17. INDEPENDENT CONTRACTOR

17.1 Franchisee Is an Independent Contractor. Nothing in this Agreement is intended to constitute you as our agent, legal representative, subsidiary, joint venturer, fiduciary partner, employee, or servant for any purpose whatsoever. You are an independent contractor and are in no way authorized by this Agreement to make any contract, warranty, or representation, or to create any obligation, express or implied, on behalf of or in the name of us. All your employees are your responsibility and not ours.

17.2 Franchise Disclosure. In all of your dealings with third parties, including customers, employees, and suppliers, you shall disclose in an appropriate manner acceptable to us that you are an independent entity. This Agreement does not create a relationship of fiduciary standards or of special trust or confidence.

17.3 Third Parties. The parties intend to confer no benefit or right on any person or entity not a party to this Agreement and no third party shall have the right to claim the benefit of any provision hereof as a third party beneficiary of any provision.

ARTICLE 18. MODIFICATIONS

18.1 Modification of Agreement. The Franchise Agreement may be modified only with the written consent of both parties as stated herein.

18.2 Franchisor's Modification Rights. We expressly reserve the right to modify our manuals and systems, the composition of the package of services offered to you and/or to change our trademarks, service marks, trade names, logotypes, commercial symbols, and specifications without your consent.

18.3 Additional Actions. The parties agree to execute such other documents and perform such further acts as may be necessary or desirable to carry out the purposes of this Agreement.

ARTICLE 19. GOVERNING LAW AND PUBLIC CHANGES

19.1 Applicable Law. This agreement shall be governed by and construed in accordance with the internal laws of the State of Maryland.

ARTICLE 20. SEVERABILITY

20.1 Severability. If this Agreement is held to violate any law, regulation or ordinance of the United States, any country, any state or municipality, the relevant portion is severable, and the balance of this Agreement shall be enforced as if such provision had not been included herein. All rights and remedies provided herein or by law are cumulative and not mutually exclusive and may be exercised serially.

ARTICLE 21. FAILURE TO ENFORCE

21.1 Failure to Enforce. Failure of either party to enforce any of the terms and conditions of this Agreement shall not constitute a waiver of right subsequently to enforce such provisions or to enforce other provisions of this Agreement.

ARTICLE 22. SUCCESSION OF BENEFITS

22.1 Succession of Benefits. In the event that you should become deceased or incapacitated, the provisions of this Agreement shall inure to the benefit of and be binding upon the heirs, executors, administrators, and assignees.

ARTICLE 23. MISCELLANEOUS

23.1 Headings, Table of Contents, Gender, and Language Usage. The headings, table of contents, gender, and language usage used herein are for purposes of convenience only and shall not be used in constructing the provisions hereof. As used herein, the male gender shall include the female and neuter genders; the singular shall include the plural, and the plural, the singular.

23.2 Injunctive Relief. You recognize the unique value and secondary meaning attached to our franchised business system, our trade names, service marks, trademarks, logotypes, commercial symbols, standards of operation, and the trade practices and agree that any noncompliance with the terms of this Agreement or any unauthorized or improper use will cause irreparable damage to us and our franchisees. You therefore agree that if you should engage in any such unauthorized or improper use, during or after the period of this franchise, we shall be entitled to apply for both permanent and temporary injunctive relief from any arbitration panel or court of competent jurisdiction in addition to any other remedies prescribed bylaw.

23.3 Arbitration.

(1) Except as specifically modified by this Article, any controversy or claim arising out of or relating to this Agreement or its breach, including, without limitation, any claim that this Agreement or any of its parts is invalid, illegal, or otherwise voidable or void, shall be submitted to arbitration before and in accordance with the arbitration rules of Franchise Arbitration and Mediation, Inc. (FAM), Maryland or, if FAM is unable to conduct said arbitration, then before the American Arbitration Association in accordance with its Commercial Arbitration Rules to be arbitrated in the State of Maryland for claims arising under the Maryland Franchise Registration and Disclosure Law. We and you agree that arbitration shall be conducted on an individual and not a class-wide basis and that there shall be three neutral arbitrators that are recognized franchise attorneys.

(2) The provisions of this Article shall be construed as independent of any other covenant or provision of this Agreement; provided that if a court of competent jurisdiction determines that any such provisions are unlawful in any way, such court shall modify or interpret such provisions to a minimum extent necessary to have them comply with the law.

   Notwithstanding any provision of this Agreement, relating to under which state laws of this Agreement shall be governed by and construed, all issues relating to arbitrational or the enforcement of the Agreement to arbitrate contained herein shall be governed by the Federal Arbitration Act (9 U.S.C. Sect. 1 et seq.) and the federal common law of arbitration.

(3) Judgment upon an arbitration award may be entered in any court having competent jurisdiction and shall be binding, final, and non-appealable. We and you (and our respective owners and guarantors, if applicable) hereby waive to the fullest extent permitted by law any right to claim for any punitive or exemplary damages against the other and agree that in the event of a dispute between us and/or them each shall be limited to the recovery of any actual damages sustained by it.

(4) Prior to any arbitration proceeding taking place, we or you may, at our respective option, elect to (1) have the arbitrator(s) conduct, in a separate proceeding prior to the actual arbitration, a preliminary hearing at which hearing testimony and other evidence may be presented and briefs may be submitted, including without limitation a brief setting forth the then-applicable statutory or common law methods of measuring damages in respect to the controversy or claim being arbitrated, or (2) submit the controversy or claim to non-bind-

ing meditation before FAM or other mutually agreeable mediator, in which event both parties shall execute a suitable confidentiality agreement.

(5) This arbitration provision shall be deemed to be self-executing and shall remain in full force and effect after expiration or termination of this Agreement. In the event either party fails to appear at any properly noticed arbitration proceeding, an award may be entered against such party by default or otherwise notwithstanding said failure to appear. Arbitration and/or mediation shall take place in Maryland unless otherwise agreed by us and you. Any limitations of claims provisions will not reduce the limitation period for bringing claims arising under the Maryland Franchise Registration and Disclosure Law. Under which such claims must be brought within three (3) years after the grant of the franchise.

(6) The obligation herein to arbitrate or mediate shall not be binding upon either party with respect to claims relating to our trademarks, service marks, patents, and copyrights; claims related to any lease or sublease or real property between the parties or their affiliated entities; requests by either party for temporary restraining orders, preliminary injunctions, or other procedures in a court of competent jurisdiction to obtain interim relief when deemed necessary by such court to preserve the status quo or prevent irreparable injury pending resolution by arbitration of the actual dispute between the parties.

ARTICLE 24. ACKNOWLEDGMENT BY A PROSPECTIVE FRANCHISEE

24.1 Acknowledgment. You, by executing this Agreement, acknowledge receipt of our Uniform Franchise Offering Circular (UFOC) and Franchise Agreement, including all exhibits required by various states, at least ten (10) business days before signing this Agreement, and that the Agreement received is substantially the form being executed this date and has been in your possession for at least five (5) business days. These representations are not intended to nor shall they act as a release, estoppel, or waiver of any liability incurred under the Maryland Franchise Registration and Disclosure Law.

24.2 Further Acknowledgment. You further acknowledge that you have entered into this Agreement in reliance upon the information set forth in this Agreement and the Uniform Franchise Offering Circular and have relied on no promises, no representations, no statements, or no undertakings made by us or our representative or others which are in conflict with any statements or representations made and not set forth in this Agreement or in the Uniform Franchise Offering Circular.

24.3 Independent Counsel. You expressly acknowledge that you have conducted an independent investigation of the contemplated association with us and you have been advised by us to seek your own independent counsel prior to sign this agreement.

24.4 Business Risk. You expressly recognize that the contemplated association with you involves business risks making the success of the association largely dependent upon the business abilities of you and external economic forces. You acknowledge that neither we nor any other person can guarantee the success of your franchised business.

24.5 No Financial Projections or Representations. You expressly acknowledge that you have not received or relied upon any warranty or assurance, expressed or implied, as to the potential sales volume, profits, or success of the association with our franchise system.

ARTICLE 25. ENTIRE AGREEMENT

25.1 Additional Provisions. Please indicate any provisions orally made that are not contained herein. If none, write "none." _____

_____

_____.

25.2 Entire Agreement. This Agreement constitutes the entire Agreement of the parties into which all prior negotiations, commitments, representations, and undertakings are merged and no modification or termination of this Agreement shall be binding unless executed in writing by all parties hereto. This Agreement is binding on the parties and their heirs, successors, and assigns.

THE UNDERSIGNED ACKNOWLEDGES THAT THEY HAVE READ THIS AGREEMENT IN FULL; HAVE BEEN SUPPLIED WITH A UNIFORM FRANCHISE OFFERING CIRCULAR IN ACCORDANCE TO FEDERAL AND STATE LAW; ARE COGNIZANT OF EACH AND EVERY ONE OF THE TERMS AND PROVISIONS HEREOF AND AGREE HERETO; THAT NO REPRESENTATIONS OR AGREEMENTS, WHETHER ORAL OR WRITTEN, EXCEPT AS HEREIN SET FORTH, HAVE BEEN MADE OR RELIED UPON; THAT THE SIGNATURES AFFIXED HERETO WERE AFFIXED AS THE WHOLLY VOLUNTARY ACT OF THE PERSONS WHO SIGNED THIS AGREEMENT; AND THAT THE TERMS AND PROVISIONS OF THIS AGREEMENT CANNOT BE CHANGED OR MODIFIED UNLESS IN WRITING SIGNED BY THE AUTHORIZED REPRESENTATIVE OF YOU AND AN AUTHORIZED CORPORATE OFFICER OF US; THAT THE UNDERSIGNED REALIZES THAT THERE CAN BE NO GUARANTEE OF SUCCESS SINCE YOUR BUSINESS ABILITY, APTITUDE, AND INDUSTRIOUS DISPOSITION ARE THE PRIMARY FACTORS IN YOUR SUCCESS.

IN WITNESS WHEREOF, the parties hereto have caused this Agreement to be duly executed in triplicate as of the day and year written herein.

FRANCHISOR:
ROCKSOLID GRANIT (USA), INC.
A Delaware corporation licensed to do business in California

Date: _____   By: _____
                                     (Typed or Printed Name and Title)

FRANCHISEE:

_____
(Typed Name of Entity)

Date: _____   By: _____
                                     (Signature and Title of Authorized Officer,
                                     if a Corporate Entity Is Involved)

Date: _____   By: _____
                                     (Signature of Sole Proprietor, if a Sole Proprietorship)

Date: _____   By: _____
                                     (Signature of a Partner; if a Partnership,
                                     All Partners Must Sign)

Date: _____   By:_____
                                         (Signature of Any Additional Partner, if a Partnership)

Date: _____   By: _____
                                         (Signature of Any Additional Partner, if a Partnership)

SHAREHOLDERS OF FRANCHISE

(If Corporate Entity is involved, all Shareholders must sign and date and by signing hereunder agree to be individually bound by all of the terms and conditions of this Agreement.)

Date: _____

(SEE TERRITORY MAP ATTACHED HERETO AS SCHEDULE 1)

Appendix B-2
Franchise Agreement
Lite For Life

sample document of a *service*-type franchise agreement (where a service is performed) is included in this Appendix B-1 to illustrate typical terms and restrictions contained in most service-type franchise agreements.

Again, as either a potential franchisor or a prospective franchisee, acquaint yourself with the evaluation pointers discussed in Chapter 2, Learning About Franchise Documents, and other portions of this book, and make your own evaluation of the sample franchise agreement.

As a franchisor, be aware of your franchisee's needs, because if the franchisee fails, so will you. You will want to supply all the support necessary to ensure the possibility of your franchisee's success.

Lite For Life Franchising Corporation, Inc.
Franchise Agreement
(1/9/03)(4/7/03)(4/14/03)(4/16/03)(6/24/03)

Table of Contents

Table of Contents (continued)

Table of Contents (continued)

* **Note:** In your franchise agreement, you must provide page numbers. They have been omitted in this sample to avoid confusion with the book's page numbers.

Lite For Life Franchising Corporation, Inc.
Franchise Agreement

THIS FRANCHISE AGREEMENT is made at Burlingame, California as of the _____day of _____, 200___, by and between Lite For Life Franchising Corporation, Inc., a California corporation, having an office located at 1199 Howard Ave., Suite 102, Burlingame, California 94010 (herein referred to as "we," "us," etc.) and _____ of _____ (herein referred to as "you"). You hereby acknowledge that this Franchise Agreement was accompanied by an Offering Circular which you received at the earlier of 1) the first personal meeting with us, 2) ten (10) business days prior to the signing of any franchise or related agreement, or 3) ten (10) business days before any payment by you. In addition, you acknowledge receipt of this Franchise Agreement containing all material terms at the time of the delivery of the offering circular.

You are desirous of obtaining a franchise in an expanding a network of independently owned weight loss centers using a proprietary diet while providing your dieters with a nutritional and behavioral approach to lifetime weight management emphasizing blood sugar stabilization and sugar addiction avoidance through private daily counseling and nutrition education along with the sale of daily nutritional supplements and fresh food products used in conjunction with a diet designed to achieve permanent weight loss.

We and you, intending to be legally bound, for and in consideration of the mutual covenants hereinafter following, do mutually covenant and agree:

I. SERVICE MARK LICENSES AND USE, TRADE PRACTICES, INFRINGEMENT, AND MODIFICATION

A. License of Service Mark. We hereby grant you the right to use the service mark "Lite For Life" in a designated territory wherein only you will have a site and where we cannot open or operate a similar operation or appoint a franchised operation to operate a location within this designated area for the purpose of servicing customers.

You also are licensed to operate the franchised business under such names and such other service marks, trademarks, and copyrights as we may designate from time to time and you are designated as a participant in our system while operating the franchise. Such business shall be conducted by you as "Lite For Life" or such other mark as we may deem.

Your approved location is located within the limits of the following territory (hereinafter called "Designated Territory"): _____

_____

_____

The specific location address from which you shall work out is: _____

_____

The Designated Territory is more particularly described and outlined in the map attached to this Franchise Agreement (Schedule 1). You agree not to open such business without our written approval nor to change the location thereafter without our written approval. You acknowledge that we may from time to time, and at our sole discretion, modify or discontinue use of any trade names, trademarks, or service marks or use one or more additional or substituted trade names, trademarks, or service marks and you agree to operate under such names, trademarks, as directed by us in our good discretion and to immediately cease using such trade names, trademarks, or service marks when directed by us in writing. You shall not use "Lite For Life" or any other of our service marks or trademarks in your corporate name or d/b/a without our prior written approval. You agree to operate your franchise under the duly acquired fictitious name of "Lite For Life" or other names designated by us in the future according to the specifications as provided from time to time by us.

B. Trade Practices. You agree that we have the sole rights to certain trade practices and that no goodwill associated with any of the trade practices shall inure to you. It is further agreed that the items of the trade practice constitute our trade secrets which are revealed to you in confidence and you will not, at any time during the term of this agreement or any time thereafter, use or attempt to use the trade practices in connection with any other entity or business in which we have an interest, direct or indirect, nor shall you disclose, duplicate, reveal, sell, or sublicense the trade practices or any part thereof or in any way transfer any rights in the trade practices except as authorized by us.

C. Use of Service Marks and Infringement. You, in conducting our franchise, shall use such service marks, trademarks, or trade names in such art form and in such logo form as specified from time to time by us, including indoor and outdoor signs identifying your service as "Lite For Life," including such designation as "Lite For Life of _____," and to indicate the required trademark, service mark, or copyright notices in the form specified by us. You may not use our trademarks or service marks in connection with the sale of unauthorized products or services or in any manner not authorized by us.

After timely written notice from you about an infringement of or challenge to your use of our mark, we shall take whatever action or inaction we think is appropriate. We alone have the right to control any legal actions or proceedings including settlements. We may, at our sole discretion, prosecute or defend any action or proceeding which we deem necessary or desirable to protect our service marks, trademarks, or logos. You agree not to contest our title in such marks and logos and to modify or discontinue the use of any names or marks or to use one or more additional or substitute name or marks at our sole discretion. While we are not required to defend you against a claim against your use of our trademark, we will reimburse you for your tangible costs of compliance in such matters of the reasonable cost of changing your exterior signs only.

D. Modification or Discontinuance of Service Mark Use. If it becomes advisable at any time in our discretion to modify or discontinue the use of any such names or marks or to use one or more additional or substituted names or marks, you are obligated to do so at your sole expense except that we shall bear the reasonable cost of changing your exterior sign.

II. FRANCHISOR ASSISTANCE

A. Pre-Opening. The obligations that we will perform for you prior to opening of your franchised business are:

1. **Operating Manual.** We will loan you one or more sets of the franchise operating manual that specifies the guidelines for site selection, decor, sign, fixtures, inventory, supplies, names of approved suppliers, suggested budgets, pre-opening advertising guides, operational techniques, financial and accounting information, marketing plans, and other items and procedures relevant to the operation of the franchised business. All of our manuals are considered confidential trade secrets. This manual is confidential and remains our property. We will modify and upgrade this manual as the occasion warrants but the modification will not alter your status and rights under the Franchise Agreement.

2. **Initial Franchise Training.** Within 10 to 60 days of your signing the Franchise Agreement, we will provide a minimum of 25 hours of training in the management and operation of the franchised business. You must attend and successfully complete the training prior to the opening of the franchised business. The training will be conducted at our main office or at the location of our choice. The initial training is mandatory. We do not charge you for this training. You must pay all of your living expenses and travel, lodging, and sustenance. All training occurs at our Los Altos or Burlingame, California or Redmond, Washington centers or a designated location of our choice and the initial training is mandatory. We will conduct additional training as we deem necessary and you will be required to bear all costs of travel, lodging, and subsistence to the training sites. It is our sole discretion as to whether or not you have successfully completed the initial training program or any subsequent training program.

3. **Initial Supplies.** We will provide initial supplies of proprietary and confidential materials.

4. **Additional Trainees.** Initial training is for one owner/manager and one other employee. Any additional employees or persons to be trained will be charged a per diem training instructor's fee of $200 per instructor. This charge is subject to consumer price increases based on annual rates as determined by the applicable CPI (Consumer Price Index) for your territory covering the inflationary price increases as compared with the year of opening of the Franchise.

5. **Territorial and Site Assistance.** We will advise you in obtaining the necessary demographics, including number of people in your territory, and assist you locating your site.

B. Post-Opening. The obligations performed by us **during the operation** of the Franchisee's business are:

1. **Advisory Services.** We will provide to you, according to the extent required by us in our sole judgment, a continuing advisory service which shall include consultation on promotional, business, or operations problems and analysis of your services, sales, marketing, and financial data at times and places and to the extent designated us.

2. **Suggested Suppliers.** We will provide to you, from time to time, a list of suggested suppliers or manufacturers of supplies and products approved by but not purchased from us.

3. **Evaluations.** We will provide you with our evaluations of sources of supplies and products recommended by you for use in the franchise system.

4. **Institutional Development.** We will develop institutional public relations, advertising, and promotional campaigns designed to benefit and assist all our franchisees and promote and enhance the value of the franchisees where possible.

5. **Advertising Supervision.** We will supervise the advertising in accordance with our advertising standards.

6. **Uniform Accounting System**. We will provide you with a uniform system of accounting and record keeping based on your usage of QuickBooks Pro, which you must purchase, and on standardized forms which we will provide to you.

7. **Subsequent Training.** We will provide subsequent training classes, both mandatory and nonmandatory, offered from time to time at our discretion with you required to pay all costs of travel, lodging, and subsistence. If you request special training, and we agree, a charge for the instructor may be added.

III. FRANCHISE FEE, TERM, AND RENEWAL FEE

A. Initial Franchise Fee. Your initial non-refundable franchise fee is Twenty Thousand Dollars ($20,000) payable upon your signing the Franchise Agreement. The initial franchise fee is non-refundable.

B. Term. The term of the Franchise Agreement is effective and binding, commencing with the date upon which the Franchise Agreement is signed, for a period of ten (10) years.

C. Renewal Fee. You can renew the Franchise Agreement for unlimited additional periods of five (5) years each, providing (1) you are not in default or in violation of the Franchise Agreement or any other agreement with us, and (2) upon execution of the then-current Franchise Agreement under the terms in effect at that time, including new royalty rates, advertising fees, etc., with the exception that the length of term or renewal terms shall not change nor shall your territory change. We may refuse to renew the Franchise Agreement if you are in default or violation of your Franchise Agreement and/or fail to execute the then-current Franchise Agreement. The renewal fee charged to you by us is One Thousand Dollars ($1,000) to cover our legal fees and administrative and overhead costs necessitated by the renewals. Should the Consumer Price Index (CPI) that is based on the annual inflationary rates in your territory increase, your renewal fee may be increased as compared with the year of opening of the franchise by the same increased CPI percentage accordingly.

IV. SERVICE FEES, ADVERTISING AND PROMOTIONAL FEES, AND TRANSFER FEES

A. Service Fees and Gross Sales. You are required to pay a monthly non-refundable service fee of five percent (5%) of your gross monthly sales after you open. The term "gross sales" is defined to include all sums or things of value received or receivable by you in and from the business from all sales of goods, products, and services, whether for cash, check, credit, or otherwise, without reserve or deduction for inability or failure to collect same including, without limitation, such sales and services where the orders thereof originated at or accepted by you at one location but delivered or performance thereof made from or at any other location. Gross sales do not include rebates, promotional sales coupons, or refunds to customers or the amount of any sales taxes or any similar taxes that you might be required to and do collect from customers to be paid to any federal, state, or local taxing authority. All such items, including non-collectible accounts which are claimed as deductions to gross sales, must be supported by proper documentation in accordance with the operating manual provided by us to you. Gross sales will be reported to us through submission of monthly profit and loss statements generated by QuickBooks Pro. The P&L, new dieter contact information, monthly Dieter Roll-Call, and the service fee shall be due and payable in full on or before the seventh business day after the close of each calendar month based on "gross sales" shown on the P&L for the previous month. Any payment not received on time shall bear interest at the maximum legal rate of interest allowable by law from date due until the date received by us. All service fees are non-refundable.

B. Local Pre-/Post-Opening Advertising and Promotions. During a period of 60 days just *prior* to opening, you agree to spend at least $2,000 on local advertising announcing the services you will provide in your territory. *After* opening, you are also required to spend a minimum sum equal to One Thousand Dollars ($1,000) per month, commencing on the first date that you open for business, on advertising to generate leads and enhance the reputation of your service on a local level in your territory, which is due and payable to the advertising media as required during each month. All advertising must be approved by us. You are required to substantiate the minimum advertising required by supplying such written information to us as we may require on a monthly basis. We reserve the right to designate or consent to the content, themes, materials, and placement of all advertising programs by you which must be tailored to your local market and without inappropriate or misleading content. You must submit all advertising to us for our approval at least five (5) business days before publication (subject to deadlines) unless specifically waived in writing by us as to each particular ad or advertising campaign. Although there are no restrictions on the areas in which you may advertise, we recommend that you concentrate on advertising in your local area as a matter of good business practice.

C. Transfer Fees. You shall be required to pay a transfer fee (except a transfer to a trained, qualified spouse or child, a corporation or entity wholly owned by you, or another franchisee in the system) of Four Thousand Five Hundred Dollars ($4,500) upon any assignment, sale, or transfer of the franchise to cover our costs of the training of the new assignee-franchisee upon approval of the assignment. The transfer fee shall be subject to consumer price increases based on annual inflationary rates as determined by the applicable CPI (Consumer Price Index) for the territory covering the inflationary price increases as compared with the year of opening of our franchise.

V. BUSINESS OPERATION

A. Employees, Inability to Conduct Business, Products and Services Sold. You shall use your best efforts to procure qualified and competent employees and shall maintain a neat, clean, safe, and orderly operation in keeping with the standards established by us through our manuals and periodic directive, including our standards set for all services and products sold by us to you. You shall not provide or sell any service or product without our prior written approval.

B. Business Records and Books of Account. You shall keep true and accurate business records and books of account and shall establish and maintain such records in accordance with the methods and procedures set forth by us.

C. Inspection. All books and records maintained by you with respect to your business shall be open to inspection by us or our duly authorized agent during regular business hours and we shall have the right to examine same, including other related records. You further consent to supply any other of its business reports upon request by us, including federal and state income tax returns, and the cost of any audit that we may conduct where the audit reveals an underpayment plus the maximum legal interest rate payment allowable by law on any amounts then due and owing.

D. Financial Statements. You further agree to have financial statements prepared, including a balance sheet and profit and loss statements made of your affairs, within sixty (60) days of the end of your fiscal year and to furnish us a copy of such audit within ten (10) days of completion thereof.

E. Claims and Liabilities, etc. You shall indemnify and save us harmless from any and all claims, liabilities, judgments, awards, or attachments arising from any sale and/or service by you and you shall promptly reimburse us for any sums expended by Franchisor as a result of such sales and/or service.

F. Uniformity in Operations. You, realizing that uniformity is a necessity in the system, agree, at our sole and complete discretion and options, to use such standard forms of reports, signs, stationery, ads, printed matter, and outside and inside decor as prescribed by us from time to time.

G. Meetings and Training Sessions. You or your manager shall attend all mandatory meetings and training sessions as designated by us in writing from time to time. Such mandatory meetings shall not exceed two per calendar year. You shall be responsible for your own travel, subsistence, and lodging expenses.

H. Signs, Stationery, Maintenance, Remodel, Appearance Specifications, etc. You shall purchase and use signs, stationery, business cards, and other trademarked items to be used in the franchise business bearing designations including the trademarks and service marks specified by us from time to time and same shall be purchased from vendors approved by us. You must maintain the appearance of the premises in a clean and attractive manner and remodel as directed by us according to our specifications.

I. Purchase of Merchandise. We are the only approved supplier for the diet supplements, paper forms, and dieting booklets used in conjunction with our diets at this time. Any scales in addition to the two (2) scales that are provided to you by us as part of your initial franchise fee must be purchased from a supplier approved by us and must include professional assembly and calibration. You must purchase or lease a commercial freezer and refrigerator with glass front doors from suppliers approved by us in writing. In the event that you believe that any such product of an equal quality can be purchased at a lower price, you must present us backup studies and data indicating the price of such items and the quality characteristics. Our sole testing procedures determine whether such items equal or exceed the quality and price reasonableness over the items approved by us. Our review typically is completed in 60 business days. If you desire to purchase any products, including supplements and food, services, equipment, and materials, from someone other than our designated supplier, you must submit a complete description of the history and credit rating of the supplier and the items you desire to purchase. You also must supply us with specifications and tests which will prove to our sole satisfaction that the products, equipment, and materials are of equal or superior quality to those which we or our designated supplier may offer for sale to you at what we feel are competitive prices and the supplier's ability to stand behind the supplier's product warranty which must meet or surpass those of our then-current designated supplier. We also require you to submit proof that the product meets USDA and FDA regulations for the type of product submitted, and the name, address, history, and ownership of the provider along with your brief business analysis of the cost, retail pricing, inventory requirements, need justification, break-even point, and marketing sales plan for the product. Suppliers of food, vitamins, and nutritional supplements also will be evaluated by compliance with appropriate USDA and FDA regulations for the type of food that you are providing, i.e., approved kitchen products, etc. Product ingredients will be evaluated by Maureen Sullivan, certified nutritionist, for healthfulness and appropriateness for the particular diet. In her absence another certified nutritionist will be designated. We also evaluate for taste, product appearance, and packaging, as well as cost and inventory requirements and how the manufacturer plans to market the product to other vendors. Six (6) samples of each product should be submitted to us for testing purposes. We will approve or disapprove a prospective supplier according to our complete and final discretion within 60 business days of receipt of your request to purchase from alternate suppliers. We may charge a fee to cover our costs in researching the product and our time spent doing so. Upon our approval of a product for sale in your franchise, we will provide written standards and specifications, including but not limited to sales methods, reporting and documentation, installation methods, etc. We may modify our specifications if changes occur in the industry based on our research and we will make this known to you in writing as the changes occur. We also may seek out and test suppliers on our own.

You might have to purchase other trademarked items to be used in the franchised business according to the specifications set forth by us in the operating manuals from time to time. We formulate and modify our specifications and standards for products and services through observations and testing that is available to you. We will provide you with a list of our approved suppliers after you have satisfactorily, in our judgment, completed your initial training. You must purchase an IBM compatible computer running a current version of Windows and possessing a CD-ROM or DVD drive, modem or DSL connection, and printer with fax capabilities. Internet Service Provider (ISP), anti-virus software, Internet browser, and email provider to be approved and compatible with our existing network systems. Current versions of QuickBooks Pro and Microsoft Office software and one (1) database program for tracking client information are required. You must update your software and hardware as we update ours and additional software may be required from time to time.

J. Audits. We reserve the right to audit your records and premises once a year (12 months) at your cost if the audit reveals a discrepancy of 2% or more with such discrepancy due and payable at the highest interest rate allowable by law.

VI. OFFICE MANAGEMENT

You (if an individual) or your principal owner or owners (if a partnership or corporation) are required to participate personally in the direct operation of the franchised business for at least thirty (30) hours per week divided equally between all locations owned. You are prohibited from the delegation of operational responsibility of the franchised business to any other person except as may otherwise be set forth in a written agreement between us and you, or approved in writing by us. You agree to hire only qualified, trained citizens meeting our standards of experience and background and you agree that you are responsible to see that your employees and independent contractors sign confidentiality agreements enforceable in your state. Preferably, your center should be operated by personnel that have successfully participated in our program. The shareholders of a corporate or other form of business entity must sign the Franchise Agreement as individuals, thereby assuming and agreeing to discharge all of the obligations of the "Franchisee" under the agreement.

VII. COMPETITION AND CONFIDENTIALITY

A. During Term. You shall not conduct or operate, directly or indirectly, or be associated or in any way employed or represent any business similar to the franchised business other than this franchise during the term of this agreement without our written consent. You further agree not to at any time furnish any information designated as confidential by us including our methods of promoting, maintaining, and operating the franchised business or any other information relative to our business. You shall: (1) strictly adhere to all security procedures prescribed by us at our sole discretion; (2) disclose such information to your employees only to the extent necessary to market your products and services and for the orderly operation of your business and only after securing a valid enforceable confidentiality agreement from such employees at your cost; (3) be prohibited from using any such information in any other business or in any manner not specifically authorized or approved in writing in advance by us; and (4) be required to exercise your highest degree of diligence to maintain the confidentiality of all such information during and after the term of the Franchise Agreement and to use its best efforts to secure confidentiality agreements enforceable under state law when required by us. You also stipulate that neither you nor your key employees will be employed or have a financial interest in a business similar to our business during the term of the franchise except for owning less than five (5%) percent of the stock of a competing company whose shares are traded on a national securities exchange.

B. Following Termination. You agree that following the termination of the franchise for any reason, you will not engage in a business similar to our business, or have a financial interest in such types of business for three (3) years after termination of this Agreement within a fifty (50) mile radius from any other of our company-owned offices or of a franchisee.

C. Public Policy. You are aware of the fact that this form of agreement is prepared for many jurisdictions with different public policies and that such public policies change and, accordingly, you hereby agree that the clauses hereinabove are severable and that the enforceability of one subclause shall not be contingent upon the enforceability or non-enforceability of any other subclause. You further agree that the prevailing non-competition restriction herein above set forth shall be modified automatically by the passage of any applicable state laws setting forth permissible non-compete clauses and that the language of such statute shall be automatically incorporated to a maximum extent herein by reference and shall constitute the limitation upon which you can compete after any termination of this Franchise Agreement.

D. Services or Products Offered for Sale. You will not conduct any other type of business or offer for sale any other services or products at such location without our prior written consent and under the terms and conditions set forth by us.

VIII. INDEPENDENT CONTRACTOR AND HOLD HARMLESS CLAUSE

You are herein granted a franchise and license to use our service marks and are therefore not authorized for or on behalf of us in any matter other than stated herein. You agree that you shall be responsible for and shall pay when due all expenses of the franchised business, including taxes and levies of any kind in connection with said business and the income arising therefrom. Failure by you to pay such encumbrances shall constitute a material violation of this Agreement subject to immediate termination by us. In addition, you agree that we shall not be liable for any expenses, taxes, levies, or disbursements otherwise paid or incurred in connection with the establishment and maintenance of your business and you hereby indemnify and hold us harmless from all liabilities, claims, suits, causes of action, demands, and expenses, including reasonable attorney's fees which may arise or be asserted against us by reason of operation of the franchise business or by reason of the use of our name. You agree that you are not authorized to use our name or other trademarks in any other capacity other than as provided herein nor to sign on our behalf any checks, drafts, leases, bonds, mortgages, documents, bills, contracts, or bills of sale or any other instruments in writing or to hold yourself out as our general partner. You shall hold yourself out as doing business as a franchisee and licensee under our name and member of our system unless otherwise provided herein. You shall immediately notify us of any lawsuits, actions, or proceedings instituted either by private parties or governmental authorities against you or us, including a complete description of the claim, action, or proceeding involved.

IX. INSURANCE AND HOLD HARMLESS

A. Insurance Premiums. At all times during the term of the Franchise Agreement, you shall maintain in effect a policy or policies of insurance naming us as an additional insured on the face of each policy at your sole cost and expense, subject to change from time to time, as follows:

1) Public liability in no less than $1,000,000 combined single limits for bodily injury and property damage, which amounts may be changed from time to time upon receipt of written demand from us.
2) Worker's compensation insurance as provided by state law for any employees you may choose to hire.
3) Comprehensive and collision auto liability insurance with deductibles not to exceed $1,000 but in no instance less than $1,000,000 combined single limits for bodily injury and property damage, which amounts may be changed upon receipt of written demand from us from time to time.
4) Business interruption insurance.

All insurance shall be with insurers acceptable to us. All policies of insurance shall be timely renewed and policies and certificates together with evidence of payment of premiums shall be delivered to us at least thirty (30) days prior to the expiration of such policies by certified mail or by hand delivery with receipt.

X. OWNERSHIP CHANGES, TRANSFER FEES, DEFAULTS, AND REMEDIES

Depending upon the entity involved, the following terms shall apply regarding transfer during the initial term or renewal term of the Franchise Agreement:

A. Sole Proprietorship. If you are a sole proprietorship, and you are not in default, the following provisions shall apply:

1) In the event of the death of the proprietor, the Franchise Agreement shall terminate unless, during the period of thirty (30) days from your death, your personal representative shall certify that you have an issue or spouse that wishes to take over the proprietorship or, in the alternative, if your personal representative shall receive a bona fide offer to purchase the deceased franchisee's business, a Franchise Agreement shall be granted accordingly for the area covered in this Agreement if said heir, spouse, or purchaser fulfills our requirements and upon receipt of written approval from us and the sum of Four Thousand Five Hundred Dollars ($4,500) is paid to us to cover our expenses in connection with effecting the transfer. Such transfer shall be contingent upon the execution by the prospective purchaser, issue, or spouse of the then-current form of our Franchise Agreement. In the event that the successor is the qualified and trained spouse or direct issue of the deceased franchisee, the transfer fee required to be paid shall be waived by us. We shall have the right of first refusal to purchase your business where the proposed sale is to a non-spouse or non-issue for the same price and upon the same terms and conditions as offered to the deceased franchisee's personal representative by a third party within thirty (30) days of receipt of written notice from said personal representative or, in absence of a third party offer, at the appraised value as appraised in accordance with the procedure as set forth hereinafter. If you do not approve the new owners, the franchisee's estate may sell the franchise to a transferee acceptable to us within three (3) months after such disapproval. If such a sale is not completed within that time, we may terminate the Franchise Agreement. If the property is stalled in probate for more than six (6) months, we have the right to place a manager in the franchised location and all necessary support systems to maintain the franchise on a cost plus ten percent (10%) basis.

2) In the event the sole proprietor desires to sell, assign, transfer, or otherwise hypothecate his/her interest during his/her lifetime, such sale shall be subject to: (1) payment to us by the sole proprietor of a transfer fee of Four Thousand Five Hundred Dollars ($4,500) to defray the expense of investigating the new purchaser and approval of same, (2) approval from us of the purchaser, which approval shall not unreasonably be withheld, (3) the purchaser executing the then-current form of our Franchise Agreement, and, if required by us, (4) our prior right to have the option of the first right of refusal to purchase the sole proprietor's business for the same price and upon the same terms and conditions as offered by the bona fide purchaser. In the event that the sole proprietor is selling to a qualified, trained spouse or issue or another franchisee in the system, the transfer fee and our right of first refusal are waived. Such transfer is subject to the transferee satisfactorily completing the training and testing required by us.

B. Partnership. If you are a partnership and the partnership is not in default, the following provisions apply:

1) This Franchise Agreement shall terminate immediately, except as otherwise provided herein, upon the dissolution of the partnership for any reason.

2) In the event of the death of a partner or partners, the franchise shall be terminated upon the expiration of one hundred twenty (120) days from the date of death. During such period, the partner surviving shall have the right to apply for permission to operate in the franchised area. Such permission shall not be unreasonably withheld by us. Upon securing such written approval of us and upon the surviving partner executing the then-current form of Franchise Agreement, a franchise shall be granted to the surviving partner for the area covered by this Agreement. If the surviving partner desires to associate a new partner into the franchise, the provisions of subparagraph B-3(a) through (d) immediately below shall also apply.

3) In the event that any partner sells, assigns, transfers, or otherwise hypothecates his/her interest in the partnership or any portion of it, the franchise shall also immediately terminate. However, the remaining partners shall have the right to continue the operation in the franchised area if, prior to such transfer, sale, assignment, or hypothecation, the following has been complied with:

a) We have been offered a first right of refusal to purchase such remaining interest which constitutes legal and entire ownership of the franchise within thirty (30) days after written notice at the price and terms of bona fide offer; and we do not so purchase the remaining interest and the remaining partner or the partnership is not in default;

b) Any proposed new partner has been approved by us after a review of the proposed new partner's financial and management qualities;

c) The remaining partner (and any proposed new partner) executes a then-current form of Franchise Agreement in use by us.

d) Payment to us by any proposed new partner of a sum representing a portion of Four Thousand Five Hundred Dollars ($4,500) based on a ratio calculated by the interest that the proposed new partner bears to the total partnership participating in the franchise. Such fee shall be for the purpose of covering our expenses in effecting such transfer. Such transfer is subject to the transferee satisfactorily completing the training and testing required by us.

4) You shall at all times immediately report to us any changes or proposed changes involving the interest of the partnership, including any dissolution of the partnership caused by death, termination, bankruptcy, or other causes.

C. Corporation. If you are a corporation and the corporation is not in default, the following provisions will apply:

1) We have been offered a first right of refusal to purchase the shares within thirty (30) days after written notice of such sale and its terms, and we do not exercise our option to purchase such shares. The present shareholders, if individually owned stock, or, if you are owned by a second corporation, the shares constituting majority control of the first and second corporation, shall not be assigned or transferred in any manner without our prior written approval, which approval will not be unreasonably withheld and must comply with the following under all circumstances:

a) Written approval by us of all proposed shareholders subject to personal interviews and subject to our first right of refusal set forth in paragraph D-2 hereinafter.

b) Execution of the then-current form of Franchise Agreement by you and all of your shareholders and all shareholders of any corporations holding any of your shares who shall agree to be individually bound by the terms and condition of this Agreement.

c) Payment to us of the transfer fee equivalent to the proportions of the issued and outstanding stock to be sold or transferred to the proposed new shareholders which bears to your total issued and outstanding stock times the sum of Four Thousand Five Hundred Dollars ($4,500) where such stock is transferred to a non-spouse or direct issue. Such transfer fee is to cover our expense in investigating and transferring said stock. The new shareholders are, at our option, required at the shareholders' cost to satisfactorily complete the training and testing required by us prior to operation of the transferred franchise by the new shareholders.

2) All of your share certificates or any corporation holding any of your shares shall be properly endorsed by you so as to contain a written notice that transfer of those shares is permitted only in accordance with the provisions of this paragraph.

3) The shareholders of the franchised corporate entity shall not sell or issue additional shares of stock of the franchised corporate entity nor shall the corporate entity controlling the franchise entity unless issued and sold to shareholders who have signed this agreement.

D. Incorporation, Transfer of Franchise Agreement, and Buy-Sell Agreements.

1) You shall not incorporate or otherwise change the form of the franchise business without our prior written consent and upon such conditions as we shall then impose. You shall not use "Lite For Life" in any corporate title without our consent.

2) You shall not sell, transfer, sublicense, or assign this Agreement or any rights, privileges, or interest accruing hereunder to any person, firm, or corporation without our written consent and upon such terms and conditions as we shall impose.

3) You shall provide us with a copy of all Buy-Sell Agreements pertaining to any transfer of a business or of the Franchise Agreement at least twenty (20) days prior to the contemplated transfer date for our prior approval.

E. Shareholder Guarantee. The shareholders of your corporate entity and the shareholders of any corporate entity that may own the shares of the corporate entity which is franchised hereunder agree by signing this Agreement to guarantee the payment of all sums which may from time to time become due to us under this Agreement and to agree to be bound by the provisions and terms of this Agreement. Such shareholders further agree that we would be entitled to injunctive relief as set forth in other portions of this Agreement.

F. Appraisal. In the absence of a bona fide offer in all cases wherein we have the first right of refusal, whether a sole proprietorship, a partnership, or a corporation, we and you will have ten (10) business days after receipt of written notice from the proposed seller to mutually agree upon the value of the interest being transferred to us and the terms on which the transfer will be made. If the parties do not reach an agreement within thirty (30) days thereafter, then each party, solely at its own cost, will hire an independent, designated, and active member of the American Society of Appraisers for the purpose of determining the value of the ownership interest being transferred. The appraisal will be completed within a reasonable period of time not to exceed thirty (30) calendar days. If the higher appraisal is less than ten percent (10%) higher than the lower appraisal, then the value of the interest being transferred will be established as the average of the two (2) appraisals. If the higher appraisal is more than ten percent (10%) higher than the lower appraisal, then the two (2) appraisers will have thirty (30) days from the date of the latter submitted appraisals to submit the name of a third, independent, designated, and active member of the American Society of Appraisers. The parties agree to cause a third appraisal to be made, by said third appraiser, within a reasonable time period but not to exceed thirty (30) days, with the expense for same to be shared equally by the parties. The value of the interest being transferred will then be established by adding the amounts of the first and second appraisers and twice the amount of the third appraiser and dividing the sum by four (4). The parties will then have thirty (30) days within which to agree on the terms of the purchase. If no agreement has been reached within said period, then, at our sole cost, the terms for the purchase will be settled by arbitration composed of three (3) arbitrators in accordance with the mutual arbitration rules of the American Arbitration Association and judgment upon a decision rendered by the arbitrators may be entered into any court having jurisdiction thereof. Within ten (10) days after receiving the arbitrator's decision, we will notify the proposed transferee of its intent to exercise its right of first refusal. If said notice is not dispatched within said ten (10) days, then Franchisor's right of first refusal will lapse. Such appraisal and repurchase price will recognize goodwill and other intangibles associated with the normal business sale.

G. Default—Material Violations—Termination. The conditions under which we may terminate subject to a thirty (30) day notice to cure unless otherwise specified include:

   (a) The attachment of any involuntary lien in the sum of $1,000 or more upon any of your business assets or property, which lien is not promptly removed.
   (b) Conduct of the franchised business in such a manner so as to affect materially and adversely our goodwill or reputation or our products and services.
   (c) Default by you under any agreement between you and us not subject to earlier termination as agreed by the parties.
   (d) Any purported assignment, transfer, or sublicense of the franchise, or any right hereunder, without our prior written consent.
   (e) Failure to make timely payment to us of any and all sums payable to us pursuant to the Franchise Agreement after five (5) days' written notice of such failure to pay.
   (f) Failure to make timely payments upon any obligation of you upon which we are acting as a guarantor or default upon or a breach of any provision of any promissory note or other evidence of indebtedness or any agreement relating thereto.
   (g) Failure to cure a default under the Franchise Agreement, within ten (10) business days after receipt of notice thereof, which default materially impairs the goodwill associated with our trade names, trademarks, service marks, logotypes, or other commercial symbols.
   (h) Failure to pay for or conduct any audit required by us or failure to secure and maintain the required insurance, including public liability and worker's compensation insurance, after ten (10) days' written notice requiring such deficiency to be cured.
   (i) Failure to supply reports on gross sales receipts and business activities to us or other reports and other product sales.
   (j) Failure to use the techniques, training, and methods promulgated by any manuals and any

periodic directives from us and/or the standards of quality and maintenance or forms, invoices, receipts, stationery, ads, and printed matter as directed by us or failure to attend mandatory training or seminar sessions required by us limited to not more than two (2) sessions per calendar year.

(k) Failure to put your full efforts into the franchised business (or at least forty [40] hours per week) or, in your excused absence, to have the franchised business managed by someone who has the proper training and aptitude in our procedures and systems.

(l) Failure to keep true and accurate business records and books in accordance with our procedures or failure to open them for inspection or provide federal and state income tax returns as requested by us or upon discovery of a deficit of two percent (2%) or more in any audit of your business.

(m) Failure to maintain and utilize fixtures, signs, exhibit booths, and decor as designated by us for the success of the franchise in order to ensure continuity of quality.

(n) Failure to maintain confidential any information designated as confidential by us.

(o) Failure to operate a weight loss center outfitted according to our specifications.

(p) Failure to purchase merchandise sold by you from vendors that are approved by us in order to ensure uniformity in the quality of the services rendered and products and goods sold in our system.

(q) Failure to participate in any purchasing or distribution cooperative that we deem will allow you cost savings for equal quality upon written notice from us or failure to purchase or lease a commercial freezer and refrigerator with glass front doors from approved suppliers and/or supplements, vitamins, protein power, paper forms, and diet books approved by us in writing; failure to use an IBM-compatible computer running a current version of Windows and possessing a CD-ROM or DVD drive, modem or DSL connection and printer with fax capabilities, Internet Service Provider (ISP), anti-virus software, Internet browser, and email provider to be approved and compatible with our existing network systems. Current versions of QuickBooks and Microsoft Office software and one (1) database program for tracking client information are required. You will update your software and hardware as we update ours and additional software may be required from time to time.

If during the period in which the franchise is in effect, there occurs any of the following events which is relevant to the franchise, immediate notice of termination without an opportunity to cure shall be deemed reasonable.

(a) The Franchise Agreement provides for termination upon bankruptcy. This provision may not be enforceable under Federal Bankruptcy Law (11 U.S.C. Section 101 et seq.).

(b) We and you agree in writing to terminate the franchise. You abandon the franchise by failing to operate the business for five (5) consecutive days during which time you are required to operate the business under the terms of the franchise, or any shorter period after which it is not unreasonable under the facts to conclude that you do not intend to continue to operate the franchise, unless such failure is due to fire, flood, earthquake, or other similar causes beyond your control.

(c) You make any material misrepresentations relating to the acquisition or operation of the franchise or you engage in conduct which reflects materially and unfavorably upon the operation and reputation of the franchise system.

(d) You fail, for a period of ten (10) days after notification of noncompliance, to comply with any federal, state, or local law or regulation applicable to the operation of the franchise.

(e) You, after curing any failure in accordance with Section D(a) through (p), engage in the same conduct or noncompliance, whether or not such conduct or noncompliance is corrected after notice.

(f) You repeatedly fail to comply with one or more requirements of the Franchise Agreement, whether or not corrected after notice.

(g) The franchise business or business premises of the franchise are seized, taken over, or foreclosed by a governmental official in the exercise of his duties, or seized, taken over, or foreclosed by a creditor, lienholder, or lessor, provided that a final judgment against you remains unsatisfied for thirty (30) days (unless supersedes or other appeal bond has been filed); or a levy of execution has been made upon the license granted by the Franchise Agreement or upon any property used in the franchised business, and it is not discharged within five (5) days of such levy.

(h) You are convicted of a felony or any other criminal misconduct which is relevant to the operation of the franchise.

(i) You fail to pay any franchise fees or other amounts due to us or our affiliate within five (5) days after receiving written notice that such fees are overdue.

(j) We make a reasonable determination that continued operation of the franchise by you will result in an imminent danger to public health or safety.

H. Discontinue Use of Trade Practices After Termination. In the event of termination of the Franchise Agreement for any reason, you lose all rights to all fees paid and may no longer use our trademarks, service marks, trade name, copyrights, systems, manuals, displays, your telephone numbers, or any other property connected with the franchise. You must immediately cease use of all of our trade names, systems, service marks, trademarks, training manuals, and other proprietary property, which must be returned to us immediately upon written notice. We have the right to enter the premises of the franchised location and to recover and remove our training material and all other proprietary property. On any termination of you due to a default by you, we have the option to purchase the equipment and tangible assets and take assignment of any lease of the weight loss center for an amount equal to the then-used fair market value of the property or assets. Any amounts due or owing us by you shall be set off against any used fair market value of the property subject to conveyance or the leases involved. You, in executing the Franchise Agreement, agree to assign all right, title, and interest to all of your business telephone numbers upon termination for any reason of your franchise and to execute any further documents or instruments or instructions necessary to further effect such transfer.

I. Monetary Obligations upon Termination. In the event of termination, we may retain all fees paid pursuant to this Agreement. In addition, all of our obligations to you and all of your rights under this Agreement shall automatically terminate; however, any of your obligations to take, or abstain from taking, any action upon termination pursuant to this Agreement shall not be affected by such termination, including the payment to us of all sums due from you at the time of termination.

J. Conflicting Law on Breach. Any provisions of this paragraph which may be determined by competent authority to be prohibited or unenforceable or contrary to the law of the jurisdiction having authority over this transaction shall be ineffective to the extent of its inconsistency with such state law and this agreement shall be deemed modified to comply with such law, but only to the extent necessary to prevent the invalidity of this Agreement or any provision hereof, the imposition of any fine or penalty or the creation of any civil or criminal liability on account thereof.

K. Termination by Franchisee.

1. You may terminate the Franchise Agreement by obtaining our written consent, which consent we are not obligated to give.

2. You may terminate the Franchise Agreement for good cause only if we have materially breached the Franchise Agreement, provided, however, prior to your terminating the Franchise Agreement for good cause, you must serve a written notice of default upon us specifying the grounds for default and granting us a reasonable opportunity, but in no case less than thirty (30) days, in which to cure the default or in which to commence diligent efforts to cure the default (if the default cannot reasonably be expected to be cured within thirty [30] days).

XI. FRANCHISEE'S OBLIGATIONS UPON TERMINATION

A. In the event of termination of this Franchise Agreement for any reason whatsoever, you shall promptly and immediately cease using our trade names, service marks, or trademarks and shall cease identifying itself as a member of our system; shall forthwith cease operating a franchise; shall promptly remove all signs bearing our names and identification; shall cause any registration of said names to be cancelled or withdrawn or, in the alternative, if requested by us, shall assign such registered names to us or our nominee; shall return to us or our representatives immediately upon written demand all customer lists, records, and books of account pertaining to your business and all training films, forms, materials, and manuals belonging to us or bearing our name or service mark, with delivery being made directly to us or our authorized representatives. You shall immediately cancel all telephone listing and yellow page ads and discontinue the use of any telephone numbers used in conjunction with the franchise business. However, upon our written request, you shall assign said telephone numbers to us or our designee and shall use your best efforts to secure the cooperation of the telephone company in assigning such numbers to us or our designee.

B. The termination of this Agreement for any reason shall not be deemed to release you from any and all sums due or to become due hereunder or from your obligations regarding non-competition and such other obligation as set forth herein.

C. Waiver of any one or more defaults you hereunder shall not operate as a waiver of successive or other defaults and all of our rights shall continue notwithstanding any such waiver or waivers.

XII. NOTICES

A. Writing. All notices, requests, demands, payments, consents, and other communications hereunder shall be transmitted in writing and shall be deemed to have been duly given when sent by registered or certified United States mail, postage prepaid, addressed as follows:

FRANCHISOR: Lite For Life Franchising Corporation, Inc.

Attn: President

Lite For Life Franchising Corporation, Inc.
A California Corporation
1199 Howard Ave., Suite 102
Burlingame, California 94010

FRANCHISEE: _____

_____

_____

B. Mailing Notice Address Change. Either party may change his/her or its mailing address for notice purposes only by giving notice of such change of address to the other party in writing.

C. Notice by Telegram or Fax. In the case of any notice required to be given by us or you hereunder, telegraphic or faxed notice with delivery verified shall be sufficient notice hereunder.

D. Mailed Notice. Mailed notices shall be deemed communicated within three (3) days from the time of mailing if mailed as provided in this paragraph.

XIII. MISCELLANEOUS

A. Injunction. You recognize the unique value and secondary meaning attached to the franchised system, its trade names, service marks, trademarks, standards of operation, and the trade practices and agree that any noncompliance with the terms of this Agreement or any unauthorized or improper use will cause irreparable damage to us and our franchisees. You therefore agree that if you should engage in any such unauthorized or improper use, during or after the period of this franchise, we shall be entitled to apply for both permanent and temporary injunctive relief from any arbitration panel or court of competent jurisdiction in addition to any other remedies prescribed by laws.

B. Additional Actions. The parties agree to execute such other documents and perform such further acts as may be necessary or desirable to carry out the purposes of this Agreement.

C. Heirs, Successors, and Assigns. This Agreement shall be binding and inure to the benefit of the parties, their heirs, successors, and assigns.

D. Entire Agreement. THE UNDERSIGNED ACKNOWLEDGE THAT THEY HAVE READ THIS AGREEMENT IN FULL, AND EACH OF THEM HAVE BEEN SUPPLIED WITH A CIRCULAR IN ACCORDANCE TO FEDERAL AND STATE LAW AND ARE COGNIZANT OF EACH AND EVERY ONE OF THE TERMS AND PROVISIONS THEREOF AND AGREEABLE THERETO; THAT NO REPRESENTATIONS OR AGREEMENTS, WHETHER ORAL OR WRITTEN, EXCEPT AS HEREINAFTER SET FORTH, HAVE BEEN MADE OR RELIED UPON; THAT THE SIGNATURES AFFIXED HERETO WERE AFFIXED AS THE WHOLLY VOLUNTARY ACT OF THE PERSONS WHO SIGNED THIS AGREEMENT; AND THAT THE TERMS AND PROVISIONS OF THIS FRANCHISE AGREEMENT CANNOT BE CHANGED OR MODIFIED UNLESS IN WRITING SIGNED BY THE AUTHORIZED REPRESENTATIVE OF YOU AND AN AUTHORIZED CORPORATE OFFICER OF US; THAT THE UNDERSIGNED REALIZE THAT THERE CAN BE NO GUARANTEE OF SUCCESS SINCE YOUR BUSINESS ABILITY, APTITUDE, AND INDUSTRIOUS DISPOSITION ARE PRIMARY IN YOUR SUCCESS.

E. Waiver of Rights. Failure by either party to enforce any rights under this Agreement shall not be construed as waiver of such rights. Any waiver, including waiver of default, in any one instance shall not constitute a continuing waiver or a waiver in any other instance. Any acceptance of money or other performance by us from you shall not constitute a waiver of any default except as to the payment of the particular payment or performance so received.

F. Interest on Past Due Obligations. Any monies past due to us from you shall bear interest at the maximum rate permitted by the state whose law governs this Agreement. The foregoing shall not affect any other right or remedy of us arising from such delinquency.

G. Validity of Parts. Any invalidity of any portion of this Agreement shall not affect the validity of the remaining portion and, unless substantial performance of this Agreement is frustrated by any such invalidity, this Agreement shall continue in effect.

H. Effectiveness. The submission of this Agreement does not constitute an offer to franchise and this Agreement shall become effective only upon execution thereof by us and you.

I. Headings and Table of Contents. The headings and Table of Contents used herein are for purposes of convenience only and shall not be used in constructing the provisions hereof. As used herein, the male gender shall include the female and neuter genders, the singular shall include the plural, and the plural, the singular.

J. Execution by Franchisor. This Agreement shall not be binding on us unless and until we shall have accepted and it shall have been signed by our authorized officer.

K. Assignment by Franchisor. This Agreement may be assigned in whole or in part by us without your prior approval and such assignment shall not modify or diminish your obligations hereunder.

L. Third Parties. The parties intend to confer no benefit or right on any person or entity not a party to this Agreement and no third party shall have the right to claim the benefit of any provision hereof as a third party beneficiary of any such provision.

M. Arbitration. Any claim or controversy arising out of or relating to this Agreement or the breach thereof shall be settled by arbitration before a panel of three (3) arbitrators duly licensed to practice law, in accordance with the rules then prevailing of the American Arbitration Association in Burlingame, California or at such American Arbitration Association office closest to the Franchisor's then-current place of business. The parties agree that the arbitrator or arbitrators may grant injunctive relief but no punitive or exemplary damages may be awarded in any dispute against either us or you or any affiliate, agent, officer, or director in any arbitration proceeding or otherwise and any rights thereto are hereby waived. The failure of one party to respond to any demand filed and served by the other party shall constitute a default by the non-responding party and any arbitration award so entered shall be binding. Judgment upon an award by the aforementioned arbitrator(s) filed in a court of competent jurisdiction shall be binding. The parties agree that any allegations regarding fraud or fraud in inducement shall be subject to arbitration and waive any statutory law to the contrary. Each party shall initially pay one-half of the expenses and fees of the neutral arbitrator(s) and other expenses of the arbitration incurred or approved by the neutral arbitrator(s), not including attorney's fees, witness fees, or other expenses incurred by one of the parties for its own benefit.

N. Governing Law. This Agreement shall be governed by and construed in accordance with the internal laws of the State of California; however, if this Agreement concerns a center located in another state and the laws of that state require terms other than those or in addition to those contained herein, then this Agreement shall be deemed modified so as to comply with the appropriate laws of such state, but only to the extent necessary to prevent the invalidity of this Agreement or any provision hereof, the imposition of fines or penalties, or the creation of civil or criminal liability on account thereof. Any provision of this Agreement which may be determined by competent authority to be prohibited or unenforceable in any jurisdiction shall, as to that jurisdiction, be ineffective to the extent of the prohibition or unenforceability without invalidating the remaining provisions of this Agreement. Any prohibition against or unenforceability of any provision of this Agreement in any jurisdiction, including the state whose law governs this Agreement, shall not invalidate the provision or render it unenforceable in any other jurisdiction. To the extent permitted by applicable law, you waive any provision of law which renders any provision of this Agreement prohibited or unenforceable in any respect.

XIV. NO PROJECTIONS OR REPRESENTATIONS

You acknowledge and represent that you have not received from us any projections or representations regarding the amount of income you can expect to earn from the franchise granted hereby. You acknowledge that no representations or warranties inconsistent with the offering circular or this agreement were made to induce you to execute this agreement.

You acknowledge that neither we nor any other person can guarantee the success of your business.

By signing this Franchise Agreement, you acknowledge that you have read same and that the Franchisor has been requested to state in writing hereafter any terms, claims, covenants, promises, or representations, including representations as to any income or gross revenue projections, that are not contained in this agreement that were made to you by the Franchisor or its representatives, including the persons making same, the location, and date. If no such representations, etc., were made, you should write the word "none" on the following line: _____

XV. ADDITIONAL REPRESENTATIONS

You make the following additional warranties and representations:

A. You are a (check one):

[ ] Partnership   [ ] Corporation   [ ] Sole Proprietorship

B. If you are a corporation or partnership, there is set forth below the name and address of each shareholder or partner holding an interest in the corporation or partnership as well as the name of the partner or shareholder who will attend training for the purpose of becoming an approved and responsible manager.

FRANCHISOR:
LITE FOR LIFE FRANCHISING CORPORATION, INC.

Date: _____   By: _____
                                        (Typed or Printed Name and Title)

FRANCHISEE:

_____
(Typed Name of Entity)

Date: _____   By: _____
                                    (Signature and Title of Authorized Officer,
                                      if a Corporate Entity)

Date: _____   By: _____
                                    (Signature of Sole Proprietor, if a Sole Proprietorship)

Date: _____   By: _____
                                    (Signature of a Partner; if a Partnership,
                                      All Partners Must Sign)

Date: _____   By:_____
                                    (Signature of Any Additional Partner, if a Partnership)

Date: _____   By: _____
                                    (Signature of Any Additional Partner, if a Partnership)

SHAREHOLDERS OF FRANCHISE
(If Corporate Entity is involved, all Shareholders must sign and date and by signing hereunder agree
to be individually bound by all of the terms and conditions of this Agreement.)

Date: _____   By: _____
                                    (Signature of Shareholder, if a Corporate Entity)

Date: _____   By: _____
                                    (Signature of Shareholder, if a Corporate Entity)

SCHEDULE 1

Map of location to be attached here.

SCHEDULE 2

List of initial supplies provided by franchisor to be attached here.

Appendix C
Background Questionnaire for Offering Circular

s a franchisor, you will be required—either by federal or state laws—to prepare and use an offering circular when offering a franchise for sale. This offering circular incorporates certain required information concerning such items as:

- The description of your business to be franchised;
- Your business's litigation and bankruptcy history;
- Your background and that of your principals as franchisors; and
- The extent of the support you plan to give your franchisees.

To help you gather this information and other important facts and figures for your offering circular, complete the background questionnaire in this appendix. When you have filled out this questionnaire, you will not only have learned more about you and your business, you will also have helped to facilitate the offering circular process. By saving time on this critical information gathering, you could even possibly reduce your attorney fees for preparing the first draft of your offering circular.

When answering the questions, be sure to attach additional sheets if needed.

This questionnaire is to be used in gathering required due diligence information from the franchisor for insertion into the new Uniform Franchise Offering Circular as adopted by NASAA on April 25, 1993, effective on or before January 1, 1995.

1. (a) Franchisor's name, principal business address (home office in the United States), and telephone number. (If a franchise corporation is to be formed, insert the name of the proposed new corporation.) (The business address cannot be a post office.)

    _____

    _____

    _____

    (b) Name, principal business address, and telephone number of international home office.

    _____

    _____

    _____

2. If the franchisor had a predecessor, i.e., a person from whom the franchisor acquired during the past 10 years or will acquire directly or indirectly the major portion of the franchisor's assets, give the name, address, and telephone number of the predecessor.

    _____

    _____

    _____

3. If the proposed franchisor has an affiliate, defined as a corporation or entity other than a natural person controlled by, controlling, or under common control with the franchisor that is offering franchises in any line of business or is providing products or services to the franchisee of the franchisor, give the name, address, and telephone number.

    _____

    _____

    _____

4. The name under which the franchisor does or intends to do business.

    _____

    _____

    _____

5. The name, address, and telephone number of person who will be listed as agent for service of process.

   _____

   _____

   _____

6. State of incorporation or business organization and the type of business organization (corporation, partnership, sole proprietorship).

   _____

   _____

   _____

7. (a) Does the franchisor operate a business of the type being franchised?   Yes ❏ No ❏
   If yes, give a brief description of the location and type of business.

   _____

   _____

   _____

   (b) Does or has the franchisor sold or granted franchises?   Yes ❏ No ❏
   If yes, please describe when, where, and to whom.

   _____

   _____

   _____

8. List the franchisor's other business activities.

   _____

   _____

   _____

9. Please give a brief description of the business to be conducted by the franchisees.

   _____

   _____

   _____

10. Describe briefly the general market for the product or service to be offered by the franchisee. Is it a relatively new product or service or is the market fairly saturated? Will the goods or services be seasonal or offered primarily to a certain group of purchasers?

_____

_____

_____

11. Are there any regulations specific to the industry in which your franchise business will operate? (Include any special licenses or legal restriction on operations set by statutes.)

_____

_____

_____

12. Give a brief description of the competition that will be faced by your franchisees.

_____

_____

_____

13. Give the prior business experience of the franchisor, including (1) the length of time the franchisor has conducted a business of the type to be operated by the franchisee; and (2) the length of time the franchisor has offered franchises for the same type of business as that to be operated by the franchisee and in which states the franchises were offered.

_____

_____

_____

14. Describe whether the franchisor has offered franchises in any other lines of business, including:
a) A description of each other line of business:

_____

_____

_____

b) The number of franchises sold in each other line of business:

_____

_____

_____

c) The length of time the franchisor has offered each other franchise:

_____

_____

_____

15. Briefly describe the business experience of any predecessor and/or affiliate of the franchisor, including (1) the length of time each predecessor or affiliate has conducted a business of the type to be operated by the franchisee; and (2) the length of time each predecessor and affiliate has offered franchises for the same type of business as that to be operated by the franchisee.

_____

_____

_____

16. Describe whether or not each predecessor and affiliate offered franchises in another line of business and, if so, include:
a) The description of each other line of business:

_____

_____

_____

b) The number of franchises sold in each other line of business:

_____

_____

c) The length of time each predecessor and affiliate offered each other franchise:

_____

_____

17. List by name and position all of the directors of the corporation or general partners of the partnership or trustees of the trust and include each person's principal occupation and employers during the past five years, with the beginning date and departure date for each job so designated, as well as the location of the job.
Director, General Partner, Trustee (strike inapplicable words):

_____

_____

_____

Director, General Partner, Trustee (strike inapplicable words):

_____

_____

_____

Director, General Partner, Trustee (strike inapplicable words):

_____

_____

_____

Director, General Partner, Trustee (strike inapplicable words):

_____

_____

_____

(**Note:** Questions 1-17 should cover only the last 10 years.)

18. List by name and present position the principal officers and other executives who will have management responsibility relating to the franchises offered by this offering circular. (Include jobs for the last five years, with beginning and departure dates.)
Chief Executive Officer:

_____

_____

_____

Chief Operating Officer:

_____

_____

_____

President:

_____

_____

_____

Treasurer or Chief Financial Officer:

_____

_____

_____

Franchise Marketing Officer:

_____

_____

_____

Franchise Training Officer:

_____

_____

_____

Franchise Operations Officer:

_____

_____

_____

Director:

_____

_____

_____

Director:

_____

_____

_____

Director:

_____

_____

_____

Other employees or consultants having management responsibilities:

_____

_____

_____

19. Does the franchisor have a franchise broker, i.e., an independent firm that specializes in selling franchises?   Yes ❑ No ❑

    If yes, please briefly state the names, addresses, and telephone numbers of the franchise broker's directors, principal officers, and executives with management responsibilities to market or service the franchisor, including their beginning and departure dates of employment for the past five years.

_____

_____

_____

20. State whether or not the franchisor, its predecessor, a person identified in Item 2, or an affiliate operating franchises under the franchisor's principal trademark has been involved in any of the following:

    (a) Please state whether or not there is an administrative, criminal, or material civil action pending against that person(s) or entity(ies) alleging a violation of a franchise, antitrust, or securities law, fraud, unfair or deceptive practices, or comparable allegations. In addition, include actions other than ordinary routine litigation incidental to the business that are significant in the context of the number of franchisees and the size, nature, or financial condition of the franchise system or its business operations.   Yes ❑ No ❑

    If yes, disclose the names of the parties and the forum, nature, and current status of pending action.

_____

_____

_____

    (b) Please state whether or not such person(s) or entity(ies) have, during the 10-year period immediately before the date of this questionnaire, been convicted of a felony or pleaded nolo contendere to a felony charge, or been held liable in a civil action by final judgment, or been the subject of a material action involving a violation of franchise, antitrust or securities law, fraud, unfair deceptive practices, or comparable allegations.   Yes ❑ No ❑

    If yes, disclose the names of the parties and the forum and date of conviction or the date the judgment was entered, penalty or damages assessed, and/or terms of the settlement, including the name of the court and the number of the action.

_____

_____

_____

c) Please state whether or not the above-named person(s) or entity(ies) are subject to a currently effective injunctive or restrictive order or decree relating to the franchise or under a federal, state, or Canadian franchise, securities, antitrust, trade regulation, or trade practice law resulting from a concluded or pending action or proceeding brought by a public agency. Yes ❑ No ❑

If yes, disclose the names of the person, the public agency and court, a summary of the allegations found by the agency or court and the date, nature, terms, and conditions of the order or decree.

_____

_____

_____

(**Note:** For the purposes of the aforementioned, "franchisor" includes the franchisor, its predecessors, persons identified in Item 2, and affiliates offering franchises under the franchisor's principal trademarks. The definition of an "action" includes any complaints, cross-claims, counterclaims, or third-party claims in a judicial proceeding and their equivalent in administrative action or arbitration proceeding. The franchisor may disclose its counterclaims. Please omit actions that were dismissed by final judgment without liability of injury of an adverse order against the franchisor. The definition of "material" is an action or an aggregate of actions that a reasonable prospective franchisee would consider important in making a decision about the franchise business. It should also be noted that settlement of action does not diminish its materiality if the franchisor agrees to pay material consideration or agrees to be bound by obligations that are materially adverse to the franchisor's interest. Also note that "held liable" includes a finding by final judgment in judicial binding arbitration or administrative proceeding that the franchisor, as a result of claims or counterclaims, must pay money or other consideration, must reduce an indebtedness by the amount of the award, cannot enforce its rights, or must take action adverse to its interest. Give the title of each action and state the case numbers or citations along with the filing date, the opposing party's name, and the opposing party's relationship with the franchisor. "Relationship" includes competitor, supplier, lessor, franchisee, former franchisee, or class of franchisees. You should also summarize the relief sought or obtained. "Conviction" involves the title of the action and state citation in parentheses with the title underlined. Include the name of the person convicted or held liable and state the crime or violation and date of conviction as well as disclose any sentence or penalty.

21. Please state whether the franchisor, its affiliates, predecessor, officers, or general partner during the 10-year period immediately before the date of this questionnaire:

a) Filed as a debtor (or had filed against it) a petition to start an action under the U.S. Bankruptcy Code?   Yes ❑ No ❑

b) Obtained a discharge of its debts under the Bankruptcy Code?   Yes ❑ No ❑ or

c) Was a principal officer of a company or a general partner in a partnership that either filed as a debtor (or had filed against it) a petition to start an action under the U.S. Bankruptcy Code or obtained a discharge of its debts under the Bankruptcy Code within one year after the officer or general partner of the franchisor held the position in the company or partnership?   Yes ❑ No ❑

If yes, disclose the name of the person or company that was the debtor under Bankruptcy Code, date of the action, and the material facts, including the name of the party that filed or had filed against it. If the debtor was an affiliate of the franchisor, state the relationship. If the debtor in the bankruptcy proceeding is unaffiliated with the franchisor, state the name, address, and principal business of the bankrupt company.

_____

_____

_____

d) Did the entity referred to in subparagraph c) file bankruptcy or reorganization under the bankruptcy law?   Yes ❑ No ❑

If so, identify the date of original filing, the bankruptcy court, the case name and number, the date the debtor obtained a discharge in bankruptcy (including a discharge under Chapter 7), and confirmation of any plans of reorganization under Chapters 11 and 13 of the Bankruptcy Code.

_____

_____

_____

Note: Cases, actions, or other proceedings under the laws of foreign nations relating to bankruptcy proceedings should be included in answers where responses are required.

22. a) State what you think would be the initial franchise fee (includes all fees and payments for services or goods received from the franchisor before the business opens) and how you arrived at this figure.

_____

_____

_____

b) State whether or not the initial franchise fee includes all fees and payments, whether payable in a lump sum or installments before the franchisee's business opens. If no, please describe fees not included.

_____
_____
_____

c) Is the initial franchise fee uniform?   Yes ❑ No ❑

If no, disclose the formula or range of initial fees paid in the previous fiscal year, if any, before the application date and the factors that determined the amount of these initial fees.

_____
_____
_____

d) If the initial franchise fee is payable in installments, disclose the installment payment terms in this portion of the questionnaire as well as in the following portion, which is dedicated to information regarding Item 10 of the offering circular, i.e., the financial arrangements.

_____
_____
_____

23. Other Fees:

Name of Fee	Amount	Due Date	Remarks[1]
Royalty	_____	_____	_____
Advertising Fund	_____	_____	_____
Cooperative Advertising	_____	_____	_____
Local Advertising	_____	_____	_____
Additional Promotional Fees	_____	_____	_____
Initial Training	_____	_____	_____
Additional Training	_____	_____	_____
Transfer Fee	_____	_____	_____
Renewal Fee	_____	_____	_____
Audit Fee	_____	_____	_____

[1]Be sure to indicate, in the Remarks column, answers to each of the following questions:
  Is the fee imposed and collected by franchisor?
  Is the fee non-refundable?

At what point in time does interest begin?

Are the fees collected by the franchisor? If no, indicate those that are and those that are not and who collects the ones that are not collected by the franchisor.

Are all of the fees listed in the above chart non-refundable? If no, which fees are refundable? Will the franchisor-owned outlets (company-owned office) have voting power on any fees imposed by cooperatives? If yes, disclose a range for the fee.

(**Note:** When listing fees, as in the above chart, please remember that fees are royalty, lease negotiation, construction and remodeling, additional training, advertising, additional assistance, audit and accounting, inventory, transfer, and renewal fees. These are fees that are paid either to you as franchisor or your affiliate or fees that you or an affiliate collect in whole or part on behalf of the third party.)

24. **Initial Investment:** Disclose in the following chart the expenditures, including high and low, to the best of your ability. If columns "Method of Payment," "When Due," and "To Whom Payment Is to Be Made" are different from that stated below, cross out reply and write in applicable wording:

Payment	Amount	Method of Payment	When Due	To Whom Payment Is to Be Made
Non-refundable Initial Franchise Fee	$_____	$_____ upon signing Deposit Agreement and $_____ upon signing Franchise Agreement	Upon execution of Franchise and Deposit Agreements	Franchisor
Area Development Option Fee	$_____ to $_____ (each additional franchise option fee within territory is $_____	Lump sum	Upon execution of Area Development Option	Franchisor
Leasehold improvements[1,2]	$_____ to $_____	Progress payments according to construction agreement until completion	Generally by agreement with contractor	General contractor
Equipment, furnishings, and fixtures[2]	$_____ to $_____	As required by vendor	As required by vendor	Vendor

Payment	Amount	Method of Payment	When Due	To Whom Payment Is to Be Made
Complete signage (interior/exterior)	$_____ to $_____	As required by vendor	As required by vendor	Sign vendor
Blueprints, plans, permits	$_____ to $_____	As required by architects and authorities	As required by architects and authorities	Architect, planner, city, county, or state
Rental approximately _____ sq. ft. and up	$_____ to $_____ per month	Lump sum (non-refundable)	Monthly	To particular landlord
Initial inventory and operating supplies	$_____ to $_____	Lump sum	As required by supplier	Supplier
Security deposits (including lease deposit, utilities, licenses, etc.)	$_____ to $_____	Lump sum	As required by landlord	Landlord
Insurance	$_____ to $_____ per month	Lump sum	Normally at time of coverage	Insurance agent
Initial advertising and promotions (includes $_____ and opening promotion expenses)	$_____ to $_____	Lump sum	As required by media	Supplier
Miscellaneous (travel and living expenses while training, permits, organizational expenses, etc.)	$_____ to $_____	Lump sum	As needed	Airlines, restaurants, motels, governmental agencies, etc.
Additional funds necessary to commence or continue operation for 3 months[3]	$_____ to $_____	Lump sum	As needed	Employees, utilities, suppliers; does not provide living expenses for franchisee
Other	$_____ to $_____			
Total	$_____ (Including initial franchise fee) to $_____ (Including initial franchise fee)[4,5]			

[1] Please note that if Franchisee is able to wholly or partially finance the construction of the entire package above or only the leasehold improvements, the initial cash requirements will be reduced by the amount financed, but the monthly interest and principal debt service must be calculated in its place by the Franchisee according to the terms of the lender. Additionally, upon negotiation of lease, on occasion, some or all of tenant improvements may be paid by the lessor of the property.

[2] If fixtures, furniture, and/or equipment is leased, the amount of the minimum and maximum initial cash requirement may be decreased depending on local terms.

[3] This estimates your initial start-up expenses. These figures are estimates and we cannot guarantee that you will not have additional expenses starting the business. Your costs will depend on factors such as how much you follow our methods and procedures, your management skills, your experience and business acumen, local economic conditions, market for your product, prevailing wage rate, competition, and sales line reached during the initial start-up period.

[4] You should review our estimated figures carefully with a business advisor before making any decision to purchase the franchise.

[5] We do not offer direct or indirect financing to franchisees for any items.

(**Note:** If a specific amount is not ascertainable, use a low/high range based on your current experience. If a building is involved, describe the probable location of the building—such as a strip shopping mall, downtown, or rural—when filling out the chart pertaining to real estate and improvement. If you or an affiliate finance a part of the initial investment, state the expenditures that you will finance, the required down payment, the annual percentage interest rate and rate factors, and the estimated loan repayments. Please make descriptions brief. Also, remember to answer this question again when referring to Item 10 of the offering circular regarding financing.)

25.   Disclose any obligations you wish to impose on the franchisee to purchase or lease from you or your designee or from suppliers approved by you as franchisor or under your specifications.

      _____

      _____

      _____

      For each obligation, disclose:

      (a) The required goods, services, supplies, fixtures, equipment, inventory, computer hardware or software, or real estate relating to establishing or operating the franchise business:

      _____

      _____

      _____

      (b) The manner in which you issue and modify specifications or grants and revoke approval for suppliers:

      _____

      _____

      _____

(c) Whether and for what categories of goods and services you as franchisor or your affiliates are approved suppliers or the only approved suppliers:

_____

_____

_____

(d) Whether you as the franchisor or your affiliates will or may derive revenue or other material consideration as a result of required purchases or leases from you or your designee or your approved supplier and, if so, the precise basis.

_____

_____

_____

(e) If you require such purchases by the franchisee from you, your designee, or your approved supplier, estimate the proportion of these required purchases and leases to all purchases and leases by the franchisee of goods and services in establishing and operating a franchise business. In other words, if you require the franchisee to purchase $100 worth of equipment from you and the franchisee will purchase and lease other goods and services from other sources for $1,000, your estimated percentage proportion would be 10% (100 divided by 1,000). _____%

26. Is there or will there be a purchasing or distribution cooperative?   Yes ❑ No ❑

If yes, please describe.

_____

_____

_____

(**Note:** Do not include goods and services provided as part of the franchise without a separate charge. For example, a fee for initial training when the cost is included in the franchise fee. Do not include fees disclosed in your previous responses.)

27. Will you require the franchisee to follow specifications and standards?   Yes ❑ No ❑

If yes, please describe what the standards will apply to such items as procedures, construction, premises, software, hardware, or uniforms, and also how you would formulate and modify these specifications.

_____

_____

_____

28. Disclose whether your specification standards are issued by you to franchisees, subfranchisors, or approved suppliers, and how and when they are updated.

_____

_____

_____

29. Describe how your suppliers are evaluated and approved or disapproved by you.

_____

_____

_____

30. Will your criteria for suppliers be available to the franchisees?   Yes ❑ No ❑

_____

_____

_____

31. State the fees, if any, that a franchisee must pay you and the procedures he or she must follow to secure your approval of his or her suppliers as well as how your approval would be removed.

_____

_____

_____

32. State the time period that it will take you to approve or disapprove a supplier.

_____

_____

_____

33. Does a designated supplier make payments to you as franchisor because of transactions with your franchisees? Yes ❑ No ❑

    If yes, disclose the basis for the payment and specify a percentage or flat amount that supplier will pay to you.

_____

_____

_____

(**Note:** When answering this question, please remember that purchases of similar goods or services by you at a lower price than available to your resale to the franchisee is a payment to you when you pass on the goods or services at a higher price to your franchisee.)

34. Do you negotiate purchase arrangements with suppliers, including price terms for the benefit of franchisees?   Yes ❑ No ❑

35. Do you provide material benefits (for example, renew or granting additional franchises) to a franchisee based on a franchisee's use of designated or approved sources?   Yes ❑ No ❑

    If yes, please describe.

    _____

    _____

    _____

36. The following items A-X include obligations that many franchisors impose upon franchisees. Please state after each obligation whether or not you desire at this time to impose such an obligation on your franchisees.
    a. site selection and acquisition/lease: Yes ❑ No ❑
    b. pre-opening purchases/lease: Yes ❑ No ❑
    c. site development and other pre-opening requirements: Yes ❑ No ❑
    d. initial and ongoing training: Yes ❑ No ❑
    e. opening obligations: Yes ❑ No ❑
    f. fees (including royalty, advertising, transfer, renewal):   Yes ❑ No ❑
    g. compliance with standards and policies/operating manual: Yes ❑ No ❑
    h. trademarks and proprietary information obligations: Yes ❑ No ❑
    i. restrictions on products and services offered: Yes ❑ No ❑
    j. warranty and other consumer service requirements: Yes ❑ No ❑
    k. territorial development and sales quota: Yes ❑ No ❑
    l. ongoing products and service purchases: Yes ❑ No ❑
    m. maintenance, appearance, and remodeling requirements: Yes ❑ No ❑
    n. insurance requirements: Yes ❑ No ❑
    o. advertising requirements: Yes ❑ No ❑
    p. indemnification: Yes ❑ No ❑
    q. owner's participation/management staffing: Yes ❑ No ❑
    r. records and reports: Yes ❑ No ❑
    s. inspections and audits: Yes ❑ No ❑
    t. transfers: Yes ❑ No ❑
    u. renewals: Yes ❑ No ❑
    v. posttermination obligations: Yes ❑ No ❑
    w. noncompetition covenants: Yes ❑ No ❑
    x. dispute resolution, such as arbitration with FAM or the American Arbitration Association:
       Yes ❑ No ❑
    y. others: Yes ❑ No ❑

If yes, describe other obligations you will impose upon your franchisees:

_____

_____

(**Note:** These obligations will be listed in the circular and cross-referenced to the sections in the circular and franchise agreement.)

37. Financing: Do you intend to finance your franchisee, including its initial franchise fee or its monetary requirements for equipment, etc.? (Remember: financing includes leasing and installment contracts. Payments due you within 90 days on an open account need not be disclosed.)   Yes ❑ No ❑

    If yes, describe the written arrangements between you, your affiliate, and any lender for the lender to offer financing to the franchisee. Any arrangement by which you, as franchisor, or your affiliate receive a benefit from a lender for franchisee financing is an "indirect offer of financing," since any benefit received from a lender is indirect financing, and it must be disclosed. (For example, if you as franchisor guarantee a note, lease, or obligation of a franchisee, it is an "indirect offer of financing.")

    _____

    _____

    _____

    If you finance, please complete this summary of financing.

Item Financed (Source)	Amount Financed	Down Payment	Term (Yrs)	APR	Monthly Payment	Prepay Penalty	Security Required	Liability upon Default	Loss of Legal Right on Default
Initial Fee (Name of Lender)									
Land/ Construct									
Lease Space (Name of Lender)									
Equipment Lease (Name of Lender)									
Equipment Purchase (Name of Lender)									
Opening Inventory									
Other Financing									

38. Franchisor's Obligations: Please describe your obligations you intend at this time to include in your agreement in assisting your client prior to opening:

Prior to Opening: The following is a list of some obligations you may impose on yourself, if you choose, and that will require a brief description:

a) Will you locate a site for the franchised business and negotiate the purchase or lease of this site for the franchisee?   Yes ❏ No ❏

If yes, will you own the premises and lease it to the franchisee?   Yes ❏ No ❏

b) Will you conform the premises to local ordinances and building codes and obtain the required permits?   Yes ❏ No ❏

c) Will you construct, remodel, or decorate the premises for the franchised business?
   Yes ❏ No ❏

d) Will you purchase or lease equipment, signs, fixtures, opening inventory, and supplies for the franchisee?   Yes ❏ No ❏

If yes, will you provide these items directly?   Yes ❏ No ❏

If no, will you merely provide the names of approved suppliers?   Yes ❏ No ❏

Do you have written specifications for these items?   Yes ❏ No ❏

Do you deliver or install these items?   Yes ❏ No ❏

e) Do you hire and train employees for the franchisee?   Yes ❏ No ❏

f) List any other obligations you wish to impose on yourself prior to the franchisee's opening.

_____

_____

_____

After Opening: The following is a list of questions about your obligations during the operation of the franchised business that you may feel should be in your agreement:

a) Do you offer products or services to the franchisee to offer to its customers during the term of the agreement?   Yes ❏ No ❏

b) Do you hire and train employees of the franchisee during the term of the agreement?
   Yes ❏ No ❏

c) Do you make improvements and developments in the franchised business during the term of the agreement?   Yes ❏ No ❏

d) Do you do pricing during the term of the agreement?   Yes ❏ No ❏

e) Do you do administrative, bookkeeping, accounting, and inventory control procedures during the term of the agreement?   Yes ❏ No ❏

f) Do you handle or troubleshoot operating problems encountered by the franchisee during the term of the agreement?   Yes ❏ No ❏

g) Do you desire an advertising program that will feature the product or service offered by your franchisee?   Yes ❏ No ❏

If yes, provide the information elicited in the following 10 sections.

1) In which media do you intend to disseminate the advertising (for example, print, radio, or television)?

_____

_____

2) Is the coverage of the media local, regional, or national in scope?

_____

_____

3) What is the source of the advertising (e.g., in-house advertising department, a national or regional advertising agency)?

_____

_____

4) Under what conditions you will permit the franchisees to use their own advertising material?

_____

_____

5) If there is an advertising council composed of franchisees that advises you on advertising policies, indicate:

a) How members of the council are selected.

_____

_____

b) Whether the council serves in an advisory capacity only or has operational or decision-making power.

_____

_____

c) Whether you as franchisor have the power to form, change, or dissolve the advertising council.

_____

_____

6) If, during the term of the agreement you feel the franchisee must participate in a local or regional advertising cooperative, indicate:

a) How the area or membership of the cooperative is defined.

_____

_____

b) How the franchisee's contribution to the cooperative is calculated.

_____

_____

c) Who is responsible for administration of the cooperative (e.g., franchisor, franchisees, advertising agency).

_____

_____

d) Whether cooperatives must operate from written governing documents and whether the documents are available for review by the franchisee.

_____

_____

e) Whether cooperatives must prepare annual or periodic financial statements and whether the statements are available for review by the franchisee.

_____

_____

f) Whether the franchisor has the power to require cooperatives to be formed, changed, dissolved, or merged.

_____

_____

7) If applicable, for each advertising fund not described in above subpart (6), indicate:
a) Who contributes to each fund (e.g., franchisees, franchisor-owned units, outside vendors, or suppliers).

_____

_____

b) Whether the franchisor-owned units must contribute to the fund and, if so, whether it is on the same basis as franchisees.

_____

_____

c) How much the franchisee must contribute to the advertising fund(s) and whether other franchisees are required to contribute at a different rate. (It is not necessary to disclose the specific rates.)

_____

_____

d) Who administers the fund(s).

_____

_____

e) Whether the fund is audited and when, and whether financial statements of the fund are available for review by the franchisee.

_____

_____

f) If you already have a fund, please provide the following for the most recently concluded fiscal year: (a) the percentage spent on production: _____%; (b) the percentage spent on media: ____%; (c) the percentage spent on administrative expenses: ____%; and (d) the percentage spent on other (define: _____: ____%; _____: ____%). Your total should equal 100%.

g) Whether you or an affiliate receives payment for providing goods or services to an advertising fund.   Yes ❑ No ❑
If yes, describe:

_____

_____

8) Will you as franchisor be obligated to spend any amount on advertising in the area or territory where the franchisee is located?   Yes ❑ No ❑
If yes, describe:

_____

_____

9) If all advertising fees are not spent in the fiscal year in which they accrue, explain how you will use the remaining amounts.

_____

_____

Will the franchisees receive a periodic accounting of how advertising fees are spent?
Yes ❑ No ❑
If yes, how frequent is the accounting?

_____

_____

10) Disclose the percentage of advertising funds, if any, used for advertising that is principally a solicitation for the sale of franchises.

_____

_____

39. If your franchise agreement will require the franchisee to buy or use an electronic cash register or computer system, provide a general description of the systems in nontechnical language. Include in your description an identification of each hardware component and software program by brand, type, and principal functions and whether or not it is your proprietary property or that of an affiliate or a third party.

    _____

    _____

    _____

40. Do you, an affiliate, or a third party have a contractual obligation to provide ongoing maintenance, repair, upgrades, or updates to the hardware and software sold to your franchisee? Yes ❑ No ❑

41. Disclose the current annual cost of any optional or required maintenance and support contracts, upgrades, and updates.

    _____

    _____

    _____

42. If the hardware component or software program is the proprietary property of a third party and no compatible equivalent is available, identify the third party by name, business address, and telephone number.

    _____

    _____

    _____

43. If the hardware component or software program is not proprietary, identify compatible equivalent components or programs that perform the same functions and indicate whether you as franchisor have approved them.

    _____

    _____

    _____

44. State whether the franchisee has any contractual obligation to upgrade or update any hardware component or software program during the term of the franchise and, if so, whether there are any contractual limitations on the frequency and cost of the obligation.

    _____

    _____

    _____

45. For each electronic cash register system or software program, describe how it will be used in the franchisee's business and the types of business information or data that will be collected and generated.

   _____

   _____

   _____

46. State whether you, as the franchisor, will have independent access to the information and data set forth above and, if so, whether there are any contractual limitations on the franchisor's right to access the information and data.

   _____

   _____

   _____

47. Attach a copy of the table of contents of your operating manual, which will be provided to the franchisee as of the franchisor's last fiscal year end or a more recent date. Please indicate the number of pages devoted to each subject listed in the table of contents and the total number of pages in the manual as of this date.
   (**Note:** An alternative disclosure can be accomplished if the prospective franchisee is allowed to view the manual before the purchase of the franchise.)

Franchisor's Methods for Selecting the Location of the Franchisee's Business:

48. Do you select the site or approve an area within which the franchisee selects a site?
   Yes ❏ No ❏
   If yes, describe.

   _____

   _____

   _____

49. Describe how and whether you must approve a franchisee's selected site.

   _____

   _____

   _____

50. List the factors that you as franchisor consider in selecting or approving sites (for example, general location and neighborhood, traffic patterns, parking, size, physical characteristics of existing buildings, and lease terms).

   _____

   _____

   _____

51. Define the time limit for you as franchisor to locate or to approve or disapprove the site.

   _____

   _____

   _____

   Describe the consequences if the franchisor and franchisee cannot agree on a site.

   _____

   _____

   _____

52. Indicate the typical length of time (a range is permissible) between the signing of the franchise agreement or the first payment of consideration for the franchise and the opening of the franchisee's business.

   _____

   _____

   _____

53. Describe any factors that may affect the time period of opening, such as a delay in obtaining a lease, financing or building permits, zoning and local ordinances, weather conditions, shortages, or delays in the installation of equipment, fixtures, and signs.

   _____

   _____

   _____

Training Program of the Franchisor:

54. Describe the location, duration, and general outline of the training program.

   _____

   _____

   _____

55. How often will the training program be conducted after the pre-opening training program and who is required to attend?

_____

_____

_____

56. List the names and experience of your instructors, in number of years and subjects.

_____

_____

_____

57. List charges to be made to the franchisee and indicate who must pay travel and living expenses of the enrollees in the training program.

_____

_____

_____

58. For all non-mandatory training programs, if available, state the percentage of new franchisees who enrolled in these non-mandatory training programs during the preceding 12 months.

_____

_____

_____

59. State whether or not any additional training programs and/or refresher courses are required.
Yes ❏ No ❏
If yes, please describe.

_____

_____

_____

For your benefit, we are listing in chart form items for you to complete regarding your training.

Subject	Time	Instructional Material	Hours of Classroom Training	Hours of on-the-Job Training	Instructor

Territory

60. Describe any exclusive territory granted to the franchisee and how its boundaries were determined—by population, ZIP code, or other method.

_____

_____

_____

61. Have you established or will you establish any franchisee who may use your trademark in another franchisee's territory?   Yes ❑ No ❑
If yes, explain.

_____

_____

_____

62. Have you established or may you establish a company-owned outlet or other channels of distribution using your name in a franchisee's territory?   Yes ❑ No ❑
If yes, explain.

_____

_____

_____

63. Describe the minimum area granted to the franchisee and how it is determined—by specific miles, specific population, or any other means.

_____

_____

_____

64. Will the franchise be granted for a specific location or a location to be approved by the franchisor?   Yes ❑ No ❑

65. State the conditions under which you will approve the relocation of the franchised business or the establishment of additional franchised outlets.

_____

_____

_____

66. Describe restrictions on you as a franchisor regarding operating company-owned stores or granting franchised outlets for a similar or competitive business within the defined area.

_____

_____

_____

(**Note:** It is not a good policy to allow any company-owned stores or franchised outlets for a similar or competitive business within a franchisee's territory.)

67. Will you restrict franchisees from soliciting or accepting orders outside of the defined territories?   Yes ❑ No ❑
If yes, describe these restrictions.

_____

_____

_____

68. Describe any restrictions on you as franchisor from soliciting or accepting orders inside the franchisee's defined territory.

_____

_____

_____

69. State any compensation that you as franchisor may pay to a franchisee for soliciting or accepting orders inside the franchisee's defined territory, if any.

    _____

    _____

    _____

70. Describe the franchisee's options, rights of first refusal, or similar rights to acquire additional franchises within his or her territory or contiguous territories.

    _____

    _____

    _____

Trademarks

71. Describe your principal trademarks, which means the primary trademarks, service marks, names, logos, and symbols to be used by the franchisee to identify the franchised business.

    _____

    _____

    _____

72. State the date and identification number of each trademark registration or registration application with the United States Patent and Trademark Office.

    _____

    _____

    _____

73. Have you filed all required affidavits?   Yes ❑ No ❑

74. Has any registration been renewed?   Yes ❑ No ❑

75. State whether the principal marks are registered on the Principal or Supplemental Register of the U.S. Patent and Trademark Office.

    _____

    _____

76. State whether or not an Intent to Use application or an application based on actual use has been filed with the U.S. Patent and Trademark Office. If so, list the trademark in question and the serial number of the application.

_____
_____
_____

77. Disclose any currently effective material determinations of the Patent and Trademark Office, the Trademark Trial and Appeal Board, the trademark administrator of your state, or any court; pending infringement, opposition, or cancellation; and pending material litigation involving the principal trademarks, including the name of the principal trademarks, a brief summary of such opposition, and the current status.

_____
_____
_____

78. Describe any litigation affecting your trademarks if it could significantly affect the ownership or use of the trademarks.

_____
_____
_____

79. Disclose any agreements currently in effect that significantly limit the rights of you as franchisor to use or license other franchisees to use the trademark in a manner material to the franchise.

_____
_____
_____

80. State whether you as franchisor will protect the franchisee's right to use the trademarks and protect the franchisee against claims or infringements or unfair competition arising out of your use of them.   Yes ❑ No ❑
If no, indicate what, if any, protection will be given to the franchisee.

_____
_____
_____

81. Do you wish to have the franchisee obligated to notify you in case of any claims?
Yes ❑ No ❑

82. Do you want the franchise agreement to require you as franchisor to take affirmative action when notified of these uses or claims?   Yes ❑ No ❑

83. Do you want to have the right to control administrative proceedings or litigation?
Yes ❑ No ❑

84. Do you wish a clause that would require the franchisee to modify or discontinue use of the trademark as a result of a proceeding or settlement or any other obstacles that you encounter?
Yes ❑ No ❑

85. Do you know of any superior prior right or any infringing use that could materially affect the franchisee's use of the principal trademarks in this state or in the state in which the franchised business is to be located?   Yes ❑ No ❑
If yes, describe.

_____

_____

_____

Patents, Copyrights, and Proprietary Information

86. If you as franchisor own any rights in patents or copyrights that are material to the franchise, describe these patents and copyrights and their relationship to the franchise. Include their duration and whether you as franchisor can and intend to renew the copyrights. If you are claiming proprietary rights in confidential information or trade secrets, describe their general subject matter and the terms and conditions for use by the franchisee.

_____

_____

_____

87. If you have any patents, give the patent number, issue date, and title for each patent. If you have any patent applications pending, give the serial number, filing date, and title for each application.

_____

_____

_____

88. If you know of any infringements or any actions affecting any patent or copyright, describe.

_____

_____

_____

Obligation to Participate in the Actual Operation of the Franchise Business

89. Will you require personal on-premises supervision?   Yes ❏ No ❏
    If not, will you recommend on-site supervision by the franchisee?   Yes ❏ No ❏

90. State any limitations on whom the franchisee can hire as an on-premises supervisor.

    _____

    _____

    _____

91. Will the on-premises supervisor be required to successfully complete your training program?
    Yes ❏ No ❏

92. If the franchisee is a business entity, state the amount of equity interest that the on-premises
    supervisor must have in the franchise, if any. _____%

93. Do you wish to require the franchisee to place restrictions on its manager, including maintain-
    ing trade secrets, non-competition, etc.?   Yes ❏ No ❏
    If yes, describe.

    _____

    _____

    _____

Restrictions on What the Franchisee May Sell

94. Do you want the franchisee to be obligated to sell only goods and services that you approve?
    Yes ❏ No ❏

95. Do you want the franchisee to sell only goods and services that you authorize?   Yes ❏ No ❏

96. Do you want to retain the right to change the types of authorized goods and services?
    Yes ❏ No ❏
    If so, are there any limits on your right to make such changes?   Yes ❏ No ❏
    If so, what are they?

    _____

    _____

    _____

97. Do you wish the franchisee to be restricted regarding customers?   Yes ❑ No ❑
If yes, describe the restrictions.

_____

_____

_____

Renewal, Termination, Transfer, and Dispute Resolution

98. The following are areas that require answers, if you can provide them at this time:
  a) Desired length of term of the franchise agreement: _____
  b) Renewal or extension of the term: _____
  c) Do you wish requirements for franchisee to renew or extend?   Yes ❑ No ❑
  d) Will you allow the franchisee to terminate other than with good cause?   Yes ❑ No ❑
  e) Do you want provisions by which you can terminate without cause?   Yes ❑ No ❑
  f) Do you want provisions by which you can terminate the agreement with cause?
     Yes ❑ No ❑
  g) Do you want obligations on the franchisee on termination or non-renewal?
     Yes ❑ No ❑
  h) Do you want the right to assign the agreement?   Yes ❑ No ❑
  i) Do you want a transfer fee in the event the franchisee desires to transfer?   Yes ❑ No ❑
     If yes, what fee do you think is reasonable? $_____
  j) Do you want approval of any transfer of the franchisee?   Yes ❑ No ❑
  k) Do you want a right of first refusal to acquire the franchise business upon any transfer?
     Yes ❑ No ❑
  l) Do you want a general option to purchase the franchise business at any time?
     Yes ❑ No ❑
  m) Do you want a non-compete covenant during the term of the franchise?   Yes ❑ No ❑
  n) Do you want a non-compete covenant after the franchise is terminated or expires?
     Yes ❑ No ❑
     If yes, put the miles, the restrictions, and the years the non-compete covenant would be
     in effect.

_____

_____

  o) Do you desire an arbitration clause?   Yes ❑ No ❑
  p) Do you desire a mediation clause?   Yes ❑ No ❑
  q) Do you want to specify a state in which any legal action should be brought?
     Yes ❑ No ❑
     If so, name the state: _____
  r) Do you want the law of your state to apply?   Yes ❑ No ❑
     If so, name the state: _____

Note: Your answers to the questions in part 98 will be placed in a table, summarized, and cross-referenced to the franchise agreement.

Public Figures

99. Will you be using a public figure to promote the franchise, i.e., a person whose name or physical appearance is generally known to the public in the geographic area where the franchisor will be located?   Yes ❑ No ❑

If yes, please disclose the name, compensation to be paid, the person's position and duties in your business structure, and the amount of his or her investment, if any, in your franchise.

_____

_____

_____

Earnings Claims

100. Do you intend to make earnings claims to your franchisees, which must be disclosed in your offering circular?   Yes ❑ No ❑

If so, describe such claims and the reasonable basis in writing that can be presented to the authorities as evidence that these earnings claims have a reasonable basis.

_____

_____

_____

List of Outlets

101. Do you have any franchises at this time?   Yes ❑ No ❑
If so, describe them.

_____

_____

_____

102. Do you have any of your own outlets at this time?   Yes ❑ No ❑
If so, list them, including name, address, telephone number, and years in business:

_____

_____

_____

103. If you have any franchisees, provide a complete list on a separate sheet, including names, addresses, and telephone numbers.

_____

_____

_____

104. Estimate the number of franchises to be sold throughout the United States during the one-year period after the close of the franchisor's most recent fiscal year.

_____

_____

_____

105. If any franchises have closed, cancelled, not renewed, been reacquired, or otherwise ceased to do business, list each of them on a separate sheet, with the name and last known address and telephone number of every franchisee.

_____

_____

_____

106. For your convenience, use the following columns to summarize the status of franchise centers for the last three fiscal years.

_____

_____

_____

Summary of Status of Franchise Centers for the Last Three Fiscal Years (years: 20__, 20__, 20__)[1]

State	Transfers	Canceled/ Terminated	Not Renewed	Reacquired by Franchisor	Left the System/ Other	Total from Left Columns[2]	Franchises Operating at Year End
Alabama							
Alaska							
Arizona							
Arkansas							
California							
Colorado							
Connecticut							
Delaware							

State	Transfers	Canceled/ Terminated	Not Renewed	Reacquired by Franchisor	Left the System/ Other	Total from Left Columns[2]	Franchises Operating at Year End
Dist. of Col.							
Florida							
Georgia							
Hawaii							
Idaho							
Illinois							
Indiana							
Iowa							
Kansas							
Kentucky							
Louisiana							
Maine							
Maryland							
Massachu.							
Michigan							
Minnesota							
Mississippi							
Missouri							
Montana							
Nebraska							
Nevada							
New Hamp.							
New Jersey							
New Mexico							
New York							
North Car.							
North Dakota							
Ohio							
Oklahoma							
Oregon							
Pennsylvania							
Rhode Island							
South Car.							
South Dakota							

State	Transfers	Canceled/ Terminated	Not Renewed	Reacquired by Franchisor	Left the System/ Other	Total from Left Columns[2]	Franchises Operating at Year End
Tennessee							
Texas							
Utah							
Vermont							
Virginia							
Washington							
West Virginia							
Wisconsin							
Wyoming							

[1] All numbers are as of December 31 for each year.

[2] The numbers in the "Total" column may exceed the number of outlets affected, because several events may have affected the same outlet. For example, an outlet may have had multiple owners.

Status of Company-Owned Centers for the Last Three Fiscal Years (years: 20__, 20__, 20__)[1]

State	Centers Closed During Year	Centers Opened During Year	Total Centers Operating at Year End
Alabama			
Alaska			
Arizona			
Arkansas			
California			
Colorado			
Connecticut			
Delaware			
Dist. of Col.			
Florida			
Georgia			
Hawaii			
Idaho			
Illinois			
Indiana			
Iowa			
Kansas			

State	Centers Closed During Year	Centers Opened During Year	Total Centers Operating at Year End
Kentucky			
Louisiana			
Maine			
Maryland			
Massachu.			
Michigan			
Minnesota			
Mississippi			
Missouri			
Montana			
Nebraska			
Nevada			
New Hamp.			
New Jersey			
New Mexico			
New York			
North Car.			
North Dakota			
Ohio			
Oklahoma			
Oregon			
Pennsylvania			
Rhode Island			
South Car.			
South Dakota			
Tennessee			
Texas			
Utah			
Vermont			
Virginia			
Washington			

State	Centers Closed During Year	Centers Opened During Year	Total Centers Operating at Year End
West Virginia			
Wisconsin			
Wyoming			

Projected Openings as of _____, 200_

State	Franchise Agreements Signed but Site Center Not Opened	Projected Franchised New Site Centers in the Next Fiscal Year	Projected Company-Owned Center Openings in the Next Fiscal Year
Alabama			
Alaska			
Arizona			
Arkansas			
California			
Colorado			
Connecticut			
Delaware			
Dist. of Col.			
Florida			
Georgia			
Hawaii			
Idaho			
Illinois			
Indiana			
Iowa			
Kansas			
Kentucky			
Louisiana			
Maine			
Maryland			
Massachu.			
Michigan			

State	Franchise Agreements Signed but Site Center Not Opened	Projected Franchised New Site Centers in the Next Fiscal Year	Projected Company-Owned Center Openings in the Next Fiscal Year
Minnesota			
Mississippi			
Missouri			
Montana			
Montana			
Nebraska			
Nevada			
New Hamp.			
New Jersey			
New Mexico			
New York			
North Car.			
North Dakota			
Ohio			
Oklahoma			
Oregon			
Pennsylvania			
Rhode Island			
South Car.			
South Dakota			
Tennessee			
Utah			
Vermont			
Virginia			
Washington			
West Virginia			
Wisconsin			
Wyoming			
Totals			

Financial Statements

107. You will be required to provide financial statements audited by an independent certified public accountant. If you will provide me with the name, address, and telephone number of your accountant, I will provide him or her with the needed information. The audited financials should include the balance sheet of the franchise corporation for the last two fiscal years before the application date or, if less than two years, the actual time that your franchise entity has been in business. In addition, you must include a Statement of Operations of stockholders' equity and of cash flow for each of the franchisor's last three fiscal years or, if less than three fiscal years, the time it has been in business. If the most recent balance sheet and statement of operations date from more than 90 days before the application date, then you must also submit an unaudited balance sheet and a Statement of Operations as of the date within 90 days of the application date.

Contracts

108. List all agreements in addition to the franchise agreement that we will prepare that will be used regarding the franchise agreement, including any leases, options, and purchase agreements that are separate from the franchise agreement but that you will require your franchisee to use.

_____

_____

_____

_____

_____

_____

_____

The undersigned has prepared the responses to this questionnaire and compiled the above material on behalf of the franchisor and declares that, to the best of his or her knowledge, they are true and correct.

_____

Signature

_____

Title

_____

Date

Your offering circular cannot be drafted until your attorney knows the above information. Please attach additional sheets as needed.

Appendix D
Background Information for Franchise Agreement

s you franchise your business, keep in mind that the more carefully you choose your franchisees, the less your agreement will need onerous "weeding out" provisions, such as minimum annual sales quotas, nonexclusive sales territories, short-term franchise agreements, and new contractual provisions upon transfer or renewal.

This questionnaire was designed to help you, as a franchisor, retain just enough control to ensure quality and consistency in the way each franchisee offers your services or products while not economically strangling the franchisee's ability to make a reasonable profit.

Pay particular attention to establishing initial franchise and royalty fees that are fair and operable. Consider each franchised location as if it were a company-owned location with the franchisee paying the bills. Never sell a franchise to a person that you would not hire for life as a manager of your company-owned operation.

After considering these ideas, you can properly frame a franchise agreement that will be workable for both parties, allowing you to achieve greater success through your franchisees than if your agreement were heavily weighted in your favor.

Attach additional sheets, if needed, for each question.

Franchisor:	Person to contact about this questionnaire:
Name: _____	Name: _____
Address: _____	Address: _____
City/State/ZIP: _____	City/State/ZIP: _____
Telephone: _____	Telephone: _____

Service Marks

Indicate the service marks or trademarks used, as well as their registration dates and registration numbers with the United States Patent and Trademark Office and/or state trademark authorities.

_____

_____

_____

Will you defend a franchise that is sued for using your service mark or trademark by a third party claiming your trademark or service mark is an infringement of its service mark or trademark?
Yes ❑ No ❑

Territory

Will each franchised territory be exclusive, meaning no other franchise or company units will be located in a territory?   Yes ❑ No ❑

Describe how your territorial boundaries will be determined. (For example, ZIP code, county, population, number of businesses.)

_____

_____

_____

Definition of Franchise Business

Give a brief description of the type of business that will be franchised.

_____

_____

_____

_____

_____

_____

Internal Franchisee Identification

Set forth any type of prefix or suffix you, as the franchisor, may require to identify each franchisee in your internal records. (For example: "McDonald's of Oakland" or "McDonald's #6.")

_____

_____

_____

_____

_____

Franchisor Training

Initial Training Prior to Opening

Locations	Number of Trainers	Number of Working Days	Hours per Day

Training at Time of Franchise Opening (Grand Opening)

Locations	Number of Trainers	Number of Working Days	Hours per Day

What additional training will be available to the franchisee throughout the term of the agreement?

_____

_____

_____

Will such training will be mandatory? Yes ❏ No ❏

Other Franchisor Assistance

Describe any other assistance the franchisor will provide the franchisee.

Prior to the Opening

Site selection:

_____

_____

Market-area survey:

_____

_____

Inventory supplies:

_____

_____

Equipment:

_____

_____

Financial assistance:

_____

_____

Hiring of personnel:

_____

_____

Local business licenses:

_____

_____

Public relations:

_____

_____

Other:

_____

_____

After the Opening

Purchasing assistance:

_____

_____

Accounting services:

_____

_____

Product updates:

_____

_____

Procedure improvements:

_____

_____

Public relations:

_____

_____

Inspections:

_____

_____

Other:

_____

_____

Franchisee Fee

Indicate the amount of the initial franchise fee you, as the franchisor, feel you can charge a franchisee. $ _____

How did you arrive at this fee?

_____

_____

_____

Terms of payment of the initial franchise fee:

Down payment $ _____ Balance payment $ _____

Monthly Royalty

Percent of gross receipts you expect to receive as a royalty each month: _____%
List reasons for estimating this percentage.

_____

_____

_____

Would any minimums be desired? Amount of these minimums: $ _____
(Consideration can also be given to reducing a monthly royalty upon the attainment of a certain amount of gross receipts per month or deferring all or part of the royalty for an initial specified period of time.)

Promotion and Advertisements

Percent of gross receipts or other formula that you desire in establishing a general advertising fee fund: _____%

List reasons for arriving at this percentage.

_____

_____

_____

What amount must the franchisee spend on local advertising?

Percentage of gross sales: _____ % or a minimum: $ _____

Must the franchisee enter into cooperative advertising with fellow franchisees?   Yes ❑ No ❑

Explain any limits upon such advertising expenditures.

_____

_____

_____

Yellow Pages

Specify the minimum Yellow Pages advertisement desired, if any: _____ inches by _____ columns

Operations Manual

Will a confidential operations manual be provided to the franchisee?   Yes ❑ No ❑

Describe the areas covered.

_____

_____

_____

Day-to-day operations:

_____

_____

Marketing:

_____

_____

Purchasing:

_____

_____

Advertising:

_____

_____

Accounting procedures:

_____

_____

Hiring of employees:

_____

_____

Training of staff:

_____

_____

Public relations:

_____

_____

Other:

_____

_____

_____

Franchise Operation

Is the franchisee allowed to sell products or render services other than those designated by the franchisor?   Yes ❑ No ❑

If so, what are the restrictions on the products or services that the franchisee can sell or render?

_____

_____

_____

Amount of supervisory time that a franchisee or approved manager must render for actual on-premises operation of the franchise: _____ hours per week _____ weeks per year

Insurance

Most franchisors desire public liability insurance in amounts of $1,000,000 combined single limits for bodily injury and property damage.

Is this satisfactory to your insurance agent for the type of franchise business in question?
Yes ❏ No ❏

Is a fidelity bond insurance requirement of $50,000 necessary and satisfactory?   Yes ❏ No ❏

If not, list the desired policy limits.

_____

_____

_____

Non-Competition Provisions

What non-competition restrictions do you desire, if any, including distance from existing franchisees and number of years in which competition is prohibited?

_____

_____

_____

Office Management Personnel

Are you agreeable to absentee management?   Yes ❏ No ❏

Do you wish to require that all franchisees' managers and personnel be trained by your personnel?
Yes ❏ No ❏

Do you wish to require that any assignee of the franchise who purchases the business also be trained by you?   Yes ❏ No ❏

Term and Transfers

Do you desire to have the franchise agreement last for an infinite amount of time, with the only contingency being that any transfer to third parties, heirs, or relatives be made with the approval of the franchisor as to financial ability and suitability?   Yes ❏ No ❏

If not, do you desire a length of franchise term in number of years, such as 10, 20, or 30? State your suggested term and renewal terms, if any: _____

Do you want a transfer fee payable to the franchisor when a franchisee sells his or her business and transfers it to another party with your approval?   Yes ❏ No ❏

If yes, what transfer fee amount would you like? $ _____ What renewal fee amount? $ _____

Franchisee's Initial Investment

As best you can, provide the projected amount a franchisee would have to pay to start up a franchise of yours, in each of the following categories:

Category	Amount
Leasehold improvements	$ _____
Equipment	$ _____
Decor	$ _____
Furnishings	$ _____
Signs	$ _____
Rent* (first and last months)	$ _____
Cash registers	$ _____
Uniforms	$ _____
Opening inventory for three months	$ _____
Working capital necessary to commence or continue operation for one month	$ _____

Deposits

Rental	$ _____
Telephone	$ _____
Electricity	$ _____

Insurance

Auto	$ _____
Errors and omissions	$ _____
Fidelity bond	$ _____
Liability	$ _____

Other

_____	$ _____
_____	$ _____

Total $ _____

*Average square footage of your franchise premises buildings is _____ sq. ft.

Obligation of Franchisee to Purchase from Franchisor or from Franchisor's Designated Supplier

Describe any obligations of the franchisee to purchase goods or services from you or from your designated supplier. (If the franchisee is required to purchase from a designated supplier, also give the name and address of the supplier, the reason for requiring the purchase from a designated supplier, and a brief description of what must be purchased.)

_____

_____

_____

If the franchisee is obligated to purchase goods or services from you or from your designated supplier, will you receive any profit or revenue from such sales?   Yes ❑ No ❑

If such purchases are required, what percent of the franchisee's total requirements of that service or product will constitute purchases from you or your designated supplier? _____ %

Financing Arrangement

Will you take back promissory notes or carry some paper from the franchisee?   Yes ❑ No ❑
If so, please describe:

_____

_____

_____

Will you assist the franchisee in securing financing from independent third parties?   Yes ❑ No ❑
If yes, please explain:

_____

_____

_____

Services the Franchisor May Provide

Describe any services you may provide although not legally obligated to do so under the franchise agreement.

Periodic visits by representatives:

_____

_____

_____

Telephone consultation (describe limits on hours of such):

_____

_____

Suggested advertising:

_____

_____

_____

Other advisory services:

_____

_____

_____

Patents and Copyrights

Describe any patents or copyrights you may offer to the franchisee.

_____

_____

_____

_____

_____

_____

Public Figures

Will you provide public figures in promotion of the franchise?   Yes ❑ No ❑

If yes, please explain, providing the names of the public figures, basic arrangement with the public figures, including compensation, duration of the agreement, and general description of the services of the public figure to the franchisee.

Public Figure	Compensation	Duration	Services

Actual Average, Projected, or Forecasted Franchise Sales, Profits, or Earnings

Do you wish to provide average, projected, or forecasted franchise sales to potential franchisees? Yes ❑ No ❑

(If so, your projections must be based on figures, data, and information that is documented and submitted to the Department of Corporations so that it can determine the feasibility of your forecast.)

If yes, provide a written substantiation showing that such projections will be valid for your franchisees operating in other locations.

_____

_____

_____

Provision for Legal Fees

Reasonable Attorney Fee to Prevailing Party

In some states, it is permissible to insert a clause to the effect that if there is a dispute and the matter is brought to arbitration or trial, the prevailing party would be entitled to reasonable attorney fees. This clause on its face seems desirable. However, the downside of the clause is that it may encourage franchisees to bring action since they feel that they will win and that the franchisor will have to pay their attorney fees. In some cases, an attorney may take the franchisee's lawsuit on a contingency basis, figuring that if he or wins the franchisor will pay his or her fees. In addition, the courts do not always award all of the attorney fees to the prevailing party. In some cases, the court will order payment of an amount less than the actual amount billed, on the grounds that this is what the courts feel is reasonable, not what the attorney charged.

As a franchisor, do you wish to have a clause inserted which would provide that the prevailing party in any law action or arbitration would have a right to an award for reasonable attorney fees?
Yes ❑ No ❑

Arbitration

More and more franchisors are utilizing arbitration to resolve problems between franchisees and franchisors. Arbitration allows the parties to pick knowledgeable arbitrators; this is far less costly and takes considerably less time. An arbitration award is unappealable, for all practical purposes, but it can eliminate many of the costly preliminary procedures, such as depositions, interrogatories, motions, etc. Some franchisors prefer not to include arbitration clauses, because they feel that if the franchisee were to go to court, he or she would eventually run out of money because of high court costs and attorney fees for court appearances. However, by the same token, if the franchisor were to have any appreciable number of lawsuits, he or she would also run out of money.

The disadvantage of an arbitration clause is that it is not appealable. However, as a practical matter, appeals are extremely expensive and time-consuming, and only the more financially endowed franchisee can make use of this procedure. In addition, in the majority of appeals, the original decision is upheld.

Do you want to have an arbitration clause in your agreement with your franchisees? Yes ❑ No ❑

Maximum Multiple Franchise Locations for One Franchisee

If a franchisee has the right to purchase more than one franchise, what total number of franchise locations will you allow a franchisee to open in one area? _____
(Some businesses, such as fine restaurants, require almost all of the time and attention of the franchisee and, therefore, allowing additional locations could cause the franchisee to fail. Take this into consideration when answering this question.)

Considerations:

_____

_____

_____

Other Desired Clauses

List your thoughts regarding additional clauses that are of particular importance to you and the business you are franchising.

_____

_____

_____

_____

_____

_____

_____

_____

_____

_____

_____

The undersigned has prepared the responses to this questionnaire and compiled the above material on behalf of the franchisor.

_____
Date

_____
Signature of party answering questionnaire

_____
Printed or typed name and title of party answering questionnaire

Appendix E
State Franchise Information Guidelines

lthough all franchises are subject to the FTC regulations, many states have additional laws governing franchises and similar business opportunities. The information contained in this appendix is a compilation of the available data from those states that have franchise registration laws or business opportunity statutes, or both. Included under each state heading, where applicable, is information on:

- State franchise and business opportunity statutes;
- Laws affecting franchise transfers, renewals, and terminations;
- State franchise law enforcement offices; and
- State advertising filings and review procedures.

The last two pages of this appendix consist of charts containing the most recent information on fees charged by states with franchise registration and business opportunity statutes.

Use these guidelines only as an initial reference resource. As a prospective franchisor or franchisee, you should consult your own state regarding its laws, especially to request updated instructions and forms for filing a uniform franchise offering circular. Registration states have personnel, usually attorneys, who examine each offering circular submitted.

Remember: any failure on the part of the franchisor in using, preparing, or filing the required circular could result in censure or penalties. Use this section of the book so you are knowledgeable when you talk to your attorney.

State Guidelines and Offices

Alabama

Alabama has enacted a Deceptive Trade Practices Act that makes it unlawful to make certain misrepresentations in any franchises, distributorships, and seller-assisted marketing plans. ALA. CODE Section 8-19-1.

Arkansas

Arkansas has a franchise relationship act known as the Franchise Practices Act that doesn't require registration or disclosure, but prohibits termination or nonrenewal of franchisees without good cause and protects franchisees from the wrongful acts of franchisors in the misuse of advertising fees. ARK. STAT. Section 70-807 and ANN. Section 4-72-201 through 4-72-210.

California

California has a Franchise Investment Act, which requires full disclosure and registration by the franchisor. CAL. CORP. CODE Section 31000 to 31516. It should be noted that California has a Seller Assisted Marketing Plan Act, which covers certain types of marketing that are akin to franchising. CAL. CIVIL CODE Section 1812-200 to 1812-221. California's Franchise Relations Act became effective January 1, 1981, and pertains to termination with good cause and prior 180-day notification if the franchisor does not intend to renew a contract. The Act further provides for compensation for franchises that have not been renewed but are intended for conversion to company-owned outlets. CAL. BUS. & PROF. CODE Section 20000-20043. Brochures and ads must be submitted in duplicate and avoid any statements regarding success, safe investments, unlikelihood of default, or earnings not supported by Item 19. The ad must be filed with the Department of Corporations at least three business days prior to publishing the ad.

Connecticut

Connecticut has a Business Opportunity Investment Act that requires registration and disclosure by any person who is engaged in the business of selling or offering for sale a business opportunity. CONN. GEN. STAT. Title 36, Ch. 662a, Section 36b-60 through 36b-80. Connecticut also has a Franchise Termination Act that requires good cause for nonrenewal or termination of franchises. CONN. GEN. STAT. Section 42-133e through 42-133g.

Delaware

Delaware has a Franchise Security Law that is a franchisee-franchisor relationship statute requiring good cause for terminations and non-renewals of franchises. DEL. CODE ANN. Title 6, Section 2551 through 2556.

Florida

Florida's Business Opportunity Act provides for filing, full disclosure, and securing an advertising number. Under certain conditions, an exception from filing can be secured. Certain misrepresentations are prohibited. FLA. STAT. 1995, Ch. 817, Section 559.8 to 559.815, effective Oct. 1, 1998. The Florida Franchise Misrepresentation Act pertains to misrepresentation by franchisors. FLA. STAT. Section 817.416.

Georgia

Georgia has a Business Opportunity Statute pertaining to fraudulent and deceptive practices in the sale of business opportunities. A disclosure must be provided in multilevel distributions. GA. CODE ANN. Section 10-1-410 through 10-1-417.

Hawaii

Hawaii has a Franchise Investment Law pertaining to filing an application and disclosure. HAW. REV. STAT. Section 482E.1 through 482E.5. Hawaii also has a Franchise Rights and

Prohibitions Act regarding prohibited actions and good cause requirements for nonrenewals and terminations and an antidiscrimination provision in regard to charges made for royalties, goods, services, equipment, rentals, advertising services unless made at different times and in different circumstances. HAW. REV. STAT. Section 482E. Hawaii does not review advertising.

Illinois

Illinois has a Franchise Disclosure Act that regulates full disclosure, registration, good cause termination, and nonrenewal provisions. ILL. COMP. STATS. 1992, Ch. 815, Section 705/19 through 705/44. Illinois has a Business Opportunity Sales Law of 1995. Illinois Laws of 1995, Public Act 89-209; ILL. COMP. STATS. 1996, Ch. 815, Section 60215-1 to 60215-135. [See also Illinois (815 IL CS 705/20).] Illinois does not require a franchisor to amend its registration when a negotiated change is made unless a material change implemented in subsequent sales.

Indiana

Indiana has a Registration Disclosure Statute in addition to a Deceptive Franchise Practices Act (IND. CODE 23-2-217) affecting good cause on nonrenewals and 90-day termination notices. IND. CODE 23-2-2.5-1 to 51. See Business Opportunity Transaction, IND. CODE, Title 24, Art. 5, Ch. 8, Section 1-21 (Par. # 5138.19). Section 23-2-2.5-25 requires advertising copy to be filed with the commission at least five business days prior to first publication.

Iowa

Iowa has two franchise acts: the 1992 Act applies to agreements prior to July 1, 2000 (1992 Act) and the 2000 Act applies to agreements after July 1, 2000 (Section 537 A.10), covering transfers, encroachments, good-cause terminations, good-cause nonrenewals, and a duty of good faith performance. IOWA CODE

(2003), Title XIII, Section 523B and 523B 13 and 523H, Section 523H.1 through 523 H.17.

Kentucky

Kentucky has a Business Opportunity Disclosure Act calling for registration of nonexempt offerings. KY. REV. STAT. Section 367.801 et seq. and 367.990.

Louisiana

Louisiana has a Business Opportunity Law that does not provide for filing, but a surety bond is required in certain instances. LA. REV. STAT. Section 51:1801 through 51:1804.

Maine

Maine has a Business Opportunity Act that includes registration of nonexempt offerings and disclosure requirements pertaining to the sale of any business opportunity. ME. REV. STAT. ANN. Chapter 69-B, Section 4691 and Chapters 542 and 597 (Sections 4696-4697).

Maryland

Maryland has a Franchise Registration and Disclosure Law regulating franchises. MD. CODE ANN. Bus. Reg. Section 14-201 et seq. to 14-233. Maryland also has an Equity Participation Investment Program Act, passed for the purpose of encouraging and developing franchises in Maryland, and the Maryland Fair Distributorship Act (1993), regarding cancellation or nonrenewal notices, repurchases, and arbitration between a grantor and a distributor. ANN. CODE of Maryland, Title 14, Section 14-101 through 14-129, Section 14-201 through 14-233, Article of Commercial Law, Title 11, Section 11-1301 through 11-1306.

Michigan

Michigan has a Franchise Investment Law that includes good cause for termination and renewal provision laws and repurchase requirements for nonrenewals. MICH. COMP. LAWS Section 445.1527(c). It also has a Business Opportunity Act requiring a notice filing (MICH. COMP.

LAWS Section 445.901 through 445.922) and a Void and Unenforceable Provisions Law (MICH. COMP. LAWS Section 445.1527). See MICH. COMP. LAWS Section 445.1525.

Minnesota

Minnesota has a Franchise Registration and Full Disclosure Act that also covers Business Opportunities in addition to Pyramid and Unfair Practice Act and requires good cause for terminations and 90 days' prior written notice with a 60-day cure period for nonrenewals. MINN. STAT. Section 80C.01 et seq. to 80C.22. It has an antidiscrimination provision and ads must be filed five business days prior to the first publication.

Mississippi

Mississippi's Franchise Termination Statute also includes provisions regarding profit projections and misrepresenting earnings. Take special notice of the Repurchase of Inventory from Retailers upon Termination of Contract Statute and required 90-day written nonrenewal and termination notices. MISS. CODE ANN. Section 75-24-51 to 75-24-61.

Missouri

Missouri's statute prohibits termination without notice, requires a nonrenewal written 90-day notice, and includes a Pyramid Sales Statute. MO. REV. STAT. Section 407.400 through 407.410, 407.420.

Nebraska

Nebraska's Franchise Practice Act has provisions regarding 60 days' prior written notice and good cause for nonrenewals and terminations. NEB. REV. STAT. Section 87-401 through 87-410. In addition, it has a Business Practice Act that is, in essence, a seller-assisted marketing plans act. NEB. REV. STAT. Section 59-1701 through 59-1761.

New Hampshire

New Hampshire has a Distributor Disclosure Act. N.H. REV. STAT. ANN. Section 339-C1 through 339-C9 and Section 358-E1 through 358-E6.

New Jersey

New Jersey has a Franchise Practice Act requiring 60 days' prior written notice and good cause for terminations, cancellations, and nonrenewals. N.J. REV. STAT. Section 56:10-1 through 56:10-12.

New York

New York's Franchise Registration and Disclosure Statute became effective January 1, 1981, N.Y. GEN. BUS. LAW Section 680 through 695, Laws of 1989 Ch. 61 approved effective April 1, 1989. Franchisors are free to negotiate with prospective franchisees.

North Carolina

North Carolina's Business Opportunities Disclosure Law requires filing two copies of the disclosure statement that are nonexempt offerings with the secretary of state. N.C. GEN. STAT. Section 66.94 to 66-100.

North Dakota

North Dakota's Franchise Investment Law governs registration, full disclosure, termination, and renewal of provisions. N.D. CENT. CODE ANN. Section 51.19.01 through Section 51.19.17.

Ohio

Ohio has a non-filing Business Opportunity Act requiring a disclosure be provided to prospective purchasers. OHIO REV. CODE Section 13340.01 through 1334.15 and 1334.99.

Oklahoma

Oklahoma's Business Opportunity Sales Act requires registration of nonexempt offerings. OKLA. STAT. Section 71-4-801 through 828.

Oregon

Oregon's Franchise Transactions Statute requires full disclosure but does not require registration. OR. REV. STAT. Section 650.005 through 650.085. It also has a little FTC Act prohibiting certain misrepresentation actions. OR. REV. STAT. Section 646.605. No advertising filing is required.

Rhode Island

Rhode Island's Franchise Distributor Investment Regulation Act requires the franchisor to fully disclose and register. R.I. GEN. LAWS Section 19-28-1 through 19-28.1-34. Franchisors can negotiate changes with prospective franchisees and ads must be filed three business days prior to first publication.

South Carolina

South Carolina's Business Opportunity Sales Act requires filing a disclosure with the secretary of state. S.C. CODE Section 39-57-10 to 39-57-80.

South Dakota

South Dakota's Franchises for Brand-Name Goods and Services Law requires registration and full disclosure. S.D. CODIFIED LAWS ANN. Section 37-5A-1 through 37-5A-87. Its Business Opportunity Statute requires filing of business opportunities. S.D. CODIFIED LAWS ANN. Section 37-25A-1 through 37-25A-54.

Texas

Texas has a Business Opportunity Act requiring registration unless the offering is exempt as a franchise offering and a notice of exemption is filed with the secretary of state. TEX. BUS. & COM. CODE, Title 4, Ch. 41, Section 41.001 through 41.303. (See Section 97.21.)

Utah

Utah has a Business Opportunity Disclosure Act in which it refers to "assisted marketing plans" and requires filing of nonexempt offerings. A notice of claim for exception can be filed with a fee. UTAH CODE ANN. Section 13-15-1 through 13-15-6.

Virginia

Virginia has a Retail Franchise Act that requires disclosure and registration (VA. CODE Section 13.1-557 through 13.1-574) and a Business Opportunity Law that does not require registration (VA. CODE Section 59.1-262 through 59.1-269). It also has a statute requiring good cause for cancellation (VA. CODE Section 13.1-564) and it gives the franchisee the right to negotiate changes.

Washington

Washington has a Franchise Investment Protection Act, which requires full disclosure and registration (WASH. REV. CODE Section 19.100.10 through 19.100.940), as well as provisions regarding renewal with buyout compensation and good cause termination (WASH. REV. CODE Section 19.100.180 and 19.100.190). It also has a Business Opportunity Fraud Act requiring registration (WASH. REV. CODE Section 19.110.010 through 19.100.930).

Washington D.C.

D.C. Franchising Act, D.C. CODE ANN. Section 29-1201, requires good cause for terminations, cancellations, failure to renew, or failure to consent to a transfer with a required 60-day cure period. D.C. has an antidiscrimination provision and franchisors can renegotiate if initiated by the franchisees.

Wisconsin

Wisconsin's Franchise Investment Law requires annual registration by notification on a prescribed form and full disclosure. WIS. STAT. Section 553.01 through 553.78. Its Fair Dealership Law requires "good cause" in order to terminate or fail to renew. WIS. STAT. Section 135.01 to 135.07.

United States

The Federal Trade Commission (FTC) has a general disclosure act covering franchises and business opportunities (Rule 436.1, entitled Disclosure Requirements and Prohibitions Concerning Franchising and Business

Opportunity Ventures). No registration is required (16 C.F.R. Part 436). Legislation is pending regarding franchisor-franchisee relations, including good-cause renewals and terminations and earnings claims.

Note: All states are subject to the FTC Act whether or not they have franchise or business opportunity statutes. The FTC will recognize the Uniform Offering Disclosure of franchise registration states, but business opportunity disclosures must also include the requirements of the FTC disclosure. The FTC does not require registration of the FTC disclosure.

Filing Fees of Franchise Registration States

State	Initial Filing	Renewal	Pre-Effective Amendment	Post-Effective Amendment	Exemption Notice	Exemption Notice Renewal
California	$675	$450	$0	$50	$450	$150
Hawaii	$250	$250	$250	N/A	$250	N/A
Illinois	$500	$100	$0	$100	N/A	N/A
Indiana	$500	$250	$0	$50	$250	N/A
Maryland	$500	$250	$0	$100	$250	$0
Michigan	$250	$0				
Minnesota	$400	$200	$0	$100	N/A	N/A
New York	$750	N/A	$0	$150	$0	$0
North Dakota	$250	$100	$0	$50	$100	$50
Oregon	(no registration but statute dictates type of circular and contracts to be used)					
Rhode Island	$500	$250	$0	$100	$300	$0
South Dakota	$250	$100	$0	$50	N/A	N/A
Virginia	$500	$250+$50 if changes made	$0	$100	$100	N/A
Washington	$600	$100	$0	$100	$100	N/A
Wisconsin	$400	$400	$0	$200	$200	$0

Business Opportunity Registration Fees

State	Reg. Fee	Renewal Fee	Amendment Fee	Exemption
Alabama	no registration			
California	$100	$100	$30	
Connecticut	$400	$100	$0	
Florida	$300	$300	$50	$100
Georgia	no registration			
Indiana	$50	$10	$10	
Iowa	$500	$250	$0	$100
Kentucky	$0	$0	$0	
Louisana	$0	$0	$0	
Maine	$25	$10	$0	
Maryland	$250	$100	$50	
Michigan	$0	$0	$0	
Minnesota	See General Franchise Law Fee			
Nebraska	$100	$50	$50	$100
New Hampshire	$0	$0	$0	
North Carolina	$10			
Ohio	$0	$0	$0	
Oklahoma	$250	$150	$0	
South Carolina	$100	$0	$0	
South Dakota	$100	$50	$0	
Texas	$195	$25	$25	$25
Utah	$0	$0	$0	
Virginia	$0	$0	$0	
Washington	$200	$125	$30	

Appendix F
Uniform Franchise Offering Circular (UFOC) Guidelines

The guidelines reprinted here outline the requirements for the Uniform Franchise Offering Circular (UFOC) as prepared and adopted by the North American Securities Administrators Association (NASAA) on April 25, 1993 and put into effect on January 1, 1995. (Consequently, the example UFOC uses 1990-1995 dates.) These guidelines assist the franchisor by listing the requirements, instructions, and sample answers to the questions raised.

The numbered items under General Instructions refer to numbered rules published by the FTC. Following the General Instructions, the guidelines cover every item of the UFOC, from the cover page and table of contents to Item 23, receipt of the offering circular by the franchisee.

This reproduction of the UFOC guidelines is designed to work together with Appendices A-1 and A-2, the sample offering circulars, and Appendix C, the background questionnaire for preparing the offering circular.

The Uniform Franchise Offering Circular Guidelines

General Instructions

90. Introduction: The Uniform Franchise Offering Circular (UFOC) Guidelines consist of the Requirements, the Instructions, and the Sample Answers. The UFOC Guidelines were prepared and adopted by the North American Securities Administrators Association (NASAA) and its predecessor, the Midwest Securities Commissioners Association. The members of NASAA cannot create statutes since that is the constitutional province of state legislatures, but NASAA intends for the UFOC Guidelines to facilitate compliance with disclosure requirements under state franchise investment laws. Where possible, NASAA has developed uniform disclosure requirements, but differences in state laws bearing on the franchise relationship may necessitate changes. In addition, state administrators will continue to review the application for deficient disclosure and additional disclosure necessitated by special problems or risks in the proposed offering.

100. Follow these General Instructions and the Requirement and Instruction for each Item in franchise registration applications and disclosures in the Uniform Franchise Offering Circular.

110. Original Registration Application—Documents to File:
  (a) Uniform Franchise Registration Application Page (also known as Facing Page);
  (b) Supplemental Information page(s);
  (c) Certification page;
  (d) Uniform Consent to Service of Process;
  (e) Sales Agent Disclosure Form;
  (f) If the applicant is a corporation or partnership, an authorizing resolution if the application is verified by a person other than applicant's officer or general partner;
  (g) Uniform Franchise Offering Circular;
  (h) Application Fee;
  (i) Auditor's consent (or a photocopy of the consent) to the use of the latest audited financial statements in the offering circular; and
  (j) Advertising or promotional materials.

Examples of forms (a) through (f) are printed at the end of these Guidelines.

120. Renewal Application: When state law requires renewal, mark "renewal" on the application page. Submit all documents required for an initial application with additions to the previously filed documents underlined. Changes must be clearly marked so that the change is noticed easily. File a renewal application before the prior registration has expired. If the prior registration has expired, mark "Registration of an Offer or Sale of Franchises" on the facing page and pay the fee charged for initial registrations. Redlining and bracketing changes from the last filing will speed a re-registration. Do not mark the amendment boxes on the application page on the first renewal filing even if documents are revised.

150. "Disclose" means to state all material facts in an accurate and unambiguous manner. Disclose clearly, concisely, and in a narrative form that is understandable by a person unfamiliar with the franchise business. For clear and concise disclosure, avoid legal antiques[1] and repetitive phrases.[2] When possible, use active, not passive voice.[3] Limit the length and complexity of disclosure through

careful organization of information in the disclosure. Avoid technical language and unnecessary detail. Make the format and chronological order consistent within each Item.

1. Avoid these legal antiques. Preferred substitutes are in parentheses: aforesaid; arising from (from); as between; as an inducement for; as part of the consideration; as set forth in (in); as the case may be; at a later point in time; binding upon and inure; commence (begin); condition precedent (before); condition subsequent (after); consist of (are); engaged in the business of offering (offers); for and in consideration of the grant of the franchise; for a period of (for); foregoing; forthwith; from time to time; further; hereby; herein; hereinafter; hereto; heretofore; if necessary; in the event (if); including but not limited to (including); in any manner whatsoever; including without limitation (including); in conjunction with; in connection with; in no event; in the event of (if); in whole or in part; it will be specifically understood that; manner in which; not later than (within, by); not less than (at least); notwithstanding; offers to an individual, corporation or partnership (offer); on behalf of (for); precedent (before); prescribed (required); prior to (before); provided however (but, unless); provided that (if, unless); purporting to; relating to (under); subsequent (after); such (this); so as to (to); so long as (while); thereafter; therefrom; thereof; thereunder; without limiting the foregoing; whatsoever; with respect to.

2. Avoid repetitive phrases. Preferred substitutes are in parentheses: agrees, acknowledges and recognizes; any and all; are and remain; based upon, related to, or growing out of (because); certified as true and correct (certified); consultation, assistance and guidance (guidance); each and every; equipment, furniture, supplies and inventory set forth on the equipment list attached as Exhibit _____ (items on Exhibit _____); necessary and appropriate; sample, test and review (test); and twenty-three (23) (write as 23).

3. The preferred phrase is in parentheses: as the franchisor prescribes (you must); being offered (offers); consist of (is); engaged in the business of offering (offer); giving rise to; if it becomes necessary for (if); inure to the benefit of (benefit); is granted the right to (can); is given an opportunity to (can); is required to (must); shall be no less than (a minimum of); shall continue in effect (continues); with the exception of (except).

160. Since prospective franchisees must have sufficient disclosure to understand economic commitments and to develop a business plan, Items 5, 6, 7, and 8 must disclose the minimum and maximum franchisee cost. The franchisor should provide reasonably available information to allow franchisees to forecast future charges listed in these Items and to be paid to persons who are independent of the franchisor. Future payments to the franchisor should be specific as is required by individual Items.

170. The disclosure for each UFOC Item should be separately titled and in the required order. Do not repeat the UFOC question in the offering circular. Respond to each question fully. If the disclosure is not applicable, respond in the negative, but if an answer is required "if applicable," respond only if the requested information applies. Do not qualify a response with a reference to another document unless permitted by the instructions to that Item.

180. For each Item in the UFOC, type the Requirement's Item title and number. Sub-items may be designated by descriptive headings, but do not use sub-item letters and numbers.

190. Separate documents (for example, a confidential Operations Manual) must not make representations or impose terms that contradict or are materially different from the disclosure in the offering circular.

200. Use 8½ by 11 inch paper for the entire application.

210. When the applicant is a master franchisor seeking to sell subfranchises, references in these

requirements and instructions to "franchisee" include the subfranchisor unless the language context requires a different meaning.

220. The offer of subfranchises is an offer separate from the offer of franchises and usually requires a separate registration or exemption. A single application may register the sale of single-unit and multi-unit franchises if the offering circular is not confusing.

230. When the applicant is a subfranchisor, disclose to the extent applicable the same information concerning the subfranchisor that is required about the franchisor.

240. In offerings by a subfranchisor, "franchisor" means both the franchisor and subfranchisor.

250. When state requirements conflict with these Guidelines, the state requirements control. The State Administrator may modify or waive these Guidelines or may require additional documentation or information.

260. Grossly deficient applications may be rejected summarily by the administrator as incomplete for filing. It is not the function of an administrator to prepare, in effect, an applicant's application. The additional examiner time reviewing the grossly deficient product delays the processing of diligently prepared and pursued applications.

265. These Guidelines are effective six months after the Federal Trade Commission and each NASAA member whose jurisdiction requires presale registration of a franchise adopt them. In any event, these Guidelines will be effective no earlier than January 1, 1994 and no later than January 1, 1995. After the effective date of these Guidelines, all initial franchise applications, renewals, and reregistrations must comply with these Guidelines.

270. The Guidelines that continue after these instructions use the following format:
   (a) The title of the Item follows the Item number. It is capitalized and centered on the page.
   (b) The "Item" is a restatement of the Uniform Franchise Offering Circular ("UFOC") Item Requirement. It is capitalized and follows the title of the Item.
   (c) The "Instruction" appears beneath the Item. It explains portions of the Item Requirements.
   (d) The "Sample Answer" at the end of each Item provides sample disclosures. Double horizontal lines divide the Sample Answer from the Instructions.

REQUIREMENTS FOR PREPARATION OF A UNIFORM FRANCHISE OFFERING CIRCULAR

Cover Page

The state cover page of the offering circular must state:

1. The title in boldface type: **Franchise Offering Circular.**
2. The franchisor's name, type of business organization, principal business address, and telephone number.
3. A sample of the primary business trademark, logotype, trade name, or commercial label or symbol under which the franchisee will conduct its business. (Place in upper left-hand corner of the cover page.)
4. A brief description of the franchised business.
5. The total amounts in Items 5 and 7 of the offering circular: Franchisee's Initial Franchisee Fee or Other Payment and Franchisee's Initial Investment.
6. The following statements:

   Information comparing franchisors is available. Call the state administrators listed in Exhibit _____ or your public library for sources of information.

   Registration of this franchise by a state does not mean that the state recommends it or has verified the information in this offering circular. If you learn that anything in the offering circular is untrue, contact the Federal Trade Commission and (State or Provincial authority).
7. Effective Date: (Leave blank until notified of effectiveness by state regulatory authority.)

Cover Page Instructions

i. Present information in the required order. Except for risk factors or when instructed by the examiner, do not capitalize or underline.
ii. The estimated cash investment should agree with the Item 7 total. This total should represent the franchisees entire initial investment minus only exclusions allowed by Item 7. Do not state what the total includes.
iii. Limit the cover page disclosure to one page unless risk factors require additional space. Disclosure on the cover page should be brief. Limit the description of the business to the product or service offered by the franchisor. Unless required by a state regulator, do not disclose financing arrangements or the franchisee's right to use the trademark. Exclude non-required information unless necessary as a risk factor or required by a state regulator.
iv. If applicable, disclose the following risk factors using the following language on the cover:

   1. THE FRANCHISE AGREEMENT PERMITS THE FRANCHISEE (TO SUE) (TO ARBITRATE WITH) _____ ONLY IN _____. OUT OF STATE (ARBITRATION) (LITIGATION) MAY FORCE YOU TO ACCEPT A LESS FAVORABLE SETTLEMENT FOR DISPUTES. IT MAY ALSO COST MORE (TO SUE) (TO ARBITRATE WITH) _____ IN _____ THAN IN YOUR HOME STATE.

   2. THE FRANCHISE AGREEMENT STATES THAT _____ LAW GOVERNS THE AGREEMENT, AND THIS LAW MAY NOT PROVIDE THE SAME PROTECTION AND BENEFITS AS LOCAL LAW. YOU MAY WANT TO COMPARE THESE LAWS.

3. THERE MAY BE OTHER RISKS CONCERNING THIS FRANCHISE.

v. In addition to the above language, disclose other risk factors required by a state regulator.

vi. Use capital letters for risk factor disclosure.

vii. In multi-state offerings in which the franchisor uses a single offering circular, refer to an exhibit to the offering circular for a list of State or Provincial authority.

SAMPLE COVER PAGE

(Logo)

Franchise Offering Circular

Belmont Mufflers, Inc.
A Minnesota Corporation
111First Street
Jackson, Minnesota 55555
(612) 266-3430

The franchisee will repair and install motor vehicle exhaust systems.

The initial franchise fee is $10,000. The estimated initial investment required ranges from $132,700 to $160,200. This sum does not include rent for the business location.

Risk Factors

THE FRANCHISE AGREEMENT REQUIRES THAT ALL DISAGREEMENTS BE SETTLED BY ARBITRATION IN MINNESOTA. OUT OF STATE ARBITRATION MAY FORCE YOU TO ACCEPT A LESS FAVORABLE SETTLEMENT FOR DISPUTES. IT MAY ALSO COST YOU MORE TO ARBITRATE WITH US IN MINNESOTA THAN IN YOUR HOME STATE.

Information about comparisons of franchisors is available. Call the state administrators listed in Exhibit _____ or your public library for sources of information.

Registration of this franchise with the state does not mean that the state recommends it or has verified the information in this offering circular. If you learn that anything in this offering circular is untrue, contact the Federal Trade Commission and (State or Provincial authority).

Effective Date:

TABLE OF CONTENTS

INCLUDE A TABLE OF CONTENTS BASED ON THE REQUIREMENTS OF THIS OFFERING CIRCULAR.

Table of Contents Instruction

i. Refer to UFOC Items and state the page where each UFOC Item disclosure begins. List exhibits by letter. Use the following format:

TABLE OF CONTENTS

Item   Title   **Page**

Sample Table of Contents

TABLE OF CONTENTS

Item Title   **Page***

1. The Franchisor, Its Predecessors, and Affiliates
2. Business Experience
3. Litigation
4. Bankruptcy
5. Initial Franchise Fee
6. Other Fees
7. Initial Investment
8. Restrictions on Sources of Products and Services
9. Franchisee's Obligations
10. Financing
11. Franchisor's Obligations
12. Territory
13. Trademarks
14. Patents, Copyrights, and Proprietary Information
15. Obligation to Participate in the Actual Operation of the Franchise Business
16. Restrictions on What the Franchisee May Sell
17. Renewal, Termination, Transfer, and Dispute Resolution
18. Public Figures
19. Earnings Claims
20. List of Outlets
21. Financial Statements
22. Contracts
23. Receipt

Exhibits

A. Franchise Agreement
B. Equipment Lease
C. Lease for Premises
D. Loan Agreement

* Note: In your actual document, page numbers must be filled in, but they have been omitted in this publication to avoid confusion with the book's page numbers.

ITEM 1. THE FRANCHISOR, ITS PREDECESSORS, AND AFFILIATES

Item 1 Instructions

i. Use the word "we," initials, or one or two words to refer to the franchisor. Use different initials or a different one or two words to refer to other persons contracting with the franchisee under the franchise agreement. Except in the 23 Item titles, use these initials or the word(s) to describe these persons or entities throughout the offering circular.

ii. Define the franchisee as "you" and use this description throughout the offering circular. If the franchisee could be a corporation, partnership or other entity, disclose whether "you" includes the franchisee's owners.

iii. "Predecessor" in Item 1 means a person from whom the franchisor acquired directly or indirectly the major portion of the franchisor's assets.

iv. The disclosure regarding Predecessors need only cover the 10 year period immediately before the close of the franchisor's most recent fiscal year.

v. "Affiliate" in Item 1 means a person (other than a natural person) controlled by, controlling, or under common control with the franchisor, which is offering franchises in any line of business or is providing products or services to the franchisees of the franchisor.

DISCLOSE IN SUMMARY FORM

A. THE NAME OF THE FRANCHISOR, ITS PREDECESSORS AND AFFILIATES

B. THE NAME UNDER WHICH THE FRANCHISOR DOES OR INTENDS TO DO BUSINESS

Item 1B Instruction

If the franchisor does business under a name different from the name disclosed in Item A, state that other name. If not, state that the franchisor does not do business under another name.

C. THE PRINCIPAL BUSINESS ADDRESS OF THE FRANCHISOR, ITS PREDECESSORS AND AFFILIATES, AND THE FRANCHISOR'S AGENT FOR SERVICE OF PROCESS

Item 1C Instructions

i. Principal business address means "home office" in the United States, not in the state for which the offering circular was prepared. If appropriate, also disclose the location of an international "home office." The business address can not be a post office box.

ii. In a multi-state offering in which the agent for service of process is required, the franchisor may use an exhibit or the acknowledgement of receipt to disclose this agent.

D. THE BUSINESS FORM OF THE FRANCHISOR

Item 1D Instructions

i. Disclose the state of incorporation or business organization and the type of business organization.

E. THE FRANCHISOR'S BUSINESS AND THE FRANCHISES TO BE OFFERED IN THIS STATE

Item 1E Instructions

Disclose the following:

i. That the franchisor sells or grants franchises;

ii. Whether the franchisor operates businesses of the type being franchised;

iii. The franchisors' other business activities;

iv. The business to be conducted by the franchisees;

v. The general market for the product or service to be offered by the franchisee. (For example, is the market developed or developing? Will the goods be sold primarily to a certain group? Are sales seasonal?)

vi. In general terms any regulations specific to the industry in which the franchise business operates. It is not necessary to include laws or regulations that apply to businesses generally.

vii. A general description of the competition.

F. THE PRIOR BUSINESS EXPERIENCE OF THE FRANCHISOR, ITS PREDECESSORS AND AFFILIATES INCLUDING:

(1) THE LENGTH OF TIME THE FRANCHISOR HAS CONDUCTED A BUSINESS OF THE TYPE TO BE OPERATED BY THE FRANCHISEE.

(2) THE LENGTH OF TIME EACH PREDECESSOR AND AFFILIATE HAS CONDUCTED A BUSINESS OF THE TYPE TO BE OPERATED BY THE FRANCHISEE.

(3) THE LENGTH OF TIME THE FRANCHISOR HAS OFFERED FRANCHISES FOR THE SAME TYPE OF BUSINESS AS THAT TO BE OPERATED BY THE FRANCHISEE.

(4) THE LENGTH OF TIME EACH PREDECESSOR AND AFFILIATE OFFERED FRANCHISES FOR THE SAME TYPE OF BUSINESS AS THAT TO BE OPERATED BY THE FRANCHISEE.

(5) WHETHER THE FRANCHISOR HAS OFFERED FRANCHISES IN OTHER LINES OF BUSINESS, INCLUDING:

(A) A DESCRIPTION OF EACH OTHER LINE OF BUSINESS;

(B) THE NUMBER OF FRANCHISES SOLD IN EACH OTHER LINE OF BUSINESS; AND

(C) THE LENGTH OF TIME THE FRANCHISOR HAS OFFERED EACH OTHER FRANCHISE.

(6) WHETHER EACH PREDECESSOR AND AFFILIATE OFFERED FRANCHISES IN OTHER LINES OF BUSINESS, INCLUDING:

(A) A DESCRIPTION OF EACH OTHER LINE OF BUSINESS;

(B) THE NUMBER OF FRANCHISES SOLD IN EACH OTHER'S LINE OF BUSINESS; AND

(C) THE LENGTH OF TIME EACH PREDECESSOR AND AFFILIATE OFFERED EACH OTHER FRANCHISE.

Item 1F Instruction

Limit disclosure about predecessors to the time before the franchisor acquired the predecessor's assets. Thus, under the 10 year limitation, if a franchisor acquired the assets of a predecessor 8 years ago, the disclosure about the predecessor should cover only the 2 year period before the acquisition.

Sample Answer 1

To simplify the language in this offering circular "Belmont" means Belmont Mufflers Inc., the franchisor. "You" means the person who buys the franchise. Belmont is a Minnesota corporation that was incorporated on September 3, 1963. Belmont does business as Belmont Muffler Shops. Our principal business address is 111 First Street, Jackson, Minnesota 55555.

Belmont's agent for service of process is disclosed in Exhibit _____.

Belmont currently operates 12 Belmont Muffler Shops and sells pipe bending machines and mufflers to various muffler shops.

Belmont franchises the right to sell and install mufflers for the public. You must honor our guarantee to replace mufflers or exhaust pipes that wear out if the vehicle ownership has not changed. Belmont's franchisees often operate their muffler shop franchise with their service stations or tire center. Your competitors include department store service departments, service stations and other national chains of muffler shops. Exhibit _____ is attached to this offering circular and contains a summary of the special regulations for muffler installation in your state.

During the past 5 years Belmont has operated 7 muffler shops that are similar to the franchised shops being offered. All these shops are located in urban areas, have approximately _____ square feet of floor space and are located on busy streets. An additional 3 muffler shops were opened in 1990. From 1968 to 1973, Belmont offered franchises for "Repair-All Transmission Shops." "Repair-All" franchisees repaired and replaced motor vehicle transmissions under a marketing plan similar to the franchise in this offering circular. Belmont sold 40 of these franchises primarily in the states of Minnesota, Michigan, Wisconsin and Illinois. In 1973, Belmont sold this transmission repair company to CTF Inc.

ITEM 2. BUSINESS EXPERIENCE

LIST BY NAME AND POSITION THE DIRECTORS, TRUSTEES AND/OR GENERAL PARTNERS, THE PRINCIPAL OFFICERS AND OTHER EXECUTIVES OR SUBFRANCHISORS WHO WILL HAVE MANAGEMENT RESPONSIBILITY RELATING TO THE FRANCHISES OFFERED BY THIS OFFERING CIRCULAR. LIST ALL FRANCHISE BROKERS. STATE EACH PERSON'S PRINCIPAL OCCUPATIONS AND EMPLOYERS DURING THE PAST FIVE YEARS.

Item 2 Instructions

i.   Principal officers include the chief executive and chief operating officer, the president, financial, franchise marketing, training and franchise operations officers.

ii. First disclose the position and the name of the person holding it. Underline this information; then skip one line.

iii. Disclose the beginning date and departure date for each job held in the five year period, whether or not this date is within the past five years. Disclose the location of the job.

iv. Do not disclose home addresses, home telephones, social security numbers or birth dates in this Item.

v.   Disclose the required information concerning the franchise broker's directors, principal officers and executives with management responsibility to market or service the franchises.

vi. In a multi-state offering in which the franchisor uses a single offering circular and franchise brokers and executives with direct management responsibility to the franchisees differs from state to state, use an exhibit to refer to these personnel.

Sample Answer 2

President: Jane J. Doe

From June, 1978, until April, 1986, Ms. Doe was Vice-President of Atlas Inc., a Houston, Texas based manufacturer of automobile wheels. In April, 1986, she joined Belmont as a Director and Vice President. She was promoted to president in June, 1987.

ITEM 3. LITIGATION

DISCLOSE WHETHER THE FRANCHISOR, ITS PREDECESSOR, A PERSON IDENTIFIED IN ITEM 2 OR AN AFFILIATE OFFERING FRANCHISES UNDER THE FRANCHISOR'S PRINCIPAL TRADE-MARK:

A. HAS AN ADMINISTRATIVE, CRIMINAL OR MATERIAL CIVIL ACTION PENDING AGAINST THAT PERSON ALLEGING A VIOLATION OF A FRANCHISE, ANTITRUST OR SECURITIES LAW, FRAUD, UNFAIR OR DECEPTIVE PRACTICES, OR COMPARABLE ALLEGATIONS. IN ADDITION, INCLUDE ACTIONS OTHER THAN ORDINARY ROUTINE LITIGATION INCI-DENTAL TO THE BUSINESS WHICH ARE SIGNIFICANT IN THE CONTEXT OF THE NUM-BER OF FRANCHISEES AND THE SIZE, NATURE OR FINANCIAL CONDITION OF THE FRANCHISE SYSTEM OR ITS BUSINESS OPERATIONS. IF SO, DISCLOSE THE NAMES OF THE PARTIES, THE FORUM, NATURE, AND CURRENT STATUS OF THE PENDING ACTION. FRANCHISOR MAY INCLUDE A SUMMARY OPINION OF COUNSEL CONCERNING THE ACTION IF A CONSENT TO USE OF THE SUMMARY OPINION IS INCLUDED AS PART OF THIS OFFERING CIRCULAR.

B. HAS DURING THE 10 YEAR PERIOD IMMEDIATELY BEFORE THE DATE OF THE OFFER-ING CIRCULAR BEEN CONVICTED OF A FELONY OR PLEADED NOLO CONTENDERE TO A FELONY CHARGE; OR BEEN HELD LIABLE IN A CIVIL ACTION BY FINAL JUDGMENT OR BEEN THE SUBJECT OF A MATERIAL ACTION INVOLVING VIOLATION OF A FRAN-CHISE, ANTITRUST OR SECURITIES LAW, FRAUD, UNFAIR OR DECEPTIVE PRACTICES, OR COMPARABLE ALLEGATIONS. IF SO, DISCLOSE THE NAMES OF THE PARTIES, THE FORUM AND DATE OF CONVICTION OR DATE JUDGMENT WAS ENTERED, PENALTY OR DAMAGES ASSESSED AND/OR TERMS OF SETTLEMENTS.

C. IS SUBJECT TO A CURRENTLY EFFECTIVE INJUNCTIVE OR RESTRICTIVE ORDER OR DECREE RELATING TO THE FRANCHISE OR UNDER A FEDERAL, STATE, OR CANADIAN FRANCHISE SECURITIES, ANTITRUST, TRADE REGULATION, OR TRADE PRACTICE LAW RESULTING FROM A CONCLUDED OR PENDING ACTION OR PROCEEDING BROUGHT BY A PUBLIC AGENCY. IF SO, DISCLOSE THE NAME OF THE PERSON, THE PUBLIC AGENCY AND COURT, A SUMMARY OF THE ALLEGATIONS OR FACTS FOUND BY THE AGENCY OR COURT, AND THE DATE, NATURE, TERMS, AND CONDITIONS OF THE ORDER OR DECREE.

Item 3 Definitions

i. For purposes of these instructions to Item 3, "franchisor" includes the franchisor, its prede-cessors, persons identified in Item 2, and affiliates offering franchises under the franchisor's principal trademarks.

ii. "Action" includes complaints, cross claims, counterclaims, and third party complaints in a judicial proceeding, and their equivalents in an administrative action or arbitration proceeding. The franchisor may disclose its counterclaims. Omit actions that were dismissed by final judgment without liability of or entry of an adverse order against the franchisor.

iii. Included in the definition of material is an action or an aggregate of actions if a reasonable prospective franchisee would consider it important in making a decision about the franchised business.

iv. In this Item, settlement of an action does not diminish its materiality if the franchisor agrees to pay material consideration or agrees to be bound by obligations which are materially adverse to its interests.

v. "Ordinary routine litigation" means actions which ordinarily result from the business and which do not depart from the normal kinds of actions in the business.

vi. "Held liable" includes a finding by final judgment in a judicial, binding arbitration or administrative proceeding that the franchisor, as a result of claims or counterclaims must pay money or other consideration, must reduce an indebtedness by the amount of an award, cannot enforce its rights, or must take action adverse to its interests.

vii. "Currently Effective": An injunctive or restrictive order, or decree is "currently effective" unless it has been vacated or rescinded by a court or by the issuing public agency. An order that has expired by its own terms is not "currently effective." If the named party(s) have fully complied with an order (for example, through registration of its franchise offer), the order is not "currently effective." A party has not fully complied with an order to act or to refrain from an act (for example to comply with the franchise law or to refrain from violating the franchise law) until the order expires by its own terms.

Item 3 Instructions

Civil Litigation, or Injunctive or Restrictive Order:

viii. Use Sample Answer 3-1 for a negative response to Item 3 if the franchisor has never been named in litigation or if the only litigation naming the franchisor is outside the scope of Item 3.

ix. Disclose in the same order as the instructions below appear.

x. Title each action and state its case number or citation in parentheses. Underline the title of the action.

xi. For each action state the action's initial filing date and the opposing party's name and relationship with the franchisor. Relationships include competitor, supplier, lessor, franchisee, former franchisee, or class of franchisees.

xii. Summarize the legal and factual nature of each claim in the action.

xiii. Summarize the relief sought or obtained. Summarize conclusions of law or fact.

xiv. State that other than these (list number of actions) no litigation is required to be disclosed in this offering circular.

Criminal Convictions or Pleas:

xv. Disclose in the same order as the following instructions appear.

xvi. Title each action and state its citation in parentheses. Underline the title of the action.

xvii. Name the person convicted or who pleaded.

xviii. Next, state the crime or violation and the date of conviction.

xix. Next, disclose the sentence or penalty imposed.

xx. Lastly, state that other than these (list the number of actions) actions, no litigation is required to be disclosed in this offering circular.

Sample Answer 3-1

No litigation is required to be disclosed in this offering circular.

Sample Answer 3-2

Doe v. Belmont Muffler Service, Inc. (cite) On March 1, 1985, our franchisee, Donald Doe, sought to enjoin us from terminating him for nonpayment of royalty fees. Doe alleged _____. On April 3, 1986, Doe withdrew the case when we repurchased his franchise for $90,000 and agreed not to enforce non-compete clauses against him.

Indiana v. Belmont Muffler Service, Inc. (cite) On April 1, 1985, the Attorney General of Indiana sought to enjoin us from offering unregistered franchises and from using false income representations. The Attorney General alleged that the earnings claims were false because .... The court found that we had offered franchises, that the offers were not registered and that we had made the alleged false representations in our earnings claims. The court enjoined us from repeating those acts. Other than these two actions, no litigation is required to be disclosed in this offering circular.

ITEM 4. BANKRUPTCY

STATE WHETHER THE FRANCHISOR, ITS AFFILIATE, ITS PREDECESSOR, OFFICERS OR GENERAL PARTNER DURING THE 10-YEAR PERIOD IMMEDIATELY BEFORE THE DATE OF THE OFFERING CIRCULAR (A) FILED AS DEBTOR (OR HAD FILED AGAINST IT) A PETITION TO START AN ACTION UNDER THE U.S. BANKRUPTCY CODE; (B) OBTAINED A DISCHARGE OF ITS DEBTS UNDER THE BANKRUPTCY CODE; OR (C) WAS A PRINCIPAL OFFICER OF A COMPANY OR A GENERAL PARTNER IN A PARTNERSHIP THAT EITHER FILED AS A DEBTOR (OR HAD FILED AGAINST IT) A PETITION TO START AN ACTION UNDER THE U.S. BANKRUPTCY CODE OR THAT OBTAINED A DISCHARGE OF ITS DEBTS UNDER THE BANKRUPTCY CODE DURING OR WITHIN 1 YEAR AFTER THE OFFICER OR GENERAL PARTNER OF THE FRANCHISOR HELD THIS POSITION IN THE COMPANY OR PARTNERSHIP. IF SO, DISCLOSE THE NAME OF THE PERSON OR COMPANY THAT WAS THE DEBTOR UNDER THE BANKRUPTCY CODE, THE DATE OF THE ACTION AND THE MATERIAL FACTS.

Item 4 Instructions

i. First, name the party that filed (or had filed against it) the petition in bankruptcy and the party's relationship to the franchisor. If the debtor in a bankruptcy proceeding was or is affiliated with the franchisor, state the relationship. If the debtor in a bankruptcy proceeding is unaffiliated with the franchisor, state the name, address and principal business of the bankrupt company.

ii. Disclose that the entity filed bankruptcy or reorganization under the bankruptcy law and the date of the original filing.

iii. Identify the bankruptcy court and the case name and number. Put this information in parentheses.

iv. State the date on which the debtor obtained a discharge in bankruptcy (including discharges under Chapter 7 and confirmation of any plans of reorganization under Chapters 11 and 13 of the U.S. Bankruptcy Code).

v. Disclose other material facts.

vi. Cases, actions and other proceedings under the laws of foreign nations relating to bankruptcy proceedings should be included in answers, where responses are required, as if those cases, actions and proceedings took place under the U.S. Bankruptcy Code.

vii. If information is disclosed in this Item, at the end of the disclosure add sample answer 4-1 with the qualification "other than these actions."

viii. Use sample answer 4-1 if no person listed in Items 1 or 2 has been involved as a debtor in bankruptcy proceedings or any person listed in Items 1 or 2 has been involved as a debtor in bankruptcy proceedings but the bankruptcy proceedings (under the U.S. Bankruptcy Code or its predecessor, the National Bankruptcy Act of 1898) were discharged more than 10 years ago. "Person" includes natural persons and legal entities listed in Items 1 and 2. Person does not include anyone acting solely as the franchisor's agent for service of process.

Sample Answer 4-1

No person previously identified in Items 1 or 2 of this offering circular has been involved as a debtor in proceedings under the U.S. Bankruptcy Code required to be disclosed in this Item.

Sample Answer 4-2

On March 2, 1984, Belmont filed a petition to reorganize under Chapter 11 of the U.S. Bankruptcy Code. We were allowed to continue to operate under bankruptcy court supervision. On October 2, 1985, the bankruptcy court approved our plan of reorganization and discharged the proceedings. (U.S. Bankruptcy Court for the District of _____ Case B 84301).

Belmont's present president, Roger Rowe, was president of Acme Muffler Service, Inc., a Houston, Texas based manufacturer of exhaust systems, from July 1, 1978, through June 14, 1983. On June 6, 1983, an involuntary petition under the U.S. Bankruptcy Code was filed against Acme by its creditors. On July 14, 1983, the court entered an order of relief. Acme sold its assets and was dissolved.

Other than these 2 actions, no person previously identified in Items 1 or 2 of this offering circular has been involved as a debtor in proceedings under the U.S. Bankruptcy Code required to be disclosed in this Item.

ITEM 5. INITIAL FRANCHISE FEE

DISCLOSE THE INITIAL FRANCHISE FEE AND STATE THE CONDITIONS WHEN THIS FEE IS REFUNDABLE.

Item 5 Instructions

i. "Initial fee" includes all fees and payments for services or goods received from the franchisor before the franchisees business opens. "Initial fee" includes all fees and payments whether payable in lump sum or installments.

   ii. If the initial fee is not uniform, disclose the formula or the range of initial fees paid in the fiscal year before the application date and the factors that determined the amount.

  iii. Disclose installment payment terms in this Item or in Item 10.

Sample Answer 5-1

All franchisees pay a $10,000 lump sum franchise fee when they sign the franchise agreement. Belmont will refund the entire amount if we do not approve your application within 45 days. Belmont will refund $9,000 of this fee if you do not satisfactorily complete your 2-week training. There are no refunds under other circumstances.

Sample Answer 5-2

You must pay a franchise license fee of $____ per thousand licensed drivers who reside within your exclusive area when the franchise agreement is signed. The number of licensed drivers is determined by the latest abstract of the state agency which issues driver's licenses. The minimum fee is $20,000. When you send your application, you must pay a non-refundable $500 application fee. You must pay an additional $10,000 when you receive your equipment. The balance of your fee is payable in 12 equal monthly installments of $_____. The first installment payment is due 1 year after your shop opens. Belmont charges 10% annual interest on the unpaid balance. Interest compounds daily and accrues from the date that you receive your equipment. All buyers pay this uniform fee and receive the same financing terms on the fee. If your application is not accepted, Belmont retains the $500 for investigative costs, but you are not liable for the $19,500 remainder. Belmont does not give refunds under other circumstances.

ITEM 6. OTHER FEES

DISCLOSE OTHER RECURRING OR ISOLATED FEES OR PAYMENTS THAT THE FRANCHISEE MUST PAY TO THE FRANCHISOR OR ITS AFFILIATES OR THAT THE FRANCHISOR OR ITS AFFILIATES IMPOSE OR COLLECT IN WHOLE OR IN PART ON BEHALF OF A THIRD PARTY. INCLUDE THE FORMULA USED TO COMPUTE THESE OTHER FEES AND PAYMENTS. IF ANY FEE IS REFUNDABLE, STATE THE CONDITIONS WHEN EACH FEE OR PAYMENT IS REFUNDABLE.

Item 6 Instructions

    i. First disclose fees in tabular form. Use footnotes or a "remarks" column to elaborate on the information in the table or to disclose caveats. If elaborations are lengthy, use footnotes instead of a "remarks" column.

   ii. Disclose the amount of each fee. A dollar amount or a percentage of gross sales is acceptable if the term gross sales is defined. If dollar amounts may increase, disclose the formula which determines the increase or the maximum amount of the increase.

  iii. Disclose the due date for recurring payments.

  iv. If all fees are payable to only the franchisor, disclose this in a footnote.

   v. If all fees are imposed and collected by the franchisor, disclose this in a footnote.

  vi. If all fees are non-refundable, state this in a footnote.

 vii. Disclose the voting power of franchisor owned outlets on any fees imposed by cooperatives.

If franchisor outlets have controlling voting power, disclose a range for the fee. Disclose this information in a footnote or a "remarks" column.

viii. The franchisor need not repeat information contained in Items 8 and 9, but the table should direct the franchisees to those Items.

ix. Examples of fees are royalty, lease negotiation, construction, remodeling, additional training, advertising, group advertising, additional assistance, audit, accounting/inventory, and transfer and renewal fee.

Sample Answer 6-1

Name of Fee	Amount	Due Date	Remarks
Royalty[1]	4% of total gross sales	Payable monthly on the 10th day of the next month	Gross sales includes all revenue from the franchise location. Gross sales does not include sales tax or use tax.
Advertising[1]	2% of total gross sales	Same as Royalty fee	
Cooperative Advertising[1]	Maximum—2% of total gross sales	Established by franchisees	Franchisees may form an advertising cooperative and establish local advertising fees. Company-owned stores have no vote in these cooperatives.
Additional Training[1]	$1,000 per person	2 weeks prior to beginning of training	Belmont trains two persons free—see Item 11.
Additional Assistance[1]	$500 per day	30 days after billing	Belmont provides opening assistance free—see Item 11.
Transfer[1]	$1,000	Prior to consummation of transfer	Payable when you sell your franchise. No charge if franchise is transferred to a corporation that you control.
Audit[1]	Cost of audit plus 10% interest on underpayment[2]	30 days after billing	Payable only if audit shows an understatement of at least 2% of gross sales for any month.
Renewal[1]	$1,000	30 days before renewal	

[1] All fees are imposed by and are payable to Belmont. All fees are nonrefundable.

[2] Interest begins from the date of the underpayment.

ITEM 7. INITIAL INVESTMENT

DISCLOSE THE FOLLOWING EXPENDITURES STATING TO WHOM THE PAYMENTS ARE MADE, WHEN PAYMENTS ARE DUE, WHETHER EACH PAYMENT IS REFUNDABLE, THE CONDITIONS

WHEN EACH PAYMENT IS REFUNDABLE, AND, IF PART OF THE FRANCHISEE'S INITIAL INVESTMENT IN THE FRANCHISE MAY BE FINANCED, AN ESTIMATE OF THE LOAN REPAYMENTS, INCLUDING INTEREST:

A. REAL PROPERTY, WHETHER PURCHASED OR LEASED. IF NEITHER ESTIMABLE NOR DESCRIBABLE BY A LOW?HIGH RANGE, DESCRIBE REQUIREMENTS, SUCH AS PROPERTY TYPE, LOCATION AND BUILDING SIZE.

B. EQUIPMENT, FIXTURES, OTHER FIXED ASSETS, CONSTRUCTION, REMODELING, LEASEHOLD IMPROVEMENTS AND DECORATING COSTS, WHETHER PURCHASED OR LEASED.

C. INVENTORY REQUIRED TO BEGIN OPERATION.

D. SECURITY DEPOSITS, UTILITY DEPOSITS, BUSINESS LICENSES, OTHER PREPAID EXPENSES.

E. ADDITIONAL FUNDS REQUIRED BY THE FRANCHISEE BEFORE OPERATIONS BEGIN AND DURING THE INITIAL PHASE OF THE FRANCHISE.

F. OTHER PAYMENTS THAT THE FRANCHISEE MUST MAKE TO BEGIN OPERATIONS.

Item 7 Instructions

i. Begin disclosure by listing expenditures in tabular form. List pre-opening expenses first. Use footnotes to comment on expected expenditures.

ii. Disclose payments required by the franchise agreement and all costs necessary to begin operation of the franchise and operate the franchise during the initial phase of the business. A reasonable time for the initial phase of the business is at least 3 months or a reasonable period for the industry. Include an entry titled "additional funds" and disclose the length of the initial phase in the entry.

iii. If a specific expenditure amount is not ascertainable, use a low-high range based on the franchisor's current experience. If real property costs cannot be estimated in a low-high range, disclose the approximate size of the property and building involved. Describe the probable location of the building (for example, strip shopping center, mall, downtown, rural, or highway).

iv. The franchisor may include additional expenditure tables to show expenditure variations caused by differences in site location, premise size, etc. Describe in general terms the factors, basis, and experience that the franchisor considered or relied upon in formulating the amount required for additional funds.

v. If the franchisor or an affiliate finances part of the initial investment, state the expenditures that it will finance. State the required down payment, annual percentage rate of interest, rate factors, and the estimated loan repayments. Make the discussion brief, and refer to Item 10.

vi. Total the initial investment. This total should be the same as the total investment on the offering circular cover.

Sample Answer 7

Your Estimated Intial Investment

Payment	Amount	Method of Payment	When Due	To Whom Payment Is to Be Made
Initial Franchise Fee[1]	$20,000[1]	Lump sum	At signing of Franchise Agreement	Belmont, Inc.
Travel and Living Expenses While Training	$2,500 to $5,000	As incurred	During training	Airlines, hotels, and restaurants
Real Estate and Improvements[2]				
Equipment	$40,000[3]	Lump sum	Prior to opening	Belmont or vendors
Signs	$2,200	Lump sum	Prior to opening	Abbey Sign Company
Miscellaneous Opening Costs	$8,000[4]	As incurred	As incurred	Suppliers, utilities, etc.
Opening Inventory	$8,000[5]	Lump sum	Prior to opening	Belmont or vendors
Advertising Fee, 3 Months	$500		Monthly	Belmont
Additional Funds, 3 Months	$50,000 to $75,000[6]	As incurred	As incurred	Employees, suppliers, utilities
Total	$132,700 to $160,200[7]	(Does not include real estate costs)		

[1] See Item 5 for the conditions when this fee is partly refundable. Belmont does not finance any fee.

[2] If you do not own adequate shop space, you must lease the land and building for the Belmont Muffler Shop. Typical locations are light industrial and commercial areas. The typical Belmont Muffler Shop has 5,000-8,000 square feet. Former three or four bay gasoline service stations have been converted with relative ease into Belmont Muffler Shops. Rent is estimated to be between $12,000-20,000 per year depending on factors such as size, condition, and location of the leased premises.

[3] This payment is fully refundable before equipment installation. After installation, Belmont deducts $3,000 installation costs from your refund.

[4] Includes security deposits, utility costs, incorporation fee.

[5] This payment is fully refundable before Belmont delivers your inventory. After delivery Belmont deducts a 10% restocking fee from your refund.

[6] This estimates your initial start-up expenses. These expenses include payroll costs. These figures are estimates and Belmont cannot guarantee that you will not have additional expenses starting the business. Your costs will depend on factors such as: how much you follow Belmont's methods and procedures; your management skill, experience, and business acumen; local economic conditions; the local market for our product; the prevailing wage rate; competition; and the sales level reached during the initial period.

[7] Belmont relied on its 30 years of experience in the muffler business to compile these estimates. You should review these figures carefully with a business advisor before making any decision to purchase the franchise.

[8] Belmont does not offer direct or indirect financing to franchisees for any items.

ITEM 8. RESTRICTIONS ON SOURCES OF PRODUCTS AND SERVICES

DISCLOSE FRANCHISEE OBLIGATIONS TO PURCHASE OR LEASE FROM THE FRANCHISOR ITS DESIGNEE OR FROM SUPPLIERS APPROVED BY THE FRANCHISOR OR UNDER THE FRANCHISOR'S SPECIFICATIONS. FOR EACH OBLIGATION DISCLOSE:

A. THE GOODS, SERVICES, SUPPLIES, FIXTURES, EQUIPMENT, INVENTORY, COMPUTER HARDWARE AND SOFTWARE, OR REAL ESTATE RELATING TO ESTABLISHING OR OPERATING THE FRANCHISED BUSINESS.

B. THE MANNER IN WHICH THE FRANCHISOR ISSUES AND MODIFIES SPECIFICATIONS OR GRANTS AND REVOKES APPROVAL TO SUPPLIERS.

C. WHETHER, AND FOR WHAT CATEGORIES OF GOODS AND SERVICES, THE FRANCHISOR OR ITS AFFILIATES ARE APPROVED SUPPLIERS OR THE ONLY APPROVED SUPPLIERS.

D. WHETHER, AND IF SO, THE PRECISE BASIS BY WHICH THE FRANCHISOR OR ITS AFFILIATES WILL OR MAY DERIVE REVENUE OR OTHER MATERIAL CONSIDERATION AS A RESULT OF REQUIRED PURCHASES OR LEASES.

E. THE ESTIMATED PROPORTION OF THESE REQUIRED PURCHASES AND LEASES TO ALL PURCHASES AND LEASES BY THE FRANCHISEE OF GOODS AND SERVICES IN ESTABLISHING AND OPERATING THE FRANCHISED BUSINESS.

F. THE EXISTENCE OF PURCHASING OR DISTRIBUTION COOPERATIVES.

Item 8 Instructions

i. An obligation includes those imposed by written agreement or by the franchisor's practice. The franchisor may include the reason for the requirement.

ii. Do not include goods or services provided as part of the franchise and without a separate charge (for example, a fee for initial training when the cost is included in the franchise fee). These fees should be described in Item 5. Do not include fees disclosed in response to Item 6.

iii. For "precise basis," disclose the franchisor's total revenues and the franchisor's revenues from all required purchases and leases of products and services. Also, disclose the percentage of the franchisor's total revenues represented by the franchisor's revenues from required purchases or leases. If the franchisor's affiliates also sell or lease products or services to franchisees, disclose affiliate revenues from those sales or leases. These amounts should be taken from the franchisor's statement of operations (or profit and loss statement) from the most recent annual audited financial statement attached to the offering circular. If the franchisor's annual audited financial statement is not required to be attached to the offering circular or if the franchisor's affiliate sells or leases required products or services to franchisees, disclose the sources of information used in computing revenues.

iv. State how the franchisor formulates and modifies specifications and standards imposed on franchisees.

v. Disclose whether specifications and standards are issued to franchisees, subfranchisors, or approved suppliers.

vi. Describe how suppliers are evaluated, approved, or disapproved. Disclose whether the franchisor's criteria for supplier approval are available to franchisees. State the fees and procedure to secure approval and how approvals are revoked. State the time period when the franchisee will receive notification of approval or disapproval.

vii. If the designated supplier will make payments to the franchisor because of transactions with franchisees, disclose the basis for the payment. Specify a percentage or a flat amount. Purchases of similar goods or services by the franchisor at a lower price than that available to franchisees is a payment.

viii. Disclose whether the franchisor negotiates purchase arrangements with suppliers (including price terms) for the benefit of franchisees.

ix. Disclose whether the franchisor provides material benefits (for example renewal or granting additional franchises) to a franchisee based on a franchisee's use of designated or approved sources.

x. Use Sample Answer 8-1 if the response to Item 8 is negative.

Sample Answer 8-1

Belmont has no required specifications, designated suppliers, or approved suppliers for goods, services, or real estate relating to your franchise business. Belmont will not derive revenue from your purchases or leases.

Sample Answer 8-2

You must purchase your pipe bending machine, hoist, cutting torch, and supplies under specifications in the operations manual. These specifications include standards for delivery, performance, design, and appearance. You may purchase this equipment from Belmont. In the year ending December 31, 1992, Belmont's revenues from the sale of this equipment to franchisees was $500,000, or 5% of Belmont's total revenues of $10,000,000. The cost of equipment purchased in accordance with specifications represents 10% of your total purchases in connection with establishment of your store.

Belmont's affiliate, Muffler Supply Co., is an approved supplier of mufflers to franchisees. In the year ending December 31, 1992, the affiliate's revenues from the sale of mufflers to franchisees was $2,000,000. The purchase of mufflers from approved sources will represent 15 to 20% of your overall purchases in operating the store. Belmont has approved other suppliers of mufflers and exhaust pipe. If you would like to purchase these items from another supplier, you may request our "Supplier Approval Criteria and Request Form." Based on the information and samples you supply to us and your payment of a $500 fee, we will test the item supplied and review the proposed supplier's financial records, business reputation, delivery performance, credit rating, and other information. Our review typically is completed in 30 days.

One of the approved suppliers of mufflers and exhaust pipes, Scottie's Pipes, Inc., pays Belmont a rebate of 1% of all franchisee purchases, which is deposited in the Belmont Advertising Fund. Another approved supplier, Michael's Clean-Air, Inc., pays Belmont 2% of all franchisee purchases of catalytic converters. This amount is used in Belmont's training center for classes in catalytic converter repair and replacement.

ITEM 9. FRANCHISEE'S OBLIGATIONS

DISCLOSE THE PRINCIPAL OBLIGATIONS OF THE FRANCHISEE UNDER THE FRANCHISE AND OTHER AGREEMENTS AFTER THE SIGNING OF THESE AGREEMENTS.

Item 9 Instructions

i. Disclose obligations in tabular form. Refer to the section of the agreement that contains the obligation and any item of the Offering Circular that further describes the obligation.

ii. The table should contain a response to each category listed below. If the response to any category is that no obligation is imposed, the table should state that. Do not change the names of the categories. Fit all obligations within the listed categories. If other material obligations fall outside the scope of all of the prescribed categories, add additional categories as needed. The categories of franchisee obligations are:

    a. Site selection and acquisition/lease

    b. Pre-opening purchases/leases

    c. Site development and other pre-opening requirements

    d. Initial and ongoing training

    e. Opening

    f. Fees

    g. Compliance with standards and policies/Operating Manual

    h. Trademarks and proprietary information

    i. Restrictions on products/services offered

    j. Warranty and customer service requirements

    k. Territorial development and sales quotas

    l. Ongoing product/service purchases

    m. Maintenance, appearance, and remodeling requirements

    n. Insurance

    o. Advertising

    p. Indemnification

    q. Owner's participation/management/staffing

    r. Records and reports

    s. Inspections and audits

    t. Transfer

    u. Renewal

      v. Post-termination obligations

      w. Non-competition covenants

      x. Dispute resolution

      y. Other (describe)

  iii. Before the table, state the following:

THIS TABLE LISTS YOUR PRINCIPAL OBLIGATIONS UNDER THE FRANCHISE AND OTHER AGREEMENTS. IT WILL HELP YOU FIND MORE DETAILED INFORMATION ABOUT YOUR OBLIGATIONS IN THESE AGREEMENTS AND IN OTHER ITEMS OF THIS OFFERING CIRCULAR.

Sample Answer 9

THIS TABLE LISTS YOUR PRINCIPAL OBLIGATIONS UNDER THE FRANCHISE AND OTHER AGREEMENTS. IT WILL HELP YOU FIND MORE DETAILED INFORMATION ABOUT YOUR OBLIGATIONS IN THESE AGREEMENTS AND IN OTHER ITEMS OF THIS OFFERING CIRCULAR.

Obligation	Section in Franchise Agreement	Item in Offering Circular
a. Site selection and acquisition/lease	2A	Items 6 and 11
b. Pre-opening purchases/lease	3D	Item 8
c. Site development and other pre-opening requirements	3A and 3B	Items 6, 7, and 11
d. Initial and ongoing training	5	Item 11
e. Opening	4	Item 11
f. Fees	6	Items 5 and 6
g. Compliance with standards and policies/Operating Manual	8A	Item 11
h. Trademarks and proprietary information	7 and 11	Items 13 and 14
i. Restrictions on products/ services offered	12	Item 16
j. Warranty and customer service requirements	8B	Item 11
k. Territorial development and sales quotas	None	
l. Ongoing product/service purchases	9	Item 8

Obligation	Section in Franchise Agreement	Item in Offering Circular
m. Maintenance, appearance, and remodeling requirements	8C and 10	Item 11
n. Insurance	13A	Items 6 and 8
o. Advertising	15	Items 6 and 11
p. Indemnification	13B	Item 6
q. Owner's participation/management/staffing	4, 5, and 14	Items 11 and 15
r. Records and reports	17A	Item 6
s. Inspections and audits	17B	Items 6 and 11
t. Transfer	18	Item 17
u. Renewal	20	Item 17
v. Post-termination obligations	22	Item 17
w. Non-competition covenants	11, 18, and 22C	Item 17
x. Dispute resolution	24	Item 17

ITEM 10. FINANCING

DISCLOSE THE TERMS AND CONDITIONS OF EACH FINANCING ARRANGEMENT THAT THE FRANCHISOR, ITS AGENT OR AFFILIATES OFFERS DIRECTLY OR INDIRECTLY TO THE FRANCHISEE, INCLUDING:

Item 10 Instructions

   i. "Financing" includes leases and installment contracts.

  ii. Payments due within 90 days on open account financing need not be disclosed under this Item.

 iii. A written arrangement between a franchisor or its affiliate and a lender for the lender to offer financing to the franchisee or an arrangement in which a franchisor or its affiliate receives a benefit from a lender for franchisee financing is an "indirect offer of financing" and must be disclosed under this Item. The franchisor's guarantee of a note, lease, or obligation of the franchisee is an "indirect offer of financing" and must be disclosed under this Item.

 iv. If financing of the initial fee is disclosed in the Item 7 disclosure, a cross reference to Item 7 is sufficient if all the disclosure which Item 10 requires is provided in Item 7.

  v. If an affiliate offers financing, identify the affiliate and its relationship to the franchisor.

 vi. The franchisor may summarize the terms of each financing arrangement in tabular form, using footnotes to entries in the chart to provide additional information required by these instructions that does not fit in the chart.

vii. If a financing arrangement is for the establishment of the franchised business, disclose what the financing covers, including:
   a) Initial franchise fee;
   b) Site acquisition;
   c) Construction or remodeling;
   d) Equipment or fixtures; and
   e) Opening inventory or supplies.

viii. If the franchisor generally offers financing for the operation of the franchised business, disclose what the financing arrangement covers, including:
   a) Inventory or supplies;
   b) Replacement equipment or fixtures; and
   c) Other continuing expenses.

ix. Disclose the terms of each financing arrangement, including:
   a) The identity of the lender(s) providing the financing and its relationship to the franchisor (for example, affiliate);
   b) The amount of financing offered or, if the amount depends on an actual cost that may vary, the percentage of the cost that will be financed;
   c) The annual percentage rate of interest ("APR") charged, computed as provided by Sections 106-107 of the Consumer Protection Credit Act, 15 U.S.C. §§ 106-107. If the APR may differ depending on when the financing is issued, disclose the APR on a specified recent date;
   d) The number of payments or the period of repayment;
   e) Nature of security interest required by the lender;
   f) Whether a person other than the franchisee (for example, spouse, shareholder of the franchisee) must personally guarantee the debt;
   g) Whether the debt can be prepaid and the nature of any prepayment penalty;
   h) The franchisee's potential liabilities upon default, including any accelerated obligation to pay the entire amount due, court costs and attorney's fees for collection, and termination of the franchise, or other cross default clauses whether directly, as a result of non-payment, or indirectly, as a result of loss of necessary facilities; and
   i) Other material financing terms.

x. Include specimen copies of the financing documents as an exhibit to Item 22. Cite the section and name of the document containing the financing terms. Put this information in parentheses at the end of the description of the term.

xi. Use Sample Answer 10-1 if the franchisor does not offer financing.

A. A WAIVER OF DEFENSES OR SIMILAR PROVISIONS IN A DOCUMENT

Item 10A Instructions:
   i. Disclose the terms of waivers of legal rights by the franchisee under the terms of the financing arrangement (for example, confession of judgment).
   ii. Describe provisions of the loan agreement that bar the franchisee from asserting a defense

   iii.   against the lender, the lender's assignee, or the franchisor.
   iii.   If the loan agreement does not contain the provisions in (i) or (ii), disclose that fact.
   iv.   Cite the section and name of the document containing these terms. Put this information in parentheses at the end of the description of the term.

B. THE FRANCHISOR'S PRACTICE OR ITS INTENT TO SELL, ASSIGN, OR DISCOUNT TO A THIRD PARTY ALL OR PART OF THE FINANCING ARRANGEMENT

Item 10B Instructions

   i.   Practice includes past or present practice and future intent to sell or assign franchisee financing arrangements.
   ii.   Disclose the assignment terms including whether the franchisor will remain primarily obligated to provide the financed goods or services.
   iii.   If the franchisor may sell or assign its rights under the financing agreement, disclose that the franchisee may lose all its defenses against the lender as a result of the sale or assignment.
   iv.   Cite the section and name of the document containing these terms. Put this information in parentheses at the end of the description of the term.
   v.   If no disclosure is required by Instruction B, disclose that fact.

C. PAYMENTS TO THE FRANCHISOR OR AFFILIATE(S) FOR THE PLACEMENT OF FINANCING WITH THE LENDER.

Item 10C Instructions:

   i.   Describe the payments.
   ii.   If no disclosure is required by Instruction 10C(i) for a financing arrangement, disclose that fact.
   iii.   Identify the source of the payment and the relationship of the source to the franchisor or its affiliates.
   iv.   Disclose the amount or the method of determining the payment.
   v.   Cite the section and name of the document containing these arrangements. Put this information in parentheses at the end of the description of the term.

Sample Answer 10-1

Belmont does not offer direct or indirect financing. Belmont does not guarantee your note, lease, or obligation.

Sample Answer 10-2

Summary of Financing Offered

Item Financed (Source)	Amount Financed	Down Payment	Term (Years)	APR %	Monthly Payment	Prepay Penalty	Security Required	Liability upon Default	Loss of Legal Right on Default
Initial Fee[1] (Belmont)	$10,000		10	18	$	None	Personal guarantee	Loss of franchise, unpaid loan	Waive notice, confess judgment
Land/Construct	None								
Leased Space[2] (Belmont)		$2,000 (Security)	7-10	N/A	$	None	Personal guarantee	Loss of franchise, back rent + 2 mos., franchise rights, atty's fees	None
Equipment Lease[3] (USA Credit Corp.)	$5,000	None	5	15	$	None	Equipment, Personal equipment	Cost of removal	Lose all defenses
Equip. Purch.[4] (Belmont)	$3,750	$1,250 (25%)	2-7	15	$	$500	Equipment, personal guarantee	Loss of franchise, atty's fees	None
Opening Investment	None								
Other Financing	None								

Notes

[1] If you meet Belmont's credit standards, Belmont will finance the $10,000 initial franchisee fee over a 10-year period at an APR of 18%, using the standard form note in Exhibit A. The only security Belmont requires is a personal guarantee of the note by you and your spouse or by all the shareholders of your corporation. (Loan Agreement Section _____) The note can be prepaid without penalty at any time during its 10-year term. (Loan Agreement Section _____) If you do not pay on time, Belmont can call the loan and demand immediate payment of the full outstanding balance and obtain court costs and attorney's fees if a collection action is neces-

sary. (Loan Agreement Section ____) Belmont also has the right to terminate your franchise if you do not make your payments on time more than three times during the note term. (Loan Agreement Section ____) You waive your rights to notice of a collection action and to assert any defenses to collection against Belmont. (Loan Agreement Section ____) Belmont discounts these notes to a third party who may be immune under the law to any defenses to payment you may have against Belmont. (Loan Agreement Section ____)

[2] In most cases Belmont will sublease the franchised premises to you but will guarantee your lease with a third party if you have acceptable credit and that is the only way to obtain an exceptional location. (Lease Section ____) The precise terms of Belmont's standard lease in Exhibit B will vary depending on the size and location of the premises, but the chart reflects a typical range of payments for Belmont's standard 6-day franchise outlet, including payment of one month's rent as a security deposit. (Lease Section ____) The only other security Belmont requires is a personal guarantee of the lease by you and your spouse or by all the shareholders of your corporation. (Lease Section ____) The lease can be prepaid without penalty at any time during its term. (Lease Section ____) If you do not make a rent payment on time, Belmont has the right to collect the unpaid rent plus an additional two months' rent, as liquidated damages. (Lease Section ____) Belmont can also obtain court costs and attorney's fees if a collection action is necessary. (Lease Section ____) If you are late with your rent more than three times during the lease term, Belmont has the right to terminate the lease, take over the premises, and terminate your franchise. If Belmont guarantees your lease, Belmont will require you to sign the guarantee agreement in Exhibit F (Lease Section ____) This gives Belmont the same legal rights as the sublease but requires you to give Belmont the right to approve your lease and pay the rent for you if you fail to pay on time. (Lease Section ____)

[3] If you want to lease the pipe bending machine and other equipment you need, Belmont has arranged an equipment lease (see Exhibit C) from USA Credit Corporation of Las Vegas, Nevada. If you choose this option, you will pay $100 a month for 60 months (5 years) at an APR of 15% based on a cash price of $5,000, with no money down. (Equipment Lease Section ____) At the end of the lease term, you may purchase the equipment with a one-time payment of $2,500. (Equipment Lease Section ____) USA Credit requires a personal guarantee from you and your spouse or from all the shareholders of your corporation and retains a security interest in the equipment. (Equipment Lease Section ____) The equipment lease can be prepaid at any time, but the interest you might otherwise save will be reduced by application of the Rule of 78's for computing finance charges. (Equipment Lease Section ____) If you do not make a payment on time, USA Credit can demand payment of all past due payments, remove the equipment, and charge you $1,000 as liquidated damages. (Equipment Lease Section ____) USA Credit can also recover its costs of collection, including court costs and attorney's fees. (Equipment Lease Section ____) While Belmont does not know USA Credit's policies, USA Credit may discount the lease to a third party who may be immune under the law to claims or defenses you may have against USA Credit, the equipment manufacturer, or Belmont. Belmont receives a referral fee of $500 from USA Credit for every franchisee who leases equipment from it.

[4] If you prefer, Belmont will sell you the pipe bending machine and other necessary equipment on time (Equipment Purchase Agreement Section ____). Belmont requires a 25% down payment of $1,250. (Equipment Purchase Agreement Section ____) Belmont will finance the remainder over a 2-7 year period at your option at an APR of 15%. (Equipment Purchase Agreement Section ____) Payments range from $228.11 a month over 7 years to $821.58 a month over 2 years. (Equipment Purchase Agreement Section ____) Belmont's standard equipment financing note in Exhibit D must be personally guaranteed by you and your spouse or by all the shareholders of your corporation, and Belmont will retain a security interest in the equipment. (Equipment Purchase Agreement Section ____) You may purchase the equipment at any time during the lease period by paying the remainder of the principal plus a $500 prepayment penalty. (Equipment Purchase Agreement Section ____) If you do not make a payment on time, Belmont can demand all overdue payments, repossess the equipment, and terminate your franchise. Belmont can also recover its costs of collection, including court costs and attorney's fees. (Equipment Purchase Agreement Section ____)

Except as disclosed in Note 1, Belmont does not offer financing that requires you to waive notice, confess judgment, or waive a defense against Belmont or the lender, although you may lose your defenses against

Belmont and others in a collection action on a note that is sold or discounted, as disclosed in Notes 2 and 3.

Except as disclosed in Note 3, Belmont does not arrange financing from other sources.

Except as disclosed in Notes 1 and 3, commercial paper from franchisees has not been and is not sold or assigned to anyone, and Belmont has no plans to do so.

Except as disclosed in Note 3, Belmont does not receive direct or indirect payments for placing financing.

Except as disclosed in Note 2, Belmont does not guarantee your obligations to third parties.

ITEM 11. FRANCHISOR'S OBLIGATIONS

DISCLOSE THE FOLLOWING:

A. THE OBLIGATIONS THAT THE FRANCHISOR WILL PERFORM BEFORE THE FRANCHISE BUSINESS OPENS. CITE BY SECTION THE PROVISIONS OF THE AGREEMENT REQUIRING PERFORMANCE.

Item 11A Instructions

i. Begin the disclosure by stating: "Except as listed below, (the franchisor) need not provide any assistance to you."

ii. Pre-opening obligations include assistance to:

    a) Locate a site for the franchised business and negotiate the purchase or lease of this site. State whether the franchisor generally owns the premises and leases it to the franchisee;

    b) Conform the premises to local ordinances and building codes and obtain the required permits (i.e., health, sanitation, building, driveway, utility, and sign permits);

    c) Construct, remodel, or decorate the premises for the franchised business;

    d) Purchase or lease equipment, signs, fixtures, opening inventory, and supplies. Disclose whether the franchisor provides these items directly or merely the names of approved suppliers. Disclose whether the franchisor provides written specifications for these items. Disclose whether the franchisor delivers or installs these items. (The franchisor may cross reference Item 8 for details.)

    e) Hire and train employees.

iii. After describing the obligation, cite the section number of the agreement imposing the obligation. Put the citation in parentheses. Use this format throughout this Item.

B. THE OBLIGATIONS TO BE MET BY THE FRANCHISOR DURING THE OPERATION OF THE FRANCHISE BUSINESS.

Item 11B Instructions

i. Include assistance in:

    a) Products or services to be offered by the franchisee to its customers;

    b) Hiring and training of employees;

    c) Improvements and developments in the franchised business;

    d) Pricing;

    e) Administrative, bookkeeping, accounting, and inventory control procedures; and

    f) Operating problems encountered by the franchisee.

ii. For the franchisor's advertising program for the product or service offered by the franchisee:

a) Disclose the media in which the advertising may be disseminated (for example, print, radio, or television).

b) Disclose whether the coverage of the media is local, regional, or national in scope.

c) Disclose the source of the advertising (for example, in-house advertising department, a national or regional advertising agency).

d) Disclose the conditions when the franchisor permits franchisees to use their own advertising material.

e) If there is an advertising council composed of franchisees that advises the franchisor on advertising policies, disclose:

   (1) How members of the council are selected.

   (2) Whether the council serves in an advisory capacity only or has operational or decision-making power.

   (3) Whether the franchisor has the power to form, change, or dissolve the advertising council.

f) If the franchisee must participate in a local or regional advertising cooperative, disclose:

   (1) How the area or membership of the cooperative is defined.

   (2) How the franchisee's contribution to the cooperative is calculated (may reference Item 6).

   (3) Who is responsible for administration of the cooperative (for example, franchisor, franchisees, advertising agency).

   (4) Whether cooperatives must operate from written governing documents and whether the documents are available for review by the franchisee.

   (5) Whether cooperatives must prepare annual or periodic financial statements and whether the statements are available for review by the franchisee.

   (6) Whether the franchisor has the power to require cooperatives to be formed, changed, dissolved, or merged.

g) If applicable, for each advertising fund not described in above sub-part (f), disclose:

   (1) Who contributes to each fund (for example, franchisees, franchisor, franchisor-owned units, outside vendors or suppliers);

   (2) Whether the franchisor-owned units must contribute to the fund and, if so, whether it is on the same basis as franchisees.

   (3) How much the franchisee must contribute to the advertising fund(s) (may reference Item 6) and whether other franchisees are required to contribute at a different rate (it is not necessary to disclose the specific rates).

   (4) Who administers the fund(s). Whether the fund is audited and when, and whether financial statements of the fund are available for review by the franchisee.

   (5) Use of the fund(s) in the most recently concluded fiscal year, the percentages spent on production, media placement, administrative expenses, and other (with a description of what constitutes "other"). Totals should equal 100%.

   (6) Whether the franchisor or an affiliate receives payment for providing goods or services to an advertising fund.

h) State whether the franchisor must spend any amount on advertising, in the area or territory where the franchisee is located.

i) If all advertising fees are not spent in the fiscal year in which they accrue, explain how the franchisor uses the remaining amounts. Indicate whether franchisees will receive a periodic accounting of how advertising fees are spent.

j) Disclose the percentage of advertising funds, if any, used for advertising that is principally a solicitation for the sale of franchises.

k) Cross-reference Items 6, 8, and 9.

iii. If the franchisor requires that franchisees buy or use electronic cash register or computer systems, provide a general description of the systems in nontechnical language:

    a) Identify each hardware component and software program by brand, type, and principal functions.

        (1) If the hardware component or software program is the proprietary property of the franchisor, an affiliate, or a third party, state whether the franchisor, an affiliate, or a third party has the contractual right or obligation to provide ongoing maintenance, repairs, upgrades, or updates. Disclose the current annual cost of any optional or required maintenance and support contracts, upgrades, and updates.

        (2) If the hardware component or software program is the proprietary property of a third party, and no compatible equivalent component or program has been approved by the franchisor for use with the system to perform the same functions, identify the third party by name, business address, and telephone number, and state the length of time the component or program has been in continuous use by the franchisor and its franchisees.

        (3) If the hardware component or software program is not proprietary, identify compatible equivalent components or programs that perform the same functions and indicate whether they have been approved by the franchisor.

    b) State whether the franchisee has any contractual obligation to upgrade or update any hardware component or software program during the term of the franchise, and if so, whether there are any contractual limitations on the frequency and cost of the obligation.

    c) For each electronic cash register system or software program, describe how it will be used in the franchisee's business, and the types of business information or data that will be collected and generated. State whether the franchisor will have independent access to the information and data, and if so, whether there are any contractual limitations on the franchisors right to access the information and data.

iv. After describing the obligation, cite the section number of the agreement imposing the obligation. Put the citation in parentheses.

v. Disclose if the franchisor is not obligated to provide or to assist the franchisee to obtain the above items or services.

vi. Do not repeat, but do cross-reference disclosure made in Item 6.

vii. Disclose the table of contents of the operating manual(s) provided to the franchisee as of the franchisor's last fiscal year end or a more recent date. State the number of pages devoted to each subject and the total number of pages in the manual as of this date. Alternatively, this disclosure may be omitted if the prospective franchisee views the manual before purchase of the franchise.

C. THE METHODS USED BY THE FRANCHISOR TO SELECT THE LOCATION OF THE FRANCHISEE'S BUSINESS.

Item 11C Instructions

   i. Disclose whether the franchisor selects the site or approves an area within which the franchisee selects a site. Disclose how and whether the franchisor must approve a franchisee selected site.

  ii. Disclose the factors which the franchisor considers in selecting or approving sites (for example, general location and neighborhood, traffic patterns, parking, size, physical characteristics of existing buildings, and lease terms).

 iii. Disclose the time limit for the franchisor to locate or to approve or disapprove the site. Disclose the consequences if the franchisor and franchisee cannot agree on a site.

 iv. Disclosures made in response to Item 11A need not be repeated or cross-referenced in the response to Item 11C.

D. THE TYPICAL LENGTH OF TIME BETWEEN THE SIGNING OF THE FRANCHISE AGREEMENT OR THE FIRST PAYMENT OF CONSIDERATION FOR THE FRANCHISE AND THE OPENING OF THE FRANCHISEE'S BUSINESS.

Item 11D Instructions

   i. Disclosure may be a range of times if the range is specific.

  ii. Describe the factors which may affect the time period such as ability to obtain a lease, financing or building permits, zoning and local ordinances, weather conditions, shortages, or delayed installation of equipment, fixtures, and signs.

E. THE TRAINING PROGRAM OF THE FRANCHISOR AS OF THE FRANCHISOR'S LAST FISCAL YEAR END OR A MORE RECENT DATE INCLUDING:

   (1) THE LOCATION, DURATION, AND GENERAL OUTLINE OF THE TRAINING PROGRAM;

   (2) HOW OFTEN THE TRAINING PROGRAM WILL BE CONDUCTED;

   (3) THE EXPERIENCE THAT THE INSTRUCTORS HAVE WITH THE FRANCHISOR;

   (4) CHARGES TO BE MADE TO THE FRANCHISEE AND WHO MUST PAY TRAVEL AND LIVING EXPENSES OF THE ENROLLEES IN THE TRAINING PROGRAM;

   (5) IF THE TRAINING PROGRAM IS NOT MANDATORY, THE PERCENTAGE OF NEW FRANCHISEES THAT ENROLLED IN THE TRAINING PROGRAM DURING THE PRECEDING 12 MONTHS; AND

   (6) WHETHER ANY ADDITIONAL TRAINING PROGRAMS AND/OR REFRESHER COURSES ARE REQUIRED.

Item 11E Instructions

   i. Use a table to state the subjects taught and the number of hours of classroom and "on the job training" devoted to each subject in the franchisor's training program. Use footnotes to explain.

  ii. For each subject disclose the training location and how often training classes are held.

 iii. Describe the location or facility where the training is held (for example, company, home, office, company-owned store.)

 iv. State how long after the signing of the agreement or before the opening date of the business the franchisee must complete the required training.

   v. Describe the nature of instructional material. Disclose the minimum experience of the instructors. Disclose only experience that is relevant to the subject taught and the franchisor's operations.

  vi. State who may and who is required to attend the training. State whether the franchisee or other persons must complete the program to the franchisor's satisfaction.

 vii. Charges for training or training materials should be disclosed in Item 5 if the obligation to pay arises before the franchise location opens.

viii. Disclose who pays the travel and living expenses of the persons receiving the training.

Sample Answer 11

Except as disclosed below, Belmont need not provide any assistance to you.

Before you open your business, Belmont will:

1) Designate your exclusive territory (Franchise Agreement – paragraph 2).

2) Assist you in selecting a business site. Your site must be at least _____ square feet in area, have ____ parking spaces, and an average of ____ cars per hour driving by. We must approve or disapprove your site within 20 days after we receive notice of the location.

3) Within 30 days of your signing the Franchise Agreement, assist you to find and negotiate the lease or purchase of a location for your muffler shop (Franchise Agreement – paragraph ___). Your store location will be purchased or leased by you from independent third parties.

4) Within 60 days of your signing the Franchise Agreement, provide written specifications for store construction or remodeling and for all required and replacement equipment, inventory, and supplies (Franchise Agreement – paragraph _____). See Item 8 of this offering circular.

5) Within 60 days of your signing the Franchise Agreement, provide blueprints for your store construction or remodeling and obtain health, sanitation, building, utility, and sign permits for your premises. You pay for the construction or remodeling. (Franchise Agreement – paragraph _____).

6) Within 60 days of your signing the Franchise Agreement, train you and one other person as follows:

Subject	Instructional Material	Time Begun	Hours of Classroom Training	Hours of on-the-Job Training	Instructor and Years of Experience

Belmont does not charge for this training or service, but you must pay the travel and living expenses for you and your employees. All training occurs at Belmont's Jackson, Minnesota headquarters. During the operation of the franchised business, Belmont will:

1) Develop new products and methods and provide you with information about developments. (Franchise Agreement – paragraph _____).

2) Loan you a copy of our operations manual which contains mandatory and suggested specifications, standards, and procedures. This manual is confidential and remains our property. Belmont will modify this manual, but the modification will not alter your status and rights under the Franchise Agreement. (Franchise Agreement – paragraph _____). The table of contents is as follows:

Each week for the first 90 days after you open your shop, Belmont will telephone to discuss your operational problems.

Belmont will hold annual conferences to discuss sales techniques, personnel training, bookkeeping, accounting, inventory control, performance standards, advertising programs, and merchandising procedures. There is no conference fee, but you must pay all your travel and living expenses. These elective conferences are held at our Jackson, Minnesota headquarters or at a location chosen by a majority vote of all franchisees.

Belmont provides advertising materials and services to you through a national advertising fund (the "National Fund"). Materials provided by the National Fund to all franchisees include video and audio tapes, mats, posters, banners, and miscellaneous point-of-sale items. You will receive one sample of each at no charge. If you want additional copies you must pay duplication costs.

You may develop advertising materials for your own use, at your own cost. Belmont must approve the advertising materials in advance and in writing.

Belmont occasionally provides for placement of advertising on behalf of the entire Belmont system, including franchisees. However, most placement is done on a local basis, typically by local advertising agencies hired by individual franchisees or advertising cooperatives. Belmont reserves the right to use advertising fees from the Belmont system to place advertising in national media (including broadcast, print, or other media) in the future. In the past Belmont has used an outside advertising agency to create and place advertising. Neither Belmont nor its affiliate receives payment from the National Fund. Advertising funds are used to promote the product sold by the franchisee and are not used to sell additional franchises.

The National Fund is a nonprofit corporation which collects advertising fees from all franchisees. Each franchisor-owned store of Belmont contributes to the National Fund on the same basis as franchisees. All payments to the National Fund must be spent on advertising, promotion, and marketing of goods and services provided by Belmont Muffler Shops. You must contribute the amounts described in Item 6, under the heading "Advertising Fees and Expenses."

The National Fund is administered by Belmont's accounting and marketing personnel under the direction of the Advertising Council. An annual audited financial statement of the National Fund is available to any franchisee upon request. During the last fiscal year of the National Fund (ending on December 31, 1990), the National Fund spent 39% of its income on the production of advertisements and other promotional materials, 36% for media placement, 18% for general and administrative expenses, and 7% for other expenses (the purchase of glassware given to customers of Belmont shops as part of a promotional campaign).

The Advertising Council acts as the board of directors of the National Fund. The Advertising Council has 8 members: the President, Treasurer, Vice President-Marketing, and Vice President-Operations of Belmont; and 4 franchisee representatives who are elected by the governing board of the Belmont Franchisee Association.

Once your shop opens, you must participate in the local advertising cooperative established in the Area of Dominant Influence (ADI) where your store is located. The amount of your contribution to the local advertising cooperative is described in Item 6 under the heading "Advertising Fees and Expenses."

Each local advertising cooperative must adopt written governing documents. A copy of the governing documents of the cooperative (if one has been established) for your ADI is available upon request. Each cooperative may determine its own voting procedures; however, each company-owned Belmont Shop will be entitled to one vote in any local advertising cooperative. The members and their elected officers are responsible for administration of the cooperative. Advertising cooperatives must prepare quarterly and annual financial statements. The annual financial statement must be prepared by an independent CPA and be made available to all franchisees in that advertising cooperative.

You select your business site within your exclusive area subject to our approval. Belmont assists in site selection by telling you the number of new car registrations, population density, traffic patterns, and proximity of the proposed site to other Belmont Muffler Shops.

Franchisees typically open their shops 4 to 7 months after they sign a franchise agreement. The factors that affect this time are the ability to obtain a lease, financing or building permits, zoning and local ordinances, weather conditions, shortages, and delayed installation of equipment, fixtures, and signs.

ITEM 12. TERRITORY

DESCRIBE ANY EXCLUSIVE TERRITORY GRANTED THE FRANCHISEE. CONCERNING THE FRANCHISEE'S LOCATION (WITH OR WITHOUT EXCLUSIVE TERRITORY), DISCLOSE WHETHER:

A. THE FRANCHISOR HAS ESTABLISHED OR MAY ESTABLISH ANOTHER FRANCHISEE WHO MAY ALSO USE THE FRANCHISOR'S TRADEMARK.

B. THE FRANCHISOR HAS ESTABLISHED OR MAY ESTABLISH A COMPANY-OWNED OUTLET OR OTHER CHANNELS OF DISTRIBUTION USING THE FRANCHISOR'S TRADEMARK.

Item 12 Instructions

i. As used in Item 12, trademark includes names, trademarks, logos, and other commercial symbols.

ii. If appropriate, describe the minimum area granted to the franchisee. The franchisor may use an area encompassed within a specific radius, a distance sufficient to encompass a specified population, or another specific designation.

iii. State whether the franchise is granted for a specific location or a location to be approved by the franchisor.

iv. If appropriate, state the conditions under which the franchisor will approve the relocation of the franchised business or the establishment of additional franchised outlets.

v. Describe restrictions on the franchisor regarding operating company-owned stores or on granting franchised outlets for a similar or competitive business within the defined area.

vi. Describe restrictions on franchisees from soliciting or accepting orders outside of their defined territories.

vii. Describe restrictions on the franchisor from soliciting or accepting orders inside the franchisee's defined territory. State compensation that the franchisor must pay for soliciting or accepting orders inside the franchisees defined territories.

viii. Describe franchisee options, rights of first refusal, or similar rights to acquire additional franchises within the territory or contiguous territories.

ix. If the franchisor does not grant territorial rights, use Sample Answer 12-1.

C. THE FRANCHISOR OR ITS AFFILIATE HAS ESTABLISHED OR MAY ESTABLISH OTHER FRANCHISES OR COMPANY-OWNED OUTLETS OR ANOTHER CHANNEL OF DISTRIBUTION SELLING OR LEASING SIMILAR PRODUCTS OR SERVICES UNDER A DIFFERENT TRADEMARK.

Item 12C Instructions

i. "Similar products and services" includes competing, interchangeable, or substitute products but not products or services which are not part of the same product or service market.

ii. If the franchisor or an affiliate operates franchises or has present plans to operate or franchise a business under a different trademark and that business sells goods or services similar to those to be offered by the franchisee, describe:

a) The similar goods and services;

b) The trade names and trademarks;

c) Whether outlets will be franchisor owned or operated;

d) Whether the franchisor or its franchisees who use the different trademark will solicit or accept orders within the franchisee's territory;

e) A timetable for the plan;

f) How the franchisor will resolve conflicts between the franchisor and the franchisees and between the franchisees of each system regarding territory, customers, or franchisor support;

g) If appropriate, disclose the principal business address of the franchisor's similar operating business. If it is the same as the franchisor's principal business address disclosed in Item 1, disclose whether the franchisor maintains (or plans to maintain) physically separate offices and training facilities for the similar competing business.

D. CONTINUATION OF THE FRANCHISEE'S TERRITORIAL EXCLUSIVITY DEPENDS ON ACHIEVEMENT OF A CERTAIN SALES VOLUME, MARKET PENETRATION, OR OTHER CONTINGENCY AND UNDER WHAT CIRCUMSTANCES THE FRANCHISEE'S TERRITORY MAY BE ALTERED.

Item 12D Instructions

i. Disclose conditions for the franchisee's keeping its territorial rights (for example, sales quotas or the opening of additional business outlets). Specify the quotas or conditions and the franchisor's rights if the franchisee fails to meet the requirements.

ii. Disclose other circumstances that permit the franchisor to modify the franchisee's territorial rights (for example, a population increase in the territory giving the franchisor the right to grant an additional franchise within the area). Disclose the effect on the franchisee's rights.

Sample Answer 12-1

You will not receive an exclusive territory. Belmont may establish other franchised or company owned outlets that may compete with your location.

Sample Answer 12-2

You will receive an exclusive territory with a minimum population of 50,000 people. You will operate from one location and must receive Belmont's permission before relocating. Belmont will not operate stores or grant franchises for a similar or competitive business within your area. Except when advertising cooperatively with appropriate franchisees, neither Belmont nor you can advertise or solicit orders within another franchisee's territory. You and Belmont can accept orders from outside your territory without special payment.

You do not receive the right to acquire additional franchises within your area.

There is no minimum sales quota. You maintain rights to your area even though the population increases.

ITEM 13. TRADEMARKS

DISCLOSE THE PRINCIPAL TRADEMARKS TO BE LICENSED TO THE FRANCHISEE INCLUDING:

Item 13 Instructions

   i. As used in Item 13, "Principal trademarks" means the primary trademarks, service marks, names, logos, and symbols to be used by the franchisee to identify the franchised business. It does not include every trademark owned by the franchisor.

   ii. The franchisor may limit Item 13 disclosure to information that is relevant to the state where the franchised business will be located. The franchisor may include all states to eliminate the need for multiple disclosure in Item 13 but must amend its offering circular to reflect any material change in the list.

A. WHETHER THE PRINCIPAL TRADEMARKS ARE REGISTERED WITH THE UNITED STATES PATENT AND TRADEMARK OFFICE. FOR EACH REGISTRATION STATE THE REGISTRATION DATE AND NUMBER AND WHETHER THE REGISTRATION IS ON THE PRINCIPAL OR SUPPLEMENTAL REGISTER.

Item 13A Instructions

   i. Identify each principal trademark which the franchisee may use. The franchisor may reproduce these trademarks in this Item.

   ii. State the date and identification number of each trademark registration or registration application listed. State whether the franchisor has filed all required affidavits. State whether any registration has been renewed.

   iii. State whether the principal trademarks are registered on the principal or supplemental register of the U.S. Patent and Trademark Office, and if not, whether an "intent to use" application or an application based on actual use has been filed with the U.S. Patent and Trademark Office. If the principal trademark to be used by the franchisee is not registered on the Principal

Register of the U.S. Patent and Trademark Office, state:

By not having a Principal Register federal registration for (name or description of symbol), (Name of Franchisor) does not have certain presumptive legal rights granted by a registration.

B. DISCLOSE CURRENTLY EFFECTIVE MATERIAL DETERMINATIONS OF THE PATENT AND TRADEMARK OFFICE, TRADEMARK TRIAL AND APPEAL BOARD, THE TRADEMARK ADMINIS-TRATOR OF THIS STATE OR ANY COURT; PENDING INFRINGEMENT, OPPOSITION, OR CANCEL-LATION; AND PENDING MATERIAL LITIGATION INVOLVING THE PRINCIPAL TRADEMARKS.

Item 13B Instructions

i. Litigation or an action is material if it could significantly affect the ownership or use of a trade-mark listed under Item 13. Describe how the determination affects the ownership, use, or licensing. Describe any decided infringement, cancellation, or opposition proceedings. Include infringement, opposition, or cancellation proceedings in which the franchisor unsuc-cessfully sought to prevent registration of a trademark in order to protect a trademark licensed by the franchisor.

ii. For pending material federal or state litigation regarding the franchisor's use or ownership rights in a trademark, disclose:

   a) The forum and case number;

   b) The nature of claims made opposing the franchisor's use or by the franchisor opposing another person's use; and

   c) Any effective court or administrative agency ruling concerning the matter.

iii. Do not repeat disclosure made in response to Item 13A.

iv. The franchisor need not disclose historical challenges to registrations of trademarks listed in Item 13 that were resolved in the franchisor's favor.

v. The franchisor may include an attorney's opinion relative to the merits of litigation or of an action if the attorney issuing the opinion consents to its use. The text of the disclosure may include a summary of the opinion if the full opinion is attached and the attorney issuing the opinion consents to the use of the summary.

C. DISCLOSE AGREEMENTS CURRENTLY IN EFFECT WHICH SIGNIFICANTLY LIMIT THE RIGHTS OF THE FRANCHISOR TO USE OR LICENSE THE USE OF TRADEMARKS LISTED IN ITEM 13 IN A MANNER MATERIAL TO THE FRANCHISE.

Item 13C Instructions

For each agreement disclose:

i. The manner and extent of the limitation or grant;

ii. The agreement's duration;

iii. The parties to the agreement;

iv. The circumstances under which the agreement may be cancelled or modified; and

v. All other material terms.

D. WHETHER THE FRANCHISOR MUST PROTECT THE FRANCHISEE'S RIGHT TO USE THE PRINCIPAL TRADEMARKS LISTED IN ITEM 13, AND MUST PROTECT THE FRANCHISEE AGAINST CLAIMS OF INFRINGEMENT OR UNFAIR COMPETITION ARISING OUT OF THE FRANCHISEE'S USE OF THEM.

Item 13D Instructions

    i.   Disclose the franchisee's obligation to notify the franchisor of the use of or claims of rights to a trademark identical to or confusingly similar to a trademark licensed to the franchisee.

   ii.   State whether the franchise agreement requires the franchisor to take affirmative action when notified of these uses or claims. Identify who has the right to control administrative, proceedings, or litigation.

  iii.   State whether the franchise agreement requires the franchisor to participate in the franchisee's defense and/or indemnify the franchisee for expenses or damages if the franchisee is a party to an administrative or judicial proceeding involving a trademark licensed by the franchisor to the franchisee, or if the proceeding is resolved unfavorably to the franchisee.

  iv.   Disclose the franchisee's rights under the franchise if the franchisor requires the franchisee to modify or discontinue the use of a trademark as a result of a proceeding or settlement.

E. WHETHER THE FRANCHISOR ACTUALLY KNOWS OF EITHER SUPERIOR PRIOR RIGHTS OR INFRINGING USES THAT COULD MATERIALLY AFFECT THE FRANCHISEE'S USE OF THE PRINCIPAL TRADEMARKS IN THIS STATE OR THE STATE IN WHICH THE FRANCHISED BUSINESS IS TO BE LOCATED.

Item 13E Instructions

For each use of a principal trademark that the franchisor believes constitutes an infringement that could materially affect the franchisee's use of a trademark, state:

    i.   The location(s) where the infringement is occurring;

   ii.   To the extent known, the length of time of the infringement; and

  iii.   Action taken by the franchisor.

If the franchisor knows of a use of a trademark by another in a geographic area relevant to the franchisee which is or is likely to be based on a claim of superior prior rights to the franchisor's, state the nature of the use by the other person and the place or area where it is occurring.

Sample Answer 13

Belmont grants you the right to operate a shop under the name Belmont Muffler Shop. You may also use our other current or future trademarks to operate your shop. By trademark Belmont means trade names, trademarks, service marks, and logos used to identify your shop. Belmont registered the below trademark on the United State Patent and Trademark Office principal register:

You must follow our rules when you use these marks. You can not use a name or mark as part of a corporate name or with modifying words, designs, or symbols except for those which Belmont licenses to you. You may not use Belmont's registered name in connection with the sale of an unauthorized product or service or in a manner not authorized in writing by Belmont.

On June 4, 1973, the United States Patent and Trademark Office rejected Belmont's application to register the mark "Super Mufflers" because the mark was found to be confusingly similar to a registered mark. Belmont's inability to register this mark on a federal level permits others to establish rights to use the mark. This use will not be in areas where our franchisees are operating, or advertising under the mark, or in the natural zone of expansion for Belmont's shops. In addition, these users must act in good faith and without actual knowledge of Belmont's prior use of the mark. However, if others establish rights to use Belmont's mark, Belmont may not be able to expand into these areas using the mark.

No agreements limit Belmont's right to use or license the use of Belmont's trademarks.

You must notify Belmont immediately when you learn about an infringement of or challenge to your use of our trademark. Belmont will take the action we think appropriate. While Belmont is not required to defend you against a claim against your use of our trademark, Belmont will reimburse you for your liability and reasonable costs in connection with defending Belmont's trademark. To receive reimbursement you must have notified Belmont immediately when you learned about the infringement or challenge.

You must modify or discontinue the use of a trademark if Belmont modifies or discontinues it. If this happens, Belmont will reimburse you for your tangible costs of compliance (for example, changing signs). You must not directly or indirectly contest our right to our trademarks, trade secrets, or business techniques that are part of our business.

Belmont does not know of any infringing uses that could materially affect your use of Belmont's trademark.

or

John E. Jones, 4231 Main Street, Reno, Nevada is currently doing business as Belmont Muffler Shoppe at 4231 Main Street, Reno, Nevada. We believe that this is an infringing use of our federally registered trademark "Belmont Muffler Shop," and we have filed an action to enjoin Mr. Jones and to recover damages. If the court holds that Mr. Jones' use is not infringing, Belmont may not be able to use Belmont's trademark in Mr. Jones' immediate area. (*Belmont Muffler Shop v. Belmont Muffler Shoppe* [cite])

ITEM 14. PATENTS, COPYRIGHTS, AND PROPRIETARY INFORMATION

IF THE FRANCHISOR OWNS RIGHTS IN PATENTS OR COPYRIGHTS THAT ARE MATERIAL TO THE FRANCHISE, DESCRIBE THESE PATENTS AND COPYRIGHTS AND THEIR RELATIONSHIP TO THE FRANCHISE. INCLUDE THEIR DURATION AND WHETHER THE FRANCHISOR CAN AND INTENDS TO RENEW THE COPYRIGHTS. TO THE EXTENT RELEVANT, DISCLOSE THE INFORMATION REQUIRED BY ITEM 13 CONCERNING THESE PATENTS AND COPYRIGHTS. IF THE FRANCHISOR CLAIMS PROPRIETARY RIGHTS IN CONFIDENTIAL INFORMATION OR TRADE SECRETS, DISCLOSE THEIR GENERAL SUBJECT MATTER AND THE TERMS AND CONDITIONS FOR USE BY THE FRANCHISEE.

Item 14 Instructions

i. State the patent number, issue date, and title for each patent. State the serial number, filing date, and title of each patent application. Describe the type of patent or patent application (for example, mechanical, process, or design). State the registration number and date of each copyright.

ii. Describe the relationship of the patent, patent application, or copyright to the franchised business.

iii. Describe any current determination of the Patent and Trademark Office, Copyright Office (Library of Congress), or court regarding the patent or copyright. Include the forum, case number, and effect on the franchised business.

iv. State the forum, case number, claims asserted, issues involved, and effective determinations for any proceedings pending in the Patent and Trademark Office or the Court of Appeals for the Federal Circuit.

v. If counsel consents, the franchisor may include a counsel's opinion or a summary of the opinion about patent or copyright issues discussed in this Item.

vi. If an agreement limits the use of the patent, patent application, or copyright, state the parties to and duration of the agreement, the extent to which the franchisee may be affected by the agreement, and other material terms of the agreement.

vii. Disclose the franchisor's obligation to protect the patent, patent application, or copyright. State:

    a) Whether franchisee must notify the franchisor of claims or infringements or if the action is discretionary.

    b) Whether the franchisor must take affirmative action when notified of infringement or if the action is discretionary.

    c) Who has the right to control litigation.

    d) Whether the franchisor must participate in the defense of a franchisee or indemnify the franchisee for expenses or damages in a proceeding involving a patent, patent application, or copyright licensed to the franchisee.

    e) Requirements that the franchises modify or discontinue use of the subject matter covered by the patent or copyright.

    f) Franchisee's rights if the franchisor requires the franchisee to modify or discontinue the use of the subject matter covered by the patent or copyright.

viii. If the franchisor actually knows of an infringement that could materially affect the franchisee state:

    a) The nature of the infringement.

    b) The locations where the infringement is occurring.

    c) The length of time of the infringement.

    d) Action taken or anticipated by the franchisor.

ix. State whether the franchisor intends to renew the copyright when the registration expires.

x. Discuss in general terms other proprietary information communicated to the franchisee (for example, whether there is a formula or recipe considered to be a trade secret).

xi. Use Sample Answer 14-1 if no patents or copyrights are material to the franchise.

Sample Answer 14-1

No patents or copyrights are material to the franchise.

Sample Answer 14-2

You do not receive the right to use an item covered by a patent or copyright, but you can use the proprietary information in Belmont's Operations Manual. The Operations Manual is described in Item 11. Although Belmont has not filed an application for a copyright registration for the operations Manual, it claims a copyright and the information is proprietary. Item 11 describes limitations on the use of this manual by you and your employees. You must also promptly tell us when you learn about unauthorized use of this proprietary information. Belmont is not obligated to take any action but will respond to this information as we think appropriate. Belmont will indemnify you for losses brought by a third party concerning your use of this information.

Sample Answer 14-3

U.S. Patent 3999442 was issued on December 14, 1980. It describes a process for exhaust system installation. The process describes the steps in making a straight length of exhaust pipe, bending this pipe, coating the inside and outside of this pipe with our Pipe Protector, and installing the exhaust pipe on a motor vehicle. You will use equipment utilizing this process.

On December 15, 1970, Belmont obtained a copyright registration for its Operations Manual under Registration A 41139. Amendments to the manual were registered on January 7, 1983 (Reg. A 521,371) and June 6, 1974 (Reg. A 541,333). Belmont intends to renew these copyrights. Item 11 of this Offering Circular describes the Operations Manual and the manner in which you are permitted to use it.

Belmont's right to use or license these patents and copyrighted items is not materially limited by any agreement or known infringing use.

You must tell us immediately if you learn about an infringement or challenge to our use of these patents or copyrights. Belmont will take the action that Belmont thinks appropriate. You must also agree not to contest Belmont's interest in these or our other trade secrets.

If Belmont decides to add, modify, or discontinue the use of an item or process covered by a patent or copyright, you must also do so. Belmont's sole obligation is to reimburse you for the tangible cost of complying with this obligation.

Although Belmont is not obligated to defend your use of these items or processes, Belmont will reimburse you for damages and reasonable costs incurred in litigation about them.

ITEM 15. OBLIGATION TO PARTICIPATE IN THE ACTUAL OPERATION OF THE FRANCHISE BUSINESS

DISCLOSE THE FRANCHISEE'S OBLIGATION TO PARTICIPATE PERSONALLY IN THE DIRECT OPERATION OF THE FRANCHISE BUSINESS AND WHETHER THE FRANCHISOR RECOMMENDS PARTICIPATION.

Item 15 Instructions

i. Include obligations arising from written agreement (including personal guaranty, confidentiality agreement, or noncompetition agreement) or from the franchisor's practice.

ii. If personal "on-premises" supervision is not required:
    a) If the franchisee is an individual, state whether the franchisor recommends "on-premises" supervision by the franchisee;
    b) State limitations on whom the franchisee can hire as an on-premises supervisor;
    c) Whether this "on-premises" supervisor must successfully complete the franchisor's training program; and
    d) If the franchisee is a business entity, state the amount of equity interest that the "on-premises" supervisor must have in the franchise.
iii. Disclose the restrictions which the franchisee must place on its manager (for example, maintain trade secrets, non-competition).
iv. The franchisor may reference Items 14 and 17 in its answer.

Sample Answer 15-1

If you are an individual, you must directly supervise the franchised business on its premises. If you are a corporation, the direct, on-site supervision must be done by a person who owns at least 1/3 of the corporate equity.

Sample Answer 15-2

Belmont does not require that you personally supervise the franchised business. The business must be directly supervised "on-premises" by a manager who has successfully completed Belmont's training program. The on-premises manager cannot have an interest or business relationship with any of Belmont's business competitors. The manager need not have an ownership interest in a corporate or partnership franchisee. The manager must sign a written agreement to maintain confidentiality of the trade secrets described in Item 14 and to conform with the covenants not to compete described in Item 17.

Each individual who owns a 5% or greater interest in the franchisee entity must sign an agreement (Exhibit _____) assuming and agreeing to discharge all obligations of the "Franchisee" under the Franchise Agreement.

ITEM 16. RESTRICTIONS ON WHAT THE FRANCHISEE MAY SELL

DISCLOSE RESTRICTIONS OR CONDITIONS IMPOSED BY THE FRANCHISOR ON THE GOODS OR SERVICES THAT THE FRANCHISEE MAY SELL OR THAT LIMIT THE CUSTOMERS TO WHOM THE FRANCHISEE MAY SELL GOODS OR SERVICES.

Item 16 Instructions

i. Describe the franchisee's obligation to sell only goods and services approved by the franchisor.
ii. Disclose any franchisee obligation to sell all goods and services authorized by the franchisor. Disclose whether the franchisor has the right to change the types of authorized goods and services and whether there are limits on the franchisor's right to make changes.
iii. If the franchisee is restricted regarding customers, disclose the restrictions.
iv. The applicant may cross-reference disclosures made in Items 8, 9, and 12.

v. Use Sample Answer 16-1 for a negative response.

Sample Answer 16-1

Belmont does not restrict the type of goods or services that you may offer.

Sample Answer 16-1

Belmont requires you to offer and sell only those goods and services that Belmont has approved (see Item 9).

You must offer all goods and services that Belmont designates as required for all franchisees. These required services are muffler inspection, repair, and replacement. Parts, supplies, and equipment used in your Belmont Muffler business must be approved by Belmont (see Item 8).

Belmont has the right to add additional authorized services that the franchisee is required to offer. There are no limits on Belmont's right to do so except that the investment required of a franchisee (for equipment, supplies, and initial inventory) will not exceed $5,000 per year.

Belmont also designates some services as optional for qualified franchisees. Current optional services are brake inspection, repair and replacement, tire rotation, wheel balancing and alignment, and rust-proofing. To offer optional goods or services, you must be in substantial compliance with all material obligations under your Franchise Agreement. In addition, Belmont may require you to comply with other requirements (such as training, marketing, insurance) before Belmont will allow you to offer certain optional services.

As long as you meet your annual agreed sales quotas (see Item 12), Belmont will not restrict you from soliciting any customers, no matter who they are or where they are located. If you do not meet your annual sales quota, Belmont may deny you the right to receive any further fleet business referrals from Belmont and may either keep the fleet business referrals for itself or give them to another franchisee. Failure to meet your annual sales quota is a default under your Franchise Agreement and grounds for termination of your franchise (see Item 17).

ITEM 17. RENEWAL, TERMINATION, TRANSFER, AND DISPUTE RESOLUTION

SUMMARIZE THE PROVISIONS OF THE FRANCHISE AND OTHER AGREEMENTS DEALING WITH TERMINATION, RENEWAL, TRANSFER, DISPUTE RESOLUTION, AND OTHER IMPORTANT ASPECTS OF THE FRANCHISE RELATIONSHIP.

Item 17 Instructions

i. Begin Item 17 disclosure with the following statement:
This table lists certain important provisions of the franchise and related agreements. You should read these provisions in the agreements attached to this offering circular.
ii. Respond in tabular form. Refer to the section of the agreement which covers each subject.
iii. Use a separate table for any other significant franchise-related agreements. If a provision in any other agreement affects the provisions of the franchise or franchise-related agreements disclosed in this Item (for example, the term of the franchise will be equal to the term of the

lease), disclose that provision in the applicable category in the table.

iv. The table should contain a "summary" column to summarize briefly the disclosed provision. The summary is intended to provide a concise overview of the provision in no more than a few words or a sentence. Do not specify in detail all matters covered by a provision.

v. The table should respond to each category listed below. Do not change the names of the categories. List all contractual provisions relevant to each category in the table. If the response to any category is that the agreement does not contain the relevant provision, the table should so state. If the agreement is silent concerning a category but the franchisor unilaterally offers to provide certain benefits or protection to franchisees as a matter of policy, a footnote should describe this policy and state whether the policy is subject to change. The categories are:

  a. Length of the term of the franchise
  b. Renewal or extension of the term
  c. Requirements for franchisee to renew or extend
  d. Termination by franchisee
  e. Termination by franchisor without cause
  f. Termination by franchisor with "cause"
  g. "Cause" defined—curable defaults
  h. "Cause" defined—defaults which cannot be cured
  i. Franchisee's obligations on termination/nonrenewal
  j. Assignment of contract by franchisor
  k. "Transfer" by franchisee—defined
  l. Franchisor approval of transfer by franchisee
  m. Conditions for franchisor approval of transfer
  n. Franchisor's right of first refusal to acquire franchisee's business
  o. Franchisor's option to purchase franchisee's business
  p. Death or disability of franchisee
  q. Non-competition covenants during the term of the franchise
  r. Non-competition covenants after the franchise is terminated or expires
  s. Modification of the agreement
  t. Integration/merger clause
  u. Dispute resolution by arbitration or mediation
  v. Choice of forum
  w. Choice of law

Sample Answer 17

This table lists important provisions of the franchise and related agreements. You should read these provisions in the agreements attached to this offering circular.

Provision	Section in Franchise Agreement	Summary
a. Term of the franchise	1 (also Section 1 of Lease, Exhibit F)	Term is equal to lease term—10 years.
b. Renewal or extension of the term	20	If you are in good standing, you can add additional term equal to renewal term of lease (10 years maximum).
c. Requirements for you to renew or extend	20	Sign new agreement, pay fee, remodel, and sign release.
d. Termination by you	None	
e. Termination by Belmont without cause	None	
f. Termination by Belmont with cause	21	Belmont can terminate only if franchisee defaults.
g. "Cause" defined—defaults which can be cured	21B	You have 30 days to cure: non-payment of fees, sanitation problems, non-submission of reports, and any other default not listed in Section 21A.
h. "Cause" defined—defaults which cannot be cured	22	Non-curable defaults: conviction of a felony, repeated defaults even if cured, abandonment, trademark misuse, and unapproved transfers.
i. Your obligations on termination/nonrenewal	22	Obligations include complete de-identification and payment of amounts due (also see "r" below).
j. Assignment of contract by Belmont	18	No restriction on Belmont's right to assign.
k. "Transfer" by you—definition	19A	Includes transfer of contract or assets or ownership change.
l. Belmont's approval of transfer by franchisee	19B	Belmont has the right to approve all transfers but will not unreasonably withhold approval.

Provision	Section in Franchise Agreement	Summary
m. Conditions for Belmont approval of transfer	19C	New franchisee qualifies, transfer fee paid, purchase agreement approved, training arranged, release signed by you, and current agreement signed by new franchisee (see also "r" below).
n. Belmont's right of first refusal to acquire your business	19F	Belmont can match any offer for the franchisee's business.
o. Belmont's option to purchase your business	None, but see policy described in Note 1	
p. Your death or disability	19D	Franchisee must be assigned by estate to approved buyer in 6 months.
q. Non-competition covenants during the term of the franchise	11	No involvement in competing business anywhere in the U.S.
r. Non-competition covenants after the franchise is terminated or expires	19C and 22C	No competing business for 2 years within 20 miles of another Belmont franchise (including after assignment).
s. Modification of the agreement	8A	No modifications generally but Operating Manual subject to change.
t. Integration/merger clause	29	Only the terms of the franchise agreement are binding (subject to state law). Any other promises may not be enforceable.
u. Dispute resolution by arbitration or mediation	24	Except for certain claims, all disputes but _____ be arbitrated in _____, _____.
v. Choice of forum	27	Litigation must be in _____.
w. Choice of law	28	_____ law applies.

Notes

[1] Franchisor is not obligated by the Agreement to do so, but, if the franchise is terminated, franchisor's policy is to buy back inventory at fair market value. This policy is subject to change at any time.

These states have statutes which may supersede the franchise agreement in your relationship with the franchisor, including the areas of termination and renewal of your franchise: ARKANSAS [Stat. Section 70-807], CALIFORNIA [Bus. & Prof. Code Sections 20000-20043], CONNECTICUT [Gen Stat. Section 42-133e et seq.], DELAWARE [Code Ann. Title 6, Sections 2551-2556], HAWAII [Rev. Stat. Section 482E-1], ILLINOIS

[Rev. Stat. Chapter 121, par 1719-1720], INDIANA [Stat. Section 23.2-2.7], IOWA [Code Sections 523H.1-523H.17], MICHIGAN [Stat. Section 19.854(27)], MINNESOTA [Stat. Section 80C.14], MISSISSIPPI [Code Section 75-24-51], MISSOURI [Stat. Section 407.400], NEBRASKA [Rev. Stat. Section 87-401], NEW JERSEY [Stat. Section 56:10-1], SOUTH DAKOTA [Codified Laws Section 37-5A-51], VIRGINIA [Code 13.1-557-574-13.1-564], WASHINGTON [Code Section 19.100.180], WISCONSIN [Stat. Section 135.03]. These and other states may have court decisions which may supersede the franchise agreement in your relationship with the franchisor including the areas of termination and renewal of your franchise.

ITEM 18. PUBLIC FIGURES

DISCLOSE THE FOLLOWING:

A. COMPENSATION OR OTHER BENEFIT GIVEN OR PROMISED TO A PUBLIC FIGURE ARISING FROM:

    (1) THE USE OF THE PUBLIC FIGURE IN THE FRANCHISE NAME OR SYMBOL OR

    (2) THE ENDORSEMENT OR RECOMMENDATION OF THE FRANCHISE TO PROSPECTIVE FRANCHISEES.

B. THE EXTENT TO WHICH THE PUBLIC FIGURE IS INVOLVED IN THE ACTUAL MANAGEMENT OR CONTROL OF THE FRANCHISOR.

C. THE TOTAL INVESTMENT OF THE PUBLIC FIGURE IN THE FRANCHISOR.

Item 18 Instructions

   i. A "public figure" is a person whose name or physical appearance is generally known to the public in the geographic area where the franchise will be located.

  ii. Disclose the compensation paid or promised for the endorsement or use of the name of the public figure.

 iii. Describe the public figure's position and duties in the franchisor's business structure.

 iv. State the amount of the public figure's investment. Describe the extent of the amount contributed in services performed or to be performed. State the type of investment (for example, common stock, promissory note).

  v. Use Sample Answer 18-1 for a negative response.

Sample Answer 18-1

Belmont does not use any public figure to promote its franchise.

Sample Answer 18-2

Belmont has paid Ralph Doister $50,000 for the use of his name in promoting the sale of our franchise. The right expires December 31, 1992. Belmont has produced newspaper ads, a brochure, and a video which feature Mr. Doister. Mr. Doister does not manage or own an interest in Belmont.

ITEM 19. EARNINGS CLAIMS

A. AN EARNINGS CLAIM MADE IN CONNECTION WITH AN OFFER OF A FRANCHISE MUST BE INCLUDED IN FULL IN THE OFFERING CIRCULAR AND MUST HAVE A REASONABLE BASIS

AT THE TIME IT IS MADE. IF NO EARNINGS CLAIM IS MADE, ITEM 19 OF THE OFFERING CIRCULAR MUST CONTAIN THE NEGATIVE DISCLOSURE PRESCRIBED IN THE INSTRUCTION.

Item 19 Instructions

i. Definition: "Earnings claim" means information given to a prospective franchisee by, on behalf of, or at the direction of the franchisor or its agent, from which a specific level or range of actual or potential sales, costs, income, or profit from franchised or non-franchised units may be easily ascertained.

   A chart, table, or mathematical calculation presented to demonstrate possible results based upon a combination of variables (such as multiples of price and quantity to reflect gross sales) is an earnings claim subject to this item.

   An earnings claim limited solely to the actual operating results of a specific unit being offered for sale need not comply with this item if it is given only to potential purchasers of that unit and is accompanied by the name and last known address of each owner of the unit during the prior three years.

ii. Supplemental earnings claim: If a franchisor has made an earnings claim in accordance with this Item 19, the franchisor may deliver to a prospective franchisee a supplemental earnings claim directed to a particular location or circumstance, apart from the offering circular. The supplemental earnings claim must be in writing, explain the departure from the earnings claim in the offering circular, be prepared in accordance with this Item 19, and be left with the prospective franchisee.

iii. Scope of requirement: An earnings claim is not required in connection with the offer of franchises; if made, however, its presentation must conform with this Item 19. If an earnings claim is not made, then Negative Disclosure 19 (below) must be used.

iv. Claims regarding future performance: A statement or prediction of future performance that is prepared as a forecast or projection in accordance with the statement on standards for accountants' services on prospective financial information (or its successor) issued by the American Institute of Certified Public Accountants, Inc., is presumed to have a reasonable basis.

v. Burden of proof: The burden is upon the franchisor to show that it had a reasonable basis for its earnings claim.

[NEGATIVE DISCLOSURE 19]
REPRESENTATIONS REGARDING EARNINGS CAPABILITY

Belmont does not furnish or authorize its salespersons to furnish any oral or written information concerning the actual or potential sales, costs, income, or profits of [a Belmont muffler shop]. Actual results vary from unit to unit and Belmont cannot estimate the results of any particular franchise.

B. AN EARNINGS CLAIMS SHALL INCLUDE A DESCRIPTION OF ITS FACTUAL BASIS AND THE MATERIAL ASSUMPTIONS UNDERLYING ITS PREPARATION AND PRESENTATION.

Item 19B Instructions

i. Factual Basis: The factual basis of an earnings claim includes significant matters upon which a franchisee's future results are expected to depend. This includes, for example, economic or market conditions which are basic to a franchisee's operation and encompass matters affecting, among other things, franchisee's sales, the cost of goods or services sold, and operating expenses.

In the absence of an adequate operating experience of its own, a franchisor may base an earnings claim upon the results of operations of a substantially similar business of a person affiliated with the franchisor or franchisees of that person; provided that disclosure is made of any material differences in the economic or market conditions known to, or reasonably ascertainable by, the franchisor.

ii. Basic Disclosures: The earnings claim must state:

a) Material assumptions, other than matters of common knowledge, underlying the claim (see Definition iii under Item 3 for the definition of "material");

b) A concise summary of the basis for the claim including a statement of whether the claim is based upon actual experience of franchised units and, if so, the percentage of franchised outlets in operation for the period covered by the earnings claim that have actually attained or surpassed the stated results;

c) A conspicuous admonition that a new franchisee's individual financial results are likely to differ from the result stated in the earnings claim; and

d) A statement that substantiation of the data used in preparing the earnings claim will be made available to the prospective franchisee on reasonable request.

ITEM 20. LIST OF OUTLETS

DISCLOSE THE FOLLOWING:

A. THE NUMBER OF FRANCHISES OF A TYPE SUBSTANTIALLY SIMILAR TO THOSE OFFERED AND THE NUMBER OF FRANCHISOR OWNED OR OPERATED OUTLETS AS OF THE CLOSE OF EACH OF THE FRANCHISOR'S LAST 3 FISCAL YEARS. SEGREGATE FRANCHISES THAT ARE OPERATIONAL FROM FRANCHISES NOT YET OPERATIONAL. SEGREGATE DISCLOSURE BY STATE. TOTAL EACH CATEGORY.

B. THE NAMES OF ALL FRANCHISEES AND THE ADDRESSES AND TELEPHONE NUMBERS OF ALL OF THEIR OUTLETS. THE FRANCHISOR MAY LIMIT ITS DISCLOSURE TO ALL FRAN-CHISEE OUTLETS IN THE STATE, BUT IF THESE FRANCHISEE OUTLETS TOTAL FEWER THAN 100, DISCLOSE FRANCHISEE OUTLETS FROM ALL CONTIGUOUS STATES AND THEN THE NEXT CLOSEST STATE(S) UNTIL AT LEAST 100 FRANCHISEE OUTLETS ARE LISTED.

C. THE ESTIMATED NUMBER OF FRANCHISES TO BE SOLD DURING THE 1-YEAR PERIOD AFTER THE CLOSE OF THE FRANCHISOR'S MOST RECENT FISCAL YEAR.

D. THE NUMBER OF FRANCHISEE OUTLETS IN THE FOLLOWING CATEGORIES THAT, FOR THE 3-YEAR PERIOD IMMEDIATELY BEFORE THE CLOSE OF FRANCHISOR'S MOST RECENT FISCAL YEAR, HAVE:

(1) TRANSFERRED CONTROLLING OWNERSHIP;

(2) BEEN CANCELLED OR TERMINATED BY THE FRANCHISOR;

(3) NOT BEEN RENEWED BY THE FRANCHISOR;

(4) BEEN REACQUIRED BY THE FRANCHISOR; OR

(5) BEEN REASONABLY KNOWN BY THE FRANCHISOR TO HAVE OTHERWISE CEASED TO DO BUSINESS IN THE SYSTEM.

E. THE NAME AND LAST KNOWN HOME ADDRESS AND TELEPHONE NUMBER OF EVERY FRANCHISEE WHO HAS HAD AN OUTLET TERMINATED, CANCELLED, NOT RENEWED, OR OTHERWISE VOLUNTARILY OR INVOLUNTARILY CEASED TO DO BUSINESS UNDER THE FRANCHISE AGREEMENT DURING THE MOST RECENTLY COMPLETED FISCAL YEAR OR WHO HAS NOT COMMUNICATED WITH THE FRANCHISOR WITHIN 10 WEEKS OF THE APPLICATION DATE.

Item 20 Instructions

i.   Do not include a transfer when beneficial ownership of the franchise does not change.

ii.   List an outlet that is reacquired by the franchisor in that column whether or not it also fits another category.

iii.   Other than the franchisee names, addresses, and telephone numbers, disclose Item 20 information in tabular form. Use footnotes or a "remarks" column to elaborate on information in the table or to disclose caveats. Disclose the number of franchised and franchisor-owned outlets sold, opened, and closed. Disclose the total number of franchised and franchisor-owned outlets open at the end of each year. Disclose information for each of the last 3 fiscal years.

iv.   If an outlet has been operated by more than one franchisee, disclose each transfer in the transfer column.

v.   Disclose information about franchisor-owned outlets that are substantially similar to the franchised outlets. In this Item "franchisor-owned" outlets include outlets owned by the franchisor and by its affiliates. Use a separate table with a format similar to the format for franchised outlets. The same table may be used if the franchisor-owned outlets are separated from franchised outlets.

vi.   For franchisees operating within the system disclose franchisee business addresses and telephone numbers. List outlets owned by the persons listed in Item 2 and their immediate families or by business entities owned by them as franchisor-owned outlets. These outlets can be identified in the table by an asterisk.

vii.   Separate information by state. List all states for which franchisor has information responsive to this Item.

viii.   When the requirement states "most recent fiscal year," the franchisor may use a more recent date if it discloses that date and uses that date for all disclosures in this Item.

ix.   When the requirement states "most recent fiscal year," the state may require a more recent date.

Sample Answer 20

Franchised Store Status Summary for Years 1992/1991/1990[1]

State	Transfers	Canceled or Terminated	Not Renewed	Reacquired by Franchisor	Left the System/ Other	Total from Left Columns[2]	Franchises Operating at Year End
Alaska							2/0/0
Arizona	2/1/0					2/1/0	8/6/2
Arkansas							6/4/2
California					1/1/0	1/1/0	4/0/0

State	Transfers	Canceled or Terminated	Not Renewed	Reacquired by Franchisor	Left the System/ Other	Total from Left Columns[2]	Franchises Operating at Year End
Colorado							3/3/3
Connecticut							5/3/1
Delaware		1/0/0				1/0/0	6/4/0
Florida							2/0/0
Georgia							2/0/0
Idaho							2/0/0
Totals	2/1/0	1/0/0	0/0/0	0/0/0	1/1/0	4/2/0	40/20/8

[1] All numbers are as of December 31 for each year. (Editor's note: This sample uses these dates because the UFOC guidelines went into effect in 1995.)

[2] The numbers in the "Total" column may exceed the number of stores affected because several events may have affected the same store. For example, the same store may have had multiple owners.

State	Stores Closed During Year	Stores Opened During Year	Total Stores Operating at Year End
Alaska			
Arizona			
Arkansas			
California			
Colorado			
Connecticut			
Delaware			
Florida			
Georgia			
Idaho			
Totals	0/0/0	0/0/0	0/0/0

Status of Company-Owned Stores for Years 1992/1991/1990

Note: Belmont no longer operates company-owned stores.

State	Franchise Agreements Signed but Store Not Open[1]	Projected Franchised New Stores in the Next Fiscal Year	Projected Company- Owned Openings in the Next Fiscal Year
Alaska	1	1	
Arizona			
Arkansas			
California			
Colorado			

State	Franchise Agreements Signed but Store Not Open[1]	Projected Franchised New Stores in the Next Fiscal Year	Projected Company-Owned Openings in the Next Fiscal Year
Connecticut		2	
Delaware			
Florida			
Georgia			
Idaho	1		
Totals	2	3	0

Projected Openings as of December 31, 1992
1. As of December 31, 1992.

ITEM 21. FINANCIAL STATEMENTS

PREPARE FINANCIAL STATEMENTS IN ACCORDANCE WITH GENERALLY ACCEPTED ACCOUNTING PRINCIPLES. THESE FINANCIAL STATEMENTS MUST BE AUDITED BY AN INDEPENDENT CERTIFIED PUBLIC ACCOUNTANT. UNAUDITED STATEMENTS MAY BE USED FOR INTERIM PERIODS. INCLUDE THE FOLLOWING FINANCIAL STATEMENTS.

A. THE FRANCHISOR'S BALANCE SHEETS FOR THE LAST TWO FISCAL YEAR ENDS BEFORE THE APPLICATION DATE. IN ADDITION INCLUDE STATEMENTS OF OPERATIONS, OF STOCKHOLDERS' EQUITY, AND OF CASH FLOWS FOR EACH OF THE FRANCHISOR'S LAST THREE FISCAL YEARS. IF THE MOST RECENT BALANCE SHEET AND STATEMENT OF OPERATIONS ARE AS OF A DATE MORE THAN 90 DAYS BEFORE THE APPLICATION DATE, THEN ALSO SUBMIT AN UNAUDITED BALANCE SHEET AND STATEMENT OF OPERATIONS AS OF A DATE WITHIN 90 DAYS OF THE APPLICATION DATE.

B. AFFILIATED COMPANY STATEMENTS. INSTEAD OF THE DISCLOSURE REQUIRED BY ITEM 21A, THE FRANCHISOR MAY INCLUDE FINANCIAL STATEMENTS OF ITS AFFILIATED COMPANY IF THE AFFILIATED COMPANY'S FINANCIAL STATEMENTS SATISFY ITEM 21A AND THE AFFILIATED COMPANY ABSOLUTELY AND UNCONDITIONALLY GUARANTEES TO ASSUME THE DUTIES AND OBLIGATIONS OF THE FRANCHISOR UNDER THE FRANCHISE AGREEMENT.

C. CONSOLIDATED AND SEPARATE STATEMENTS:
   (1) WHEN A FRANCHISOR OWNS A DIRECT OR BENEFICIAL, CONTROLLING FINANCIAL INTEREST IN ANOTHER CORPORATION, ITS FINANCIAL STATEMENTS SHOULD REFLECT THE FINANCIAL CONDITION OF THE FRANCHISOR AND ITS SUBSIDIARIES.
   (2) IF THE APPLICANT IS A SUBFRANCHISOR INCLUDE SEPARATE FINANCIAL STATEMENTS FOR THE FRANCHISOR AND SUBFRANCHISOR RELATED ENTITY.
   (3) PREPARE CONSOLIDATED AND SEPARATE FINANCIAL STATEMENTS IN ACCORDANCE WITH GENERALLY ACCEPTED ACCOUNTING PRINCIPLES.

Item 21 Instructions

  i. States may require financial statements additional to those listed in this Item.

  ii. A company controlling 80% or more of a franchisor may be required to include its financial statements.

  iii. Present required financial in a format of columns which compare at least 2 fiscal years.

  iv. In Item 21A, the required financial statements for a franchisor with a calendar fiscal year end and a July 15, 1989 application filing date are:

      a) Unaudited balance sheet as of either April 30, May 31, or June 30, 1989 with an unaudited income statement for the period from January 1, 1989 to the date of the balance sheet;

      b) Balance sheets, statements of operations, of stockholders' equity, and of cash flow. The balance sheets should be audited and as of December 31, 1987 and 1988. The remaining statements should be audited and should be for periods ending December 31, 1986, 1987, and 1988; and

      c) If the franchisor has never had an audit, it need not supply the financial statement required by (b) if it supplies either an audit as of its last fiscal year end or the statements required by (a) in an audited form.

  v. In the Item 21B response, the affiliate's guarantee need cover only the franchisor's obligations to the franchisee. The guarantee need not extend to third parties. A sample guarantee is on page _____ in Exhibit _____.

  vi. In the Item 21B Response the filing state may permit a surety bond instead of the parent company's guarantee.

  vii. Disclose the existence of a guarantee.

ITEM 22. CONTRACTS

ATTACH A COPY OF ALL AGREEMENTS PROPOSED FOR USE OR IN USE IN THIS STATE REGARDING THE OFFERING OF A FRANCHISE, INCLUDING THE FRANCHISE AGREEMENT, LEASES, OPTIONS, AND PURCHASE AGREEMENTS.

Item 22 Instructions

  i. Copies of agreements attached to the offering circular under Item 22 are part of the offering circular. Each offering circular delivered to a prospective franchisee must include copies of all agreements to be offered.

  ii. The franchisor may cross-reference Item 10 for financing agreements.

ITEM 23. RECEIPT

THE LAST PAGE OF THE OFFERING CIRCULAR IS A DETACHABLE DOCUMENT ACKNOWLEDGING RECEIPT OF THE OFFERING CIRCULAR BY THE PROSPECTIVE FRANCHISEE. IT MUST CONTAIN THE FOLLOWING STATEMENT IN BOLDFACE TYPE:

THIS OFFERING CIRCULAR SUMMARIZES CERTAIN PROVISIONS OF THE FRANCHISE AGREEMENT AND OTHER INFORMATION IN PLAIN LANGUAGE. READ THIS OFFERING CIRCULAR AND ALL AGREEMENTS CAREFULLY.

IF _____ OFFERS YOU A FRANCHISE, _____ MUST PROVIDE THIS OFFERING CIR-
CULAR TO YOU BY THE EARLIEST OF:

    (1) THE FIRST PERSONAL MEETING TO DISCUSS OUR FRANCHISE; OR

    (2) TEN BUSINESS DAYS BEFORE THE SIGNING OF A BINDING AGREEMENT; OR

    (3) TEN BUSINESS DAYS BEFORE A PAYMENT TO _____.

YOU MUST ALSO RECEIVE A FRANCHISE AGREEMENT CONTAINING ALL MATERIAL TERMS
AT LEAST FIVE BUSINESS DAYS BEFORE YOU SIGN A FRANCHISE AGREEMENT.

IF _____ DOES NOT DELIVER THIS OFFERING CIRCULAR ON TIME OR IF IT CONTAINS A
FALSE OR MISLEADING STATEMENT OR A MATERIAL OMISSION, A VIOLATION OF FEDERAL
AND STATE LAW MAY HAVE OCCURRED AND SHOULD BE REPORTED TO THE FEDERAL TRADE
COMMISSION, WASHINGTON, DC 20580 AND (STATE AGENCY). (ANY ADDITIONAL STATE DIS-
CLOSURE TIME OR REQUIRED STATUTORY LANGUAGE.)

Item 23 Instructions

    i.   Place the name of the franchisor in the blank.

    ii. Make two copies of the Receipt: one for retention by the franchisee and one by the franchisor.

   iii. Disclose the name, principal business address, and telephone number of the subfranchisor or franchise broker offering the franchise in this state.

   iv. List the title of all attached exhibits.

    v. Effective Date: (Leave blank until notified of effectiveness by state regulatory authority.)

   vi. The name and address of the franchisor's registered agent authorized to receive service of process if not disclosed in Item 1. _____

Sample Answer 23

RECEIPT

THIS OFFERING CIRCULAR SUMMARIZES CERTAIN PROVISIONS OF THE FRANCHISE
AGREEMENT AND OTHER INFORMATION IN PLAIN LANGUAGE. READ THIS OFFERING CIR-
CULAR AND ALL AGREEMENTS CAREFULLY.

IF BELMONT OFFERS YOU A FRANCHISE, BELMONT MUST PROVIDE THIS OFFERING CIR-
CULAR TO YOU BY THE EARLIEST OF:

    (1) THE FIRST PERSONAL MEETING TO DISCUSS OUR FRANCHISE; OR

    (2) TEN BUSINESS DAYS BEFORE THE SIGNING OF A BINDING AGREEMENT; OR

    (3) TEN BUSINESS DAYS BEFORE A PAYMENT TO BELMONT.

YOU MUST ALSO RECEIVE A FRANCHISE AGREEMENT CONTAINING ALL MATERIAL
TERMS AT LEAST FIVE BUSINESS DAYS BEFORE YOU SIGN A FRANCHISE AGREEMENT.

IF BELMONT DOES NOT DELIVER THIS OFFERING CIRCULAR ON TIME OR IF IT CONTAINS
A FALSE OR MISLEADING STATEMENT OR A MATERIAL OMISSION, A VIOLATION OF FED-
ERAL AND STATE LAW MAY HAVE OCCURRED AND SHOULD BE REPORTED TO THE FEDER-
AL TRADE COMMISSION, WASHINGTON, DC 20580 AND (STATE AGENCY).

Belmont authorizes Legal Process Corp. at 448 West Washington Avenue, City, State to receive service of process for Belmont.

I have received a Uniform Franchise Offering Circular dated _____. This offering circular included the following Exhibits:

A. License Agreement

B. Equipment Lease

C. Lease for Premises

D. Loan Agreement

_____   _____

Date   Franchisee

JRH:ufoc

FORM A–UNIFORM FRANCHISE REGISTRATION APPLICATION

(Insert file number
of previous filings
of Applicant)

FEE: _____
(Enclosed when application
is initially filed)

APPLICATION FOR (CHECK ONLY ONE):

_____ REGISTRATION OF AN OFFER AND SALE OF FRANCHISES

_____ REGISTRATION RENEWAL STATEMENT OR ANNUAL REPORT

     AMENDMENT NUMBER _____ TO APPLICATION

_____ POST-EFFECTIVE   FILED UNDER SECTION _____

_____ PRE-EFFECTIVE   DATED _____

1. Name of Franchisor. (If applicant is subfranchisor, the name of the subfranchisor.)
   Name under which the Franchisor is doing or intends to do business. _____

   _____

   _____

2. Franchisor's principal business address.

   _____

   _____

   Name and address of Franchisor's agent in the State of (Name of State) authorized to receive
   process.

   _____

   _____

3. Name, address, and telephone number of subfranchisors, if any, for this state.

   _____

   _____

4. Name, address, and telephone number of person to whom communications regarding this
   application should be directed.

   _____

   _____

FORM B—SUPPLEMENTAL INFORMATION

1. Disclose:

    A. The states in which this proposed registration application is effective.

    B. The states in which this proposed registration application is or will be shortly on file.

    C. The states that have refused to register this franchise offering.

    D. The states that have revoked or suspended the right to offer franchises.

    E. The states in which this proposed registration of these franchises has been withdrawn within the last five years, and the reasons for revocation or suspension.

2. Source of Funds for Establishing New Franchises

    Disclose franchisor's total costs for performing its pre-opening obligations to provide goods or services in connection with establishing each franchise, including real estate, improvements, equipment, inventory, training, and other items stated in the offering. State separately the sources of all required funds.

FORM C—CERTIFICATION

I certify under penalty of law that I have read and know the contents of this application and the documents attached as exhibits and incorporated by reference and that the statements in all these documents are true and correct.

Executed at _____, _____, 20_____

_____
(Signature(s) of Franchisor and/or
Subfranchisor)

By _____
Title _____

(Seal)

STATE OF _____)
) ss.
COUNTY OF _____)

Personally appeared before me this _____day of _____, 20_____ the above-named _____ _____ and _____ _____ to me known to be the person(s) who executed the foregoing application (_____ and _____, respectively, of the above-named applicant) and (each), being first duly sworn, stated upon oath that said application, and all exhibits submitted herewith, are true and correct.

_____

_____

(Notary)

CORPORATE ACKNOWLEDGMENT

STATE OF _____)

) ss.

COUNTY OF _____)

On this _____ day of _____, 20_____, before me _____ (Name of Notary), the undersigned officer, personally appeared _____ and _____, known personally to me to be the _____ President and _____ Secretary, respectively, of the above-named corporation, and that they, as such officers, being authorized to do so, executed the foregoing instrument for the purposes therein contained, by signing the name of the corporation by themselves as such officers.

IN WITNESS WHEREOF I have hereunto set my hand and official seal.

_____
(Notary Public)

(Notarial Seal)   My commission expires: _____

INDIVIDUAL OR PARTNERSHIP ACKNOWLEDGMENT

STATE OF _____)
) ss.
COUNTY OF _____)

On this _____ day of _____, 20_____, before me
_____, (Name of Notary) the undersigned officer, personally
appeared _____ to me personally known and known to me to be the
same person(s) whose name(s) is (are) signed to the foregoing instrument, and acknowledged the

execution thereof for the uses and purposes therein set forth.

IN WITNESS WHEREOF I have hereunto set my hand and official seal.

_____

(Notary Public)

(Notarial Seal)   My commission expires: _____

FORM D—UNIFORM CONSENT TO SERVICE OF PROCESS

_____, (a corporation organized under the laws of

the State of _____) (a partnership) (an individual) _____

_____, irrevocably appoints the _____

_____ (name of regulatory authority) and the succes-

sors in office, its attorney in the State of _____ for service of notice, process or pleading in an

action or proceeding against it arising out of or in connection with the sale of franchises, or a vio-

lation of the franchise laws of _____, and consents that an action or pro-

ceeding against it may be commenced in a court of competent jurisdiction and proper venue with-

in _____ by service of process upon this officer with the same effect as if the

undersigned was organized or created under the laws of _____ and

had lawfully been served with process in _____. It is requested that

a copy of any notice, process, or pleading served this consent be mailed to:

_____

_____

(Name and address)

Dated: _____, 20_____

By _____

Title _____

(Seal)

By _____

Title _____

FORM E–SALES AGENT DISCLOSURE FORM

1. List the persons who will offer or sell franchises in this state. For each person state:
   A. Name;
   B. Business address and telephone number;
   C. Home address and telephone number;
   D. Present employer;
   E. Present title;
   F. Social Security Number;
   G. Birth date; and
   H. Employment during the past five years. For each employment, state the name of the employer, position held, and beginning and ending dates.

2. State whether any person identified in 1. above:
   A. Has any administrative, civil, or criminal action pending alleging a violation of franchise or securities law, fraud, embezzlement, fraudulent conversion, restraint of trade, unfair or deceptive practices, misappropriation of property, or any comparable allegations?
   YES _____ NO _____

   B. Had during the ten-year period immediately before the offering circular date:
      (1) Been convicted of a felony or pleaded nolo contendere to a felony charge or been held liable in a civil action by final judgment if the felony or civil action involved a violation of franchise or securities law, fraud, embezzlement, fraudulent conversion, restraint of trade, unfair or deceptive practices, misappropriation of property, or comparable violations of law? YES _____ NO _____
      (2) Entered into or been named in a consent judgment, decree, order, or assurance under federal or state franchise, securities, anti-trust, monopoly, trade practice, or trade regulation law? YES _____ NO _____
      (3) Been subject to an order or national securities association or national securities exchange as defined in the Securities and Exchange Act of 1934 suspending or expelling the person from membership in the association or exchange?

YES _____ NO _____

   C. For each above question answered "YES" state:
      (1) The name of the person or entity involved;
      (2) The court, agency, association, or exchange involved;
      (3) A summary of the allegations;
      (4) If applicable, the date of the conviction, judgment, decree, order, or assurance; and
      (5) The penalty imposed, damages assessed, terms and conditions of the judgment, decree, order, or assurance.

FORM F—GUARANTEE OF PERFORMANCE

For value received _____, located at _____,
                                                    (Address)

absolutely and unconditionally guarantees the performance by _____,

located at _____, of all of the obligations of
         (Address)
_____ under its franchise registration in the State

of _____ dated _____ and of its Franchise
  (Name of state or province)   (Effective date of renewal)

Agreement.

This guarantee continues until all obligations of _____ under the

franchise registration and franchise agreement are satisfied. _____ is not

discharged from liability if a claim by the franchisee against _____

remains outstanding. Notice of acceptance is waived. Notice of default on the part of

_____ is not waived.

This guarantee is binding on _____ and on its successors and assignees.

_____ executes this guarantee at _____ on the
  (Parent)
_____ day of _____ 20___.

Index

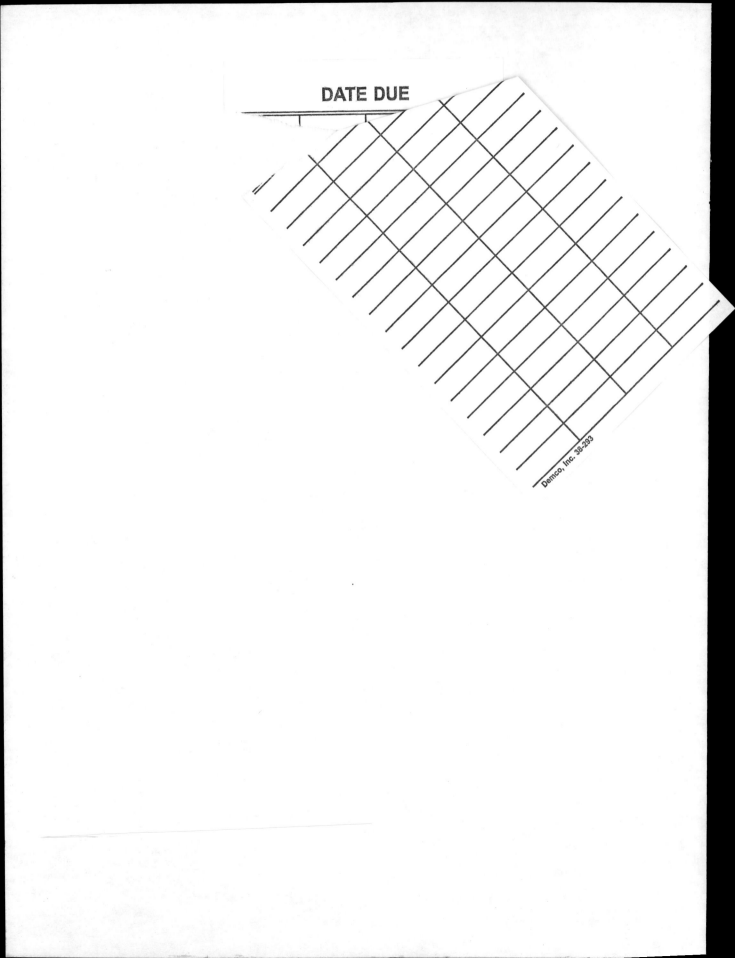

DATE DUE

Demco, Inc. 38-293